NETSCAPE
IFC

IN A NUTSHELL

*A Desktop Quick Reference
for Java Programmers*

NETSCAPE
IFC
IN A NUTSHELL

*A Desktop Quick Reference
for Java Programmers*

Dean Petrich with David Flanagan

O'REILLY™

Cambridge · Köln · Paris · Sebastopol · Tokyo

Netscape IFC in a Nutshell: A Desktop Quick Reference for Java Programmers
by Dean Petrich with David Flanagan

Published by O'Reilly & Associates, Inc., 101 Morris Street, Sebastopol, CA 95472.

Editor: David Flanagan

Production Editor: David Futato

Printing History:

August 1997:   First Edition

This book is printed on acid-free paper with 85% recycled content, 15% post-consumer
waste. O'Reilly & Associates is committed to using paper with the highest recycled
content available consistent with high quality.

ISBN: 1-56592-343-X

Table of Contents

Part IV. Advanced Topics

Part V. Quick Reference

Preface

The Netscape Internet Foundation Classes

The Internet Foundation Classes (IFC) is a Java class library containing nearly one hundred classes designed to simplify the development of large-scale Java applications. The IFC is written entirely in Java and its classes provide a new and *complete* framework for event-handling, graphical user interfaces, and indeed, applications, that is far easier to work with than the framework built into Java proper.

Who Is This Book For?

This book assumes you have at least some knowledge of Java: for instance, its syntax, and the concepts of classes, interfaces, and inheritance. If you're unfamiliar with this, there are several excellent books that cover Java at an introductory level, among them O'Reilly & Associates' *Exploring Java* and *Java in a Nutshell*. However, this book does not assume you are an expert Java programmer. The classes in the IFC provide a relatively complete framework for developing applications, so you could easily start with some knowledge of Java, a handy reference manual (such as *Java in a Nutshell*), and this book, and learn how to develop powerful Java applications quickly.

What Is in This Book?

Part 1 is an introductory section. Chapter 1 presents the contents of the IFC in more detail—read it, and you'll have an understanding of what's available to you in the IFC. In the remaining chapter of the first section, Chapter 2, we'll look at the Application class and show how to use it to create an applet. The four chapters of Part 2 cover the View class, the base class for all IFC GUI components. Part 3 covers graphical user interfaces and two related topics, animation and drag-and-drop. Part 4 covers a few miscellaneous but still useful topics, and Part 5 provides a complete reference to the IFC classes.

Conventions Used in This Book

Italic is used for:

- Pathnames, filenames, and program names.

- New terms where they are defined.

- Internet addresses, such as domain names, newsgroups, and URLs.

Boldface is used for:

- Particular keys on a computer keyboard.

- Names of user interface buttons and menus.

`Letter Gothic` is used for:

- Anything that appears literally in a Java program, including keywords, data types, constants, method names, variables, class names, and interface names.

- Command lines and options that should be typed verbatim on the screen.

- All Java code listings.

- HTML documents, tags, and attributes.

`Letter Gothic Oblique` is used for:

- Method parameters, and general placeholders that indicate that an item is replaced by some actual value in your own program.

- Variable expressions in command-line options.

Franklin Gothic Compressed is used for:

- Java class synopses in the quick-reference section. This very narrow font allows us to fit a lot of information on the page without as many distracting line breaks.

Franklin Gothic Compressed Bold is used for:

- Highlighting class, method, field, and constructor names in the quick-reference section, which makes it easier to scan the class synopses.

Franklin Gothic Compressed Italic is used for:

- Method parameter names and comments in the quick reference section.

How to Use This Book

First of all, you need the Java JDK, available from Sun. You'll also need the IFC class library, which you can get in two ways:

1. By downloading the IFC class library from Netscape

2. By using the IFC class library built into Netscape Communicator

Netscape includes installation instructions if you decide on the first option. I recommend you download the IFC, including the source, from Netscape. If you're new to Java, you can learn a lot by looking through the source code.

It's not necessary to read this book cover-to-cover in order to begin programming with the IFC. The critical chapters are chapters 2 (the `Application` class), 4 (the `View` hierarchy), and 8 (the `Target` interface). If you'd like to jump right in and design applications that don't require custom views (i.e., custom components), at a minimum you should read chapters 2, 4, and 8, and whatever chapters of the GUI section you consider relevant. If your application needs custom components or does any kind of custom drawing, you'll need to supplement that with chapters 5 (drawing in views) and 6 (mouse and keyboard events). After that, you can read the other chapters piecemeal, as necessary.

The book contains a great deal of example code, which you can download from *ftp://ftp.oreilly.com/published/oreilly/nutshell/ifc/*. I *strongly* recommend you compile, run, and modify the example code, then follow that up by writing your own examples. If you do so, you'll be writing awe-inspiring Java applications in no time!

Acknowledgments

Writing this book was a long haul, but it was made much easier with the encouragement of friends and family, including Bill, Yong, Ron, Carol, Michelle, Andrea, Stephanie, Kyle, Dirk, Ken, and Bernadette. Most of all, I would like to acknowledge my parents for their continuing support.

The content of this book benefitted greatly from the comments of the technical reviewers: James White, Director of Technology for Adventure Online Gaming, Inc. and Warren Woodford of WE Design. Several people from Netscape's IFC group were also quite helpful, particularly David Kloba, Scott Love, and Arnaud Weber.

Finally, I want to thank my editor, David Flanagan, for his steady stream of common sense advice. David is the author of the quick-reference section, and I can only hope that some of his writing and programming expertise will show through in the other chapters of this book!

David Futato was the production editor and proofreader for this book; he oversaw the entire process of converting it from a Word document to the final form you see here. Clairemarie Fisher O'Leary copyedited the book, and Sheryl Avruch, Paula Ferguson, and Nancy Wolfe Kotary did quality-assurance checks. Seth Maislin had the thankless task of creating the index. Edie Freedman designed the cover, and Robert Romano produced the illustrations. My thanks go to them all.

Part 1

Introduction

CHAPTER 1

The Internet Foundation Classes

The Internet Foundataion Classes (IFC) from Netscape are a collection of Java classes for the creation and display of graphical user interfaces (GUIs). The IFC provides a welcome alternative to the AWT (Abstract Windowing Toolkit), which, although it is part of the core Java distribution, has always been one of the stumbling blocks for Java application development.

Figure 1-1 shows an excellent example of the type of real-world programs that can be written using the IFC. It shows the *superMail* application, implemented by the Digerati Corporation using the IFC (and using some custom IFC controls in addition to the standard controls). You can learn more about this application at *http://www.digerati.net/products/supermail/*.

The IFC is implemented as a layer of functionality on top of the AWT. While the IFC completely replaces the GUI components of the AWT, it still must rely on the underlying windowing and drawing capabilities of the AWT. The IFC provides its own version of all the AWT graphics classes such as Graphics, Font, and Color, so that an IFC programmer need only use IFC classes. The IFC does provide compatibility with the AWT, however, so that it is possible to use AWT classes, and even GUI components from the AWT in IFC programs.

IFC Features

There are a number of important features that make the IFC a useful toolkit for application and GUI development. The subsections below explore these features.

Pure Java

Because the IFC relies on the native windowing and graphics facilities provided by the AWT, it is written entirely in Java and does not rely on any platform-dependent native libraries of its own. Furthermore, it complies with Sun's "100% Pure

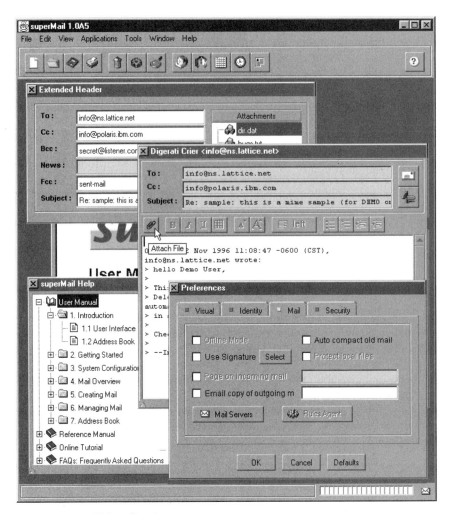

Figure 1-1: An IFC application

Java" guidelines, guaranteeing that any IFC program will run (and run correctly) on any Java platform.

Platform Independent Look-and-Feel

The IFC does not use any of the native GUI components provided in the AWT; this is its most significant divergence from the AWT. Instead, it implements all of its own GUI components, using only the basic graphics and windowing facilities provided by the AWT. This means that an IFC program will look and behave identically on any platform. AWT programs, on the other hand, have a platform-dependent look-and-feel. While there are good arguments to be made for both platform-dependent and platform-independent GUIs, it is the platform-independent model that seems to be gaining favor, and Sun has even announced plans to define a platform-independent look-and-feel for a future version of the AWT.

Customizable Look

One of the goals of the IFC developers was to allow easy customization of the appearance of IFC applications and GUI components. It is easy to modify the appearance of any IFC "view" (as IFC GUI components are called) by creating a simple subclass. While there are good human factors and usability arguments for adopting a standard GUI look, they are countered by the arguments that a standard look quickly becomes tedious and boring, is unnecessary for simple applications, and provides little opportunity for establishing product or brand identity. The trend in web site design is towards heavily customized, graphics-intensive sites. With the IFC, programmers and designers can create applets that integrate very cleanly with web sites. For example, both Figures 1-1 and 1-2 show applications that have customized the default appearance of the IFC views they use.

IFC Constructor

One of the most important IFC-related features is Netscape Constructor, a GUI builder program (pictured in Figure 1-2) for use with the IFC. Constructor allows a programmer to graphically create a GUI, and to save a description of that GUI to a file. Then, at run time, an application can read in such a GUI description file and easily recreate the entire GUI. There are a number of advantages to using a tool such as Constructor:

- It makes it easy for designers to be involved in the programming process, and allows them to tweak and adjust the layout, fonts, and colors of a GUI as they desire.

- It enables rapid prototyping.

- It saves the programmer from writing the simple but tedious and repetitive code to create GUI components "manually."

- It increases modularity by enforcing a separation of application from interface.

- It increases GUI portability by making it easier to upgrade from an IFC interface to a JFC interface when the JFC replaces the IFC in the future. (The JFC will be described later in this chapter.)

Figure 1-2 shows a simple GUI being developed in Constructor.

High-Level Components

One of the attractions of the IFC is that it provides GUI components and services that are not available elsewhere. The most notable example is the TextView class that supports the display and editing of multiline, multi-font formatted text, and even supports simple HTML parsing. There is no equivalent functionality in the AWT, and this one GUI component alone may be reason enough to use the IFC for some applications.

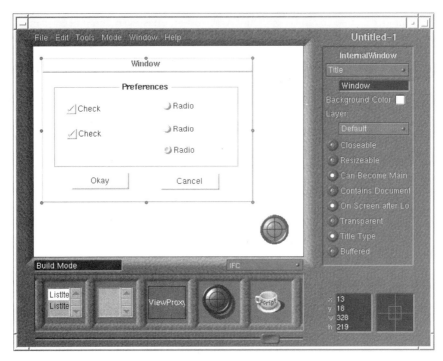

Figure 1-2: Developing an IFC GUI in Constructor

Similarly, the IFC provides a popup menu component, which is not available in the Java 1.0 AWT. (Popup menus are now available in Java 1.1, however.) The IFC also provides the very important drag-and-drop applicaiton service, which is not available through the AWT in either Java 1.0 or Java 1.1.

Availability

Another factor that argues in favor of the IFC is its availability. Version 1.1 of the IFC library and its source code are freely available from Netscape, and Netscape encourages their broad use and dissemination. Furthermore, IFC 1.1 is built into Netscape's Communicator suite, and is thus the platform of choice for developing Java applets to run in Navigator 4.0. IFC applets can also be run in other web browsers, of course. One way is to download all the necessary IFC classes along with the applet. Alternatively, the IFC classes can simply be installed on the local hard drive allowing Internet Explorer and other browers to run IFC applets as efficiently as Navigator does.

Besides its free availability, the IFC's current availability is also a strong factor arguing for its use. As this is written, both the Application Foundation Classes and the Java Foundation Classes have been announced, but have yet to be released, even in beta form. (There is more information about the AFC and the JFC later in this chapter.) While these competing toolkits may eventually be superior to the IFC, the fact is that the IFC is available *now*.

Easy to Use

IFC is in many ways easier to program with than AWT is. For example, the IFC was designed to avoid the use of threads, substituting instead a `Timer` abstraction to support things such as animation. This is especially important for beginning programmers for whom threads can be particularly confusing. Similarly, the IFC uses a callback model for handling events, which is much easier to use than the original event model in the Java 1.0 AWT. (In Java 1.1 AWT switched to a callback-based event model.)

Efficient

Although IFC adds a layer of abstraction to the AWT, it is nevertheless more efficient than the AWT in some ways. By abandoning native GUI components, it avoids the use of a native window for each component. It also avoids the memory-wasting AWT duality between the native GUI object and its Java "peer" object.

Another important efficiency gain for the IFC is that it does not support threads. IFC methods are not `synchronized`. This means that they are not re-entrant, and that an IFC program may never have more than one thread performing GUI calls. Invoking a `synchronized` method is significantly more time consuming than invoking a non-`synchronized` method, however, so the IFC gets a big performance boost by ruling out the use of multiple threads. Using more than one thread to implement a GUI is generally a sign of poor design, so this IFC restriction is not a serious one.

IFC Shortcomings

There are some shortcomings to the IFC, of course. It seems more hastily designed than the AWT and other core Java libraries, and I find that the IFC API (Application Programming Interface) iis not quite as elegant as the AWT API. Programmers accustomed to the naming conventions of AWT may find the IFC conventions just a little off at first.

A weakness of the IFC architecture is in the area of layout management—i.e., of automatically positioning GUI components within their containers. The IFC approaches this problem in two distinct ways (see Chapter 15, *Layout Managers*), but neither way is a fully general or adequate solution. In practice, many IFC applications abandon layout management altogether and rely instead on hard-coded layouts. Fortunately, the Netscape Constructor builder application makes it simple to use this hard-coded approach.

Another shortcoming of IFC is that its GUI components are not compliant with the naming conventions of the JavaBeans API, and thus, IFC "views" are not beans, and cannot be manipulated by builder applications that support Java Beans.

Other GUI Toolkits

In order to understand the IFC, it is important to understand it in the context of other GUI development options that are now available or will become available. We discuss some of these options in this section:

AWT

The Abstract Windowing Toolkit, a core Java class library, is what the IFC was written to avoid. While it is technically sound, the AWT has been criticised for its reliance on platform-dependent controls, and for not supporting enough controls. A number of the limitations of the AWT have been resolved in Java 1.1, but it is still not an ideal GUI development platform. The JFC, described below, will be a kind of second-generation AWT, and shows promise to be a very useful GUI toolkit.

AFC

The AFC, or Application Foundation Classes, is Microsoft's answer to the IFC. It, too, is a pure-Java class library designed to augment the AWT. Just as the IFC will be built into Netscape's Communicator (Navigator 4.0), the AFC will be built into Microsoft's Internet Explorer 4.0. And just as Netscape is making the IFC classes freely available for downloading, Microsoft will make the AFC classes freely available. (Microsoft is not planning to release source code, as Netscape has, however.) Where the AFC differs from the IFC is that it is not a completely new GUI environment; it is essentially nothing more than a collection of custom AWT GUI controls. As this book goes to press, the AFC library is in beta testing.

JFC

The JFC, or Java Foundation Classes, is (it seems) Sun and Netscape's answer to the AFC. Sun and Netscape have teamed up, along with IBM and Apple, to create a second-generation GUI toolkit. The JFC will integrate ideas from both the AWT and the IFC, and will hopefully learn from the shortcomings of those two toolkits. The JFC has not yet been released for beta testing, and it is not clear exactly what form it will take. Although it will not be directly compatible with the IFC, the developers have promised an upgrade path from the IFC to the JFC. It seems likely that the JFC will use the Java 2D library, and will take advantage of the "lightweight components" introduced in Java 1.1 to provide a platform-independent look-and-feel. It will also certainly provide a much richer assortment of GUI controls. As an official class library from Sun, it seems likely that the JFC will become the GUI development platform of choice. Until it becomes available, the IFC may be an appropriate second choice.

Java Beans

The term "Java Beans" does not actually refer to a GUI toolkit. Instead, it refers to a framework for defining GUI controls that can be visually manipulated with a builder tool. The controls in the IFC are unfortunately not Beans. The controls in the JFC will be.

Third-Party Controls

Another option for the Java GUI developer searching for the GUI tools she needs is to define her own controls, or to buy them from third parties.

There are a number of Java class libraries now for sale, including some GUI components.

An Overview of the IFC

The following sections provide an overview of the main features of the IFC, and act as a road map for the rest of the book.

Event Handling and the Application Class

The IFC defines its own `Runnable` object, `Application`, to act as the base class for all applications written with the IFC, whether they are intended to be run as applets or as standalone applications. `Application` provides a framework for IFC event handling. The IFC's event handling is built around *callbacks*: for example, when a button is pressed, it executes a specific method in its *target*, the object interested in handling the button press. The callback framework is very straightforward and powerful. Although it doesn't affect IFC programming, it's interesting to note that Java 1.1 uses callbacks as its event-handling model as well. The `Application` class is covered in Chapter 2, *The Application Class*, and events and event handling are covered in Chapter 6, *Mouse and Keyboard Events*.

The View Class

The IFC provides a class called `View`, which acts as the base class for all GUI components. At the lowest level, a `View` represents a rectangular area on the screen. Each view is a member of a containment hierarchy, called the *view hierarchy*, that provides a simple way to organize the layout of a large number of views. The view hierarchy is covered in Chapter 4, *The View Hierarchy*.

`View` has methods for drawing, mouse and keyboard event handling, resizing, and drag-and-drop support, and if you're planning on developing custom GUI controls, you'll need to know about these `View` features, too. Drawing is covered in Chapter 5, *Drawing in Views*, event handling in Chapter 6, and drag-and-drop in Chapter 19, *Drag-and-Drop*.

GUI Controls

The IFC provides a set of classes for GUI controls (`Button`, `Label`, `ListView`, `Menu`, `Popup`, `ScrollBar`, `Slider`, `TextField`, and `TextView`), and two layout managers to aid in the creation of complex user interfaces. The IFC's event-handling framework makes handling the events generated by these controls simple and uniform. The IFC's classes for creating graphical user interfaces are covered in Chapters 7-15.

Windows

The IFC provides an interface, `Window`, that encapsulates the behavior of a window, and two classes, `InternalWindow` and `ExternalWindow`, that implement the `Window` interface. An `InternalWindow` appears within another window or applet, and an `ExternalWindow` appears as a native, platform-dependent window. Windows are covered in Chapter 7, *Windows*, and a related topic, dialog boxes, is covered in Chapter 17, *Dialog Boxes*.

Animation

The IFC provides several classes for simplifying animation. The `Image` class can be used to display static images such as GIF or JPEG files, or animation through its subclasses `DrawingSequence` and `ImageSequence`. `DrawingSequence` uses an internal `Timer`, another IFC class, which eliminates the need for creating a secondary thread for animation. Animation is covered in Chapter 18, *Animation and Images*.

Drag-and-drop

Most modern applications support drag-and-drop in some form. The IFC provides support for implementing drag-and-drop within an application. (Since Java itself doesn't provide an interface to the *native* drag-and-drop API, there is as yet no way to drag-and-drop objects in to or out of a Java application.) Most of the dirty work is handled by the IFC, so implementing drag-and-drop is simply a matter implementing an interface or two and overriding a method in the `View` class. Drag-and-drop is covered in Chapter 19.

Archiving and Constructor

Large-scale applications often need a way to save information about internal Java objects in such a way that the object can be reconstructed later, even after the original application instance has been destroyed. The IFC has an `Archive` class that makes it easy to save information about Java objects; in particular, every relevant IFC class can be archived and unarchived in just a few lines of code. Java 1.1 now supports its own form of "archiving," known as serialization, which is a more general form of the archiving capabilities of the IFC. Archiving still plays a very important role in the IFC, however. The *.plan* files produced by the Constructor application are IFC archives—they allow a complete GUI to be saved to a file, and then read back in and recreated. Archiving is covered in Chapter 21, *Archives*, and the Constructor application is covered in Chapter 22, *Constructor and Plan Files*.

CHAPTER 2

The Application Class

In this chapter we introduce the `Application` class, the base class for all IFC applications, and show how to run an `Application` as an applet or from the command line.

The Application Class

The `Application` class is the base class for all IFC applications. The IFC uses a completely different event-handling and component containment scheme than the AWT, so `Application` does not extend `Applet`; rather, it extends `Object` and implements `Runnable`. Even though `Application` doesn't extend `Applet`, applications can be run as applets by using a trivial subclass of `FoundationApplet` to load the `Application` into an applet framework. The example programs shipped with the IFC include just such a trivial subclass, named `NetscapeApplet`, which can be used to run any `Application` as an applet. An `Application` can also be run as a standalone application by providing an implementation for the `main()` method, as usual. Bear in mind, though, that the name `Application` is slightly misleading. Like any Java program, it needs to be run in conjunction with the Java interpreter, either through *appletviewer* or a browser, or from the command line with *java*. In this chapter we'll see examples of both.

`Application`'s constructor is where the entire IFC framework is set up. Since the IFC replaces the AWT's event handling and containment hierarchy with its own, `Application` creates an `EventLoop`, and in the case of an applet, a `RootView`. The `EventLoop` is the object responsible for communicating with the underlying AWT components, and is covered in detail in Chapter 21, *Archives.** An `Application`'s `RootView` acts as the background component, and provides the top node for the view hierarchy. Chapter 3, *An Introduction to Views*, covers the `View` class

---

* Although an IFC programmer rarely interacts directly with the AWT, the IFC is written entirely in Java, so the implementation of the IFC itself involves AWT components.

and the view hierarchy in detail, so we'll defer the discussion of an Application's RootView until then.

Enough talk. Let's see some code!

"Hello, World" with the IFC

In keeping with tradition, in Example 2-1 we show how to write "Hello, World"
using an IFC application called IFCHello. IFCHello uses Label, an IFC class, to
display its message. Figure 2-1 shows what the application looks like on-screen.

Example 2-1: Hello, World!

```
// Import the IFC
import netscape.application.*;
import netscape.util.*;

// An IFC application that says "Hello, World!"
// IFCHello extends netscape.application.Application, not Applet
public class IFCHello extends Application{
  Label hello;

  // Note:  no constructor.
  // All the setup code goes into init(), the entry
  // point into every Application.
  public void init(){
    super.init();
    // create a new Label with a message
    hello = new Label("Hello, World!", Font.fontNamed("Helvetica",
                                                       Font.BOLD,48));
    // make it the size of the applet
    hello.setBounds(mainRootView().bounds());
    // center the message
    hello.setJustification(Graphics.CENTERED);
    // add it to the view hierarchy
    mainRootView().addSubview(hello);
  }

  // Use cleanup() to take care of any system resources
  // (windows, streams, etc.) that the application may have used.
  // IFCHello doesn't use any, so we don't bother to implement it.
  // public void cleanup(){}
}
```

Before we look at the details of IFCHello, let's look at the overall structure.

Life Cycle of an Application

IFCHello has only two methods, init() and cleanup(). Often, these will be
the only two methods you'll implement in an Application subclass.

When an IFC application is run as an applet, the entry point into the code you
write is the init() method, *not* the constructor. Generally you won't even write
a constructor! The init() method is called only once, and in init() you should
do all the setup work for your application: create views, build the view hierarchy,
start timers, open windows, and so on. Since init() contains application-specific

Figure 2-1: The IFCHello application

setup code, you'll always have to write an init() method for your applications. In fact, it's the only method you must implement. Once init() returns, the application starts processing events.

The cleanup() method is called after the application has stopped processing events, normally because the underlying NetscapeApplet (see below) is being destroyed. In cleanup(), you should free any system resources, such as windows or streams, that the application has allocated. The cleanup() method is optional. Simple applications that don't use any system resources don't need to implement cleanup().

IFCHello in Detail

Let's go through the code in IFCHello's init(). First, IFCHello calls super.init(). This isn't strictly necessary for IFCHello, because Application.init() does nothing. However, since IFCHello.init() is not empty, if you extended IFCHello, it would be necessary to call super.init() in the subclass init() method. That's why it's always a good idea to call super.init(): if your Application subclass lies several levels beneath Application in the class hierarchy, each of the classes above your subclass is liable to have its own initialization routines. If each level in the class hierachy calls super.init(), each subclass will have a chance to initialize itself, and your subclass will be initialized properly.

The init() method then creates a Label that does nothing but display a String. In our case, we give it a simple message: "Hello, World!" We then specify the label's bounds; in this case we make it the size of the applet. Next we set the justification of the message so that it appears in the center of the window. Finally, we add the label to the *view hierarchy* as a subview of the RootView. In short, this makes the label visible. The view hierarchy is an very important topic in IFC programming and we'll cover it in detail in Chapter 4, *The View Hierarchy.*

Although `init()` is the only method you need to override to create an IFC application, the `Application` class has a number of other methods you might find useful. Here are three:

`public static Application application();`

> A `static` method that returns the current `Application` instance–that is, the `Application` instance for the current thread. (Most IFC programs use only a single thread and have only a single instance of their `Application` class.)

`public boolean isApplet();`

> Returns `true` if the `Application` is being run as an `Applet`.

`public URL codeBase();`

> Returns the `URL` of the `Application`'s class file.

Running an IFC Application as an Applet

Well, we've seen some code, but how do we run `IFCHello`? Since `Application` doesn't extend `Applet`, to run an IFC `Application` as an applet we need an additional file, `NetscapeApplet.java`. If you downloaded the IFC from Netscape, you'll find `NetscapeApplet` included in their files—look in their *Examples* directories. Using *javac*, compile `NetscapeApplet.java` and `IFCHello.java` in the same directory. `NetscapeApplet` is just a very simple subclass of the IFC `FoundationApplet` class. Netscape's implementation of this subclass is shown below. You can retype and rename this subclass however you like. For somewhat obscure reasons, the `classForName()` method cannot be implemented directly by `FoundationApplet`, and must be part of the code that is downloaded from the same source as the `Application` class to be run. Thus every IFC `Application` to be run as an applet must have a class just like this one:

```
// NetscapeApplet.java
// Copyright 1996, 1997 Netscape Communications Corp.  All
// rights reserved.
import netscape.application.*;
import netscape.util.*;
public class NetscapeApplet extends FoundationApplet {
    public Class classForName(String className)
                throws ClassNotFoundException {
        return Class.forName(className);
    }
}
```

To load an applet into a web browser, an HTML file is required. The file we used for the `IFCHello` program is shown here. Note that the `<APPLET>` tag loads the `NetscapeApplet` class, which reads the value of the parameter named `ApplicationClass` to determine the name of the IFC `Application` subclass that it should load and run.

```
<html>
  <head>
    <title>IFCHello</title>
  </head>
  <body>
    <applet code="NetscapeApplet" width=300 height=200>
      <param name="ApplicationClass" value="IFCHello">
    </applet>
```

```
</body>
</html>
```

Figure 2-2 shows the IFCHello program running as an applet in a web browser.

Figure 2-2: Hello, World in a browser

If your Application is being run as an Applet, you can use a static method in the IFC's AWTCompatibility class to recover the underlying Applet object:

```
public static Applet awtApplet();
```

The java.applet.Applet class has about 20 methods; for details, please refer to your favorite Java reference manual. You might find these two Applet methods useful for IFC programming:

- public URL getDocumentBase();

  Returns the path for the HTML document. Remember, Application has a codeBase() method.

- public void showStatus(String *message*);

  Displays *message* on the status bar of the browser.

AWTCompatibility has other methods that return the AWT components underlying several IFC objects. If you find yourself in need of an AWT component's method, take a look at the AWTCompatibility API.

Standalone Applications

Applets are suitable for web pages, but due to security restrictions they can't take advantage of the full power of Java. Standalone applications, on the other hand, have no security restrictions and can take full advantage of everything in the language: they can read and write files, open and close sockets to arbitrary hosts, and so on. In this section we present a class to simplify the creation of standalone IFC applications.

Like all Java applications, IFC applications can be run as standalone applications by providing an implementation of the main() method. This method must instantiate the Application, create a window for it, and start it running. Example 2-2 shows a simplistic implementation of such a main() method.

Example 2-2: Running an Application from the Command Line

```
public static void main(String args[]) {
    Application app = new IFCHello();              // instantiate app
    ExternalWindow win = new ExternalWindow();     // create window for it
    app.setMainRootView(win.rootView());           // place app in window
    Size size = win.windowSizeForContentSize(400, 200); // compute win size
    win.sizeTo(size.width, size.height);           // set window size
    mainWindow.show();                             // display the window
    app.run();                              // start the app running
    System.exit(0);                         // exit when app stops running
}
```

The shortcoming of the code shown in Example 2-2 is that the Application cannot detect when the user closes its window, and thus the user can close the window and leave the application running. A proper implementation that detects window closing requires some more code and involves working with the Window class and the WindowOwner interface, both covered in Chapter 7, *Windows*. As an alternative to a premature discussion of Window, we present an Application-Viewer class in Example 2-3 that you can use to easily run applications from the command line. The ApplicationViewer class works like *appletviewer*: based on a command-line argument, it creates a new instance of an Application and a window to show it in. Don't worry if you don't understand ApplicationViewer yet. Once we've covered Window and WindowOwner, it will become a lot clearer.

Example 2-3: ApplicationViewer—Useful for Standalone Applications

```
// import the IFC
import netscape.application.*;
import netscape.util.*;

public class ApplicationViewer implements WindowOwner {
  ExternalWindow win;  // a window to show the application in
  Application app;     // the application that will be 'viewed.'

  // The main() method.  Invoked when run from the command line.
  // Create and run an Application with name args[0] in a window
  // with width and height specified by optional args[1] and args[2].
  public static void main(String[] args){
    ApplicationViewer appViewer = new ApplicationViewer();
    int width = 600;
    int height = 400;
    if (args.length >= 2) width = Integer.parseInt(args[1]);
    if (args.length >= 3) height = Integer.parseInt(args[2]);
    appViewer.createApplication(args[0], width, height);
    System.exit(0);
  }
```

```
// The next two methods run Applications from within other programs.
// Create and run an Application with name className in the default window.
public static void runApplication(String className) {
  ApplicationViewer appViewer = new ApplicationViewer();
  appViewer.createApplication(className, 600, 400);
}

// Create and run an Application with name className in a
// window with the specified width and height
public static void runApplication(String className, int width, int height){
  ApplicationViewer appViewer = new ApplicationViewer();
  appViewer.createApplication(className, width, height);
}

// This is the method that does all the real work of running an
// Application. Load and instantiate the Application class, create
// a window for it, place it in the window, and start it running.
private void createApplication(String className, int width, int height) {
  // Try to load the Application class
  Class appClass = null;
  try { appClass = Class.forName(className); }
  catch (ClassNotFoundException e) {
    System.err.println(className + " not found.  Exiting.");
    System.exit(0);
  }

  // Try to instantiate the Application
  Object o = null;
  try { o = appClass.newInstance(); }
  catch (InstantiationException e) {
    System.err.println(className + ": could not instantiate.  Exiting.");
    System.exit(0);
  }
  catch(IllegalAccessException e) {
    System.err.println(className +
                      " is not public or has no public constructor.  " +
                      " Exiting.");
    System.exit(0);
  }

  // Make sure it really is an Application subclass
  if (!(o instanceof Application)) {
    System.err.println(className + " is not an Application.  Exiting.");
    System.exit(0);
  }
  app = (Application) o;

  // Now create a window for the application.  Set the window size, etc.
  win = new ExternalWindow();
  Size s = win.windowSizeForContentSize(width, height);
  win.sizeTo(s.width, s.height);
  win.setTitle(className);
  win.setOwner(this);

  app.setMainRootView(win.rootView()); // Put app in the window
  win.show();                          // Pop the window up
  app.run();                           // Start running the application
}
```

Example 2-3: ApplicationViewer—Useful for Standalone Applications (continued)

```
    // This WindowOwner method is called when the user closes the window.
    public void windowDidHide(Window win) {
      this.win.dispose();           // Get rid of the window.
      app.stopRunning();            // Tell the application to stop.
    }

    // These other WindowOwner methods are given no-op implementations.
    public void windowDidShow(Window win){}
    public boolean windowWillHide(Window win){return true;}
    public void windowDidBecomeMain(Window win){}
    public void windowDidResignMain(Window win){}
    public void windowWillSizeBy(Window win,Size size){}
    public boolean windowWillShow(Window win){return true;}
}
```

As you can see, ApplicationViewer has three public methods, and as a result, it can be used in three different ways. The simplest way to use Application-Viewer with IFCHello is to compile IFCHello and ApplicationViewer, then go to the command line and type:

```
% java ApplicationViewer IFCHello
```

ApplicationViewer will create an instance of IFCHello and show it in a default window with size (600,400).

The other two ways of using ApplicationViewer require you to add a main() method to IFCHello. Either of the following two possibilities will work.

```
public static void main(String[] args){
  ApplicationViewer.runApplication("IFCHello");
  System.exit(0);
}
```

In this case, IFCHello will run in ApplicationViewer's default window with the default size (600,400).

```
public static void main(String[] args){
  ApplicationViewer.runApplication("IFCHello",400, 150);
  System.exit(0);
}
```

And in this case, IFCHello will run in a window with size (400, 150).

Once you've included one of the above main() methods and compiled both ApplicationViewer and IFCHello, you can run IFCHello by typing the following on the command line:

```
% java IFCHello
```

Since ApplicationViewer creates an Application based on the application's name, to use ApplicationViewer with an application other than IFCHello simply substitute that application's name everywhere you see IFCHello.

Finally, it's best to put the compiled version of ApplicationViewer in your CLASSPATH so you won't need to copy it into every directory containing a standalone application.

Part 2

The View Class

CHAPTER 3

An Introduction to Views

The View class is by far the most important class in the IFC. At heart, a View represents a rectangular area on the screen. View also acts as the base class for all the IFC's GUI classes, from Button to InternalWindow to ScrollBar, and defines methods for drawing, resizing, event handling, and drag-and-drop support. The role of the View class in an application can be broken down into three main parts:

1. Maintain a containment hierarchy that specifies the sizes and relative positions of all the views in an application

2. Perform custom drawing

3. Handle mouse and keyboard events

Following this short overview chapter, these three functions are covered in succession in Chapter 4, *The View Hierarchy*, Chapter 5, *Drawing in Views*, and Chapter 6, *Mouse and Keyboard Events*.

View Overview

The View class represents a rectangular area on the screen. All IFC graphical user interfaces, no matter how complicated, are composed of a number of nested, hierarchically arranged views. As such, the View class plays a very important role in the IFC.

First, View provides a framework for a *containment hierarchy*, in which each view can act as a parent view and can have any number of child views, called *subviews*. All subviews always lie within their parents' bounds, and the subview's positions are specified relative to the parent's position. Since each subview can have its own subviews, views in an application form a hierarchy, called the *view hierarchy*. The IFC provides a special class, RootView, that is always at the top of the view hierarchy. The view hierarchy greatly simplifies the organization of complicated graphical user interfaces and is covered in detail in Chapter 4.

21

Second, each View has a method that is responsible for drawing itself within its bounds. The View class itself provides an empty implementation for its drawing method, but View subclasses can override the method in order to specify what drawing should be done within the View's borders. This makes perfect sense. Since View acts as the base class for all IFC GUI components, a subclass must be able to dictate its appearance on the screen: a button draws itself so it looks like a button, a scroll bar draws itself so it looks like a scroll bar, and so on. By subclassing View and overriding View's drawing method, you can design your own custom GUI components. Drawing in views is covered in Chapter 5.

Third, View provides a framework for handling mouse and keyboard events. Consider, for instance, a mouse click. Since IFC graphical user interfaces are constructed of views, every mouse click that occurs in an IFC application will occur in a view. The IFC notifies the relevant view when a mouse is clicked above it by calling certain View methods. By overriding these methods, you can create a View subclass with custom event handling. Handling mouse and keyboard events in views is covered in Chapter 6.

To Subclass or Not to Subclass

One of the major design goals of the IFC was to develop a set of classes that could be used as is, without subclassing. As such, the IFC provides a number of View subclasses that are ready to be plugged in to applications: Button, ContainerView, ListView, Popup, ScrollBar, Slider, TextField, and TextView. Since these classes are already quite powerful, the issue of subclassing them is hardly ever mentioned in this book.

There is one notable exception to the "no subclassing" rule in the IFC. Although you'll rarely find it necessary to subclass the IFC GUI components, if you want to design your own component that does custom drawing or event handling in a View, you'll to need to subclass View directly. As mentioned above, drawing and event handling are covered in Chapters 5 and 6. If you're not planning on developing your own components, you'll only need to take a quick look at Chapters 5 and 6 before proceeding to Chapter 7, *Windows*.

Attributes

Many IFC objects have *properties* or *attributes* that can be specified by a programmer. Examples are the background color or image of a ContainerView, the current font of a TextField, the minimum and maximum values of a Slider, and so on. The attributes themselves are stored in private fields, but each attribute has a pair of methods that allow a program to read and write (or query and set) the attribute value.

The IFC adopts a standard naming convention for these attribute accessor methods. A few examples should make the pattern clear: the TextField method to set the current font is setFont(), and the method that returns the font is font(). The ContainerView method to set the background color is setBackgroundColor() and the method that returns the background color is backgroundColor(). The method to set a Slider's border is setBorder(), and the method that returns the border is border(). In other words, for every property there are setProperty() and property() methods. When the attribute has a boolean type, however, the method to query the attribute value is often named isProperty() instead of property(). Since this naming convention is relatively consistent throughout the IFC, in order to save a few trees, when a new IFC class is introduced we won't reproduce a complete list of all the methods related to the class's attributes, but will merely show a table or list of the attributes alone. If you're unable to deduce the names of the methods associated with an attribute, flip to the reference section in the back of the book.

CHAPTER 4

The View Hierarchy

View represents a rectangular area on the screen, and acts as the base class for all the IFC GUI classes. In the IFC, views are organized into a *view hierarchy*, where each view can have one parent view and any number of child views. Child views, called *subviews*, always appear within their parent's bounds, and further, a subview's coordinates are always specified relative to the parent's top-left corner. A moment's thought should convince you that this is extremely convenient. When a parent view is moved, all of its subviews are moved along with it, since their coordinates are specified with respect to the parent's top-left corner, no matter where it lies! Moreover, the IFC view hierarchy encourages object-oriented programming: a programmer can develop a custom GUI component by subclassing View, then subsequently use the component in any application by simply adding it to the application's view hierarchy. The IFC's GUI components, all of which extend View, are perfect examples of this design philosophy. The IFC's view hierarchy is an example of a *containment hierarchy*.

A Real, Not Virtual, Example

To further understand the idea behind the IFC view hierarchy, let's consider a simple real-world example. Consider four square pieces of paper, each a different color and size: one black, size 4"×4", one blue, size 3"×3", one green, size 2"×2", and one yellow, size 1"×1". Now, imagine placing the black square on a table, then putting the blue square on top such that it lies completely within the black square's boundaries. Similarly, place the green square within the blue square, and the yellow square within the green square. Clearly, a little bit of each square will be visible. This is all there is to the view hierarchy! Each square represents a View. Their order within the pile represents their position within the view hierarchy, and you'll notice that the child views always obscure part of their parent view. See Figure 4-1 for a snapshot of this view hierarchy.

In view hierarchy parlance, the black square is at the *top* of the view hierarchy, and as we proceed *down* the view hierarchy, we encounter the blue view, the

Figure 4-1: The Colors1 application

green view, and the yellow view. Note carefully that the view hierarchy terminology is such that the background view, in this case represented by the black
square, is at the top, not the bottom, of the view hierarchy. This terminology
should be clearer if you visualize the view hierarchy as being like a family tree,
where the parents always appear above the children.

The example given above is very simple. In real applications, graphical user interfaces can consist of 20 or more such squares or rectangles. The black square
would represent the background view, known in the IFC as a `RootView`, and the
other squares would represent GUI controls like buttons, scrollbars, or sliders,
each of which extends `View`. You could imagine adding squares to the black
square in many possible ways. For instance, in the four-square example, we had
everything arranged in a single pile, and thus there was only one branch to the
view hierarchy. More branches are possible. In addition to the four squares
above, imagine having a 2"×2" orange square and a 1"×1" pink square at our
disposal. We could create a more complicated view hierarchy in this way: take
the black square and place the green square in the upper-left corner, the orange
one in the lower-right corner. Now, to the orange square, add the yellow square
to the upper-left corner and the pink square to the lower-left corner. (A glance
ahead at Figure 4-2 should clarify this.) In view hierarchy parlance, the black view
would have two subviews, green and orange. The green view would have no
subviews, while the orange view would have two, the yellow and pink. The view
hierarchy thus has two branches, and one of the branches even splits into two
sub-branches.

You'll notice that in each of the examples above, we placed the colored squares
such that each subsquare lay completely within its parent square. The corresponding concept in the IFC view hierarchy is that subviews always lie within
their parent's bounds. In other words, a subview is *contained* by its superview.

If these examples seem simple, great! Returning to the virtual world, we present
the `Colors1` and `Colors2` examples, which provide IFC implementations of the
examples above.

The Colors1 Example

Colors1, shown in Example 4-1, implements the view hierarchy associated with the black, blue, green, and yellow view example just described.

Example 4-1: A View Hierarchy

```
import netscape.application.*;
import netscape.util.*;

// An application showing a view hierarchy
public class Colors1 extends Application{
  ColorView blue,green,yellow;

  public void init(){
    // set the background color
    mainRootView().setColor(Color.black);

    Rect rect = mainRootView().bounds();
    int w = 4*rect.width/5;
    int h = 4*rect.height/5;

    // create a blue view and add it to the view hierarchy
    blue = new ColorView(0,0,w,h,Color.blue);
    mainRootView().addSubview(blue);

    w = 4*w/5;
    h = 4*h/5;
    // create a green view and add it to the view hierarchy
    green = new ColorView(0,0,w,h,Color.green);
    blue.addSubview(green);

    w = 4*w/5;
    h = 4*h/5;
    // create a yellow view and add it to the view hierarchy
    yellow = new ColorView(0,0,w,h,Color.yellow);
    green.addSubview(yellow);
  }
}

// a view subclass that draws itself with a solid color
class ColorView extends View{
  Color color;

  // The arguments to the constructor are:
  // x position, y position, width, height, color
  public ColorView(int x,int y,int w,int h,Color c){
    super(x,y,w,h);
    color = c;
  }

  public void drawView(Graphics g){
    g.setColor(color);
    g.fillRect(0,0,bounds.width,bounds.height);
  }
}
```

Let's go through the code in Colors1 in detail, starting with init().

The Application's RootView

The first line of Color1's init() method, mainRootView().setColor-(Color.black), effectively consists of two parts: a call to Application.mainRootView() and a call to RootView.setColor(color). So what's a RootView?

RootView extends View. When an Application is run as an applet, a RootView is automatically created. This RootView, known as the main RootView, is always at the top of the Application's view hierarchy. If the views that you add to the view hierarchy don't completely cover the *appletviewer* window, it's the RootView that will appear in the background.

If your Application is run from the command line and if it uses any views, you need to specify a RootView for the Application by using the Application.setMainRootView() method. As an example, take a look ahead at Example 4-2. In either case, if an Application has a main RootView, it can be retrieved by the Application.mainRootView() method.

In the Colors1 example, we've set the color of the RootView to black so that it's in keeping with the "real-world" squares example discussed above. Colors in the IFC are represented by the Color class, which has 16 different class variables representing commonly used colors (e.g., Color.black), as well as methods for constructing colors with RGB (Red/Green/Blue) or HSB (Hue/Saturation/Brightness) values.

In addition to acting as the top node for the view hierarchy, RootViews have other uses within IFC programming, and we'll be seeing them throughout the book.

Rectangles

Continuing our discussion of the Colors1 example, the second line in Colors1.init() is:

```
Rect rect = mainRootView().bounds();
```

A Rect object obviously represents a rectangle. Rectangles in the IFC are specified by four coordinates: x, y, width, and height. View.bounds() returns the view's bounding Rect, and since RootView extends View, mainRootView().bounds() returns the main RootView's bounding Rect, the size of the applet.

As mentioned at the beginning of the chapter, a view's coordinates are specified *relative* to its parent view. The IFC uses a coordinate system in which (0,0) is in the upper left corner, the positive x-direction is to the right, and the positive y-direction is down. Therefore a view with a bounding rectangle of (10, 10, 30, 40) will appear in its parent view with its upper left corner at (10,10) and its lower right corner at (40,50). It's easy to forget that the position of a subview is specified relative to its parent's top-left corner; if your view isn't being drawn properly, check the coordinates of the bounding rectangle!

The Colors1 View Hierarchy

The rest of `Colors1.init()` creates three views and adds them to the `Application`'s view hierarchy. For instance, consider the `blue` view. It is constructed by the following code:

```
blue = new ColorView(0,0,w,h,Color.blue);
```

After it is created, `blue` is added to the view hierarchy as a subview of the main `RootView` with the `addSubview()` method:

```
mainRootView().addSubview(blue);
```

The `addSubview()` method is a member of the `View` class, and is one of the most important methods in the IFC. You'll find yourself using it repeatedly.

The `green` view is added to the view hierarchy as a subview of `blue` by `blue.addSubview(green)`, and the `yellow` view is added to the view hierarchy as a subview of `green` by `green.addSubview(yellow)`. The `Colors1` example therefore has a view hierarchy with four members: a `RootView`, the `blue` view, the `green` view, and the `yellow` view.

By the way, don't worry if you don't understand the `ColorView` class yet—we'll get to that in the next chapter.

The Colors2 Example

The view hierarchy of the `Colors1` example is simple because it has only one branch. In general, a view hierarchy will have several branches, because a view can be added to the hierarchy by using the `addSubview()` method of *any* member of the view hierarchy. The `Colors2` example, shown in Example 4-2, constructs the view hierarchy of the five-square "real-world" example described earlier. The results are shown in Figure 4-2. Note the coordinates supplied to the `ColorView` constructor; remember, IFC coordinates are relative. The code for the `ColorView` class has been omitted for brevity.

Example 4-2: A More Complicated View Hierarchy

```
import netscape.application.*;
import netscape.util.*;

// An Application with a two-branch view hierarchy
public class Colors2 extends Application{
  ColorView green,orange,pink,yellow;

  public void init(){
    mainRootView().setColor(Color.black);

    int w = mainRootView().bounds().width;
    int h = mainRootView().bounds().height;

    // create four ColorViews.
    green = new ColorView(0,0,w/2,h/2,Color.green);
    orange = new ColorView(w/2,h/2,w/2,h/2,Color.orange);
    pink = new ColorView(0,0,w/4,h/4,Color.pink);
    yellow = new ColorView(0,h/4,w/4,h/4,Color.yellow);
```

Example 4-2: A More Complicated View Hierarchy (continued)

```
    // add them to the view hierarchy
    mainRootView().addSubview(green);
    mainRootView().addSubview(orange);
    orange.addSubview(pink);
    orange.addSubview(yellow);
  }
}
```

Figure 4-2: The Colors2 application

The view hierarchy of `Colors2` has five members: the `RootView`, with two subviews, `green` and `orange`. `Green` has no subviews, while `orange` has two, `pink` and `yellow`. Since the `RootView` has two subviews, this hierarchy has two main branches, unlike the `Colors1` hierarchy, which had only one branch.

View Hierarchy Terminology

The view hierarchy has certain terminology associated with it. A view's immediate container—i.e., the view directly above a view in the view hierarchy—is called its *superview*. The collection of all the views above a given view are known as its *ancestors*. (Thus a view's superview is also one of its ancestors, and a view is contained by each of its ancestors.) A view directly below a view in the view hierarchy is known as a *subview*, and the collection of all the views below a given view are known as its *descendants*. (Thus any subview is also a descendant, and a view contains all of its descendants.) To give a concrete example, consider the `green` view in the `Colors1` example. The `blue` view is its superview, and the `yellow` view is its subview. The root and `blue` views are its ancestors, and the `yellow` view is its single descendant. When views are drawn, they obscure their ancestors. You can see this in action in both of the `Colors` examples. The superview of a view is sometimes called the view's *parent*, and the subviews of a view are sometimes called the view's *children*. Because a view must be completely contained within the bounds of its superview, the superview is occasionally referred to as a *container*.

Note that a view must be in the view hierarchy to be visible. Don't forget to call `addSubview()` after you create a view!

Other View Hierarchy Methods

There are several methods in the `View` class that deal with the view hierarchy. We've seen the most important one, `addSubview()`. Here are a few other useful methods:

`public boolean isInViewHierarchy();`
> Returns `true` if the specified view is in the view hierarchy.

`public void removeFromSuperview();`
> Removes the specified view (and all of its descendants) from the view hierarchy by removing it from its superview.

`protected void removeSubview(View);`
> Removes the specified subview from the view.

`public View superview();`
> Returns a view's superview.

`public Vector subviews();`
> Returns a `Vector` containing all of a view's subviews. The IFC documentation warns you against modifying this vector. If you want to add or remove subviews, use the `addSubview()` and `removeSubview()` methods instead, and let the IFC modify the subview vector for you.

A Realistic Hierarchy

Example 4-3 is a more realistic hierarchy that includes `Button`s, a `Slider`, a `TextField`, and several `ContainerView`s. Each of these GUI controls extends `View`, so they can be added to the view hierarchy. The `GUIHierarchy` application doesn't actually do anything except create and display all the views in its hierarchy. Figure 4-3 shows what the application looks like, and Example 4-3 shows the code that creates it.

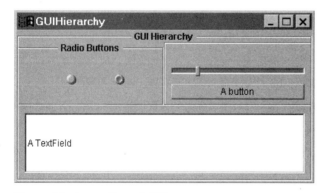

Figure 4-3: A complicated GUI

Example 4-3: A GUI Hierarchy

```
import netscape.application.*;
import netscape.util.*;
```

Example 4-3: A GUI Hierarchy (continued)

```
// An application with a realistic view hierarchy
public class GUIHierarchy extends Application{
  int wMid,hMid;
  // ContainerView, Button, Slider, and TextField all extend View,
  // so we can add them to the view hierarchy.
  ContainerView guiContainer;
  ContainerView radioContainer, sliderContainer, popContainer;
  Button radio1, radio2, button;
  Slider slider;
  TextField textField;

  public void init(){
    mainRootView().setColor(Color.lightGray);

    wMid = mainRootView().bounds().width/2;
    hMid = mainRootView().bounds().height/2;

    // Create a number of views and add them to the view hierarchy.
    guiContainer = new ContainerView(mainRootView().bounds());
    guiContainer.setTitle("GUI Hierarchy");

    radioContainer = new ContainerView(0, 15, wMid, hMid-15);
    radioContainer.setTitle("Radio Buttons");
    radio1 = Button.createRadioButton(wMid/3, (hMid-15)/2, 15, 15);
    radio2 = Button.createRadioButton(2*wMid/3, (hMid-15)/2, 15, 15);
    radioContainer.addSubview(radio1);
    radioContainer.addSubview(radio2);

    textField = new TextField(10, hMid+10, 2*wMid-20, hMid-20);
    textField.setStringValue("A TextField");

    sliderContainer = new ContainerView(wMid, 15, wMid, hMid-15);
    slider = new Slider(10, (hMid-15)/3, wMid-20, 20);
    button = new Button(10, 2*(hMid-15)/3, wMid-20, 20);
    button.setTitle("A button");
    sliderContainer.addSubview(slider);
    sliderContainer.addSubview(button);

    mainRootView().addSubview(guiContainer);
    guiContainer.addSubview(radioContainer);
    guiContainer.addSubview(textField);
    guiContainer.addSubview(sliderContainer);
  }
}
```

There are ten views involved in the GUIHierarchy example, and we can reconstruct the view hierarchy by looking at the code. As usual, mainRootView() is at
the top of the view hierarchy. Its single subview is guiContainer, which has
three subviews: radioContainer, textField, and sliderContainer. The
ContainerView radioContainer has two subviews, radio1 and radio2, and
the ContainerView sliderContainer also has two subviews, slider and
button. The TextField textField has no subviews. Figure 4-4 is a schematic of
GUIHierarchy's view hierarchy.

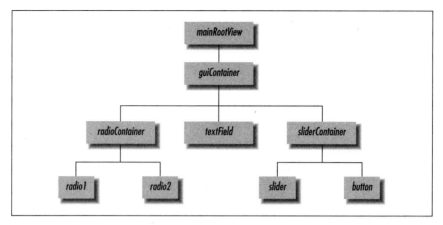

Figure 4-4: GUIHierarchy's view hierarchy

Moving and Resizing Views

There are five relatively self-explanatory `View` methods for moving and/or resizing views:

`public void moveBy(int dx, int dy);`
> Moves the view horizontally *dx* units, and vertically *dy* units. *dx* and *dy* can be either positive or negative.

`public void moveTo(int x, int y);`
> Moves the view's upper-left corner to *x* and *y*.

`public void setBounds(int x, int y, int width, int height);`
> Fixes the view's bounding rectangle to be (*x*, *y*, *width*, *height*). There is also a `setBounds(Rect)` method.

`public void sizeBy(int dx, int dy);`
> Adds *dx* to the view's width and *dy* to the view's height. *dx* and *dy* can be either positive or negative.

`public void sizeTo(int width, int height);`
> Sets the view's width and height.

The IFC doesn't allow negative sizes, so be careful when using the `sizeBy()` method!

Layout Management

In a complicated view hierarchy, the issue of *layout management* arises: there needs to be a way to position views so that the user interface is both aesthetic and functional. There are several possible approaches, and you'll see examples of them in the following chapters. In particular, resizing rules and layout managers are covered in detail in Chapter 15, *Layout Managers*. Four general approaches to layout management are:

- Hard code the size and position of every view. This is the simplest way to create a graphical user interface. One problem with this approach is that fonts have slightly different sizes on different platforms, so an interface that looks good on your platform may not look quite so good on another platform. This approach to layout mangement becomes much easier when you use a tool like the IFC Constructor application.

- Do arithmetic to place subviews according to their superview's sizes. As an example, you could place a subview in the middle of its superview, leaving a 10-pixel border, with the following command:

```
myView.setBounds(10, 10, superview().width()-20, superview.height()-20);
```

This is essentially a variant of the first approach.

- Use resize instructions. Views can be given resize instructions that determine how they are resized and repositioned when their superviews are resized. While this adds flexibility to layout management, the resize instructions are not a fully general solution to the problem. View resizing is covered in detail in Chapter 15.

- Use layout managers. The IFC has two layout managers that can be used to both position views and handle subsequent application resizing. Unfortunately, the IFC layout managers aren't very versatile, so if you want to use layout managers, you'll have to make do with the IFC layout managers, or write your own. See Chapter 15 for more details on the IFC layout managers.

Netscape has developed an extremely useful IFC application called Constructor that allows you to lay out IFC graphical user interfaces by drag-and-drop. If you plan on developing an application with a number of views, give Constructor a try.

CHAPTER 5

Drawing in Views

All IFC GUI components, such as buttons, scrollbars, and the like, extend the View class. They do so by subclassing View and providing custom drawing and event-handling instructions. Similarly, if you'd like to create your own custom components, you'll have to do the same: subclass View and implement your own drawing and event-handling instructions. In this chapter, we'll learn how to do custom drawing, and in Chapter 6, *Mouse and Keyboard Events*, we'll learn how to handle mouse and keyboard events.

If you simply want to use the IFC's powerful predefined GUI controls, you can skip ahead to Chapter 7, *Windows*.

Drawing in Views

Drawing in views is a two-step process. First, to give a View the ability to draw in its bounds, you need to provide an implementation of the view's drawView() method. The drawView() method contains the rule for drawing in the given view: put a rectangle here, a circle there, some text in between, and so on. Second, to get a view to draw—i.e., force an immediate update on the screen— call the view's draw() method. In this case, there's a distinction between the method you implement (drawView()) and the method you call (draw()). The IFC's implementation of draw() does some preliminary calculations, then calls drawView().*

In this chapter, we'll first learn how to implement drawView(), then learn how to use the draw() method by seeing it in action in an animation example.

---

* If you're familiar with AWT programming, you'll recognize the roles of drawView() and draw() as being similar to paint() and repaint().

The drawView( ) Method

The drawView( ) method is the primitive method called by the system when a view needs to be drawn on the screen, and is the single method that needs to be overridden in order to do custom drawing with a View subclass. The prototype of drawView( ) is:

```
public void drawView(Graphics g);
```

An IFC Graphics object contains information about the currently selected font, color, and so on. Before we proceed, let's take a more detailed look at Graphics.

The Graphics Class

The ColorView class, from the previous chapter, is a good example of how to use a Graphics object in drawView( ). Here is the code for ColorView:

```
class ColorView extends View{
    Color color;

    public ColorView(int x,int y,int w,int h,Color c){
        super(x,y,w,h);
        color = c;
    }

    public void drawView(Graphics g){
        g.setColor(color);
        g.fillRect(0,0,bounds.width,bounds.height);
    }
}
```

As you can see, drawView( ) is passed an IFC Graphics object *g* as an argument. The Graphics class represents a *graphics context* for drawing on the screen. A Graphics object contains important information about how any drawing should be done: where it should appear on the screen, what color, what font, and so on. Graphics also has a (large!) number of methods to simplify drawing geometrical shapes and text. The code snippet above contains two methods that you will undoubtedly use frequently: public void setColor(Color); and public void fillRect(int, int, int, int), which also comes in a second variety, public void fillRect(Rect). You should always set the color before drawing in a Graphics object; otherwise, you can't be sure about what color you're going to get. The fillRect(*r*) method simply fills the given rectangle *r* with the Graphics object's current color.

The Graphics class also contains methods to draw arcs, Bitmaps (see Chapter 18, *Animation and Images*), characters, lines, ovals, points, polygons, rounded rectangles, and strings. We'll see an example using some of these methods below. If you're familiar with AWT programming, you'll recognize that the IFC Graphics class is simply a wrapper around the AWT's Graphics class.

A Graphics object can be created directly by a View, by using the create-Graphics( ) method, which has the following prototype:

```
public Graphics createGraphics(View);
```

Since graphics contexts use system resources, if you create a Graphics object in this way, you should always remember to call its dispose() method when you are done with it.

Rectangles Revisited

The IFC coordinate system was introduced in Chapter 4, *The View Hierarchy*, but we repeat it here because it relates to the topic at hand. In the IFC coordinate system, (0,0) is located at the upper-left corner of the view, the positive x-direction is to the right, and the positive y-direction is down. See Figure 5-1.

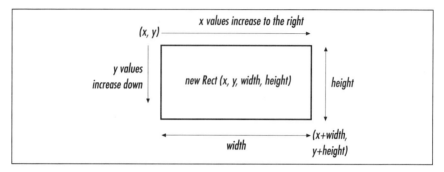

Figure 5-1: A rectangle in the IFC coordinate system

Rectangles in the IFC are represented by the Rect class, and their positions are defined by relative coordinates: the x and y fields contain the location of the upper-left corner of the rectangle in its view, and the width and height fields define the width and height of the rectangle. As an example, recall the second line of the ColorView.drawView():

```
g.fillRect(0,0,bounds.width,bounds.height);
```

It fills a Rect, given by the four arguments, with a solid color. The bounds() method is a public method of the View class, and returns the Rect that defines where the view lies in its superView. The x and y variables of the Rect to be filled are both zero, so the upper left hand corner of the Rect lies at the upper-left corner of the ColorView, and the width and height fields are bounds.width and bounds.height, which means that this command completely fills the view with a solid color. It may be slightly counterintuitive, but note that the command g.fillRect(bounds()) generally does *not* completely fill a view! Can you see why?* To eliminate this minor inconvenience, View defines the localBounds() method, which returns the Rect given by (0,0,bounds.width,bounds.height). Therefore, a cleaner alternative to the line of code shown previously is g.fillRect(localBounds()).

---

* g.fillRect(bounds()) doesn't necessarily fill an entire view because the view's bounds.x and bounds.y variables are not necessarily zero: they define where the view lies in the super-view.

`ColorView`'s implementation of `drawView()` simply fills its bounding `Rect` with a solid `Color`. Far more complicated drawing is possible, of course! Below, we'll see an example that draws a number of different geometrical shapes.

The draw( ) Method

If you want a view to be redrawn according to your implementation of `draw-View()`, call its `draw()` method, *not* its `drawView()` method. The `draw()` method comes in three forms:

```
public void draw();
public void draw(Rect rect);
public void draw(Graphics g, Rect rect);
```

Generally you'll only need the first two methods. Calling `draw()` causes an immediate redraw of the entire view, but calling `draw(rect)` causes an immediate update of the area bounded by *rect*, and not the entire view.

Roughly speaking, `View`'s implementation of `draw()` creates a `Graphics` object g, does some preliminary calculations involving the view hierarchy, then calls `draw-View(g)`. Since `draw()` goes through the extra trouble of making sure the entire view hierarchy will be drawn correctly, you should never call `drawView()` directly. Let `draw()` call it for you.

A Drawing Example

The `Drawings` example (Example 5-1) implements `drawView()`, and uses `draw()` to parade some shapes around the screen. You'll probably notice that this example suffers from severe "flickering." The IFC provides a simple way to eliminate flickering, and we'll learn about that shortly.

Notice that `Drawings` uses a `Timer` to do its animation. Every time the `Timer` fires, it notifies its `Target`, in this case the `shapes` view, which responds by redrawing itself. It's important that this example use a `Timer` rather than a second thread because *the IFC is not thread safe.* All drawing should be done by the main thread. `Targets` are covered in Chapter 8, *The Target Interface,* and `Timers` are covered in Chapter 18.

Example 5-1: Drawing in a View

```
import netscape.application.*;
import netscape.util.*;

// this application animates some shapes and strings
public class Drawings extends Application{
    Shapes shapes;
    Timer timer;

    public void init(){
        // create a new Shapes view and add it to the view hierarchy
        shapes = new Shapes(mainRootView().localBounds());
        mainRootView().addSubview(shapes);
        // create a Timer
        timer = new Timer(shapes,"moveShapes",50);
```

Example 5-1: Drawing in a View (continued)

```
        // start the animation
        timer.start();
    }

    public void cleanup(){
        // stop the timer
        timer.stop();
        super.cleanup();
    }
}

class Shapes extends View implements Target{
    Thread thread = null;
    int h1,dx,w;
    int t = 0;
    Font font;

    public Shapes(Rect r){
        super(r);
        h1 = bounds().height/3;
        dx = bounds().width/4;
        w = bounds().width;
        font = new Font("Helvetica",Font.PLAIN,12);
        // see the section "Drawing Buffers" for an explanantion of this line
        // setBuffered(true);
    }

    // overrides View.drawView() and does custom drawing
    public void drawView(Graphics g){
        // fill the background with cyan
        g.setColor(Color.cyan);
        g.fillRect(localBounds());
        // set the color to blue
        g.setColor(Color.blue);
        // draw some shapes and strings
        // their positions depend on the variable t
        g.fillRect(t%w,h1*ycoord(t),20,20);
        g.fillRoundedRect((t+dx)%w,h1*ycoord(t+dx),20,20,5,5);
        g.drawOval((t+2*dx)%w,h1*ycoord(t+2*dx),20,20);
        g.drawRoundedRect((t+3*dx)%w,h1*ycoord(t+3*dx),20,20,5,5);
        // set the font or drawStringInRect won't work
        g.setFont(font);
        g.drawStringInRect("Moving",(t+4*dx)%w,h1*ycoord(t+4*dx),
                           20,20,Graphics.CENTERED);
        g.drawStringInRect("Shapes",(t+5*dx)%w,h1*ycoord(t+5*dx),
                           20,20,Graphics.CENTERED);
        g.drawLine((t+6*dx)%w,h1*ycoord(t+6*dx),(t+6*dx)%w+20,
                   h1*ycoord(t+6*dx)+20);
        g.fillOval((t+7*dx)%w,h1*ycoord(t+7*dx),20,20);
        g.drawRect((t+8*dx)%w,h1*ycoord(t+8*dx),20,20);
    }

    // a method to compute the y coordinate of a shape.
    private int ycoord(int a){return ((a%(3*w))/w);}

    // called each time the timer fires
    public void performCommand(String command, Object data){
        if(command.equals("moveShapes")){
```

Example 5-1: Drawing in a View (continued)

```
    t += 4;  // update the time
    draw();  // redraw the view
    }
  }
}
```

Figure 5-2 shows the application created by the code in Example 5-1.

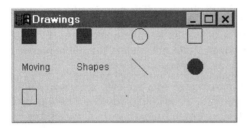

Figure 5-2: The Drawings application

Drawing Summary

In summary, then, to do custom drawing we subclass View and override the View.drawView() method, which tells the system how to draw in our view subclass. In order to force a redrawing of the view, we call the draw() method, which redraws the view using the information we have provided in the draw-View() method. This is enough to get started doing simple programming with the IFC, and you're encouraged to do so! Try starting with something relatively simple like the ColorView class. Once you're comfortable with custom drawing and the view hierarchy, try writing an Application like Drawings that creates a Timer and performs some animation.

The rest of the chapter covers other helpful methods and classes related to drawing.

Drawing Buffers

When the draw() method is called, the IFC erases the view, then calls draw-View() to redraw itself completely. A typical implementation of drawView() will draw a solid-colored background, then do further drawing of text or shapes over the solid background. Hence, for the split second before drawView() is called, and again in the split second before the text or shapes of drawView() are drawn, only a single solid color exists in the view region. If a view is required to redraw itself frequently, say several times per second, the eye will perceive these split seconds of solid color, and the view will appear to "flicker" between the solid-colored background and the text or shapes superimposed on it. You probably saw flickering in the Drawings example.

A technique known as *double buffering* or *buffered drawing* is often used to prevent flickering. To implement buffered drawing, all drawing is first done on an off-screen buffer, and then the contents of the off-screen buffer are transferred to the physical screen all at once. This completely eliminates flickering but decreases performance.

The IFC provides support for double-buffered drawing through its View.setBuffered(boolean) method. To eliminate the flickering in the Drawings example, we need to add only one line of code to the Shapes constructor, setBuffered(true). (It was commented out in the orginial example.)

Now if you compile and run the Shapes example, you'll see that the flickering has disappeared. However, you may notice that the shapes seem to move more slowly! This gives some indication of the decrease in performance when an IFC drawing buffer is used. Bear in mind that Shapes is an extreme example: most applications won't need buffered drawing at all, and the IFC's built-in buffered drawing support should be sufficient for most other applications.

For high-performance drawing, you'll have to create your own off-screen buffer with the Bitmap class and also use *clipping*, a technique in which only the part of the view that has changed is updated. Chapter 18, *Animation and Images*, has an example that uses both clipping and an off-screen buffer.

Debugging Graphics

The DebugGraphics class extends Graphics and overrides many of its methods in such a way that it's useful for graphics debugging. To use a DebugGraphics object rather than a Graphics object, a view subclass only needs to call one method:

```
public void setGraphicsDebugOptions(int option);
```

The parameter *option* can take one of four values:

DebugGraphics.FLASH_OPTION
> The portion of the graphics object that is being altered will flash several times while being drawn. Use the static DebugGraphics methods setFlashCount(), setFlashTime(), and setFlashColor() to set the parameters of the flashing.

DebugGraphics.LOG_OPTION
> The application keeps a text log of all graphics operations. Use the static DebugGraphics method setLogStream() to set the PrintStream.

DebugGraphics.BUFFERED_OPTION
> The application displays an ExternalWindow containing any off-screen drawing.

DebugGraphics.NONE_OPTION
> Turns off Graphics debugging.

It is possible to use more than one option at once. Calling setDebugGraphics-Options(NONE_OPTION) turns off the Graphics debugging, no matter what the current option is. The other three options can be used in any combination by using the | operator. For instance, to use the FLASH_OPTION and the LOG_OPTION, call:

```
setDebugGraphicsOptions(DebugGraphics.FLASH_OPTION |
                        DebugGraphics.LOG_OPTION);
```

To get an idea of what the graphics debugging looks like, try using one or more of the debugging options with `Shapes`, `FlickerView`, or one of your own `View` subclasses. All three options are quite effective in keeping track of `Graphics` operations, and the `FLASH_OPTION` is an interesting effect in its own right!

Asynchronous Drawing

The `draw()` method is synchronous, and thus all drawing is completed before `draw()` returns. If this isn't necessary, you can use `View`'s `setDirty()` method:

```
public void setDirty(boolean b);
```

Calling `setDirty(true)` marks the entire view as dirty, and conversely, calling `setDirty(false)` marks it as clean.

As we'll learn in Chapter 6, the IFC processes events one at a time. To make sure the application's user interface always remains in sync with the current state of the application, as one of the last steps of processing an event the IFC calls the `RootView`'s `drawDirtyViews()` method and redraws all the views marked as "dirty." Therefore, you have a choice about when you want views to be drawn. You can force an immediate update by calling `draw()`, or you can call `setDirty()` and let the IFC call `draw()` itself after it's done processing the current event.

As an example of when you might want to use asynchronous drawing, consider the case where an application is doing a calculation that involves changing many of its views. The application could do this sequentially: each time it finishes a calculation involving a view, it could update the view immediately by calling the given view's `draw()` method, then proceed with its calculations involving the next view, and so on. Alternatively, it could do the complete calculation without pausing to `draw()`. The application could mark the views that need updating by calling their `setDirty()` methods. Then, when the calculation was done, the application would update all the dirty views at once.

The IFC also allows you to mark individual rectangular regions as being dirty with `View`'s `addDirtyRect()` method:

```
public void addDirtyRect(Rect r);
```

The `addDirtyRect()` method marks the view as being dirty; however, the IFC also saves the information that only the `Rect` `r`, and not the entire view, needs updating. In other words, marking a view as dirty tells the IFC that some portion of the view needs to be redrawn. Without further information, the IFC simply redraws the entire view. When you use `addDirtyRect()`, it marks the view as dirty, but it also tells the IFC that it's not necessary to update the entire view. Only the rectangle (or rectangles, if `addDirtyRect()` is called multiple times) marked as dirty will be redrawn. Calling `addDirtyRect(null)` is equivalent to calling `setDirty(true)`.

A good way to implement asynchronous drawing in a view subclass is to mark part or all of the view as dirty every time the view's internal state is changed and requires redrawing. When the system is done processing the event at hand, it will redraw every dirty view, all at once. We'll see examples of both synchronous and asynchronous drawing in this book. Which technique you use is up to you.

Transparent Views

Sometimes the drawing performed by a view's drawView() method won't completely fill its bounding rectangle. For example, if we replaced fillRect() by fillOval() in the ColorView class above, the drawing done by drawView() wouldn't cover the corners of its bounds. In this case, the drawing done by the view's superview would show through the regions that are left untouched by drawView(), and the view would be referred to as being partially *transparent*. If a view's drawView() method completely covers its bounding rectangle, you can override the isTransparent() method so that it returns false. Since all drawing in the IFC is done in a step-by-step fashion, proceeding down the view hierarchy, by overriding the isTransparent() method you notify the IFC that it doesn't have to draw in the region underneath the opaque view, thus improving performance. If your drawing performance is satisfactory, it's generally better to let isTransparent() fall through to the default implementation (that returns true), since it guarantees that your views will be drawn correctly.

Background Images

If you want to display an image or a solid color in the background of your application, subclassing is unnecessary, since the RootView class has a method to set the color, setColor(), and a method to display a background image, setImage(). The Background application in Example 5-2 loads an image and centers it in the background. Figure 5-3 displays the results.

Example 5-2: Displaying a Figure in the Background

```
import netscape.application.*;
import netscape.util.*;

// Displays a JPEG file in the background
public class Background extends Application{
  Bitmap bitmap;
  java.net.URL url;

  public void init(){
    // create the URL
    try{url = new java.net.URL(codeBase(),"test.jpg");}
    catch(java.net.MalformedURLException e){
      System.out.println("bad URL");
      System.exit(0);
    }
    // create the Bitmap
    bitmap = Bitmap.bitmapFromURL(url);

    // show the bitmap in the RootView
    mainRootView().setColor(Color.green);
    mainRootView().setImage(bitmap);
    mainRootView().setImageDisplayStyle(Image.TILED);
  }
}
```

Most of the code for the Background application is self-explanatory, but there are a few things we haven't seen yet. First of all, the Bitmap class is an IFC class used

Figure 5-3: Displaying a JPEG file

to display images, typically GIF or JPEG files. We use the static `Bitmap` method `bitmapFromURL()` to create a bitmap that displays the given image. After that, we set the `RootView`'s background color, image, and display style, in this case `Image.TILED`. We'll learn more about the IFC classes `Bitmap` and `Image` in Chapter 18, but for now, we simply note that another possibility for the display style is `Image.CENTERED`.

Cursors

Many applications use different cursors for the mouse pointer depending on where the mouse pointer is and what it can do in its current location. The IFC provides a number of cursors other than the default arrow cursor. These are the standard Java cursors, and are shown in Figure 5-4. As you can see, there's a cursor for nearly every occasion.

Each of the cursors in Figure 5-4 is associated with a static integer in the `View` class. For example, the default is cursor `View.ARROW_CURSOR`, and others are `View.HAND_CURSOR`, `View.MOVE_CURSOR`, `View.SW_RESIZE_CURSOR`, and so on.

Custom Cursor Behavior

Getting a `View` subclass to use a cursor other than the default arrow cursor is a simple matter. All you need to do is override `View`'s `cursorForPoint()` method:

```
public int cursorForPoint(int x, int y);
```

`cursorForPoint()` should return one of the `View` cursor constants discussed above. Typically this method will ignore the x and y coordinates and just return a constant cursor value. Some `View` subclasses, however may need to display a different cursor at different spots and can use `cursorForPoint()` to do this. Once you've overridden `cursorForPoint()`, the IFC does the rest! The IFC automatically updates the cursor based on the mouse pointer's position within the `View`.

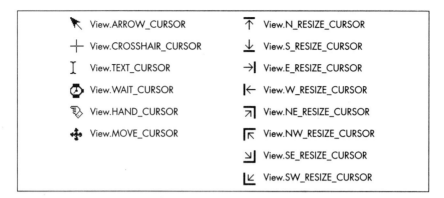

Figure 5-4: The 14 IFC cursors (on a UNIX platform)

RootView and the Cursor

The cursor is actually updated by the RootView, which calls the correct View's cursorForPoint() method, then updates the cursor accordingly. Since the Root-View plays a special role in updating the cursor, RootView has a few additional methods for working with cursors.

Using the RootView's setOverrideCursor(), you can notify the RootView that it should ignore all cursorForPoint() methods and display a single specified cursor. Here is the prototype:

```
public void setOverrideCursor(int cursor);
```

Again, cursor should be one of the View cursor constants. Calling remove-OverrideCursor() returns cursor control to the cursorForPoint() methods. Use this method, for example, to display a WAIT_CURSOR when your program is loading a large file or doing some other time-consuming task with the main thread. This lets your users know that the application is working, and has not frozen up.

A related RootView method is updateCursor(). The RootView normally only calls cursorForPoint() and updates the cursor when the mouse moves. Calling updateCursor() tells it to update the cursor immediately. This is useful when something has changed that would cause cursorForPoint() to return a different value. Unfortunately, Java has problems with cursor updating: on some platforms, even though the RootView has notified the AWT that it wants a new cursor, the AWT won't draw a new cursor until the mouse is moved.

CHAPTER 6

Mouse and Keyboard Events

Most Java applications, and IFC applications in particular, are event-driven. When a user performs an action, such as moving the mouse or hitting a key, the operating system creates an *event object* and notifies the application by placing the event on the application's event queue. Normally, the application's main thread sits in an infinite loop, taking events off the queue and processing them, one at a time. If there are no events on the queue, the application's main thread does nothing while it waits for an event to arrive.

In this chapter, we'll learn how to implement methods to handle mouse and keyboard events. In Chapter 8, *The Target Interface*, we'll learn about how most other events, such as button presses, are handled.

Handling Mouse Events

In the IFC, mouse events have their own class, MouseEvent. When the user presses the mouse button, the IFC creates a MouseEvent. When it's the MouseEvent's turn to be processed, the IFC determines which View should handle the MouseEvent, then calls that view's mouseDown() method. The mouse-Down() method takes only the MouseEvent as an argument, so to handle a MouseEvent by setting the integers mouseX and mouseY equal to the mouse coordinates, we could write:

```
public boolean mouseDown(MouseEvent e) {
  mouseX = e.x;
  mouseY = e.y;
  return true;
}
```

As you can see, the MouseEvent class has two public member variables, x and y, that represent the coordinates of the mouse at the time of the event. Moreover, notice that mouseDown() returns a boolean. Every mouse click consists of three parts: a mouse down, followed by zero or more mouse drags, and then, finally, a single mouse up. If mouseDown() returns true, the RootView calls its

45

setMouseView() method and specifies that the mouse events associated with subsequent mouse drags and mouse ups should be handled by the same view that processed the mouse down. Therefore any subsequent MouseEvents representing a mouse drag result in calls to the view's mouseDragged() method, and the final MouseEvent representing the mouse up results in a call to the view's mouseUp() method. If mouseDown() returns false, no further processing will be done on the MouseEvent, and mouseDragged() and mouseUp() won't be called at all.

The default implementations of mouseDragged() and mouseUp() in View do nothing.

Normally mouseDragged() is only called as long as the mouse remains in the view's bounds, but by overriding View's wantsAutoscrollEvents() method to return true, you can still collect mouse events even if the mouse is dragged outside the view's bounds.

The View class also implements three other methods related to MouseEvents: mouseEntered(), mouseExited(), and mouseMoved().

The Scribble example (listed in Example 6-1 and shown in Figure 6-1), familiar to *Java in a Nutshell* readers, allows a user to draw in a view. ScribbleView handles mouseDown() events by setting the value of two variables, lastx and lasty, and returns true because we want mouseDragged() to be called. The mouseDragged() method draws a line from (lastx, lasty), to the current mouse position and saves the segment in a vector of Lines.

Example 6-1: Handling Mouse Events

```
import netscape.application.*;
import netscape.util.*;

// an example that shows how to handle mouse events in a view
public class Scribble extends Application{
  ScribbleView sview;

  public void init(){
    super.init();
    // create a ScribbleView and add it to the hierarchy
    sview = new ScribbleView(mainRootView().localBounds());
    mainRootView().addSubview(sview);
  }
}

// a view that you can scribble in
class ScribbleView extends View{
  Vector linelist;
  int lastx,lasty;
  boolean drawLastLineOnly = false;

  public ScribbleView(Rect r){
    super(r);
    // linelist is a vector that keeps track of all the lines
    // that have been drawn
    linelist = new Vector(1000);
    setBuffered(true);
  }
```

Example 6-1: Handling Mouse Events (continued)

```
public void drawView(Graphics g){
  // fill the background
  g.setColor(Color.cyan);
  g.fillRect(localBounds());

  // set the line color
  g.setColor(Color.black);

  // draw the lines
  Line line;
  if(!linelist.isEmpty()){
    for(int k = 0;k < linelist.size();k++){
      line = (Line) linelist.elementAt(k);
      g.drawLine(line.x1,line.y1,line.x2,line.y2);
    }
  }
}

public boolean mouseDown(MouseEvent e){
  lastx = e.x;
  lasty = e.y;
  // return true so mouseDragged() will be called
  return true;
}

public void mouseDragged(MouseEvent e){
  // ignore the dragging if the mouse is outside of the view
  if(!containsPointInVisibleRect(e.x,e.y)) return;

  // add the new line to the list
  linelist.addElement(new Line(lastx,lasty,e.x,e.y));

  // draw the line
  Graphics gr = createGraphics();
  gr.drawLine(lastx,lasty,e.x,e.y);
  gr.dispose();  // don't forget this!

  // update the coordinates
  lastx = e.x;
  lasty = e.y;
  }
}

// helper class that represents a line segment
class Line{
  public int x1,x2,y1,y2;

  public Line(int x1,int y1,int x2,int y2){
    this.x1 = x1;
    this.x2 = x2;
    this.y1 = y1;
    this.y2 = y2;
  }
}
```

Events

Figure 6-1: The Scribble application

Mouse Event Modifiers

The status of modifier keys can be found using the following four MouseEvent methods: isControlKeyDown(), isShiftKeyDown(), isMetaKeyDown(), and isAltKeyDown(). The last two methods provide a way of identifying which mouse button was clicked on platforms with a 2- or 3-button mouse. If the **Meta** key is down, the MouseEvent corresponds to a right-click on either a 2- or 3-button mouse, and if the **Alt** key is down, the MouseEvent corresponds to a center button click on a 3-button mouse. Since Java and the IFC are designed to be platform-independent, it's best to assume that the user will have only a single-button mouse. On the other hand, users with one-button mice can simulate other buttons by pressing the **Meta** and **Alt** keys.

MouseEvents also have a method clickCount(), which returns the number of times the button was clicked. For instance, a double-click MouseEvent will have a click count of 2.

The Circles program, in Example 6-2 and shown in Figure 6-2, is a more complex example that handles double-clicks and right-clicks, as well as single left-clicks. When a user first clicks in the view, a circle appears where the MouseEvent occured. Once a circle is in the view, it can be dragged around by using the left mouse button. More circles can be created by using the left mouse button, provided the MouseEvent doesn't occur in an existing circle. And finally, if a user right-clicks or double-clicks on a circle, it disappears. If the MouseEvent represents a right- or double-click, mouseDown() returns false, because we don't want the IFC to make any further calls to mouseDragged(). After all, right- or double-clicking destroys a circle, and it makes no sense to drag something that's just been destroyed!

If you try double-clicking outside of a circle, you'll see a circle appear on the first click, then disappear on the second. This is because the IFC is sending *two* MouseEvents: one for the first click, with a click count of 1, followed by another for the second click, with a click count of 2. Keep this in mind if you're planning on using both single- and double-clicks in an application.

Unlike ScribbleView, CircleView calls setDirty(true) to do its drawing. This redraws the whole view, but is acceptable because in general there will only be a few Circles in the view at any one time, as opposed to potentially hundreds of Lines as in a ScribbleView. Finally, CircleView uses a drawing buffer to prevent flickering while a circle is being dragged.

Example 6-2: Using MouseEvent Modifiers

```
import netscape.application.*;
import netscape.util.*;

public class Circles extends Application{
  CircleView cview;

  public void init(){
    cview = new CircleView(mainRootView().localBounds());
    mainRootView().addSubview(cview);
    mainRootView().setColor(Color.green);
  }
}

class CircleView extends View{
  Vector circles;
  Color circlecolor;
  int dragnumber;

  public CircleView(Rect rect){
    super(rect);
    circles = new Vector();
    circlecolor = Color.blue;
    setBuffered(true);          .
  }

  public void drawView(Graphics g){
    g.setColor(circlecolor);
    if(!circles.isEmpty()){
      Circle circle;
      for(int k=0;k<circles.size();k++){
        circle = (Circle) circles.elementAt(k);
        g.fillOval(circle.x-circle.r, circle.y-circle.r, 2*circle.r,
                   2*circle.r);
      }
    }
  }

  public boolean mouseDown(MouseEvent e){
    if(!circles.isEmpty()){
      Circle circle;
      for(int k = 0;k<circles.size();k++){
        circle = (Circle) circles.elementAt(k);
        if(circle.isInside(e.x,e.y)){
          if(e.isMetaKeyDown() || e.clickCount() > 1){
```

Example 6-2: Using MouseEvent Modifiers (continued)

```
                // There was a right-click or double-click
                // in an existing circle.  Remove it.
                circles.removeElementAt(k);
                // Mark the view as dirty so it gets redrawn
                setDirty(true);
                return false;
              }
              else{
                // A single click in a circle.
                // Set it up so the user can drag the circle.
                dragnumber = k;
                return true;
              }
          }
        }
      }

      // We're not inside a circle.  Ignore
      // double-clicks and right-clicks.
      if(e.isMetaKeyDown() || e.clickCount() > 1) return false;
      circles.addElement(new Circle(e.x,e.y));
      // Make the new circle the circle eligible to
      // be dragged.
      dragnumber = circles.size()-1;
      // redraw the view
      setDirty(true);
      return true;
  }

  public void mouseDragged(MouseEvent e){
    Circle circle = (Circle) circles.elementAt(dragnumber);
    // Move the circle and redraw the view.
    circle.moveTo(e.x,e.y);
    setDirty(true);
  }
}

// a simple class representing a circle
class Circle {
  public int x,y;
  public int r=10;

  public Circle(int x, int y){
    this.x = x;
    this.y = y;
  }

  public boolean isInside(int a,int b){
    if(((x-a)*(x-a) + (y-b)*(y-b)) <= r*r)
      return true;
    else return false;
  }

  public void moveTo(int x,int y){
    this.x = x;
    this.y = y;
  }
}
```

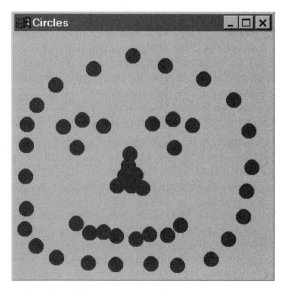

Figure 6-2: The Circles application

The Circles example shows how to move objects around inside a view. If you'd like some practice with mouse events, try modifying Circles so that right-clicking on a circle resizes it rather than deletes it.

Finally, a word of warning: if you're used to programming with the AWT, note *carefully* that some of the names of the IFC mouse event-handling methods are slightly different than those found in the AWT, and *javac* won't issue an error if you forget and use the AWT name rather than the IFC name. If you forget, you'll soon discover that your application doesn't work as expected! In particular, note that the AWT uses mouseDrag() and the IFC uses mouseDragged(). One simple solution to this is to always call the superclass' method when you override the method in a derived class. If you accidentally misspelled the name, *javac* will notice and give you a "no such method" error.

Handling Keyboard Events

The IFC class that represents keyboard events is the KeyEvent class. To handle a KeyEvent in a View, you need to provide an implementation for keyDown(), and, if desired, keyUp(). These two methods have the following prototypes:

```
public void keyDown(KeyEvent e);
public void keyUp(KeyEvent e);
```

The key that was pressed is contained in the key field of a KeyEvent object. The key field is an integer, so to find the corresponding character you need to explicitly typecast the key; i.e., if evt is a KeyEvent, use:

```
char c = (char) evt.key;
```

Special keys, such as function keys, are covered in more detail later in the chapter.

Focus Management

Only one view can receive KeyEvents at a time. The specified view is said to have the *focus*. If you want a view to have the focus, call its setFocusedView() method. When a View gains the focus of the application, its startFocus() method is called, and when it loses the focus, its stopFocus() method is called. If you would like a view to have special behavior when it is in focus (for example, displaying a special border), provide an implementation of the start-Focus() and stopFocus() methods.

As an example of when the focus might be relevant, consider an Application with two InternalWindows, each of which has an editable TextField. We'll cover InternalWindow and TextField later, but for now, it's enough to know that InternalWindow is a View that acts like a window: an InternalWindow can be moved, resized, and closed, for instance. TextField is also a View subclass, and is used to edit and display single-line text. If the user wants to edit one of the TextFields, he could click on the frame of the InternalWindow surrounding the TextField. The InternalWindow could then respond by calling the setFocused-View() method of its TextField to give it the focus. As part of giving the focus to the TextField, the IFC would call the TextField's startFocus() method. The TextField responds by displaying a blinking cursor. If the user later clicked on the second InternalWindow, and the second InternalWindow called setFo-cusedView() to give the focus to its TextField, the IFC would call the stopFocus() method of the first TextField, and would follow that up with a call to the startFocus() method of the second TextField.

If the Application loses focus (because the user has decided to use another application, for instance) the IFC calls the pauseFocus() method of the view that is currently in focus. Correspondingly, when the Application regains the focus (usually by the user clicking in the application's window), the IFC calls its resumeFocus() method.

The Keyboard User Interface

Although mouse-driven user interfaces are visual and intuitive, once users gain familiarity with an application they often find keyboard-driven interfaces faster and more convenient. As such, the IFC has a *keyboard user interface* that allows a user to select views without pointing and clicking with the mouse. By pressing the **Tab** key, the user can select the different views in the active RootView in succession. The selected view, highlighted (by default) by a small arrow, receives and processes relevant keyboard events. For instance, if a TextField is selected, it will process keyboard events normally, but if a Slider is selected, it will ignore all keyboard events except for the left and right arrow keys, which will move the Slider's knob back and forth. Pressing **Shift-Tab** traverses the views in reverse order, and if you want to change the selected view programmatically, take a look at the RootView API in the reference section.

View subclasses that have overridden the canBecomeSelectedView() method to return true are eligible to be the selected view. Nearly all the IFC's GUI components are selectable. Handling keyboard events for the keyboard user interface is different from the keyboard event handling covered in this chapter, and in Chapter 8, we'll learn more about how to write keyboard user interfaces.

The keyboard user interface is enabled by default; if you want to disable it, call setKeyboardUIEnabled(false) in the Application's init() method. Once an application is started, there's no way to enable or disable the keyboard user interface, so you need to decide in init() whether or not to disable it.

Function Keys and Modifier Keys

The KeyEvent class contains a host of methods for identifying modifier or other special keys. Some representative examples are isShiftKeyDown(), isAltKey-Down(), isFunctionKey(), and isArrowKey(). Please see the reference section at the end of the book for a complete list.

One thing to be aware of is that the browser or underlying operating system may intercept certain key events before an IFC Application has a chance to process them. You can expect your IFC application to receive alphanumeric characters properly, but unfortunately you might find that the behavior of the **Alt**, **Control**, and function keys is browser- and platform-dependent.

The Keys example (Example 6-3) shows how KeyEvents can be handled in an Application. It creates two KeyView instances, each of which simply displays a message indicating which key was typed. It checks for six special keys and two modifier keys. In order for a KeyView to gain the focus, a user must click in the view. KeyView also indicates when it is not in focus, and when its focus has been paused. If focus management is not yet clear to you, give this example a try. Figure 6-3 displays the results.

Example 6-3: Handling KeyEvents

```
import netscape.application.*;
import netscape.util.*;

// an example application that handles keyboard events
public class Keys extends Application{
  KeyView kview1,kview2;

  public void init(){
    int w = mainRootView().bounds().width;
    int h = mainRootView().bounds().height;
    kview1 = new KeyView(w/5,h/5,3*w/5,h/5,Color.blue);
    mainRootView().addSubview(kview1);
    kview2 = new KeyView(w/5,3*h/5,3*w/5,h/5,Color.green);
    mainRootView().addSubview(kview2);
  }
}

// handles keyboard events
class KeyView extends View{
  Color color;
  int keynum;
  String key;
  boolean focusPaused = false;
  boolean inFocus = false;
  boolean focusStarted = false;
```

Example 6-3: Handling KeyEvents (continued)

```
public KeyView(int x, int y, int w, int h,Color c){
  super(x,y,w,h);
  color = c;
  keynum = 0;
  setBuffered(true);
}

public void drawView(Graphics g){
  g.setColor(color);
  g.fillRect(localBounds());
  g.setColor(Color.black);
  // The application has lost the focus, so the view's
  // focus has been paused.
  if(focusPaused){
    g.drawString("Focus paused",10,20);
    return;
  }
  // The user has clicked in the view, but hasn't typed a key yet.
  if(focusStarted){
    g.drawString("In focus",10,20);
    focusStarted = false;
    return;
  }
  // The view is in focus and the user typed a key.
  if(inFocus) {
    g.drawString("You pressed the " + key + " key",10,20);
  }
  // The view is not in focus.
  else g.drawString("Not in Focus",10,20);
}

public void keyDown(KeyEvent e){
  keynum = e.key;

  // Sort through some different possibilities for the key.
  if(e.isReturnKey()) key = "return";
  else if(e.isFunctionKey() != 0) key = "F" + e.isFunctionKey();
  else if(e.isRightArrowKey()) key = "right arrow";
  else if(e.isLeftArrowKey()) key = "left arrow";
  else if(e.isUpArrowKey()) key = "up arrow";
  else if(e.isDownArrowKey()) key = "down arrow";
  else key = String.valueOf((char) e.key);

  if(e.isAltKeyDown()) key = "Alt key and the " + key;
  if(e.isControlKeyDown()){
    // Do a conversion to find out which key was pressed.
    char newKey = (char) (e.key - 1);
    newKey += 'a';
    key = String.valueOf(newKey);
    key = "Ctrl key and the " + key;
  }
  setDirty(true);
}

// Set this to be the focused view when clicked on.
public boolean mouseDown(MouseEvent e){
  setFocusedView();
  return false;  // no need to handle mouseDragged()
```

Example 6-3: Handling KeyEvents (continued)

```
}

// Called when this is the focused view, and the application loses focus.
public void pauseFocus(){ focusPaused = true; draw(); }

// Called when the application regains the focus.
public void resumeFocus(){ focusPaused = false; draw(); }

// Called when the view gains the focus.
public void startFocus(){
  inFocus = true;
  focusStarted = true;
  draw();
}

// Called when the view loses the focus.
public void stopFocus(){ inFocus = false; draw(); }
}
```

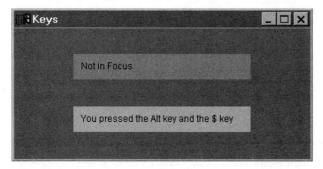

Figure 6-3: The Keys application

Event Processing and the EventLoop

As explained earlier in this chapter, IFC applications are event-driven. User actions such as mouse clicks and key presses generate events that are placed on an event queue, and an IFC application sits in an infinite loop, processing the events on the queue one at a time. In this section, we'll examine the details of IFC event processing.

The IFC and the AWT

The core Java classes have an event-handling scheme built into the java.awt package. When the operating system notifies the Java virtual machine of an event, the virtual machine creates a java.awt.Event and passes it to the applet. From there, AWT internals send it to the correct component.

Since the IFC is written entirely in Java, the AWT event-processing scheme underlies every Application. However, the IFC event-handling scheme is quite different from the AWT scheme. How can this be? An IFC Application has *two* threads. The first thread does nothing but handle AWT events by creating corresponding IFC events and placing the IFC events on the Application's internal queue of events. The second thread takes the events off the internal queue of events, one by one. The first thread is invisible to an IFC programmer, and it's the *second* thread that executes the code that you've written. Because of this separation of duties between the two threads, the IFC application is free to handle the IFC events in its own way. To a programmer, the presence of the AWT beneath the IFC is as irrelevant as the Java Virtual Machine beneath the AWT—all that matters is that IFC events are delivered to an IFC event queue.

The Application's EventLoop

An IFC application's event queue is an instance of the `EventLoop` class. The `EventLoop` processes an event in three steps: it 1) calls the application's `willProcessEvent()` method, 2) calls the event's *processor*, and when this method returns, and 3) calls the application's `didProcessEvent()` method. Each `Event` subclass has a processor that gets first crack at handling an event. For instance, the `RootView` is the event processor for keyboard and mouse events, and it processes such events by calling the `keyDown()` or `mouseDown()` methods of the correct view. That said, unless you write an `Event` subclass, you won't have to worry about event processors! On the other hand, you might find the `willProcessEvent()` and `didProcessEvent()` methods helpful. By overriding `willProcessEvent()` and `didProcessEvent()` in an application subclass, you can implement special event handling. Here we cover the `EventFilter` interface, which is yet another method of implementing special event handling.

`Application` gives a programmer access to its internal `EventLoop` through the following method:

```
public EventLoop eventLoop();
```

The `EventLoop` class provides methods to add and remove, as well as process, events. See the reference section for details.

While manipulating the `EventLoop` directly is a fairly uncommon thing to do, there is an `Application` method, `performCommandLater()`, that places a command on the event queue for later execution:

```
public void performCommandLater(Target target, String command,
                                Object data)
```

This method creates a `CommandEvent` object that contains the specified target, command, and data, and places this event on the event queue. When it reaches the front of the queue and is removed, the IFC will pass the command and data to the `performCommand()` method of the target. Although it is perfectly acceptable for an IFC application to invoke the `performCommand()` method of a `Target` directly, calling `performCommandLater()` is a somewhat more elegant way to do it. Also, there are times in which `performCommandLater()` is necessary. For example, a `TextFieldOwner` object has its `textEditingWillEnd()` method invoked when the user finishes editing a value. You might use this method to validate the value and pop up an error dialog box to report invalid input. If you do so, however, the dialog box will take the keyboard focus. When the dialog is dismissed, focus reverts to the `TextField`, and as a result, the `textEditingWill-End()` method is invoked again! The problem is that `textEditingWillEnd()` should not pop up the dialog box directly, but should delay this action using `performCommandLater()`.

Part 3

The User Interface

CHAPTER 7

Windows

The previous four chapters discussed the View class and the techniques you must understand to implement custom View subclasses. The following nine chapters discuss the use of the predefined View subclasses that are part of the IFC. These are the GUI building blocks that you'll use most often in your IFC programming. We begin our discussion of graphical user interfaces by covering windows. The IFC has two classes that represent windows, ExternalWindow and Internal-Window. An ExternalWindow is a native, platform-dependent window, and appears outside the browser. An InternalWindow appears inside the main Root-View's bounds—in fact, InternalWindow is a View subclass. Figure 7-1 shows the two different IFC windows.

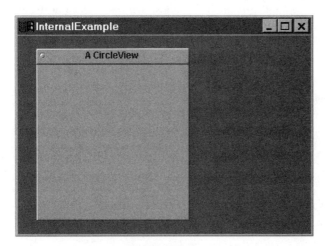

Figure 7-1: An InternalWindow inside an ExternalWindow

In this chapter we'll cover the Window interface, the ExternalWindow class, the InternalWindow class, and the WindowOwner interface. All four of these objects are complicated, and I encourage you to take a look at the reference section after you've read this chapter if you want further information.

The Window Interface

The IFC uses the Window interface to encapsulate the common behavior of the two types of windows. It's a complicated interface, containing 33 methods in all. In this section we'll briefly describe some of the different methods, and in the two sections following this one, we'll cover material more specific to ExternalWindow and InternalWindow.

The different Window methods can be broken into groups depending on what they do.

Initialization Methods

Creating a Window doesn't automatically make it visible on the screen. To make a window visible, you need to *show* it. Window has three methods related to · showing windows.

`public abstract void show();`
> Makes a window visible. We'll see examples of the relation between creating and showing a window later in the chapter.

`public abstract void hide();`
> This method hides but does not destroy a window.

`public void showModally();`
> Shows the window *modally*. When a modal window is present, the modal window gets the input focus, and the rest of the application can't be accessed by the user until the modal window has been dealt with and dismissed. Dialog boxes often use modal windows.

View Methods

Window has two methods related to views:

`public void addSubview(View view);`
> Adds *view* to the window's view hierarchy. In both of the IFC implementations of Window, this method adds *view* to the window's client area, the area bounded by the window's border.

`public View viewForMouse(int x, int y);`
> Returns the View containing the point (*x,y*). If the view hierarchy is such that more than one view contains (*x,y*), it returns the *lowest* view, the view furthest away from the RootView in the view hierarchy.

Resizing Methods

There are several methods related to resizing:

```
public abstract void setBounds(Rect r);
```
Sets the window's bounds to *r*.

```
public void setBounds(int x, int y, int w, int h);
```
Sets the window's bounds to (*x*, *y*, *w*, *h*).

```
public abstract void sizeBy(int dx, int dy);
```
Changes the width of the window by *dx* and the height of the window by *dy*. *dx* and *dy* can be positive or negative.

```
public abstract void sizeTo(int x, int y);
```
Sets the size of the window to (*x*, *y*).

```
public abstract Size windowSizeForContentSize(int width, int height);
```
Returns the window Size necessary to fit a content view of size (*width*, *height*). The window will be slightly bigger than (*width*, *height*) because windows have borders.

```
public abstract void setResizeable(boolean b);
```
Allows the user to resize the window if *b* is true, and prohibits resizing if *b* is false.

The first four methods set the overall size of the window, including the window's border. If you want to set the size of the "client area" (i.e., the area inside the border) to a given width and height, use the windowSizeForContentSize() method in the following way:

```
Size windowSize = myWindow.windowSizeForContentSize(width, height);
myWindow.sizeTo(windowSize.width, windowSize.height);
```

This will size the window so that it accommodates a client area of size (width, height) exactly.

Movement Methods

Window has five methods for moving windows:

```
public abstract void moveTo(int x, int y);
```
Moves the upper-left corner of the window to (*x*, *y*).

```
public abstract void moveBy(int dx, int dy);
```
Moves the window by *dx* and *dy*.

```
public abstract void moveToBack();
```
Moves the window behind the other windows on the screen.

```
public abstract void moveToFront();
```
Moves the window in front of the other windows on the screen.

```
public void center();
```
In the case of an ExternalWindow, center() positions the window in the center of the screen, and in the case of an InternalWindow, center() positions the window in the center of the RootView.

Note that the coordinate system is different for the two different types of windows. For an ExternalWindow, the origin (0,0) is in the upper-left corner of the screen, while for an InternalWindow, the origin (0,0) is in the upper-left corner of the RootView it's appearing in.

Document Methods

Every application has one Window that's denoted the *document* window, which typically contains the view that is currently receiving keyboard events. If a Window is eligible to become the document window, it is said to *contain* a document. Here are four methods related to documents:

public abstract void setContainsDocument();
> Notifies the application that the window is eligible to become the document window.

public abstract boolean isCurrentDocument();
> Returns true if the window is the current document window.

public abstract void didBecomeCurrentDocument();
> Called by the IFC when the window becomes the current document window. You can override this in a subclass.

public abstract void didResignCurrentDocument();
> Called by the IFC when the window loses its status as the current document window. You can override this in a subclass.

The document window is given special treatment by the application's TargetChain, which we'll learn about in Chapter 8, *The Target Interface*.

Static Variables

Finally, Window has two important static variables: TITLE_TYPE, and BLANK_TYPE. A TITLE_TYPE window has a title, and a BLANK_TYPE does not. Both External-Window and InternalWindow create TITLE_TYPE windows by default, but they have constructors to create BLANK_TYPE windows as well.

If all this seems overwhelming or confusing, don't worry! We'll see how to use Window methods in examples in the next two sections.

The ExternalWindow Class

An ExternalWindow is a native, platform-dependent window that appears outside *appletviewer* or a browser. They do little more than implement the Window interface and provide a RootView for subviews.

Creating an ExternalWindow

Creating an ExternalWindow typically takes several steps, shown here:

```
ExternalWindow window = new ExternalWindow();
Size size = window.windowSizeForContentSize(250, 250);
window.sizeTo(size.width, size.height);
window.moveTo(10, 10);
window.show();
```

As you can see, first you create an ExternalWindow. The windowSizeForContentSize() method returns the Size that the window needs to be in order to fit

---

a view of the given size, in this case (250, 250). The sizeTo() method sizes the window to the appropriate size. Calling moveTo() specifies where the ExternalWindow should appear on the screen; if you omit moveTo(), the IFC will choose where to place the window. Finally, calling show() makes the ExternalWindow visible.

ExternalWindow and the View Hierarchy

Since ExternalWindow represents a native window, ExternalWindow does not extend View, and an ExternalWindow is not a part of the main view hierarchy. However, an ExternalWindow's client area is a RootView, and therefore each ExternalWindow has its own view hierarchy, with its RootView at the top. When subviews are added to an ExternalWindow, they are added to the ExternalWindow's RootView. For example:

```
MyView myView = new MyView(new Rect(0, 0, 250, 250));
window.addSubview(myView);
```

An ExternalWindow's RootView can be retrieved with the rootView() method. Since each ExternalWindow has its own RootView, when more than one ExternalWindow is present it's unclear which should be the *main* RootView. Application provides two methods, mainRootView() and setMainRootView(), to remove this ambiguity.

There is no difference between an ExternalWindow's RootView and a RootView that's created when an IFC Application is run as an applet, which makes it easy to write IFC applications that can be run both as applets or standalone applications.

Closing an ExternalWindow

ExternalWindow has two methods related to closing an ExternalWindow, and it's important to keep the distinction between the two in mind.

The hide() method removes the window from the screen, but does *not* destroy the window. Calling a hidden window's show() method will make it reappear.

The dispose() method, on the other hand, *does* destroy the window, once and for all, by destroying the underlying native window. Calling show(), or any other window method after you've called dispose() will cause an error. Since windows often use system resources, you should always call dispose() when you're done with an ExternalWindow.

An ExternalWindow Example

Example 7-1 is an example application that creates an ExternalWindow and adds a CircleView (from Chapter 6, *Mouse and Keyboard Events*) to its view hierarchy. In cleanup() we destroy the window if it hasn't been destroyed already. Figure 7-2 shows ExternalExample being run as an applet.

Example 7-1: An Application with an ExternalWindow

```
import netscape.application.*;
import netscape.util.*;
```

Windows

Example 7-1: An Application with an ExternalWindow (continued)

```
// An application with an ExternalWindow
public class ExternalExample extends Application{
  ExternalWindow eWindow;
  CircleView cView1,cView2;

  public void init(){
    // create a CircleView and put it in the RootView
    cView1 = new CircleView(mainRootView().bounds());
    mainRootView().addSubview(cView1);

    // create a CircleView
    cView2 = new CircleView(new Rect(0,0,200,200));
    eWindow = new ExternalWindow();
    // size the ExternalWindow
    Size s = eWindow.windowSizeForContentSize(cView2.width(),
                                              cView2.height());
    eWindow.sizeTo(s.width,s.height);
    // add the CircleView to the ExternalWindow
    eWindow.addSubview(cView2);
    eWindow.moveTo(50,50);
    eWindow.setTitle("A CircleView");
    eWindow.show();  // show the ExternalWindow
  }

  public void cleanup(){
    if(eWindow != null) eWindow.dispose();  // destroy the window
  }
}
```

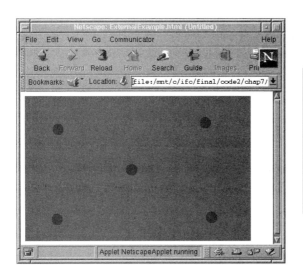

Figure 7-2: An applet with an ExternalWindow

The InternalWindow Class

Since `InternalWindow` extends `View`, an `InternalWindow` can be a member of the main view hierarchy and is therefore more complicated than `External-Window`. Like any other view, an `InternalWindow` can be resized and moved, and will be visible as long as it remains within the application's main `RootView`. Though an `InternalWindow` is a `View`, it isn't added to the view hierarchy in the usual way.

Creating and Showing an InternalWindow

`InternalWindow` has three nontrivial constructors:

```
public InternalWindow(Rect r);
public InternalWindow(int x, int y, int w, int h);
public InternalWindow(int type, int x, int y, int w, int h);
```
> Creates an `InternalWindow` of the given type and bounds Rect (x, y, w, h). The type argument can be either `Window.BLANK_TYPE` or `Window.TITLE_TYPE`.

Once an `InternalWindow` is created, you can make it appear by calling its `show()` method. Don't add it to the view hierarchy as you would any other view! As we'll see below, internal windows appear in "layers" above the main `Root-View`'s view hierarchy, so you need to add them to the application's view hierarchy using `show()` rather than `addSubview()`.

InternalWindow and the View Hierarchy

An `InternalWindow` has a complicated border. If subviews were added directly to an `InternalWindow`, they could potentially obscure parts of the `Internal-Window`'s border. To accommodate for this, `InternalWindow`'s implementation of `addSubview()` adds subviews only to the region bounded by the inner edge of the border. In fact, this area has its own IFC `View` subclass, `WindowContentView`. In summary, then, adding a subview to an `InternalWindow` with `addSubview()` does not add the subview to the window as a whole; rather, it adds the subview to the `WindowContentView`, the region bounded by the inner edge of the `Inter-nalWindow`'s border.

Borders are covered in more detail in Chapter 13, *Borders*, but for now, you might want to make a mental note of how `InternalWindow` implements `addSub-view()` in the presence of a complicated border. If you're designing a `View` subclass with a border, you might want to implement `addSubview()` in a similar way.

Closing an InternalWindow

`InternalWindow` implements the `hide()` method, which removes an `Internal-Window` from the view hierarchy, but doesn't destroy it. Since `InternalWindow` is just a `View`, destroying an `InternalWindow` doesn't require any special method calls analogous to `ExternalWindow`'s `dispose()`. If Java's garbage collector discovers an `InternalWindow` that's not referred to by any other object, the `InternalWindow` will be garbage collected like any other Java object.

The Main Window

An application can have any number of `InternalWindow` instances, but only one can be the *main* window. The concept is similar to that of the document window, but it applies only to `InternalWindows`. The main window's border is drawn differently to indicate its special status. Often dialog boxes, covered in Chapter 17, *Dialog Boxes*, will operate only on the document or main window.

Calling `setCanBecomeMain(false)` prevents an `InternalWindow` from becoming the main window.

Layers

`InternalWindows` are treated as special views that can reside in five different "layers." Windows in a given layer will always obscure windows in lower layers. In order from top to bottom the layers are: DRAG_LAYER, POPUP_LAYER, MODAL_LAYER, PALETTE_LAYER, and DEFAULT_LAYER. The default layer exists above the layer defined by the views that are added directly to the main `RootView` with `addSubview()`; in other words, an `InternalWindow` will always obscure views that are added directly to the `RootView`. Example 7-2 is an application with a window residing in each of the five layers; the results are illustrated in Figure 7-3.

Example 7-2: Layered Windows

```
import netscape.application.*;
import netscape.util.*;

// an application that has InternalWindows in 5 different layers
public class LayerTest extends Application{
  int x = 150;

  public void init(){
    // create the windows and set their titles and layers
    InternalWindow def = new InternalWindow(0,0,x,x);
    def.setLayer(InternalWindow.DEFAULT_LAYER);
    def.setTitle("default");
    InternalWindow pal = new InternalWindow(20,20,x,x);
    pal.setLayer(InternalWindow.PALETTE_LAYER);
    pal.setTitle("palette");
    InternalWindow modal = new InternalWindow(40,40,x,x);
    modal.setLayer(InternalWindow.MODAL_LAYER);
    modal.setTitle("modal");
    InternalWindow popup = new InternalWindow(60,60,x,x);
    popup.setLayer(InternalWindow.POPUP_LAYER);
    popup.setTitle("popup");
    InternalWindow drag = new InternalWindow(80,80,x,x);
    drag.setLayer(InternalWindow.DRAG_LAYER);
    drag.setTitle("drag");

    // show them all
    def.show();
    pal.show();
    modal.show();
```

Example 7-2: Layered Windows (continued)

```
    popup.show();
    drag.show();
  }
}
```

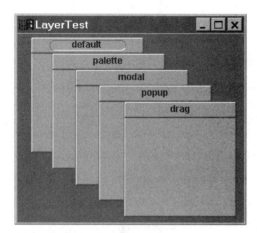

Figure 7-3: Layered windows

Another InternalWindow Example

Example 7-3 is another `InternalWindow` example, similar to the `ExternalEx-ample`. In it, we create an `InternalWindow` and add a `CircleView`. Notice that there's no need for a `cleanup()` method, because Java's garbage collector destroys `InternalWindows` automatically. Figure 7-4 shows `InternalExample` being run as an applet.

Example 7-3: An InternalWindow with a CircleView

```
import netscape.application.*;
import netscape.util.*;

// an application with an InternalWindow
public class InternalExample extends Application{
  InternalWindow iWindow;
  CircleView cView1,cView2;

  public void init(){
    // create a CircleView and put it in the RootView
    cView1 = new CircleView(mainRootView().bounds());
    mainRootView().addSubview(cView1);

    // create a CircleView
    cView2 = new CircleView(new Rect(0,0,200,200));
    iWindow = new InternalWindow();
    // size the InternalWindow
    Size s = iWindow.windowSizeForContentSize(cView2.width(),
                                               cView2.height());
    iWindow.sizeTo(s.width,s.height);
```

Windows

Example 7-3: An InternalWindow with a CircleView (continued)

```
    // add the CircleView to the InternalWindow
    iWindow.addSubview(cView2);
    iWindow.moveTo(50,50);
    iWindow.setTitle("A CircleView");
    iWindow.setCloseable(true); // add a close button to the window
    iWindow.show();            // show the InternalWindow
  }
}
```

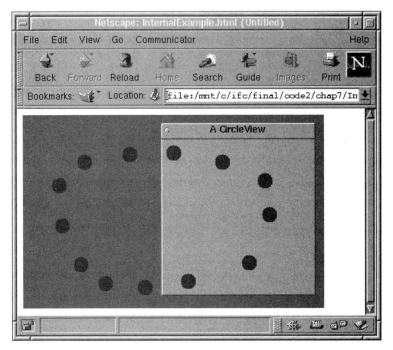

Figure 7-4: An application with an InternalWindow

The WindowOwner Interface

An object implementing the WindowOwner interface is notified when the window it "owns" is shown, hidden, resized, or becomes the main window. In fact, the WindowOwner is the only object that will be notified if a window is hidden or shown, so in some cases it's very important to implement WindowOwner. (The ApplicationViewer example from Chapter 2, *The Application Class*, is a perfect example of an application where it's important that the application implement WindowOwner.) A WindowOwner can own either an ExternalWindow or an InternalWindow.

Here are the methods that compose WindowOwner:

```
public abstract void windowDidBecomeMain(Window window);
public abstract void windowDidHide(Window window);
public abstract void windowDidResignMain(Window window);
```

```
public abstract void windowDidShow(Window window);
public abstract boolean windowWillHide(Window window);
public abstract boolean windowWillShow(Window window);
public abstract void windowWillSizeBy(Window window, Size s);
```

The first four methods are called after the associated event occurs, and the remaining three methods are called before the associated event occurs. By returning `false` from `windowWillHide()` or `windowWillShow()`, the window owner can prevent a window from being hidden or shown. Returning `true` allows the window to be hidden or shown in the normal way.

Calling a window's `setOwner(WindowOwner)` method sets its owner.

CHAPTER 8

The Target Interface

In Chapter 6, *Mouse and Keyboard Events*, we learned about the View methods for handling mouse and keyboard events. Most other events are handled in a completely different way using a framework built around the Target interface. In this chapter, we'll learn how to use Target.

The Target Interface

In Chapters 3 through 6, we learned about the View class. The designers of the IFC built on the framework provided by View and created a number of useful View subclasses that represent GUI controls: Buttons, Sliders, and the like. These GUI classes use an extremely flexible event-handling method based on the Target interface. With Target, the IFC implements an event-handling scheme built on *callbacks*. When a button is pressed, it notifies its Target. When a Slider is moved, it notifies its Target. When a ListItem is selected, it notifies its Target. What makes this system so flexible is that Target is an interface, not a class, and can therefore be implemented by any object.

To give a concrete example, consider an IFC Button. Button extends View. Button overrides View's MouseEvent-handling methods so that when a user clicks in a button's bounds, the button redraws itself to give the illusion of being pressed. Based on your knowledge of the material in Chapter 4, *The View Hierarchy*, and Chapter 5, *Drawing in Views*, you could write a View subclass to do this. But a Button has to do more—for a Button to be useful, it has to notify another object when it has been pressed. When an IFC button is pressed, a String known as the button's *command* is sent to the button's *target*, an object that implements the Target interface. The target, in turn, can then take further action after it has been notified that the button has been pressed.

As mentioned above, the power of this mechanism is that any object can be a target, provided it implements the Target interface. *Any* object—a View, an Application, anything! Target consists of one method:

```
public interface Target{
  public void performCommand(String command, Object data);
}
```

When a button is pressed, the performCommand() method of its target is called. The *data* is the button itself, and the *command* is chosen by you, the programmer. It's good programming practice to choose the command to be something descriptive that indicates what kind of action the target should take. For example, a good command for a button that starts some animation would be "start," and a good command for a button that stops some animation would be "stop."

To summarize, using an IFC GUI control involves the following steps: create the GUI control, set its command, and set its target. The target must implement the Target interface, and in particular, performCommand() should be tailored so that it takes appropriate action when it's called with the GUI control's command as an argument.

In order to understand how the Target interface works, let's look at some code that implements exactly what we discussed above, the example of a button being pushed. (We'll learn more about buttons in Chapter 9, *Buttons.*) Example 8-1 shows how this example could be implemented, and Figure 8-1 shows what it looks like.

Example 8-1: Using a Target

```
import netscape.application.*;
import netscape.util.*;

public class TargetTest extends Application implements Target{
  Button addButton,clearButton;
  TextField tField;
  int pressnumber = 0;

  public void init(){
      mainRootView().setColor(Color.green);

      // Create a button. (More on this in Chapter 9.)
      addButton = new Button(10, 10, 80,3 0);
      // Set its command to something descriptive.
      addButton.setCommand("addOne");
      // Set its target. Note that TargetTest implements Target.
      addButton.setTarget(this);
      addButton.setTitle("Press me");
      // Button extends View, so to use a button, it must be
      // added to the view hierarchy.
      mainRootView().addSubview(addButton);

      // Create another button.
      clearButton = new Button(100, 10, 80, 30);
      clearButton.setCommand("clear");     // set its command
      clearButton.setTarget(this);         // set its target
      clearButton.setTitle("Clear");
```

Example 8-1: Using a Target (continued)

```
        // Add it to the view hierarchy.
        mainRootView().addSubview(clearButton);

        // tField is a TextField that will display the number
        // of times the addButton has been pressed.
        Rect r = mainRootView().bounds;
        tField = new TextField(0, r.height/2, r.width, r.height/2);
        tField.setTransparent(true);
        tField.setJustification(Graphics.CENTERED);
        tField.setEditable(false);
        tField.setBuffered(true);
        mainRootView().addSubview(tField);
    }

    // We must define this method, since TargetTest implements Target.
    public void performCommand(String command, Object data) {
        // take appropriate action based on the command
        if(command.equals("addOne")) addOne();
        else if(command.equals("clear")) clear();
    }

    // Add one to pressnumber and redraw the TextField.
    private void addOne(){
        pressnumber++;
        tField.setStringValue("The button has been pressed " +  pressnumber +
                              " times.");
        tField.setDirty(true);
    }

    // Set pressnumber to zero and redraw the TextField.
    private void clear(){
        pressnumber = 0;
        tField.setStringValue("");
        tField.setDirty(true);
    }
}
```

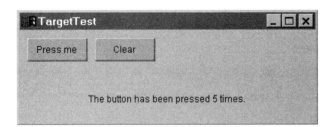

Figure 8-1: A button and its target

Notice in particular the following lines from `TargetTest`:

```
        addButton.setCommand("addOne");
        addButton.setTarget(this);
```

Button's `setCommand()` method specifies the command string that is passed to the `Target`, and Button's `setTarget()` method specifies the target.

TargetTest implements the Target interface by providing an implementation for performCommand(). When the Button titled **Press me** is pushed, TargetTest's performCommand() is called with the command set to addOne and the data set to be the addButton itself, and when the button titled **Clear** is pushed, TargetTest's performCommand() is called with the command set to clear and the data set to be the clearButton.

The performCommand() method sorts through the different possibilities and takes the appropriate action based on the command. If the command is addOne, a short message is displayed showing the number of times the addButton has been pressed, and if the command is clear, the message is erased and pressnumber, which keeps track of the number of times addButton has been pressed, is reset to zero.

Keep in mind that it's not necessary that the Application implement the Target interface. Example 8-2 is functionally identical to the TargetTest example, but rather than having the Application as the Target, we use a custom TextField subclass called TargetField as the Target. Note that the steps taken to use a button in TargetTest2 are the same as in TargetTest: create the button, set its command, set its target, and provide an implementation of Target that handles the command you've chosen. TextField implements Target already, so we have to make sure to call super.performCommand() in the implementation of Target-Field's performCommand().

Example 8-2: Another Target Example

```
import netscape.application.*;
import netscape.util.*;

public class TargetTest2 extends Application{
  Button addButton, clearButton;
  TargetField tField;

  public void init(){
      mainRootView().setColor(Color.green);

      Rect r = mainRootView().bounds;
      tField = new TargetField(0, r.height/2, r.width, r.height/2);
      mainRootView().addSubview(tField);

      // create a button
      addButton = new Button(10,10,80,30);
      addButton.setTitle("Press me");
      addButton.setCommand("addOne");  // set its command
      addButton.setTarget(tField);     // set its target
      mainRootView().addSubview(addButton);

      // create another button
      clearButton = new Button(100,10,80,30);
      clearButton.setTitle("Clear");
      clearButton.setCommand("clear");  // set its command
      clearButton.setTarget(tField);    // set its target
      mainRootView().addSubview(clearButton);
  }
}
```

Example 8-2: Another Target Example (continued)

```
// TargetField is a TextField subclass that can handle the two commands,
// "addOne" and "clear".
class TargetField extends TextField implements Target{
  int pressnumber = 0;

  public TargetField(int x,int y,int w,int h){
    super(x,y,w,h);
    setTransparent(true);
    setJustification(Graphics.CENTERED);
    setEditable(false);
    setBuffered(true);
  }

  // we must define this because TargetField implements Target
  public void performCommand(String command,Object data){
    if(command.equals("addOne")) addOne();
    else if(command.equals("clear")) clear();
    else super.performCommand(command,data);
  }

  // add one to pressnumber and redraw
  private void addOne(){
    pressnumber++;
    setStringValue("The button has been pressed " + pressnumber + " times.");
    setDirty(true);
  }

  // set pressnumber to zero and redraw
  private void clear(){
    pressnumber = 0;
    setStringValue("");
    setDirty(true);
  }
}
```

The Keyboard User Interface

If you recall Chapter 6, we introduced the keyboard user interface, which allows a user to operate a graphical user interface with the keyboard instead of the mouse, but we didn't cover how a View implements keyboard user interface event-handling. The way a View interacts with the keyboard user interface is through the Target interface. With View's setCommandForKey(), you can set the command a View subclass will receive when the user types on the keyboard. Here is the prototype:

```
public void setCommandForKey(String command, Object data, int key,
                             int modifiers, int mask);
```

The *mask* variable can take on one of three values: View.WHEN_SELECTED, View.WHEN_IN_MAIN_WINDOW, or View.ALWAYS. If the user types the *key* with the specified *modifiers*, and the key event makes it past the *mask*, the View subclass' performCommand() will be called with the given *command* and *data*. If you write a custom GUI subclass with a keyboard user interface, you may also want to override canBecomeSelectedView() to return true.

The ExtendedTarget Interface

The `ExtendedTarget` interface extends the `Target` interface. Objects implementing `ExtendedTarget` can be queried about which commands they can perform by calling the single method in the interface definition:

```
public boolean canPerformCommand(String command);
```

The `canPerformCommand()` method should return `true` if the `ExtendedTarget` can perform the indicated command. In addition, the interface definition includes seven static strings: `CUT`, `COPY`, `PASTE`, `NEW_FONT_SELECTION`, `SET_FONT`, `SHOW_COLOR_CHOOSER`, and `SHOW_FONT_CHOOSER`. `ExtendedTarget` is designed to work with the `TargetChain` class, which we turn to next.

The TargetChain Class

It's not always easy to determine where events should be handled. In the case of a mouse click, the system calls the `mouseDown()` method of the innermost view in the view hierarchy containing the mouse pointer, and in the case of a button press, the button's target gets called. But what happens when the user selects `PASTE` from a window menu? The view with the mouse pointer, for instance, may not be the correct object to handle `PASTE`, and moreover, it may not be able to handle a `PASTE` command at all! The `TargetChain` class is what the IFC uses to resolve these difficulties. `TargetChain` contains an ordered list of objects implementing `ExtendedTarget`, and in fact, `TargetChain` itself implements `ExtendedTarget`. When a `TargetChain` is called upon to perform a *command*, *command* is sent to the first `ExtendedTarget` returning `true` to `canPerformCommand(command)`. If no target can perform the command, the command is ignored. The `TargetChain` class also provides methods for adding and subtracting elements from its target list. An `Application`'s `TargetChain` is returned by `TargetChain`'s `applicationChain()` method:

```
public static TargetChain applicationChain();
```

An `ExtendedTarget` can be added to an application's `TargetChain` with the `addTarget()` method:

```
public synchronized void addTarget(ExtendedTarget target,
                                   boolean queryFirst);
```

If *queryFirst* is `true`, *target* will be added to the head of the target chain and queried first. If *queryFirst* is `false`, *target* will be added to the end of the target chain and be queried last.

The full order in which the objects appear in the application's `TargetChain` is:

1. Objects that have been added to the application's `TargetChain` with *queryFirst* set to `true`.

2. The focused `View` in the first `RootView`.

3. If there is a document window, `TargetChain` queries the document window's focused view, the document window's owner, and finally, the document window itself.

4. If there is no document window and the first `RootView` is different from the main `RootView`, `TargetChain` queries the main `RootView`'s focused view.

5. The first `RootView`'s window.

6. The first `RootView`'s owner.

7. The first `RootView`.

8. The `Application`.

9. Objects that have been added to the application's `TargetChain` with *query-First* set to `false`.

Undoubtedly, this is a little confusing! Bear in mind that each `ExternalWindow` has its own `RootView`, so it's possible that the main `RootView`, as returned by the application's `mainRootView()` method, is different from the one that's actually processing keyboard events.

CHAPTER 9

Buttons

In this chapter, we begin our coverage of IFC GUI controls by studying the Button. class. Button is quite representative of IFC GUI controls: they are very simple to create, use, and customize.

In Chapter 8, *The Target Interface*, we saw how to implement the Target interface, and in the TargetTest example, we saw how to create a default IFC button and set its target and command. If you understood that, you understood the most important concepts about buttons in the IFC, and you could begin using them in your applications right away! However, if you want to create a button with behavior other than the default behavior, read on.

Button Basics

Here is some code similar to the code we used to create a button in TargetTest in Chapter 8:

```
button = new Button(10,10,80,30);
button.setTitle("Press me");
button.setCommand("addOne");
button.setTarget(this);
mainRootView().addSubview(button);
```

The first line creates a Button with the given coordinates (remember, Button extends View), the next three set its title, command, and target, and the last line adds button to the view hierarchy as a subview of the main RootView. That's all you need to do to use an IFC Button! (Provided, of course, you've implemented the performCommand() method in your Target to handle the button's command.)

Since Button extends View, you can take advantage of View methods to move or resize a button, as well as add or remove it from the view hierarchy.

Button Attributes

The `TargetTest` example in Chapter 8 created a default IFC button; the only things that we set were its bounds, target, command, and title. However, IFC buttons are highly customizable, and in general it's unnecessary to create a custom `Button` subclass for IFC applications. Table 9-1 contains a description of some of the button attributes you'll likely need for your applications. The last section of this chapter describes some of the more advanced features of IFC buttons. Remember, for each attribute, the IFC normally has a `setAttribute()` method to set the attribute's value and an `attribute()` method that returns the attribute's value. (Or, for attributes that have a `boolean` value, there is an `isAttribute()` method for testing the value.)

Table 9-1: Basic Button Attributes

Attribute	Description
`Target`	The button's target.
`Command`	A `String` that is sent to the button's target when the button is pressed.
`Title`	The `String` displayed on the button.
`Font`	The title's `Font`. The default is `Application`'s default font, Helvetica 12.
`TitleColor`	The title's `Color`. The default is black.
`Image`	The `Image` displayed on the button. The default is no image.
`AltImage`	The `Image` that is displayed when the button is depressed.
`ImagePosition`	Specifies where the button's image appears in relation to the title text. The default image position is to the left of the title.
`Enabled`	Enables or disables the buttons. Disabled buttons are displayed in a different color, light gray by default.
`Type`	Sets the button's type (see below). The default is `PUSH_TYPE`.

Let's look at some of these attributes in detail.

Displaying Images

Most buttons in complicated graphical user interfaces display images rather than text to represent their function. For instance, my text editor has a button with scissors on it, and not surprisingly, it represents a cut command! IFC `Image` objects typically represent GIF or JPEG files and are covered in detail in Chapter 18, *Animation and Images*. Using `setImage()`, it's easy to display images rather than text on buttons. As indicated in Table 9-1, it's possible to have different images for the default state and the depressed state, and if you want both image and text on the button, you can set the position of the image in relation to the button's title with the `setImagePosition()` method.

Enabling and Disabling Buttons

Often applications need to enable or disable buttons according to the state of the application. As an example, consider an application that does some animation and has two buttons, "Start" and "Stop." Only one of these buttons should be enabled at a time: when the animation is proceeding, "Start" should be disabled and "Stop" should be enabled, and when the animation is halted, "Start" should be enabled, and "Stop" should be disabled.

The text on disabled buttons is drawn in light gray by default.

Button Types

The Button class provides four different types of buttons: PUSH_TYPE, TOGGLE_ TYPE, CONTINUOUS_TYPE, and RADIO_TYPE.

Push Buttons

When a push button is clicked on, it sends its command to its target once, and returns to its original state. The Button constructor creates a push button by default, but there is also a static Button method that can be used to create a push button:

```
public static Button createPushButton(int x, int y, int w, int h);
```

Figure 9-1 shows a push button.

Figure 9-1: A push button

Continuous Buttons

A CONTINUOUS_TYPE button sends its command to its target once when it is pressed, and then continues to send its command at regular intervals as long as the user holds the button down. The time between the calls to its target can be set by using the setRepeatDelay() method. As an example of a continuous button, consider the buttons that appear on either end of a scroll bar. Normally one mouse click on the button moves the scroll bar a small amount, and holding the button down causes the scroll bar to move continuously. In fact, the scroll bar button is a "continuous" button: when the user holds the button down, the button sends its command repeatedly, with such a short time interval between firings that the scrolling appears to be continuous.

Creating a continuous button is a two-step process. First create a push button, then use setType() to further specify that it is of the CONTINUOUS_TYPE.

Toggle Buttons

A TOGGLE_TYPE button behaves like an "on-off" switch. When the user presses a toggle button when it is in its default state, it redraws itself so that it looks like it's depressed, and *remains* there. It sends its command to its target once in this process. When the user clicks on it a second time, the button returns to its original state, and again sends its command to its target. The target can determine the current state of a toggle button (or any button, for that matter), by calling its state() method. Often a toggle button will display a different image when it is depressed.

To create a toggle button, you need to first create a push button, then use setType() to further specify that it is of the TOGGLE_TYPE. Check buttons and radio buttons are special types of toggle buttons, and are explained below.

Check Buttons

Check buttons are toggle buttons that display a "check" image when they are in the true state, and no image when they are in the false state. Figure 9-2 shows two check buttons, one in the true state, and one in the false state.

Figure 9-2: Two check buttons

To create a check button, use the following static Button method:

```
public static Button createCheckButton(int x, int y, int w, int h);
```

The check button image is always square, even though the check button itself may not be—after all, a check button is a View, and like any View, it can have its bounds specified arbitrarily. The difficulty with this is that the user doesn't have to click on the check button image to get the check button to send its command to its target. The user can click *anywhere* in the check button. This can be slightly confusing because check buttons typically do not have a border, and it's difficult for a user to determine the bounds of a check button. If this is a problem in your application, try using the setBorder() method to give the check button a border. (Borders are covered in detail in Chapter 13, *Borders*.) To see how this aspect of a check button works, compile and run the SuperScribble example below.

Radio Buttons

A RADIO_TYPE button acts like a toggle button, except that a view can have only one radio button subview in the "on" state at a time. When a radio button is selected by the user to be in the "on" state, any radio button in the same view that was previously "on" gets changed to "off" by the IFC. Only the radio button

---

that was pressed notifies its target. Typically a group of radio buttons is used when a user has to pick one of several different choices.

Radio buttons have a default image and alternate image, but as usual, the images can be changed with the setImage() and setAltImage() methods. Figure 9-3 shows a group of radio buttons with the default images.

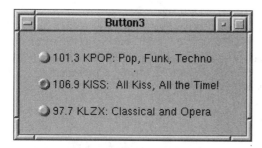

Figure 9-3: Radio buttons

A radio button is created in one step by a static Button method:

```
public static Button createRadioButton(int x, int y, int w, int h);
```

The ContainerView Class

Before we get to a Button example, let's take a quick look at a class that's often used in conjunction with radio buttons. The ContainerView class is a View subclass that can display an optional border, title, and background image or color. Figure 9-4 shows a grouping of radio buttons in a ContainerView.

Figure 9-4: Radio buttons in a ContainerView

ContainerView has the usual two constructors:

```
public ContainerView(Rect r);
public ContainerView(int x, int y, int width, int height);
```

A ContainerView's attributes can be specfied by calling its various set() methods. In Table 9-2, we present a number of ContainerView's attributes. A ContainerView can display an Image, just like the RootView.

Buttons

Table 9-2: ContainerView Attributes

Attribute	Description
BackgroundColor	The ContainerView's background Color.
Border	The ContainerView's Border. (See Chapter 13, *Borders*.)
Image	The ContainerView's Image.
ImageDisplayStyle	This attribute takes on one of three values: Image.CENTERED, Image.TILED, and Image.SCALED.
Title	A String that appears as the ContainerView's title. The title obscures the border when it is present; for example, see Figure 9-4.
TitleColor	The title's Color.
TitleFont	The title's Font.

We'll see ContainerView again in Example 9-1, and in many other examples throughout the book.

An Example

The SuperScribble example, shown in Example 9-1, is similar to the Scribble example of Chapter 6, *Mouse and Keyboard Events*, but adds a "Clear" push button, a "Thick Lines" check button, and three radio buttons, "Red," "Green," and "Blue." Note in particular the setupButton() method of SuperScribbleView. It's a convenient way of setting a button's title, target, and command. Including a method like setupButton() can cut down on the length of your code if one of your applications has a number of buttons; in fact, it's surprising that Button doesn't have a constructor or method like setupButton(). Since SuperScribbleView acts as the button's target, SuperScribbleView's performCommand() method handles each of the button's commands accordingly. Finally, note how the "Thick Lines" check button is larger than its Image and title indicate. It's possible to change from thin lines to thick lines by clicking anywhere in the "Thick Lines" button, not just on the Image or title.

The use of buttons in SuperScribble is typical of how buttons are used in an application. See Figure 9-5.

Example 9-1: Scribble with Buttons

```
import netscape.application.*;
import netscape.util.*;

// a drawing application
public class SuperScribble extends Application {
  SuperScribbleView sview;

  public void init(){
    sview = new SuperScribbleView(mainRootView().localBounds());
    mainRootView().addSubview(sview);
  }
}
```

Example 9-1: Scribble with Buttons (continued)

```
// a View to draw in, with 5 buttons to set the color and line width
class SuperScribbleView extends View implements Target{
  int lastx, lasty;
  Button clearButton, thickButton;
  Button red, green, blue;
  ContainerView radioContainer;
  Color currentColor;
  boolean wasOutOfBounds = false;
  boolean thickLines = false;

  public SuperScribbleView(Rect r){
    super(r);
    currentColor = Color.blue;

    // create the buttons
    red = Button.createRadioButton(0, 0, r.width/3, 50);
    setupButton(red, "Red", this, "red");
    blue = Button.createRadioButton(r. width/3,0, r.width/3, 50);
    setupButton(blue, "Blue", this, "blue");
    blue.setState(true);            // blue is the initial line color
    green = Button.createRadioButton(2*r.width/3, 0, r.width/3, 50);
    setupButton(green, "Green", this, "green");
    clearButton = new Button(10, 10, 100, 30);
    setupButton(clearButton, "Clear All", this, "clear");
    thickButton = Button.createCheckButton(10, 60, 100, 30);
    setupButton(thickButton, "Thick Lines", this, "thickLines");

    // put the radio buttons in a ContainerView
    radioContainer = new ContainerView(0, r.height-50, r.width, 50);
    radioContainer.setTitle("Colors");

    radioContainer.addSubview(red);
    radioContainer.addSubview(blue);
    radioContainer.addSubview(green);
    addSubview(radioContainer);

    addSubview(clearButton);
    addSubview(thickButton);
  }

  // a convenient method to set a button's attributes
  protected void setupButton(Button b, String title, Target target,
                             String command){
    b.setTitle(title);
    b.setCommand(command);
    b.setTarget(target);
  }

  public void performCommand(String command,Object data){
    if(command.equals("red")) currentColor = Color.red;
    if(command.equals("blue")) currentColor = Color.blue;
    if(command.equals("green")) currentColor = Color.green;
    if(command.equals("thickLines")) thickLines = thickButton.state();
    if(command.equals("clear")) draw();
  }

  public void drawView(Graphics g){
    g.setColor(Color.white);
```

Example 9-1: Scribble with Buttons (continued)

```
   g.fillRect(localBounds());
 }

 public boolean mouseDown(MouseEvent e){
   wasOutOfBounds = false;            // the MouseEvent is in the view
   lastx = e.x;
   lasty = e.y;
   return true;
 }

 public void mouseDragged(MouseEvent e){
   // if the mouse is dragged out of the view
   // or over a button, set a flag and return
   if(!containsPointInVisibleRect(e.x, e.y) ||
      viewForMouse(e.x, e.y) != this) {
     wasOutOfBounds = true;
     return;
   }

   // if the mouse is dragged out of the view
   // or over a button, ignore it
   if(wasOutOfBounds) return;

   // prepare to draw
   Graphics gr = createGraphics();
   gr.setColor(currentColor);
   int dx = lastx - e.x;
   int dy = lasty - e.x;

   // draw the line
   gr.drawLine(lastx, lasty, e.x, e.y);

   // if the lines are "thick", draw four lines around the center line
   if(thickLines){
     gr.drawLine(lastx-1, lasty, e.x-1, e.y);
     gr.drawLine(lastx+1, lasty, e.x+1, e.y);
     gr.drawLine(lastx, lasty-1, e.x, e.y-1);
     gr.drawLine(lastx, lasty+1, e.x, e.y+1);
   }

   gr.dispose();                      // dispose of the Graphics object

   // update the mouse position
   lastx = e.x;
   lasty = e.y;
 }
}
```

Advanced Buttons

I'll bet you thought that by now you knew everything about buttons! In fact, buttons have even more functionality than we have discussed. The designers at Netscape clearly wanted to put an end to the need to subclass buttons. You can learn more by reading the reference section in the back of the book, but here we

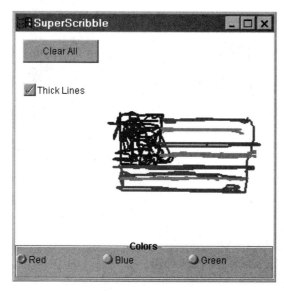

Figure 9-5: Buttons in an application

take a brief look at some of the other things an IFC button can do. In Table 9-3, we list a number of advanced button attributes.

Table 9-3: Advanced Button Attributes

Attribute	Description
LoweredBorder	The Border when the button is depressed
RaisedBorder	The Border when the button is raised
MouseDownSound	The Sound a button makes when a mouse button is pressed in its bounds
MouseUpSound	The Sound a button makes when a mouse button is raised in its bounds
LoweredColor	The title's color when the button is depressed
RaisedColor	The title's color when the button is raised

As we saw above, buttons can display static images; in fact, radio buttons and check buttons do exactly that. Buttons can also display animated images, because they implement the DrawingSequenceOwner interface, which we'll learn about in Chapter 18.

Finally, if you would like to do custom drawing, Button subclasses can override the drawViewBackground(), drawViewInterior(), and drawViewTitleIn-Rect() methods to specify how the button draws itself. Most applications won't require all these methods, but the IFC makes it easy to make complicated buttons.

Buttons

CHAPTER 10

Lists

The IFC provides the ListView class as a convenient way for displaying a list of choices, represented by the ListItem class. A ListView can have a target and each ListItem a command, allowing an application to take action when a specific ListItem is selected. This chapter takes a brief look at the ListItem and ListView classes.

The ListItem Class

Before we get started, take a look at Figure 10-1. It displays a list of three choices, one of which is selected.

Figure 10-1: A ListView in an application

The ListView class is responsible for displaying the entire list, allowing the user to select from the list, and highlighting the selected item. The individual choices displayed by the ListView are instances of the ListItem class.

ListItem is a relatively simple class. Normally you won't create a ListItem directly with the ListItem constructor; rather, you'll use ListView's addItem() method to create a new ListItem or use a ListItem's clone() method to create a ListItem from an existing one. Below, we'll see an example using List-View's addItem() method to create a ListItem. As usual, once you have a ListItem, you can set its attributes. Table 10-1 presents a list of ListItem's most important attributes.

Table 10-1: ListItem Attributes

Attribute	Description
Command	A String that's sent to the ListItem's target when the ListItem is selected.
Data	The Object that is sent to the ListItem's target when the ListItem is selected.
Enabled	Enables or disables the ListItem. Disabled ListItems are displayed in a different color, light gray by default.
Font	The title's Font. The default is Application's default font, Helvetica 12.
Image	The ListItem's Image, which can be displayed instead of or in addition to a title. The default is no image.
Selected	Specifies whether the user has selected the item, and allows the item to be programmatically selected or de-selected.
Title	The String that represents the ListItem in the ListView.

The two attributes that every ListItem should set are the command and title, and often the data attribute will be set as well. There is no target attribute since the ListView, not the ListItem, has a target. Note that a ListItem can display an Image; this is convenient because it is often easier to glance through a list of images than a list of titles.

Now, let's move on to ListView, where we'll see how to use ListItems in conjunction with ListViews.

The ListView Class

We've seen that a ListItem can have a command. ListView supplies the target. A ListView displays a vertical list of ListItem instances, and when the user selects an item from the list, the selected ListItem's command is sent to the ListView's target. For displaying large lists, ListView is often used in conjunction with a scroll bar, the subject of Chapter 12, *Scroll Bars and Scrolling*.

ListView is a subclass of View, and it must therefore be added to the view hierarchy if it is to be visible.

The two useful ListView constructors are:

```
public ListView(Rect r);
public ListView(int x, int y, int w, int h);
```

Once you have a ListView, there are two methods you will undoubtedly need to use:

```
public void setTarget(Target target);
```
       Sets the ListView's Target. When a ListItem is selected, the ListItem's command is sent to the ListView's target.

```
public ListItem addItem();
```
       Adds a new ListItem to the ListView.

The following code snippet creates a `ListView` with target `myTarget` and adds two items to it:

```
ListView listView = new ListView(0,0,50,50);
listView.setTarget(myTarget);

ListItem listItem = listView.addItem();
listItem.setTitle("Mike");
listItem.setCommand("mike");

listItem = listView.addItem();
listItem.setTitle("Jane");
listItem.setCommand("jane");
```

Unfortunately, there's no `ListView` method to add a `ListItem` with a given title and command in just one line of code. If your application has a `ListView` with a number of `ListItems`, you might find it convenient to have a method like this:

```
public void addListItem(ListView listView, String title, String command) {
    ListItem listItem = listView.addItem();
    listItem.setTitle(title);
    listItem.setCommand(command);
}
```

Advanced ListView Features

The `ListView` class provides several methods that are useful for creating and updating more complex lists. Some are shown below. Please refer to the reference section if you'd like a complete list.

`public void sizeToMinSize();`
Resizes the `ListView`'s height so that it accommodates all its items. Its width is left unchanged.

`public void minItemWidth();`
Returns the width of the largest `ListItem`. Use this in conjunction with `sizeToMinSize()` to resize the `ListView`.

`public void removeItem(ListItem item);`
Removes the `ListItem` *item*.

`public void setDoubleCommand(String command);`
Sets the command that is sent to the target when a user double-clicks on the `ListView`. The double-click command can be distinct from the single-click command, and the double-click command is the same no matter what `ListItem` is clicked on.

`public void setAllowsMultipleSelection(boolean b);`
Enables a user to select multiple list items.

Of these, probably the most important are the `sizeToMinSize()` and `minItem-Width()` methods. Since `ListView` does *not* automatically resize itself to accommodate its items, you need to call `sizeToMinSize()` and `minItem-Width()`, or set the bounds yourself manually using `setBounds()`.

CHAPTER 11

TextFields

This chapter examines one of the IFC GUI classes for displaying and entering text, TextField. TextField is used for editing a single line of text, and is often used in dialog boxes. The TextView class, used for multi-line text editing, is covered in Chapter 20, *TextView*, after we cover FontChooser, ColorChooser, Image, and drag-and-drop.

The TextField Class

The TextField class is used for entering or displaying a single line of text. When a user clicks in a TextField's bounds, the TextField gets the Application's focus and becomes eligible for keyboard events. When the user is done entering or editing text and hits **Return**, the TextField notifies its Target (and, as we'll see below, its TextFieldOwner).

A TextField is created using one of two constructors:

```
public TextField(Rect rect);
public TextField(int x, int y, int width, int height);
```

Using a TextField is as simple as creating it and setting its command and target. A TextField, however, can have *two* targets: one that is notified when the user hits return, and one that is notified if the TextField's contents are changed.

To get the value of the String contained in the TextField, use the stringValue() method. If you'd like to set the string's value yourself, use the setStringValue() method. This is often useful to give an initial value for the string. If you're expecting the value entered into the TextField to be an integer, you can use the intValue() and setIntValue() methods.

Table 11-1 lists TextField's most important attributes..

Table 11-1: TextField Attributes

Attribute	Description
StringValue	The String currently in the TextField.
Target	The object that is notified after the user hits **Return**.
Command	The command sent to the TextField's target.
ContentsChangedTarget	The object that is notified when the TextField's contents are changed and the user is done editing. (See below.)
ContentsChangedCommand	The String that is passed to the "Contents Changed Target" when to be notified when the TextField's contents are changed and the user is done editing. (See below.)
IntValue	Set or query the TextField value as an integer instead of as a string.
Editable	Allows or prohibits editing.
Selectable	Allows or prohibits the user to select the text with the mouse. (Also, see the "Tabbing Between Text Fields" section later in the chapter.)
Border	The TextField's Border.
Owner	A TextFieldOwner object notified when the field value is edited.
Filter	A TextFilter object, used to filter all user input to the text field.
DrawableCharacter	The TextField's *echo character*, the character that will appear on the screen when the user types. The asterisk (*) is often used as an echo character when entering a password into a Text-Field.

The "contents changed" target is notified when the user is done editing and the contents have changed. In addition to a **Return** key, there are several reasons why the editing could end: the user could have hit a **Tab** or **Backtab** key, which moves the focus to a different TextField, or the TextField could have lost or resigned the focus. In any of these cases, if the TextField's contents have changed, the "contents changed" target is notified. Unfortunately, this is one example of where the IFC naming convention has not been followed. There is a single method, setContentsChangedCommandAndTarget(), that sets both the command and target, but there are no setContentsChangedCommand() or setContentsChangedTarget() methods. On the other hand, there are contentsChangedCommand() and contentsChangedTarget() methods.

Copying, Cutting, and Pasting

A TextField can copy, cut, and paste text to and from the application's clipboard. The copy() method copies the selected text to the application's clipboard, leaving the TextField's contents unchanged. The cut() method copies the selected text to the application's clipboard, but also deletes it from the Text-Field's contents. Finally, the paste() method inserts the clipboard text at the current cursor position.

Other objects can set or retrieve the clipboard text directly from the Application object with Application's static setClipboardText() and clipboardText() methods.

Tabbing Between Text Fields

Often a View will have multiple text fields in it. For instance, imagine a form in which the user has to enter values in three fields: a name, an employee number, and an age. Once the user has finished editing the name field and hits the **Tab** or **Return** key, we want the cursor to appear in the employee field immediately, without the user having to click on it. We can do this by setting the *tab field* for a TextField. The method is:

```
public void setTabField(TextField nextField);
```

If no tab field is set, the TextField simply resigns the focus.

When the user hits the **Tab** key to cause the focus to jump to the tab field, any text that's in the tab field is selected. This means that any TextField that's going to be a tab field *must* be selectable.

There is also a setBackTabField() method.

The TextFieldOwner Interface

A TextField can have an "owner," an object that is notified when a TextField is being edited or has finished editing. TextFieldOwner has four methods:

```
public void textEditingDidBegin(TextField t);
```
> Called when the TextField gains the keyboard input focus.

```
public void textEditingDidEnd(TextField t, int reason,
                              boolean modified);
```
> Called when the editing is finished. *reason* can take one of five values: TAB_KEY, BACKTAB_KEY, RETURN_KEY, LOST_FOCUS, and RESIGNED_FOCUS. If modified is true, the TextField's contents have been changed.

```
public boolean textEditingWillEnd(TextField t, int reason,
                                  boolean modified);
```
> Called when the editing is about to finish. *reason* can take one of the five values listed in the textEditingDidEnd() method. Unless the TextField has lost or resigned the focus, returning false from this method will prevent the editing from ending. If modified is true, the TextField's contents have been changed.

```
public void textWasModified(TextField t);
```
> Called after every keystroke in the TextField.

The TextFieldOwner interface is especially useful if you'd like to monitor the validity of the TextField's input. You can do this on a character-by-character basis with textWasModified(), or wait until the editing is about to end, and check the validity of the TextField's string in textEditingWillEnd(). If text-EditingWillEnd() discovers an invalid string, it can notify the user (with a dialog box, say), then return false, which returns the focus to the TextField. Below we'll see an example of this in an application that compares the TextField input against a password.

The TextFilter Interface

Using a TextFilter, you can intercept keyboard events before the characters are displayed on the screen. This is often useful for capturing special keyboard events beginning with control characters, for example. If you skipped Chapter 6, *Mouse and Keyboard Events*, you might want to skip back and read the section on keyboard events before using TextFilter.

TextFilter consists of only one method:

```
public abstract boolean acceptsEvent(Object textObject,
                                     KeyEvent keyEvent,
                                     Vector eventVector);
```

The *textObject* argument represents the TextField (or TextView) that is having its key events filtered. The *keyEvent* argument represents the KeyEvent the TextField just received, and the final argument, *eventVector*, is the *textObject*'s vector of keyboard events. With a TextFilter, you can inspect the KeyEvent, and if you want the *textObject* to process it unmodified, return true. Otherwise, return false and add whatever replacement KeyEvent or KeyEvents you would like to *eventVector*.

As an example TextFilter, consider a TextField that accepts only numerical input: a zip code, for instance. We could use an acceptsEvent() method like this to rule out all characters except the numbers 0–9:

```
public boolean acceptsEvent(Object textObject, KeyEvent keyEvent,
                            Vector eventVector) {
  if(((char) keyEvent.key < '0') || ((char) keyEvent.key > '9'))
     return false;
  else return true;
}
```

Another use for a TextFilter is to create macros. For instance, to define a macro that shows "IFC is cool" in the TextField every time the user hits CTRL–M, we could use an acceptsEvent() like this:

```
public boolean acceptsEvent(Object textObject, KeyEvent keyEvent,
                            Vector eventVector) {
  char macroKey = 'm' - 'a' + 1;            // ASCII for Ctrl-m
  if((char) keyEvent.key == macroKey){
    String message = "IFC is cool";         // our macro
    // add the message's characters to the eventVector
    for(int i = 0;i<message.length();i++){
      KeyEvent newKeyEvent = new KeyEvent();
      newKeyEvent.key = (int) message.charAt(i);
      eventVector.addElement(newKeyEvent);
    }
    // we've actively filtered things, so return false.
    return false;
  }
}
```

```
    // let everything else pass through unmodified.
    else return true;
  }
```

An Example

The `Form` example below uses `TextField` labels and the `acceptsEvent()`
method explained above to implement a three-field form, which asks the user to
enter a name, an employee number, and a password, shown in Figure 11-1.
`InfoInput` uses a `TextFilter` to allow only integers to be typed in the
employee number field. The password field uses an asterisk as an echo character.
Also note the use of the `TextFieldOwner` interface to allow validation of the
user's input into each field.

Incidentally, the way the views are laid out in Example 11-1 is quite primitive.
We'll cover layout managers in more detail in Chapter 15, *Layout Managers*.

Example 11-1: Tabbing Between Text Fields

```
import netscape.application.*;
import netscape.util.*;

public class Form extends Application{
  InfoInput infoInput;

  public void init(){
    infoInput = new InfoInput(mainRootView().localBounds());
    mainRootView().addSubview(infoInput);
  }
}

class InfoInput extends View implements TextFieldOwner, TextFilter{
  TextField nameField, empNumberField, passField;
  Label nameLabel, numberLabel, passLabel;

  public InfoInput(Rect r){
    this(r.x, r.y, r.width, r.height);
  }
  public InfoInput(int x, int y, int w, int h){
    super(x,y, w,h);
    int fieldHeight = 30;    // TextField height
    int fieldWidth = w-20;   // TextField width
    int spacing = 10;        // spacing between TextFields

    // create the "Employee Name" label and associated TextField
    nameLabel = new Label("Employee Name:", Font.defaultFont());
    nameLabel.moveTo(spacing,fieldHeight + 2*spacing - nameLabel.height());

    nameField = new TextField(spacing, fieldHeight+2*spacing,
                              fieldWidth, fieldHeight);

    // create the "Employee Number" label and associated TextField
    numberLabel = new Label("Employee Number:", Font.defaultFont());
    numberLabel.moveTo(spacing,
                3*fieldHeight+4*spacing-numberLabel.height());

    empNumberField = new TextField(spacing, 3*fieldHeight+4*spacing,
                                   fieldWidth, fieldHeight);
```

Example 11-1: Tabbing Between Text Fields (continued)

```
      // create the "Password" label and associated TextField
      passLabel = new Label("Password:", Font.defaultFont());
      passLabel.moveTo(spacing, 5*fieldHeight+6*spacing-passLabel.height());

      passField = new TextField(spacing, 5*fieldHeight+6*spacing,
                                fieldWidth, fieldHeight);

      // set the tab fields
      nameField.setTabField(empNumberField);
      empNumberField.setTabField(passField);

      // set owners
      nameField.setOwner(this);
      empNumberField.setOwner(this);
      passField.setOwner(this);
      // filter the employee number field to allow only integers
      empNumberField.setFilter(this);
      // set * as the echo character
      passField.setDrawableCharacter('*');

      addSubview(nameLabel);
      addSubview(nameField);
      addSubview(numberLabel);
      addSubview(empNumberField);
      addSubview(passLabel);
      addSubview(passField);

   }

   // TextFieldOwner methods
   // check for valid input before allowing editing to end
   public boolean textEditingWillEnd(TextField tf, int why, boolean altered) {
      if(tf==nameField) {
         // check for valid name here...
      }
      else if(tf==empNumberField) {
         // check employee number validity here...
      }
      else if(tf==passField) {
         // check validity of the password here...
      }
      return true;
   }
   public void textEditingDidBegin(TextField tf) {}
   public void textEditingDidEnd(TextField tf, int why, boolean altered) {}
   public void textWasModified(TextField tf) {}

   // TextFilter method.  Allows only integers in empNumberField
   public boolean acceptsEvent(Object tf, KeyEvent keyEvent,
                               Vector eventVector) {
      if(tf==empNumberField){
         // let the tab and return keys pass through unmodified
         if((char) keyEvent.key == '\t' ||
            (char) keyEvent.key == '\n') return true;
         // otherwise, only let integers appear
         if((char) keyEvent.key < '0' || (char) keyEvent.key > '9'){
         return false;
         }
```

Example 11-1: Tabbing Between Text Fields (continued)

```
    }
    return true;
  }
}
```

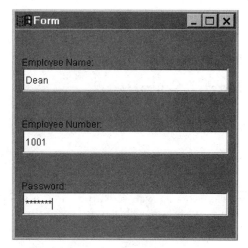

Figure 11-1: Multiple text fields

CHAPTER 12

Scroll Bars and Scrolling

The IFC provides several different ways of working with scroll bars, and in this section, we'll show how to use each one. We'll start with the easiest and most useful way to use a scroll bar first, then proceed to the more complicated methods.

The ScrollGroup Class

A ScrollGroup is an IFC View subclass that attaches vertical and/or horizontal scroll bars to a View, and automatically scrolls that View within a smaller area. Since ScrollGroup handles the scrolling and updating of views internally, it's by far the easiest way to use scroll bars. If you have a large View that you'd like to use in conjunction with scroll bars, use a ScrollGroup whenever possible. To give you an idea of how easy it is to create a scrolling view with a ScrollGroup, here's the code to add a vertical scroll bar to a View called myView:

```
ScrollGroup sGroup = new ScrollGroup(0,0,200,200);
sGroup.setHasVertScrollBar(true);
sGroup.setContentView(myView);
```

Simply add sGroup to the view hierarchy and *voila!* You have a view with an attached scroll bar. myView will be displayed within a 200×200 rectangle. sGroup's bounding rectangle is chosen simply for illustrative purposes. Since ScrollGroup extends View, you can set a ScrollGroup's bounds just as you would any other view.

By default, a ScrollGroup doesn't have any scroll bars until they are added with setHasVertScrollBar() or setHasHorizScrollBar(), as above. ScrollGroup also has a related option to remove the scroll bars when the ScrollGroup's content view is smaller than the ScrollGroup itself. For instance, to make the vertical scroll bar on sGroup appear only when the content view is larger than the ScrollGroup, call:

```
sGroup.setVertScrollBarDisplay(ScrollGroup.AS_NEEDED_DISPLAY);
```

We present two examples, one with a `TextView` and one with a `ListView`. (We haven't seen `TextView` yet, but it's perfect for this example. `TextView` is used for editing multiline text.) The examples are easy, but that's a good thing: they are typical of how a `ScrollGroup` would be used in a real `Application`.

Example 12-1 creates a `ScrollGroup` and sets a large (800×800) `TextView` to be its content view. The results are shown in Figure 12-1.

Example 12-1: Using a ScrollGroup and a TextView

```
import netscape.application.*;
import netscape.util.*;

// an application with a scrolling TextView
public class ScrollGroupExample1 extends Application{
  TextView textView;
  ScrollGroup sGroup;

  public void init(){
    // create a big View
    textView = new TextView(0,0,800,800);

    // create a ScrollGroup
    sGroup = new ScrollGroup(mainRootView().bounds);
    // give it vertical and horizontal scroll bars
    sGroup.setHasVertScrollBar(true);
    sGroup.setHasHorizScrollBar(true);
    // add the textView as the ScrollGroup's content view
    sGroup.setContentView(textView);

    // make the scroll bars appear only when needed
    sGroup.setVertScrollBarDisplay(ScrollGroup.AS_NEEDED_DISPLAY);
    sGroup.setHorizScrollBarDisplay(ScrollGroup.AS_NEEDED_DISPLAY);

    // add it to the view hierarchy
    mainRootView().addSubview(sGroup);
  }
}
```

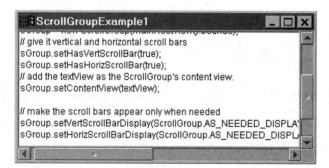

Figure 12-1: A TextView with scroll bars (default positions)

Example 12-2 shows how to use a scroll bar with a `ListView`. The `ListView` represents a number of different gray scale values. When one is selected, the

Application's background color is changed. Notice how we've set the List-View's bounds:

```
listView.sizeToMinSize();
```

After calling `sizeToMinSize()`, the `ListView`'s bounds accommodate its items perfectly.

Similarly, we've set the `ScrollGroup`'s bounds with:

```
listGroup.setBounds(0,0,listView.width() + listGroup.minSize().width,150);
```

The `ScrollGroup`'s height is fixed at 150 for illustrative purposes.

Example 12-2: Using a ScrollGroup and a ListView

```
import netscape.application.*;
import netscape.util.*;

// a ScrollGroup + ListView example
public class ScrollGroupExample2 extends Application implements Target{
  ListView listView;
  ScrollGroup listGroup;

  public void init(){
    // set up the listView
    setupListView();

    // create a ScrollGroup
    listGroup = new ScrollGroup();
    listGroup.setHasVertScrollBar(true);
    listGroup.setBounds(20,20,
                      listView.width() + listGroup.minSize().width,150);

    // add the listView as the ScrollGroup's content view
    listGroup.setContentView(listView);

    mainRootView().setBuffered(true);
    mainRootView().addSubview(listGroup);
  }

  private void setupListView(){
    listView = new ListView();
    listView.setTarget(this);
    ListItem item;
    for(int j=0;j<=255;j+=5){
      item = listView.addItem();
      item.setCommand(Integer.toString(j));
      item.setTitle(Integer.toString(j));
    }

    // size the listView to its minimum size
    listView.sizeTo(listView.minItemWidth(),listView.minSize().height);
  }

  public void performCommand(String command, Object data){
    try{
      int j = Integer.parseInt(command);
      mainRootView().setColor(new Color(j,j,j));
      mainRootView().setDirty(true);
    }
```

Example 12-2: Using a ScrollGroup and a ListView (continued)

```
    catch(NumberFormatException e){}
  }
}
```

The ScrollView Class

The scroll bars of a `ScrollGroup` always appear immediately below and/or to the right of the `ScrollGroup`'s content view. If you want the scroll bars to appear somewhere else, say above or to the left, you can use a `ScrollView` in conjunction with a `ScrollBar`. In fact, since `ScrollView` and `ScrollBar` both extend `View`, you can set their bounds independently and they can appear anywhere in relation to each other!

Creating a `ScrollView` and an associated `ScrollBar` is a four-step process: create a `ScrollBar`, create a `ScrollView`, attach the `ScrollView` to the `ScrollBar`, and finally, attach the `ScrollBar` to the `ScrollView`. Let's look at the steps in detail.

There are several ways to create a new scroll bar:

`public ScrollBar(Rect r);`
> Creates a vertical `ScrollBar` with bounds `Rect r`.

`public ScrollBar(int x, int y, int w, int h);`
> Creates a vertical `ScrollBar` with bounds `Rect (x,y,w,h)`.

`public ScrollBar(int x, int y, int w, int h, int axis);`
> Creates a `ScrollBar` with bounds `Rect (x, y, w, h)` and orientation specified by `axis`, which can take two possible values: `Scrollable.HORIZONTAL` or `Scrollable.VERTICAL`. This version is the only way to create a horizontal `ScrollBar`.

`ScrollView` is a `View` subclass, and can be created in one of two ways:

`public ScrollView(Rect r);`
`public ScrollView(int x, int y, int w, int h);`

Now that we have a `ScrollView` and a `ScrollBar`, we need to inform them that they are associated with each other. To specify what object the scroll bar should notify when its knob is moved, use `ScrollBar`'s `setScrollableObject()` method:

```
    public void setScrollableObject(Scrollable);
```

`Scrollable` is an interface that objects interacting with a `ScrollBar` must implement. `ScrollView` implements `Scrollable`.

To specify which object the `ScrollView` should notify when its content view has moved, use `ScrollView`'s `addScrollBar()` method:

```
    public void addScrollBar(Target);
```

Note that this method takes a `Target` as an argument, and thus it can be used to notify objects other than a `ScrollBar` that its content view has moved. `ScrollBar` implements `Target`.

Now, you're ready to go! The ScrollBar and ScrollView are set up. The final step is to give the ScrollView something to scroll by setting its content view:

```
public void setContentView(View);
```

Example 12-3 example shows how to use a ScrollView in conjunction with a ScrollBar. Figure 12-2 displays the application. Example 12-3 is similar to Example 12-1, except that we position the scroll bars above and to the left of the large TextView.

Example 12-3: Using a ScrollView and a ScrollBar

```
import netscape.application.*;
import netscape.util.*;

public class ScrollViewExample extends Application{
  ScrollView scrollView;
  ScrollBar vertBar,horizBar;
  TextView textView;

  public void init(){
    textView = new TextView(0, 0, 800, 800);

    // create the ScrollBars with proper bounds
    Rect r = mainRootView().bounds;
    // a ScrollBar is vertical by default
    vertBar = new ScrollBar(0, 20, 20, r.height-20);
    // specify horizBar to be a horizontal scroll bar
    horizBar = new ScrollBar(20, 0, r.width-20, 20, Scrollable.HORIZONTAL);

    // create the ScrollView
    scrollView = new ScrollView(20, 20, r.width-20, r.height-20);

    // connect the scroll bars and the scroll view
    vertBar.setScrollableObject(scrollView);
    horizBar.setScrollableObject(scrollView);
    scrollView.addScrollBar(vertBar);
    scrollView.addScrollBar(horizBar);

    // set the scroll view's content view
    scrollView.setContentView(textView);

    // add everything to the view hierarchy
    mainRootView().addSubview(vertBar);
    mainRootView().addSubview(horizBar);
    mainRootView().addSubview(scrollView);
  }
}
```

The Scrollable Interface

The final, and most complicated, way to use a ScrollBar is to use it with an object that implements the Scrollable interface. Since Scrollable is an interface, the Scrollable object can be anything, not necessarily a View. Since using scroll bars in this way can be confusing, we'll go over it in detail.

We've already seen the two Scrollable static member variables Scrollable.HORIZONTAL and Scrollable.VERTICAL. In addition, the Scrollable

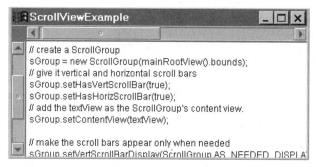

```
// create a ScrollGroup
sGroup = new ScrollGroup(mainRootView().bounds);
// give it vertical and horizontal scroll bars
sGroup.setHasVertScrollBar(true);
sGroup.setHasHorizScrollBar(true);
// add the textView as the ScrollGroup's content view.
sGroup.setContentView(textView);

// make the scroll bars appear only when needed
sGroup.setVertScrollBarDisplay(ScrollGroup.AS_NEEDED_DISPLA
```

Figure 12-2: A TextView with scroll bars (custom positions)

interface has five methods. It's helpful to refer to Figure 12-3 for further clarification of the different lengths involved in the Scrollable interface.

public abstract int lengthOfContentViewForAxis(int *axis*);
> Returns the total length of the content view. In Figure 12-3, this is 1000 for the vertical axis, and 800 for the horizontal axis.

public abstract int lengthOfScrollViewForAxis(int *axis*);
> Returns the length of the visible region. In Figure 12-3, this is 400 for both the vertical and horizontal axes.

public abstract int positionOfContentViewForAxis(int *axis*);
> Returns the position of the visible part of the view. In Figure 12-3, this is −300 for the vertical axis, and −200 for the horizontal axis. See later in this section for more information about the sign!

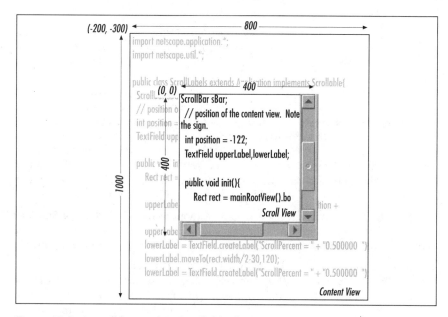

Figure 12-3: A scroll bar and its Scrollable object

```
public abstract void scrollTo(int x, int y);
```
This method is called when the scroll bar's knob is dragged. Based on the information passed to scrollTo( ), you should update the value returned by positionOfContentViewForAxis( ), redraw the Scrollable object, and update the scroll bar (see below).

```
public abstract void scrollBy(int dx, int dy);
```
This method is called when one of the buttons at the end of the bar is pressed, or when the user clicks somewhere in the tray between the knob and one of the end buttons. In the first case, the scroll bar scrolls one *line increment*, and in the second, it scrolls one *page*. Keep in mind that in either of these cases, the scroll bar calls scrollBy( ), not scrollTo( ). One way to implement scrollBy( ) is to have it call scrollTo( ), which is what we do in Example 12-4. The arguments *dx* and *dy* can be positive or negative.

An IFC scroll bar is drawn with a proportional knob, which is why there is a lengthOfContentViewForAxis( ) method as well as a lengthOfScrollViewFor-Axis( ) method. The IFC sets the knob length such that the ratio of the knob length to the scroll tray length is equal to the ratio of the content view length to the scroll view length.

It's important to remember that when you use a scroll bar in this way, it *never* updates itself. You're always responsible for updating the scroll bar after each call to scrollTo( ) or scrollBy( ). The easiest way to update a scroll bar is to call its performCommand( ) method directly. For example, if your Scrollable object has a scroll bar called sBar that needs to be redrawn, call:

```
sBar.performCommand(ScrollBar.UPDATE,this);
```
Here, the this argument is the Scrollable object.

Finally, there are some strange things about ScrollBar and Scrollable that you should be aware of. The integers passed to scrollTo( ) are *negative*, and run from 0 to -(lengthOfContentViewForAxis( ) - lengthOfScrollViewFor-Axis( )). For example, in Example 12-4, the variable *x* passed to scrollTo( ) will be in the range (0,-245). Second, a scroll bar's scrollValue( ) method returns the position of the knob in *pixels*. Therefore it depends on the absolute size of the scroll bar as it is drawn on the screen, and is not useful in determining the *relative* position of the scroll bar's knob. To find the relative position of the scroll bar's knob, use the scrollPercent( ) method, which returns a float between 0 and 1. To set the position of the knob, use the setScrollPercent( ) method, which takes a float between 0 and 1. The setScrollPercent( ) method ultimately calls the scrollable object's scrollTo( ) method.

So, in short, if you want to use a scroll bar without using ScrollView or Scroll-Group, the two main things to keep in mind are 1) you're always reponsible for redrawing the scroll bar, and 2) the numbers passed to scrollTo( ) are negative.

If you want to use a scroll bar with a view, it's better to use the ScrollView class, or better yet, the ScrollGroup class, since these two classes take care of the communication between the scroll bar and the scrollable view. The Slider class, covered at the end of the chapter, provides another, simpler, alternative to a scroll bar.

Example 12-4 implements `Scrollable` and shows how to use a scroll bar. It displays the scroll knob's current position and its scroll percent. Working with this example should clarify some of the more confusing aspects of `Scrollable` and `ScrollBar`.

Example 12-4: A ScrollBar and a Scrollable Object

```
import netscape.application.*;
import netscape.util.*;

public class ScrollLabels extends Application implements Scrollable{
  ScrollBar sBar;
  // position of the content view  (note the sign)
  int position = -122;
  TextField upperLabel,lowerLabel;

  public void init(){
      Rect rect = mainRootView().bounds();

      upperLabel = TextField.createLabel("Postion = " + position + "    ");
      upperLabel.moveTo(rect.width/2-30, 60);
      lowerLabel = TextField.createLabel("ScrollPercent = " + "0.500000  ");
      lowerLabel.moveTo(rect.width/2-30, 120);

      sBar = new ScrollBar(10, 10, rect.width-20, 20, Scrollable.HORIZONTAL);
      sBar.setScrollableObject(this);
      sBar.setScrollPercent((float) 0.5);

      mainRootView().setBuffered(true);
      mainRootView().addSubview(sBar);
      mainRootView().addSubview(upperLabel);
      mainRootView().addSubview(lowerLabel);

  }

  public int lengthOfScrollViewForAxis(int axis){
      if(axis == Scrollable.HORIZONTAL) return 10;
      else return 0;  // vertical axis not used in this application
  }

  public int lengthOfContentViewForAxis(int axis){
      if(axis == Scrollable.HORIZONTAL)  return 255;
      else return 0;  // vertical axis not used in this application
  }

  public int positionOfContentViewForAxis(int axis){
      if(axis == Scrollable.HORIZONTAL) return position;
      else return 0;  // vertical axis not used in this application
  }

  public void scrollTo(int x, int y){
    position = x;

    // don't let position get larger than its maximum value
    if(position > 0) position = 0;

    // don't let position get smaller than its minimum value
    int length = lengthOfContentViewForAxis(Scrollable.HORIZONTAL) -
            lengthOfScrollViewForAxis(Scrollable.HORIZONTAL);
```

Example 12-4: A ScrollBar and a Scrollable Object (continued)

```
        if(position < -length) position = -length;

        // redraw the the scroll bar
        sBar.performCommand(ScrollBar.UPDATE,this);

        // change the labels; they get redrawn automatically
        upperLabel.setStringValue("Position = " + position + " ");
        lowerLabel.setStringValue("ScrollPercent = " + sBar.scrollPercent() +
                                   " ");
    }

    public void scrollBy(int x, int y){ scrollTo(position + x, y); }
}
```

Sliders

A Slider is a stripped-down scroll bar; see Figure 12-4 to see what an IFC Slider looks like. It has a knob and a horizontal groove in which the knob "slides," but it lacks the buttons that appear on the end of a scroll bar, and clicking on the slider's track does nothing. IFC sliders are always oriented horizontally.

Sliders are used as analog controls; for instance, you might use a slider to allow the user to vary the playback rate of an animation sequence between a minimum and maximum value. You could do this with a scroll bar, but there is no natural "line increment" or "page," so it's better to use a slider. A slider's appearance is also less complex than a scroll bar, which makes the user interface less cluttered. In general, scroll bars are used to scroll entire views, and appear only on the outside edges of a view.

Slider has the usual two constructors:

```
public Slider(Rect r);
public Slider(int x, int y, int w, int h);
```

Once you have a Slider, you need to set its minimum and maximum values with its setLimits() method:

```
public void setLimits(int minimum, int maximum);
```

The final steps in setting up a Slider are setting its target and its command. When a slider's knob is moved by the user, it sends its command to its target.

You can retrieve a Slider's current value with the value() method, and you can set its current value to v with setValue(int v). Typically the target's perform-Command() method will determine the slider's current value by calling the slider's value() method, then take appropriate action.

Example 12-5, the RGBView example that follows, is a View subclass with three sliders, each running from 0 to 255; the results are shown in Figure 12-4. Taken together, their three values are used to create a Color from an RGB value, and the color is displayed in a ContainerView below the sliders. RGBView is similar to (but simpler than) the ColorChooser class we'll learn about in Chapter 16,

Color, Font, and File Choosers. We'll use this class again in Chapter 17, *Dialog Boxes.*

Example 12-5: A View Subclass That Uses Sliders

```
import netscape.application.*;
import netscape.util.*;

// a view to select a color
public class RGBView extends View implements Target{
  Slider sliders[];
  String sliderName[] = {"red", "green", "blue"};
  ContainerView container;
  TextField textFields[];
  ContainerView colorContainer;

  public RGBView(Rect r){ this(r.x, r.y, r.width, r.height);}

  public RGBView(int x, int y, int w, int h){
    super(x, y, w, h);
    setBuffered(true);
    container = new ContainerView(localBounds());

    sliders = new Slider[3];
    textFields = new TextField[3];
    int sliderHeight = 15;

    // create three sliders and three labels,
    // one pair for each of red, green, and blue
    for(int j = 0;j<3;j++){
      sliders[j] = new Slider(10, 10+2*j*sliderHeight, w-100, sliderHeight);
      sliders[j].setCommand("updateColors");
      sliders[j].setLimits(0, 255);
      sliders[j].setValue(127);
      sliders[j].setTarget(this);

      textFields[j] = TextField.createLabel(sliderName[j] + " = 127 ");
      textFields[j].moveTo(w-80,10+2*j*sliderHeight);
      container.addSubview(sliders[j]);
      container.addSubview(textFields[j]);
    }

    // a ContainerView to display the current color
    colorContainer = new ContainerView(10, 10+6*sliderHeight, w-20,
                                       sliderHeight);

    colorContainer.setBorder(null);
    container.addSubview(colorContainer);
    addSubview(container);
    updateColor();
  }

  public void performCommand(String command, Object arg) {
    if (command.equals("updateColors")) updateColor();
  }

  // update the current color and redraw the RGBView
  protected void updateColor() {
    for(int j = 0;j<3;j++)
```

Example 12-5: A View Subclass That Uses Sliders (continued)

```
        textFields[j].setStringValue(sliderName[j] + " = " +
                                    sliders[j].value());
    Color c = new Color(sliders[0].value(), sliders[1].value(),
                        sliders[2].value());
    colorContainer.setBackgroundColor(c);
    container.setBorder(new LineBorder(c));
    setDirty(true);
}

// a public method to retrieve the color of the RGBView
public Color color() {
    Color c = new Color(sliders[0].value(), sliders[1].value(),
                        sliders[2].value());

    return c;
}

// a public method to set the color of the RGBView
public void setColor(Color c) {
    sliders[0].setValue(c.red());
    sliders[1].setValue(c.green());
    sliders[2].setValue(c.blue());
    updateColor();
}
}
```

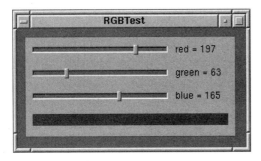

Figure 12-4: Three sliders in an application

CHAPTER 13

Borders

Many GUI components are displayed with borders. Normally each component has a default IFC border (BezelBorder, LineBorder, InternalWindowBorder, or EmptyBorder), but most components allow you set a non-default border using the setBorder() method. This short chapter covers the Border class and its four subclasses.

Border Basics

The View class does *not* have built-in support for adding a Border, but certain IFC GUI components, such as Button and ContainerView, have implemented code for adding an arbitrary Border. View subclasses with a border set aside a Border-dependent number of pixels, called the *margin,* around the inside edge of their bounds. Since the precise number of pixels in the margin depends on the specific type of Border, every non-abstract Border subclass is required to implement public methods that return the size of its margins. That way, the View can query the Border and determine how much area it should set aside for it. The rectangular area inside the margin is called the *interior rectangle.* Figure 13-1 shows the relation between a view, its border, and its interior rectangle.

The Border Class

Border is an abstract class with five abstract methods and a few implemented methods, mostly related to margin sizes. The five abstract methods are:

```
public abstract void drawInRect(Graphics g, int x, int y, int w,
                                int h);
```
Does the drawing for a Border subclass. The rectangle (x, y, w, h) is the rectangle defining the view that the border surrounds. A Border subclass should draw only in the area given by the specified margin sizes.

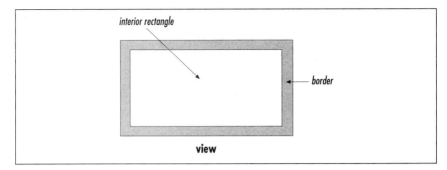

interior rectangle

border

view

Figure 13-1: A view, its border, and its interior rectangle

```
public abstract int bottomMargin();
```
Returns the number of pixels required to draw the bottom edge of the border.

```
public abstract int topMargin();
```
Returns the number of pixels required to draw the top edge of the border.

```
public abstract int leftMargin();
```
Returns the number of pixels required to draw the left edge of the border.

```
public abstract int rightMargin();
```
Returns the number of pixels required to draw the right edge of the border.

Border provides implementations of two interiorRect() methods that you can use to determine the rectangle the Border surrounds.

Now that we've seen the five Border methods, it's easy to see what a View needs to do to draw a border. When a View subclass with a Border is required to draw itself, the View subclass has to do it in two steps: first, it draws the Border by calling drawInRect(localBounds()), and second, it does any remaining drawing in the interior rectangle. The important point is that a Border appears inside a View's bounds, and a View subclass designed to work with an arbitrary Border needs to implement some special drawing code that sets aside some space for the Border.

The IFC has two general-purpose Border subclasses, BezelBorder and LineBorder. InternalWindowBorder and EmptyBorder also extend Border, but in general you won't work with them directly. In the following sections we give a short summary of the two general-purpose subclasses.

BezelBorder

A BezelBorder is a border that makes a component look raised or lowered with respect to its background by drawing different colors on different sides of the component. BezelBorder can draw five different variations: RAISED, LOWERED, RAISED_BUTTON, LOWERED_BUTTON, and GROOVED. Figure 13-2 shows all five. The grooved, raised, and lowered options allow you to set the color of the border, but the raised button and lowered button do not.

Figure 13-2: The five different BezelBorders

There are a multitude of different ways of creating a BezelBorder, which you can read about in the reference section. Here we will cover two ways:

```
public BezelBorder(int type, Color color);
public BezelBorder(int type, Color lighterColor, Color color,
                Color darkerColor);
```

A BezelBorder actually consists of two or three colored and slightly offset rectangles. The *color* argument is the base color. On a raised bezel, a line drawn with the *lighterColor* is drawn on the left and top sides of the GUI component, and a line drawn with the *darkerColor* is drawn on the right and bottom sides of the component. This gives the appearance of having a raised component lit from the upper-left corner of the screen. Reversing the colors gives a lowered bezel. The first constructor determines the lighter and darker colors from the base color by calls to the base color's lighterColor() and darkerColor() methods.

LineBorder

A LineBorder is a 1-pixel border with a uniform color. To create a LineBorder, use:

```
public LineBorder(Color color);
```

LineBorder has two static member methods for creating gray and black line borders:

```
public static LineBorder blackLine();
public static LineBorder grayLine();
```

Custom Borders

You can create a custom border by subclassing the abstract Border class. You need to provide implementations for the five abstract methods of Border. The only thing to keep in mind is that the drawInRect() method should draw only within the margins specified by your implementation of the four margin methods. Besides that, there are no restrictions on what kinds of drawing a Border subclass can do—consider, for instance, an InternalWindow's border, which is very complicated indeed. Example 13-1 is similar to LineBorder but replaces the 1-pixel line width with a variable line width and color.

Example 13-1: A Custom Border

```
import netscape.application.*;
import netscape.util.*;

// a Border subclass with a variable width and color
public class WideLineBorder extends Border {
```

Example 13-1: A Custom Border (continued)

```
Color color;
int margin;

public WideLineBorder(int width, Color c) {
  margin = width;
  color = c;
}

// The following five methods are the abstract methods from Border.
public int bottomMargin(){return margin;};
public int topMargin(){return margin;};
public int leftMargin(){return margin;};
public int rightMargin(){return margin;};

// This method draws the WideLineBorder. Note that it draws
// only in the area specified by the four margin methods above.
public void drawInRect(Graphics g,int x,int y,int w,int h) {
  g.setColor(color);
  g.fillRect(x,y,w,margin);
  g.fillRect(x,y,margin,h);
  g.fillRect(w-margin,y,margin,h);
  g.fillRect(x,h-margin,w,margin);
}
}
```

An Example

Example 13-2 lists the Borders class. If you compile and run it, you'll see what some of the IFC borders look like on a ContainerView (see Figure 13-3). Three borders are shown: a BezelBorder with a non-standard color, a LineBorder, and our custom border from above, WideLineBorder.

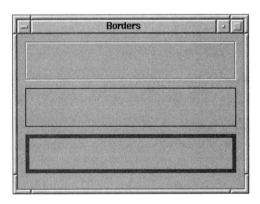

Figure 13-3: Three example borders

Example 13-2: Container Views with Borders

```
import netscape.application.*;
import netscape.util.*;

public class Borders extends Application{
  ContainerView cview1,cview2,cview3;
```

Example 13-2: Container Views with Borders (continued)

```
public void init(){
    Rect rect = mainRootView().localBounds();
    int cviewHeight = (rect.height-30)/3;

    cview1 = new ContainerView(0, 0, rect.width, cviewHeight);
    cview1.setBorder(new BezelBorder(BezelBorder.GROOVED, Color.cyan));
    mainRootView().addSubview(cview1);

    cview2 = new ContainerView(0, cviewHeight+10, rect.width,cviewHeight);
    cview2.setBorder(new LineBorder(Color.green));
    mainRootView().addSubview(cview2);

    cview3 = new ContainerView(0,2*cviewHeight+20,rect.width,cviewHeight);

    cview3.setBorder(new WideLineBorder(4, Color.blue));
    mainRootView().addSubview(cview3);
    }
}
```

CHAPTER 14

Menus

This chapter covers the two types of IFC menus, encapsulated by the Popup and Menu classes. A Popup menu contains an internal ListView with a list of possible menu choices. When it is inactive, the popup appears as a button with the currently selected ListItem as the button's title. When the user clicks on the button, the button disappears and a window containing the ListView "pops up," exposing the popup's entire list of options. Popup menus reduce the clutter in complicated graphical user interfaces because the full list of choices appears only when the popup is selected by the user. The Menu class represents a traditional menu bar and its associated menu items. A Menu can be added to an External-Window directly, or can be used to create a MenuView, which can be added to either an ExternalWindow or an InternalWindow.

The Popup Class

See Figure 14-1 for a snapshot of popup menus in their selected and default states.

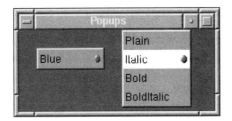

Figure 14-1: Popup menus

As with all the IFC GUI classes, Popup extends View and has two useful constructors:

```
public Popup(Rect r);
public Popup(int x, int y, int w, int h);
```

Once you've created a Popup, you need to set its target with the setTarget() command. When a ListItem is selected, the ListItem's command is sent to the popup's target.

A PopupItem can be added to the Popup with addItem():

```
public ListItem addItem(String title, String command);
```

Alternatively, a Popup can be used with an existing ListView with the setPopup-List() method. You can retrieve the Popup's internal ListView with the popup-List() method if you need to manipulate it directly. Popup displays a default image next to the selected ListItem. You can change the default Image with setPopupImage().

The TextPop class, Example 14-1, is an implementation of a class that acts some-what like a dropdown menu: it has a Popup working in conjunction with a TextField. If the user makes a selection from the Popup's ListView, the Text-Field is updated and the TextPop sends the ListItem's command. Similarly, if the user types a valid selection into the TextField, the Popup is updated, and the ListItem's command is sent to the TextPop's target. Items can be added to a TextPop by accessing the TextPop's internal Popup with the popup() method. Figure 14-2 shows what the TextPop class looks like.

Example 14-1: A Popup Menu and a TextField

```
import netscape.application.*;
import netscape.util.*;

// an object that acts like a dropdown menu
public class TextPop extends View implements Target, TextFieldOwner {
    Target target;
    TextField textField;
    Popup popup;
    ContainerView container;

    public TextPop(int x, int y, int w, int h){
        super(x,y,w,h);
        setBuffered(true);
        // put the whole works in a ContainerView
        container = new ContainerView(localBounds());

        // a Popup menu
        popup = new Popup(5, 5, (w-10)/3, h-10);
        popup.setTarget(this);

        // a TextField
        textField = new TextField(5+2*(w-10)/3, 5, (w-10)/3, h-10);
        textField.setOwner(this);

        addSubview(container);
        container.addSubview(textField);
        container.addSubview(popup);
    }

    // allow the user to set the TextPop's target
    public void setTarget(Target t){
        target = t;
    }
```

Example 14-1: A Popup Menu and a TextField (continued)

```
// notify the target if a valid command has been selected
public void performCommand(String command, Object arg) {
  for(int j = 0;j<popup.count();j++){
    ListItem item = popup.itemAt(j);
    if(command.equals(item.command())){
      textField.setStringValue(item.title());
      draw();
      target.performCommand(item.command(), item.data());
    }
  }
}

// give public access to the popup so items can be added to it
public Popup popup() { return popup; }

// TextFieldOwner methods:
// We only care if editing will end.
public boolean textEditingWillEnd(TextField t, int reason,
                                  boolean altered) {
  for(int j = 0;j<popup.count();j++) {
    ListItem item = popup.itemAt(j);
    // if the entered string matches a command, inform the target
    if(t.stringValue().equals(item.command())){
      popup.selectItem(item);
      draw();
      target.performCommand(item.command(), item.data());
      return true;
    }
  }
  // invalid string, ignore it.
  textField.setStringValue(popup.selectedItem().title());
  return false;
}

public void textEditingDidEnd(TextField t, int reason,
                              boolean altered){}
public void textWasModified(TextField t){}
public void textEditingDidBegin(TextField t){}
}
```

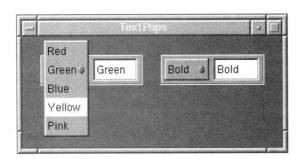

Figure 14-2: A Popup combined with a TextField

Menus for Windows

The `Menu` class represents a menu bar and its associated menu items. A `Menu` can be used in two ways. First, it can be used to create a `MenuView`, a `View` subclass that can be added to either an `InternalWindow` or an `ExternalWindow`. Second, a `Menu` can be added directly to an `ExternalWindow` (but not an `Internal-Window`). In the second case, the resulting menu is an AWT menu, which has a slightly different look than the `MenuView`. For an `ExternalWindow`, either menu works perfectly well, so the choice is simply a matter of taste.

The way IFC menus are set up is a little confusing, so I'll step through it in detail, then summarize it again at the end of this section.

The source of all `Menu` confusion is that an IFC `Menu` object can represent *either* a menu bar *or* one of the menu bar's submenus. A menu bar is created by using the `Menu` constructor with an argument of `true`:

```
Menu menuBar = new Menu(true);
```

The `true` argument signals that a menu bar rather than a submenu should be created. Giving a top-level menu a name like `menuBar` makes it clear that it's a top-level menu and not a submenu.

Once a menu bar is created, `MenuItem` objects can be added to it. Menu items themselves fall into two classes: those that have submenus, and those that don't. Typically all the items on the menu bar will have submenus. To add a `MenuItem` with a submenu, use the `addItemWithSubmenu()` method. For instance, the following code adds a **File** submenu to our menu bar:

```
MenuItem fileItem = menuBar.addItemWithSubmenu("File");
```

Note that this creates a submenu automatically; there's no need to call a constructor.

We can now add menu items to menuItem's **File** submenu, using the submenu's `addItem()` method. Each menu item has a command and a target. To add an **Open** item to menuItem's submenu, we use its submenu in the following way:

```
fileItem.submenu().addItem("Open","open",target);
```

In this snippet of code, **Open** is the word that will appear in the menu and "open" is the command that will be sent to its `target` when **Open** is selected.

Now that you have a menu, you can create a `MenuView` using the `MenuView` constructor:

```
menuView = new MenuView(menuBar);
```

Finally, the menuView can now be added to an `ExternalWindow` or an `Internal-Window` using the `setMenuView()` method:

```
internalWindow.setMenuView(menuView);
```

If you're adding a `MenuView` to an `ExternalWindow`, call the MenuView's `size-ToMinSize()` method first:

```
menuView.sizeToMinSize();
externalWindow.setMenuView(menuView);
```

The call to `sizeToMinSize()` is optional before adding a `MenuView` to an `InternalWindow`.

Summarizing, to create a menu, take the following steps:

1. Create a menu bar:

   ```
   Menu menuBar = new Menu(true);
   ```

2. Add items to the menu bar (typically the top-level menu items will have submenus):

   ```
   MenuItem fileItem = menuBar.addItemWithSubmenu("File");
   ```

3. Add items to the submenus:

   ```
   fileItem.submenu().addItem("Open","open",target);
   ```

4. Create a `MenuView`:

   ```
   menuView = new MenuView(menuBar);
   ```

5. Size the `MenuView`:

   ```
   menuView.sizeToMinSize();
   ```

6. Add the `MenuView` to a window:

   ```
   internalWindow.setMenuView(menuView);
   ```

A top-level menu (i.e., a menu bar) can be added directly to an `ExternalWindow` with the `setMenu()` method. There is one restriction, however: if you add a `Menu` to an `ExternalWindow` with `setMenu()`, any menu item added directly to a menu bar *must* have a submenu. Since menu items on a menu bar typically have submenus, this isn't a large restriction.

Menus often need to be updated to be kept in sync with the current state of the application. Usually, this means you'll need to disable or enable a `MenuItem` programmatically. To enable a `MenuItem`, call `setEnabled(true)`, and to disable it, call `setEnabled(false)`. A disabled `MenuItem` appears grayed out. In some cases, you may want to change rather than disable a menu. To do so, you can use the `addItem()` and `removeItem()` methods. If you want to add an entire `MenuView` to an existing `MenuView`, use the `setOwner()` method.

Note that even though a menu item has been added or removed, the changes will only appear when the menu is redrawn. If you use a `MenuView`, you can force an immediate redraw of the menu bar with a call to the `MenuView`'s `draw()` method, as usual.

Finally, menu separators can be added with Menu's `addSeparator()` method.

Example 14-2 shows a simple `Application` that creates a set of pulldown menus in an `InternalWindow`. It is pictured in Figure 14-3. Note the use of the convenience method `fillMenuPane()` to easily create the `MenuItem` objects for each menu pane.

Example 14-2: Creating Menus for an InternalWindow

```
import netscape.application.*;
import netscape.util.*;

public class MenuTest extends Application implements Target {
  InternalWindow win;
  static final String[] fileitems = { "New", "Open", "Save", "Save As..." };
  static final String[] edititems = { "Cut", "Copy", "Paste" };
  static final String[] helpitems = { "About" };

  public void init() {
    // create menubar
    Menu menubar = new Menu(true);
    // add items and pulldown panes to the menubar
    MenuItem file = menubar.addItemWithSubmenu("File");
    MenuItem edit = menubar.addItemWithSubmenu("Edit");
    MenuItem help = menubar.addItemWithSubmenu("Help");
    // put menu items in those pulldown panes
    fillMenuPane(file, this, fileitems);
    fillMenuPane(edit, this, edititems);
    fillMenuPane(help, this, helpitems);
    // create a MenuView so the menu can be displayed in an InternalWindow
    MenuView mview = new MenuView(menubar);

    win = new InternalWindow();  // create the InternalWindow
    win.setMenuView(mview);      // set the MenuView in it
    win.moveTo(20, 20);          // set window position and size
    win.sizeTo(250, 150);
    win.show();                  // display it
  }

  // A convenience routine for creating an array of menu items
  // It uses the menu item title as the command string, too.
  public void fillMenuPane(MenuItem item, Target target, String[] items) {
    Menu pane = item.submenu();
    for(int i = 0; i < items.length; i++)
      pane.addItem(items[i], items[i], target);
  }

  // A dummy target method that sets the window title to the command string
  public void performCommand(String command, Object data) {
    win.setTitle(command);
  }
}
```

Checkboxes and Menu Shortcuts

Menu has three other addItem() methods that can be used to create MenuItems with a checkbox, keyboard shortcut, or both. For instance, to create a MenuItem with a keyboard shortcut and a checkbox, use the following method:

```
public MenuItem addItem(String title, char shortcutChar, String command,
                        Target target, boolean showCheckbox);
```

When the user hits **Ctrl**-*shortcutChar*, the new menu item will notify its target with its command. Only the menu associated with the focused RootView will receive keyboard shortcut requests.

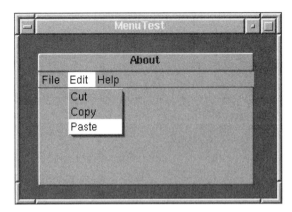

Figure 14-3: An InternalWindow with a MenuView

Since a `Menu` added directly to an `ExternalWindow` is actually an AWT `Menu`, it implements Java1.1's menu shortcut system. Java1.1's shortcut system has a number of nice features in addition to the shortcut key: for instance, it allows a user to navigate the menu with the arrow keys. Please see your favorite Java reference book for complete documentation.

O'REILLY™

PUBLISHING · SOFTWARE · RESEARCH

PRESS RELEASE

1 October 1997

Dear Colleague

Please find enclosed a selection of new books from O'Reilly & Associates.

WEB SECURITY
A Matter of Trust
World Wide Web Journal Vol 2 Issue 3
£21.95

Second Edition
JAVA LANGUAGE REFERENCE
Mark Grand
£24.50

ADVANCED PERL PROGRAMMING

Sriram Srinivasan

£25.95

LEARNING PERL ON WIN32 SYSTEMS

Randal L Schwartz, Erik Olson & Tom Christiansen

£21.95

NETSCAPE IFC IN A NUTSHELL

Dean Petrich with David Flanagan

£14.95

I would love to receive two copies of each review when published.

Many thanks

Josette Garcia
Marketing Manager

O'REILLY & ASSOCIATES, INC.

CHERITON HOUSE · NORTH WAY · ANDOVER, SP10 5BE · UK

+44 (0) 1264 342988 · FAX +44 (0) 1264 342732

ora.orders@itps.co.uk

http://www.ora.com

CHAPTER 15

Layout Managers

With many applications having 20 or more views in a user interface, it's useful to automate some of the layout so the application looks good even if it is resized by the user. The issue of layout management can be divided up into two parts:

1. Calculating the initial layout of views

2. Responding to resizing events

In this chapter, we cover some of the different possibilities for handling these two aspects of layout management. First, we cover in a little more detail what we've been doing up until now, i.e., hard-coding view sizes and positions. Then, we cover the IFC's view resizing rules, and finally, we cover IFC layout managers. In principle, layout managers are the most robust means of laying out views, because they can compute the initial view size and positioning, as well as handle subsequent resize events.

Simple Layout Management

Up until now, the views we have worked with have been static; we've hard-coded their sizes, and they don't respond to resizing events. Although user interfaces can be designed this way, it's very time-consuming.

Fortunately, Netscape has come to the rescue. Netscape has written an IFC application called Constructor that greatly simplifies IFC GUI development by allowing you to create graphical user interface by drag-and-drop. It's a huge improvement over trial-and-error hard-coding of sizes. Constructor doesn't produce Java code, but instead creates a "plan file" that can later be used to reconstruct the view hierarchy. Once you've created the views that compose a user interface, you can give those views resizing rules or use them in conjunction with a layout manager, just like any other views. An explanation of how to load Constructor plan files into an IFC application is given in Chapter 22, *Constructor and Plan Files*. In this chapter, we cover resizing rules and layout managers in detail.

Resizing Rules

Java applications are designed to run on many different platforms, and hard-coded sizes that look good on one platform may not look good on another. Robust applications, particularly Java applications, should be able to handle resizing. One way of handling resizing is through *resizing rules* that specify how a view is to be resized when its superview is resized. The two View methods that fix the resizing rules of a view are:

public void setHorizResizeInstruction(int *instruction*);
> Specifies what the view should do when its superview is resized horizontally. *instruction* can take on one of four values: LEFT_MARGIN_CAN_ CHANGE, RIGHT_MARGIN_CAN_CHANGE, WIDTH_CAN_CHANGE, and CENTER_ HORIZ.

public void setVertResizeInstruction(int *instruction*);
> Specifies what the view should do when its superview is resized vertically. *instruction* can take on one of four values: TOP_MARGIN_CAN_CHANGE, BOTTOM_MARGIN_CAN_CHANGE, HEIGHT_CAN_CHANGE, and CENTER_VERT.

Sizing, in Example 15-1, demonstrates nine possible combinations of horizontal and vertical resizing instructions. The only rules it omits are CENTER_HORIZ and CENTER_VERT. Try running Sizing with ApplicationViewer, then resize the window, as shown in Figure 15-1. The labels in the figure indicate what is changing. Thus the view label Width, Top means that its width and top margin are configured to change when the superview resizes.

Example 15-1: View Resizing Rules

```
import netscape.application.*;
import netscape.util.*;

// An example to demonstrate resizing instructions.
// Create 9 Labels with 9 possible combinations of instructions.
// This example omits the CENTER_HORIZ and CENTER_VERT rules.
public class Sizing extends Application {
  int[] hrules = { View.RIGHT_MARGIN_CAN_CHANGE, View.WIDTH_CAN_CHANGE,
                   View.LEFT_MARGIN_CAN_CHANGE };
  int[] vrules = { View.BOTTOM_MARGIN_CAN_CHANGE, View.HEIGHT_CAN_CHANGE,
                   View.TOP_MARGIN_CAN_CHANGE };
  String[] htitles = { "Right", "Width", "Left" };
  String[] vtitles = { "Bottom", "Height", "Top" };

  public void init() {
    for(int x = 0; x < hrules.length; x++) {
      for(int y = 0; y < vrules.length; y++) {
        TextField t = new TextField(x*100, y*50, 100, 50);
        t.setStringValue(htitles[x] + "," + vtitles[y]);
        t.setJustification(Graphics.CENTERED);
        t.setHorizResizeInstruction(hrules[x]);
        t.setVertResizeInstruction(vrules[y]);
        mainRootView().addSubview(t);
      }
    }
  }
}
```

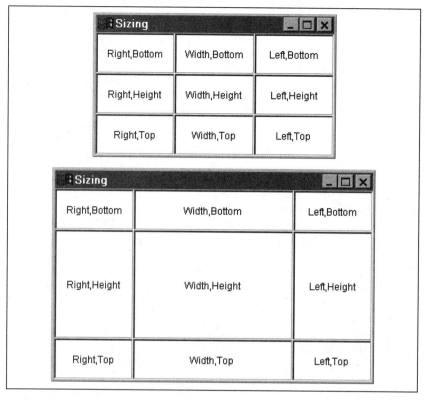

Figure 15-1: The Sizing application before and after a resizing

Layout Managers

Layout managers also lay out views according to rules, but layout managers are far more flexible than the resizing rules we just saw. Essentially *any* layout or resizing rule can be implemented. The IFC has two layout managers, and the simpler one, GridLayout, is a good example of a simple layout manager. Grid-Layout divides a view into equal-sized cells, and places one subview in each cell. If the user resizes the application, the GridLayout automatically adjusts the size and position of the cells to reflect the new size of the view and subsequently moves all the view's subviews into the new cells.

Other layout managers lay out their views according to *constraints*. In a constraint-based layout manager, each subview has a set of constraints associated with it that the layout manager tries to satisfy: one subview may be constrained to lie near the upper-left corner of the superview, another subview may be constrained to lie near the right hand side of the the superview, and so on. It's up to the particular layout algorithm to satisfy all the constraints as well as possible. The IFC has one constraint-based layout manager, PackLayout.

IFC layout managers can successively layout subviews when a view further up in the hierarchy has been resized, so if you use a layout manager for every View, in principle the entire application can easily respond to resizing events.

Unfortunately, the IFC's two layout managers appear to have been added as an afterthought. The saving grace is that LayoutManager is a public interface, so Netscape has made it possible for others to write layout managers that integrate seamlessly into the IFC architecture. In the following sections, after an introduction to what's happening behind the scenes, we cover GridLayout and PackLayout. The LayoutManager interface is so simple that it's left to the reference section.

Behind the Scenes: How a Layout Manager Works

There are two separate ways of implementing layout managers. There is a View method, layoutView(), and an interface, LayoutManager. View's layoutView() method can be overridden to implement virtually any layout and resizing rule. In short, when a view is resized by its superview, the view's didSizeBy() method is called. The didSizeBy() method subsequently calls layoutView(), and you can override layoutView() so that the view lays out its subviews in precisely the way you want. If you do things this way, effectively the view is acting as its own layout manager.

The LayoutManager interface simplifies matters somewhat. Each View can have a layout manager. The key method in the LayoutManager interface is also layoutView(), and if you give a View a layout manager, ultimately it's the layout manager's layoutView() that gets called on to lay out subviews. Again, since the implementation of layoutView() is totally arbitrary, you can implement any resizing rule. As you might imagine, in the face of all this flexibility, the key is to have layout managers with good general-purpose implementations of layoutView(). Below, we present the two IFC implementations of LayoutManager.

The GridLayout Class

As explained above, GridLayout represents a layout in which subviews are positioned in regular rows and columns. To create a new GridLayout, use the constructor:

```
public GridLayout(int rows, int columns);
```

Once you have a layout manager, connect it to a view by calling the view's setLayoutManager() method.

Subviews are positioned in the GridLayout's cells according to the order in which they are added to the view. By default, the order in which subviews appear in the GridLayout's cells is from left to right in the top row, then from left to right in the second row, and so on, although this order can be changed by using the setFlowDirection() method. Figure 15-2 shows the configuration of GridLayout's cells.

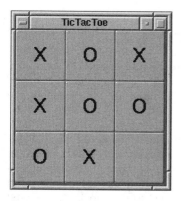

Figure 15-2: A GridLayout

Once views have been added to view and you have set its layout manager with setLayoutManager(), there are two ways you can instruct the layout manager to lay out a view's subviews. The first is to call the view's layoutView() method:

```
public void layoutView(int dx, int dy);
```

This method is called by a view when it's resized. In this case, the arguments *dx* and *dy* represent the change in size. If you want to do an initial layout of a view, or have just added or subtracted a subview and want to update the user interface, call layoutView(0,0).

The second method to lay out a view is to call the layout manager's layout-View() method:

```
public void layoutView(View view, int dx, int dy);
```

The parameters *dx* and *dy* have the same meaning as before—the change in size of a view.

The layoutView() method operates by resizing a view's direct descendants. If the descendants have a layout manager, this resizing has the effect of calling the subview's layoutView(), which resizes its subviews, and so on. In this way, the resizing continues down the view hierarchy. However, if one view does not have a layout manager, it doesn't resize its subviews, and the resizing ends there for that part of the hierarchy—which could make for some strange-looking user interfaces! If you expect your application to be resized, make sure you use a layout manager for every view that has subviews.

The PackLayout Class

The PackLayout class contains an implementation of a constraint-based layout algorithm. Each subview has a set of constraints associated with it, and Pack-Layout places each subview in turn, taking the subview's constraints into account. The algorithm is outlined below, and if you're planning to use Pack-Layout, I recommend that you study it carefully, then experiment by laying out some small view hierarchies.

The TK Packer algorithm

In the explanation below, the "cavity" is the rectangular area remaining to be laid out; initially, then, the cavity is the entire view.

1. PackLayout takes a subview and allocates a rectangular "parcel" of area for it. The parcel is positioned according to the subview's specified *side*: SIDE_TOP, SIDE_BOTTOM, SIDE_RIGHT, or SIDE_LEFT. If the side is the top or bottom, the width of the parcel will be the cavity's width, and the parcel's height will be the subview's minimum height plus two times the *external padding* in the y direction plus two times the *internal padding* in the y direction. If the side is left or right, the parcel will be the cavity's height and the subview's minimum width plus two times the padding in the x direction and two times the internal padding in the x direction. The difference between internal padding and external padding is that internal padding is added to the subview's preferred size in the layout process, effectively increasing a subview's preferred size, while external padding is used to provide separation between subviews. The side, external padding, and internal padding are three members of the subview's set of constraints.

2. If the *expand* constraint is set to true, PackLayout expands the parcel in such a way that all the remaining subviews set to expand will share any leftover space equally. For example, if the current subview's side is top, PackLayout cycles through all the remaining subviews, adding up their preferred heights and counting the number of subviews with expand set to true. If the sum of the preferred heights is less than the cavity's height by a distance delta-Height, and there are N subviews set to expand, the current parcel is expanded in the y direction by the amount deltaHeight/N.

3. PackLayout sizes the subview to be its preferred size plus two times any internal padding. The preferred size for a view with no subviews is returned by the minSize() method. If a view has subviews, the preferred size depends on the preferred size of its subviews. (This is an important point with Pack-Layout, and it's discussed in more detail below.) If the subview is set to *fill* in the x or y direction, the subview is further resized to take up the entire parcel in the specified direction, minus two times the external padding.

4. PackLayout then places the subview in the parcel according to its *anchor*. If a subview fills a parcel, there is no choice about where the subview should lie in the parcel, but if a subview does not fill its parcel, the anchor specifies where in the parcel the subview should lie. The anchor can take on one of nine values: ANCHOR_CENTER, ANCHOR_NORTH, ANCHOR_NORTHEAST, ANCHOR_EAST, ANCHOR_SOUTHEAST, ANCHOR_SOUTH, ANCHOR_SOUTHWEST, ANCHOR_WEST, and ANCHOR_NORTHWEST. The subview placement respects any external padding that has been specified.

5. PackLayout subtracts the parcel from the cavity, takes the next subview, and proceeds back to step 1.

As an example, consider a root view of size (400, 400), and two subviews, view1 and view2, both of size (100, 100). Take the constraints for view1 to be side = SIDE_TOP, anchor = ANCHOR_CENTER, all padding = 0, fillx = true, filly = false, and expand = true, and the constraints for view2 to be side = SIDE_LEFT, anchor = ANCHOR_WEST, all padding = 0, fillx = false, filly = false, and expand = false. According to the above, placing two views is a nine-step process. If you can work through this example, you'll be a PackLayout expert.

If we place view1 first, the cavity will be the entire 400x400 view, or in terms of its bounding rectangle, (0, 0, 400, 400).

1. Since view1's side is top and its height is 100, view1's parcel will be the rectangle with bounds (0, 0, 400, 100).

2. View1 has been set to expand. The remaining subview, view2, is not set to expand, and view2's height is 100, which means view1's parcel can expand in the y-direction by (cavity.height - view1.height - view2.height) / (number of expanding top or bottom subviews) = (400 − 100 − 100) / 1 = 200. After expanding, view1's parcel occupies (0, 0, 400, 300).

3. Since view1 has no subviews, its preferred size is minSize(). Moreover, it has no padding, so view1 is sized to (100, 100). However, view1 is set to fill in the x-direction, so it's resized in the x-direction to fill its parcel. After this, its size is (400, 100).

4. View1 doesn't fill its entire parcel, so it's positioned according to its anchor, in this case ANCHOR_CENTER. After this step, its bounding rect is (0, 100, 400, 100), which is its final size and position.

5. After we subtract view1's parcel from the cavity, we're left with a cavity with bounding rectangle (0, 300, 400, 100).

Now, proceed back to step1 and place view2.

1. Since view2's side is left and its width is 100, its parcel is (0, 300, 100, 100).

2. View2 doesn't expand, so its bounding rectangle is still (0, 300, 100, 100).

3. View2 doesn't fill, so again its bounding rectangle remains (0, 300, 100, 100).

4. Since view2 fills its parcel, there's no need to use an anchor to determine where to place it. There are no subviews left to place, so we're done! As an exercise, try figuring out what their final bounding rectangles would be if view2 were placed before view1.

If the cavity becomes smaller than the subview's minSize() plus its padding, PackLayout will allocate space for the external padding and give the subview all the remaining space. If there are other subviews remaining to be placed, they won't appear at all!

The key method in the PackLayout class is the preferredLayoutSize() method, which calculates the preferred size of a subview in step 3 of the Pack-Layout algorithm. The default implementation returns a subview's minSize(), but since preferredLayoutSize() is public, you can override the default and create your own custom layout manager. As an example, you might want to calculate the preferred size of a subview based on the preferred size of *its* subviews, and so on.

Setting the packing constraints

The IFC uses the `PackConstraints` class to set a view's constraints. First you create an instance of the `PackConstraints` class, then call the `PackLayout`'s `setConstraints()` method to connect the constraints with a given view. The `PackConstraints` constructor is a doozey:

```
public PackConstraints(int anchor, boolean expand, boolean fillx,
                       boolean filly, int ipadx, int ipady, int padx,
                       int pady, int side);
```

`PackConstraints` also has an empty constructor, which creates an instance with default constraints, and several methods that can be used to set the constraints individually. Please see the reference section for details.

Once you have a `PackConstraints` instance, you need to connect it to a view with `PackLayout`'s `setConstraints()` method:

```
public void setConstraints(View view, PackConstraints constraints);
```

The `setConstraints()` method actually creates a clone of the `PackConstraints` instance, which means you can use the same `PackConstraints` instance to set the constraints for several different views; just change the constraints that need changing, and pass the same `PackConstraints` instance back in.

Finally, `PackLayout` allows you to set default constraints with its `setDefaultConstraints()` method.

If you look at the `LayoutManager` and `PackLayout` API in the reference section, you'll see that there's an `addSubview()` method. You don't have to worry about calling `PackLayout`'s `addSubview()` method directly because `setConstraints()` calls `PackLayout`'s `addSubview()`. Add your view to the view hierarchy as usual, and set its constraints using `setConstraints()`.

A Layout Manager Example

Finally, an example! Example 15-2 uses a `GridLayout` and a `PackLayout` to arrange ten views. The top half of the `RootView` is covered with a `ContainerView` that uses a 2×2 `GridLayout` to position four views, and the bottom half of the `RootView` is covered with a `ContainerView` that uses a `PackLayout` to position four other views. Figure 15-3 shows the `Layouts` example with two different sizes.

Example 15-2: Using IFC Layout Managers

```
import netscape.application.*;
import netscape.util.*;

// a layout manager example
public class Layouts extends Application{
  GridLayout layout, mainLayout;
  PackLayout packLayout;
  Button button1, button2, button3;
  TextField label1, label2, label3, label4, textfield;
  PackConstraints button1Constraints, button2Constraints;
  PackConstraints button3Constraints, textfieldConstraints;
```

Example 15-2: Using IFC Layout Managers (continued)

```
ContainerView cview, cview2;

public void init(){
    // Create the Container Views.
    // The sizes used here are totally irrelevant.
    // All views are resized by the LayoutManagers.
    int w = mainRootView().bounds().width/2;
    int h = mainRootView().bounds().height/2;

    // cview covers the upper half of the RootView
    // and contains four TextFields in a 2x2 GridLayout.
    cview = new ContainerView(0, 0, 2*w, h);

    // cview2 covers the lower half of the RootView
    // and contains four Views positioned by a PackLayout.
    cview2 = new ContainerView(0, h, 2*w, h);
    mainRootView().addSubview(cview);
    mainRootView().addSubview(cview2);

    // Create and set the layout managers.
    layout = new GridLayout(2, 2);      // cview's layout manager
    cview.setLayoutManager(layout);
    packLayout = new PackLayout();      // cview2's layout manager
    cview2.setLayoutManager(packLayout);
    mainLayout = new GridLayout(2, 1);  // RootView's layout manager
    mainRootView().setLayoutManager(mainLayout);

    // Create subviews for cview1.
    // These will be positioned by a 2x2 GridLayout.
    label1 = createCenteredLabel("Label 1");
    label2 = createCenteredLabel("Label 2");
    label3 = createCenteredLabel("Label 3");
    label4 = createCenteredLabel("Label 4");

    // Note: *order* matters, not the initial bounds rects.
    cview.addSubview(label1);
    cview.addSubview(label2);
    cview.addSubview(label3);
    cview.addSubview(label4);

    // Create subviews for cview2.
    // These will be positioned by a PackLayout.
    button1 = new Button(0, 0, 40, 40);
    button1.setTitle("button 1");
    button2 = new Button(0, 0, 40, 40);
    button2.setTitle("button 2");
    button3 = new Button(0, 0, 30, 30);
    button3.setTitle("button 3");
    textfield = new TextField(0, 10, 100, 40);

    // Set the properties for cview2's subviews.
    // Remember, the order is anchor, expand, fillx, filly,
    // ipadx, ipady, padx, pady, and side.
    button1Constraints=new PackConstraints(PackConstraints.ANCHOR_NORTHWEST,
                                    false,false,false,0,0,10,10,
                                    PackConstraints.SIDE_LEFT);
    button2Constraints=new PackConstraints(PackConstraints.ANCHOR_NORTHEAST,
                                    false,false,false,0,0,10,10,
```

Example 15-2: Using IFC Layout Managers (continued)

```
                                        PackConstraints.SIDE_RIGHT);
    button3Constraints = new PackConstraints(PackConstraints.ANCHOR_CENTER,
                                        false,false,false,0,0,10,40,
                                        PackConstraints.SIDE_TOP);
    textfieldConstraints = new PackConstraints(PackConstraints.ANCHOR_SOUTH,
                                        false,true,false,0,0,10,10,
                                        PackConstraints.SIDE_BOTTOM);
    // textfieldConstraints fills in the X direction.

    packLayout.setConstraints(button1, button1Constraints);
    packLayout.setConstraints(button2, button2Constraints);
    packLayout.setConstraints(button3, button3Constraints);
    packLayout.setConstraints(textfield, textfieldConstraints);

    // Add subviews to cview2.
    cview2.addSubview(button1);
    cview2.addSubview(button2);
    cview2.addSubview(button3);
    cview2.addSubview(textfield);

    // Force the layout managers to lay out their views.
    cview2.layoutView(0, 0);
    cview.layoutView(0, 0);
    mainRootView().layoutView(0, 0);
  }

  // Create a label with a LineBorder and a centered message.
  protected TextField createCenteredLabel(String message) {
    TextField tf = new TextField();
    tf.setStringValue(message);
    tf.setEditable(false);
    tf.setTransparent(true);
    tf.setBorder(new LineBorder(Color.black));
    tf.setJustification(Graphics.CENTERED);
    return tf;
  }
}
```

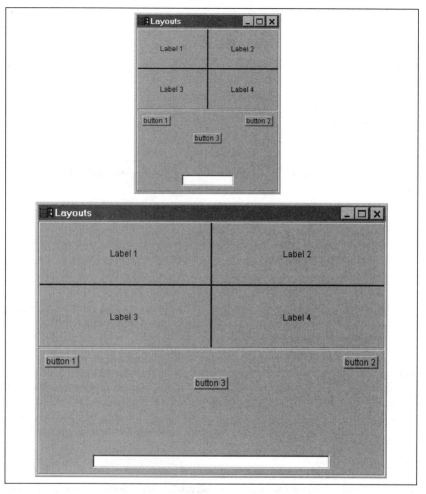

Figure 15-3: The Layouts application, shown in two different sizes

CHAPTER 16

Color, Font, and File Choosers

The previous chapters covered the primitive GUI building blocks provided by the IFC. The remaining chapters of the book cover higher-level GUI constructs such as dialog boxes, and advanced features of IFC programming such as animation and drag-and-drop. We begin with a discussion of the predefined "chooser" dialog boxes provided by the IFC.

Many families of applications today use the same dialog boxes for routine tasks—opening and saving files, choosing a color, and so on. The reuse of dialog boxes (and user interface components in general) helps makes applications easier to understand and use. The IFC has three classes of this nature: FileChooser, a dialog box for loading or saving files, ColorChooser, a dialog box for choosing a color by drag-and-drop, and FontChooser, a dialog box for choosing a font.

ColorChooser

The ColorChooser class creates a view hierarchy that allows a user to choose a color based on RGB values. This hierarchy is typically displayed within a modeless dialog box. Once a color is selected in the chooser, a small swatch of it can be "dragged and dropped" onto other user interface components. A few IFC classes (such as TextView and ColorWell) respond to dropped colors directly and in Chapter 19, *Drag-and-Drop*, we'll learn about how to implement drag-and-drop in our own View subclasses. To use a ColorChooser, all you have to do is create it and provide drag destinations (more about that in Chapter 19); the ColorChooser does the rest.

The simplest way to create and show a ColorChooser is to call the RootView's showColorChooser() method. A ColorChooser will automatically be hidden if the user closes the InternalWindow it appears in; alternatively it can be hidden programmatically by calling its hide() method. Figure 16-1 shows a ColorChooser.

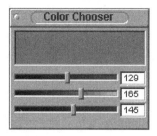

Figure 16-1: A ColorChooser

FontChooser

The `FontChooser` class creates a view hierarchy (again, typically displayed within a modeless dialog box) that allows a user to select a font name, style, and size. When the user selects a font and clicks the `FontChooser`'s "Set" button, the `FontChooser` sends an `ExtendedTarget.SET_FONT` command to the application's `TargetChain`. All you need to do to use a `FontChooser` is create an `Extended-Target` that responds to the `SET_FONT` command, make sure it's in the application's `TargetChain`, then show the `FontChooser`.

The `FontChooser` is allowed to become the main window, so when you're using a `FontChooser` you should be careful that the object requiring a new font remains in the `TargetChain` when the user selects the `FontChooser`. We'll see an example of this in Chapter 20, *TextView*, which covers the `TextView` class. As with `ColorChooser`, the simplest way to create and show a `FontChooser` is to call the `RootView`'s `showFontChooser()` method. Again, like `ColorChooser`, `FontChooser` also has a `hide()` method. Figure 16-2 shows a `FontChooser`.

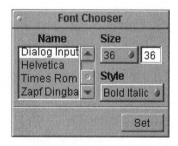

Figure 16-2: A FontChooser

FileChooser

The `FileChooser` class creates a modal dialog that is used to allow the user to enter a filename. Since `FileChooser` is modal, it's different from `ColorChooser` and `FontChooser`; the user must select a file or cancel the selection before the application can resume. Figure 16-3 shows a `FileChooser`.

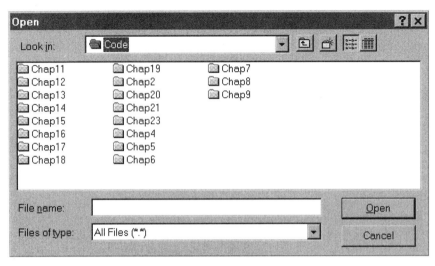

Figure 16-3: A FileChooser

The `FileChooser` constructor looks like this:

```
public FileChooser(RootView rootView, String title, int type);
```

The type argument can take on one of two values, `LOAD_TYPE` or `SAVE_TYPE`. The *title* argument is the title of the `FileChooser`'s window. Once the `FileChooser` is created, you can show it by calling its `showModally()` method. This method does not return until the user has selected a file or typed a filename. Once it returns, you can find out what file the user selected by calling `directory()` and `file()`.

Table 16-1 lists `FileChooser`'s attributes.

Table 16-1: FileChooser Attributes

Attribute	Description
Directory	The current directory, a `String`.
File	The current file, a `String`.
FilenameFilter	A `java.io.FilenameFilter`. Only the accepted filenames will appear in the `FileChooser`.
Title	A `String` that appears as the title of the `FileChooser`'s window.

An Example

The `Choosers` example shows how to use the three chooser classes. Remember, the `FileChooser` is modal and therefore must be dismissed before the application can continue! When the `FileChooser` is dismissed, the application proceeds and displays the selected file in a `Label` in the upper-left corner of the `RootView`.

Note how colors can be dragged out of the `ColorChooser`. The `ColorChooser` implements the "drag" part of drag-and-drop, but the `Choosers` application doesn't implement the "drop" part, so when the swatch of color is dropped, it simply returns to the source. (To see drag-and-drop in action, modify `Choosers` so it shows two `ColorChoosers`, and then drag and drop colors from one `Color-Chooser` to the other.)

As discussed above, when the user selects the **Set** button on the `FontChooser`, a `SET_FONT` command is sent to the application's `TargetChain`. To demonstrate this, Example 16-1 implements `ExtendedTarget` and it displays a message in the current font in a `Label`.

Example 16-1: Choosers

```
import netscape.application.*;
import netscape.util.*;

// demonstrates the 3 IFC "chooser" dialog boxes
public class Choosers extends Application implements ExtendedTarget {
  FileChooser filechooser;
  ColorChooser colorchooser;
  FontChooser fontchooser;
  InternalWindow colorwindow, fontwindow;
  Label label;

  public void init(){
    // create and show a FileChooser
    filechooser = new FileChooser(mainRootView(), "Press Cancel to Dismiss",
                                  FileChooser.LOAD_TYPE);
    filechooser.showModally();
    // create a label and display the chosen file's name
    label = new Label("You chose the file " + filechooser.file(),
                  Font.defaultFont());
    label.moveTo(0,0);
    mainRootView().addSubview(label);

    // use RootView methods to show a ColorChooser and a FontChooser

    mainRootView().showColorChooser();
    mainRootView().showFontChooser();
  }

  public void performCommand(String command, Object arg) {
    if(command.equals(ExtendedTarget.SET_FONT)) {
      Font font = (Font) arg;
      // remove the old label
      label.removeFromSuperview();
      mainRootView().addDirtyRect(label.bounds());
      // make a new one with the new font
      label = new Label("You set the font to " + font.name(), font);
      label.moveTo(0,0);
      // add it to the view hierarchy and draw it
      mainRootView().addSubview(label);
      mainRootView().addDirtyRect(label.bounds());
    }
  }
}
```

Example 16-1: Choosers (continued)

```
// ExtendedTarget method
public boolean canPerformCommand(String command) {
  // handle the FontChooser's command
  if(command.equals("setFont")) return true;
  else return false;
}
}
```

CHAPTER 17

Dialog Boxes

Many applications use dialog boxes to present information to the user. In this chapter we cover the IFC's modal dialog box class, `Alert`, and present example code that illustrates how to create your own dialog boxes with `ExternalWindow` and `InternalWindow`.

Some Terminology

There are two types of dialog boxes: *modal* and *modeless*. When a modal dialog box appears on the screen, the modal dialog box gains the application's focus and doesn't relinquish it until the modal dialog is dismissed. All keyboard events get directed to the dialog box, and all mouse events outside the dialog box are ignored. The point of a modal dialog is to force the user to deal with the modal dialog before proceeding, and as such, modal dialog boxes are typically used to query a user for important information. As an example of when a modal dialog would be useful, consider a text editor. If the user selected **Exit** from the menu and there were unsaved changes to the text, a user-friendly application would pop up a modal dialog and ask the user if he or she wanted to "Save Changes Before Exiting?" and provide three possible responses, **Yes**, **No**, and **Cancel**. The application would not exit or proceed until the user had selected one of the responses. The IFC `Alert` class, covered below, is a good general-purpose modal dialog box. If you want to design your own modal dialog box, you can always use an `ExternalWindow` or `InternalWindow` and show it with `showModally()` rather than `show()`.

A modeless dialog box does not affect the main application's event handling. A user can work with other parts of the application normally even when a modeless dialog box is present. Modeless dialog boxes are often used for setting the properties of other objects in an application; for instance, `ColorChooser` and `FontChooser`, covered in Chapter 16, *Color, Font, and File Choosers*, are good examples of modeless dialog boxes. Note, however, that since the IFC doesn't have a `Dialog` class, there really isn't a modeless dialog box *per se*—a modeless dialog box is indistinguishable from any other modeless window.

Modal Dialog Boxes: The Alert Class

The `Alert` class represents a general-purpose modal dialog box. Figure 17-1 shows three `Alert` dialogs, using standard images that represent a notification alert, a question alert, and a warning alert.

Figure 17-1: Notification, question, and warning alerts

An `Alert` has an optional image, and up to five strings associated with it: a title, a message, and up to three button titles, each representing a possible choice for the user, typically something like `Yes`, `No`, and `Cancel`. An `Alert` can be run internally, appearing in a window in the browser, or externally, appearing in an outside window. To show an `Alert`, use one of the following methods:

```
public static int runAlertInternally(String title, String message,
                             String option1, String option2,
                             String option3);
public static int runAlertExternally(String title, String message,
                             String option1, String option2,
                             String option3);
public static int runAlertInternally(Image image, String title,
                             String message, String option1,
                             String option2, String option3);
public static int runAlertExternally(Image image, String title,
                             String message, String option1,
                             String option2, String option3);
```

Passing *null* as *option3* will create a two-option `Alert`, and passing *null* as *option2* and *option3* will create a one-option `Alert`. `Alert` returns one of three values: `Alert.DEFAULT_OPTION`, `Alert.SECOND_OPTION`, and `Alert.THIRD_OPTION`. If one of the first two methods are used, `Alert` supplies a default image.

For your convenience, `Alert` provides three images, each returned by a static method: a notification image, accessed by `notificationImage()`, a question image, accessed by `questionImage()`, and a warning image, accessed by `warningImage()`. Of course, you're not required to use any of these images. You can use any `Image` you want as an argument to an `Alert`.

If `Alert` is not sufficient for your application, you can create your own modal dialog box by following a procedure similar to the one outlined below for creating a modeless dialog box. Remember, however, to use `showModally()` to show the window, and if you're using an `InternalWindow`, be sure to put it in the modal layer.

Modeless Dialog Boxes by Example

Since the IFC has no `Dialog` class, you'll have to use an `InternalWindow` or `ExternalWindow` to show a modeless dialog box. In this section, we present two home-brewed dialog box examples to give you a taste of what's involved in designing dialog boxes. The first is of general utility, and creates a modeless dialog box that looks similar to an `Alert`. The second example is a dialog box designed for a specific application.

A General-Purpose Modeless Dialog Box

The first step in creating a dialog box is to decide on a user interface and program a `View` subclass to implement it. The `DialogView` class, shown in Example 17-1, is an example. `DialogView` lays out an image, a title, a message, and a button for the dialog box shown in Figure 17-2. Since `DialogView` is merely a `View`, it can be added to either an `InternalWindow` or `ExternalWindow` to create a dialog box; by burying the complicated part of dialog box construction in a `View` subclass rather than an `InternalWindow` or `ExternalWindow` subclass, you can get both types of modeless dialog boxes for the price of one. `DialogView` has a target and a command, and its target is notified when its button is pressed. Typically the button will read **OK**, and the `DialogView`'s target will be the window it's appearing in, which will hide itself when the **OK** button is pressed.

Figure 17-2: An informative dialog box

Notice the layout management in `DialogView` is done by brute force arithmetic. This is a good example of how to lay out views in the absence of robust layout managers.

Example 17-1: A View Class for Laying Out a Dialog Box

```
import netscape.application.*;
import netscape.util.*;

// a View class for a modeless dialog box
public class DialogView extends View implements Target {
  Image image;
  String title, message, buttonTitle, command;
  Label titleField, messageField;
  Button button;
  ContainerView imageView;
  int padding = 10;
  Target target;

  public DialogView(Image image, String title, String message,
                    String buttonTitle) {
    this.image = image;
    this.title = title;
    this.message = message;
    this.buttonTitle = buttonTitle;

    createThings();

    Size sz = computeMinSize();
    sizeTo(sz.width,sz.height);
    // fix the button's x coordinate
    button.moveTo(width()/2-button.width()/2, button.y());

    addSubview(imageView);
    addSubview(titleField);
    addSubview(messageField);
    addSubview(button);
  }

  // create the Labels and the Button
  protected void createThings(){
    if(image != null){
      imageView = new ContainerView(10, 10, image.width(), image.height());
      imageView.setBorder(null);
      imageView.setImage(image);
      imageView.setImageDisplayStyle(Image.CENTERED);
    }
    titleField = new Label(title, new Font("Helvetica", Font.BOLD, 24));

    if(image != null) {
      titleField.moveTo(image.width() + 2*padding,padding +
                        Math.max(0,image.height()-titleField.bounds.height));
    }
    else titleField.moveTo(padding,padding);

    messageField = new Label(message,Font.defaultFont());
    messageField.moveTo(padding,titleField.y() + titleField.height() +
                        2*padding);
```

Example 17-1: A View Class for Laying Out a Dialog Box (continued)

```
    button = new Button();
    button.setTitle(buttonTitle);
    button.sizeToMinSize();
    // fix the button's y coordinate
    // we can't fix the x coordinate yet because we don't know
    // how big the DialogView will be yet
    button.moveTo(0, messageField.y() + messageField.height() + 2*padding);

    button.setTarget(this);
    button.setCommand("buttonPressed");
  }

  // find the minimum size
  protected Size computeMinSize(){
    Size size = new Size();
    size.width = size.height = 0;
    if(image != null){
      size.width = padding + image.width() + padding + titleField.width() +
                   padding;
      size.height = padding + Math.max(image.height(),titleField.height()) +
                    padding;
    }
    else{
      size.width = titleField.width() + 2*padding;
      size.height = titleField.height() + 2*padding;
    }
    size.width = Math.max(size.width,2*padding + messageField.width());
    size.height += messageField.height() + 2*padding;

    size.width = Math.max(size.width,2*padding + button.width());
    size.height += 2*padding + button.height();

    return size;
  }

  // give the DialogView a target
  public void setTarget(Target t){ target = t;}
  public void setCommand(String s){ command = s;}

  // notify the target with the button is pressed
  public void performCommand(String com, Object arg){
    if(com.equals("buttonPressed"))
      if(target != null) target.performCommand(command,this);
  }
}
```

Once we have a DialogView, creating a dialog box is easy: simply add the DialogView to a Window's view hierarchy! The InternalInfoDialog class, shown in Example 17-2, automates this for the case of an InternalWindow. When the DialogView's button is pressed, the InternalInfoDialog hides itself. You can alter this behavior as necessary.

Example 17-2: An InternalWindow Subclass for Use with DialogView

```
import netscape.application.*;
import netscape.util.*;
```

Example 17-2: An InternalWindow Subclass for Use with DialogView (continued)

```
public class InternalInfoDialog extends InternalWindow implements Target {
  DialogView dialogView;

  public InternalInfoDialog(Image image, String title, String message,
                            String buttonTitle) {
    super();
    // create the DialogView
    dialogView = new DialogView(image, title, message, buttonTitle);
    // size the window
    Size size = windowSizeForContentSize(dialogView.width(),
                                         dialogView.height());
    sizeTo(size.width,size.height);
    // add the dialog view
    addSubview(dialogView);
    setCanBecomeMain(false);
    dialogView.setTarget(this);
    dialogView.setCommand("dialogViewDismissed");
  }

  public void performCommand(String command, Object arg) {
    // hide the window when the button is pressed
    if(command.equals("dialogViewDismissed")){
      hide();
      return;
    }
    // pass other commands through to the superclass
    super.performCommand(command, arg);
  }
}
```

An Application-Specific Dialog Box

InfoDialog is a good general-purpose dialog box, but most applications will require other, application-specific dialog boxes. Together, the OptionView and OptionDialog classes form an application-specific dialog box for a drawing application. The user enters information about line width and color choices into OptionDialog, and when he or she presses a button, a setOptions command along with the data is sent to the application's target chain. In this case, the data is an instance of the Parameters class, a simple two-member class. The example code in this section is quite long. You'll understand the code better if you compile and run it first, before you attempt to look through windows.

Again, all the hard work in designing the dialog box is done in a View subclass, here called OptionView (in Example 17-3 and Figure 17-3). OptionView has a number of lines of code dedicated to laying out its subviews. (Since PackLayout resizes views with subviews, PackLayout has trouble with some of OptionView's complicated subviews. This is unfortunate, as you can see by the length of OptionView!) OptionView is an example of a complicated user interface that could have been built quickly with a GUI builder such as Netscape's Constructor.

OptionView presents the user with two-line width choices and a color choice, represented by an RGBView, from Chapter 12, *Scroll Bars and Scrolling*. Finally, it has a **Clear** button, and a **Set** button, which sends the line width and color values to its target.

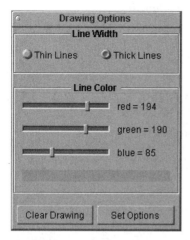

Figure 17-3: A custom dialog box

Example 17-3: A Custom View for a Dialog Box

```
import netscape.application.*;
import netscape.util.*;

public class OptionView extends View implements Target {
  RGBView rgb;
  Button clear,thick,thin,setOptions;
  ContainerView lineWidthContainer,buttonContainer;
  Target target;

  public OptionView(){
    super(0,0,220,260);  // hard code the size
    setBuffered(true);  // looks better
    // Put everything in one big ContainerView.  This makes the background
    // a uniform color.
    ContainerView overallContainer = new ContainerView(localBounds());
    overallContainer.setBorder(null);

    // Make a ContainerView for the line width radio buttons.
    lineWidthContainer = new ContainerView(0,0,width(),60);
    lineWidthContainer.setTitle("Line Width");
    // The title is a subview, and thus if you use a LayoutManager
    // with a ContainerView with a title, it doesn't look right.
    // Make a separate ContainerView for the radio buttons.
    // Use a GridLayout to position the buttons.
    ContainerView radioContainer = new ContainerView(0,14,width(),42);
    radioContainer.setBorder(null);
    GridLayout gridLayout = new GridLayout(1,2);
    gridLayout.setHorizGap(10);
    radioContainer.setLayoutManager(gridLayout);
    lineWidthContainer.addSubview(radioContainer);
    // Create the thin line and thick line buttons.
    thick = Button.createRadioButton(1,1,1,1);
    thick.setTitle("Thick Lines");
    thin = Button.createRadioButton(1,1,1,1);
    thin.setTitle("Thin Lines");
    // Add the buttons and lay out the view.
```

Example 17-3: A Custom View for a Dialog Box (continued)

```
    radioContainer.addSubview(thin);
    radioContainer.addSubview(thick);
    gridLayout.layoutView(radioContainer,0,0);

    // Make another ContainerView for the RGBView.
    ContainerView colorContainer =
                        new ContainerView(0,lineWidthContainer.height()+10,
                                            width(),145);
    colorContainer.setTitle("Line Color");
    rgb = new RGBView(2,14,width()-4,colorContainer.height()-16);
    colorContainer.addSubview(rgb);

    // Make a ContainerView for the "Clear All" and "Set Options" buttons.
    ContainerView buttonContainer =
                    new ContainerView(0,colorContainer.y() +
                                        colorContainer.height()+10,width(),35);

    // Use a GridLayout again.
    GridLayout gridLayout2 = new GridLayout(1,2);
    buttonContainer.setBorder(null);
    buttonContainer.setLayoutManager(gridLayout2);
    gridLayout2.setVertGap(5);
    gridLayout2.setHorizGap(5);
    // Create the buttons.
    clear = new Button();
    clear.setTitle("Clear Drawing");
    clear.setCommand("clearAll");
    clear.setTarget(this);
    setOptions = new Button();
    setOptions.setTitle("Set Options");
    setOptions.setCommand("setOptions");
    setOptions.setTarget(this);
    // Add the buttons and lay out the view.
    buttonContainer.addSubview(clear);
    buttonContainer.addSubview(setOptions);
    gridLayout2.layoutView(buttonContainer,0,0);

    // Add the container views to the view hierarchy.
    overallContainer.addSubview(buttonContainer);
    overallContainer.addSubview(colorContainer);
    overallContainer.addSubview(lineWidthContainer);

    addSubview(overallContainer);
  }

  public void performCommand(String command,Object arg){
    if(command.equals("clearAll")){
      if(TargetChain.applicationChain().canPerformCommand("clearAll")) {
        TargetChain.applicationChain().performCommand("clearAll", null);
      }
    }
    if(command.equals("setOptions")){
      Parameters params = new Parameters(rgb.color(),thick.state());
      if(TargetChain.applicationChain().canPerformCommand("setOptions")) {
        TargetChain.applicationChain().performCommand("setOptions", params);
      }
    }
  }
}
```

InternalOptionDialog, shown here in Example 17-4, extends InternalWindow, and creates an OptionView and adds it to its view hierarchy. We prevent users from resizing the InternalOptionDialog by calling setResizable(false), and we also prevent it from becoming the main window by calling setCanBecome-Main(false). Although we have left InternalOptionDialog in the default window layer, it could have been placed in the palette layer.

Example 17-4: A Window for a Dialog Box

```
import netscape.application.*;
import netscape.util.*;

public class InternalOptionDialog extends InternalWindow{
   OptionView optionView;
   public InternalOptionDialog(){
      super();
      optionView = new OptionView();
      setTitle("Drawing Options");
      addSubview(optionView);
      Size size = windowSizeForContentSize(optionView.width(),
                                           optionView.height());
      sizeTo(size.width, size.height);
      setResizable(false);
      setCloseable(true);
      setCanBecomeMain(false);
   }
}
```

An Application with Dialog Boxes

Well, after all that, how about an application? The Scribbler, shown is Example 17-5 and Figure 17-4, is another Application similar to the Scribble application of Chapter 6, *Mouse and Keyboard Events.* There are four classes presented here: Scribbler, ScribbleView, ScribbleWindow, and Parameters. Scribbler is the application, ScribbleView is the view that the user can draw in, and Scrib-bleWindow is an InternalWindow subclass that contains a ScribbleView. ScribbleView is capable of supporting lines of different color, and two different line thicknesses. Parameters is a helper class, used for passing information from a dialog box to a ScribbleView.

Scribbler also uses five classes that we've seen already: RGBView, DialogView, InternalInfoDialog, OptionView, and InternalOptionDialog.

Example 17-5: Four Classes for an Application with Dialog Boxes

```
import netscape.application.*;
import netscape.util.*;

public class Scribbler extends Application implements Target{
   InternalOptionDialog optionDialog;
   InternalInfoDialog infoDialog;
   Menu menuBar;
   MenuItem fileItem, optionItem, aboutItem, infoItem, newScribbler;
   InternalWindow scribbleWindow;

   public void init(){
```

```
    // create a window to scribble in
    scribbleWindow = new ScribbleWindow();
    scribbleWindow.show();

    // create and add the menu
    menuBar = new Menu(true);
    fileItem = menuBar.addItemWithSubmenu("File");
    optionItem = fileItem.submenu().addItem("Options", "options", this);
    newScribbler = fileItem.submenu().addItem("New Scribbler",
                                              "newScribbler", this);
    infoItem = menuBar.addItemWithSubmenu("Help");
    aboutItem = infoItem.submenu().addItem("About", "about", this);
    if(mainRootView().externalWindow() != null)
      mainRootView().externalWindow().setMenu(menuBar);
  }

  public void performCommand(String command, Object data){
    if(command.equals("options")) onOptions();
    if(command.equals("about")) onAbout();
    if(command.equals("newScribbler")) createNewScribbler();
  }

  // create the drawing options dialog box
  protected void onOptions(){
    if(optionDialog != null && !optionDialog.isVisible()){
      optionDialog.moveTo(100,100);
      optionDialog.show();
    }
    if(optionDialog == null){
      optionDialog = new InternalOptionDialog();
      optionDialog.moveTo(100,100);
      optionDialog.show();
    }
  }

  protected void onAbout(){  // create a new information dialog box
    if(infoDialog != null && !infoDialog.isVisible()){
      infoDialog.moveTo(100,100);
      infoDialog.show();
    }
    if(infoDialog == null) {
      infoDialog =
          new InternalInfoDialog(Alert.notificationImage(), "Scribbler",
                                 "By Dean Petrich, 1997.", "OK");
      infoDialog.moveTo(100,100);
      infoDialog.show();
    }
  }

  // create a new scribble window
  protected void createNewScribbler() {
    ScribbleWindow newWindow = new ScribbleWindow();
    newWindow.show();
  }
}

// A View to draw in
import netscape.application.*;
```

Example 17-5: Four Classes for an Application with Dialog Boxes (continued)

```
import netscape.util.*;

public class ScribbleView extends View implements Target, ExtendedTarget {
  int lastx,lasty;
  Graphics gr;
  Color currentColor;
  boolean wasOutOfBounds = false;
  boolean thickLines = false;

  public ScribbleView(Rect r) {
    super(r);
    currentColor = Color.blue;
  }

  public void performCommand(String command, Object data) {
    if(command.equals("clearAll")) draw();  // calls drawView()
    if(command.equals("setOptions")){      // set the drawing options
      Parameters p = (Parameters) data;
      currentColor = p.color;
      thickLines = p.thickLines;
    }
  }

  public void drawView(Graphics g) {
    g.setColor(Color.white);
    g.fillRect(localBounds());
  }

  public boolean mouseDown(MouseEvent e) {
    wasOutOfBounds = false;
    gr = createGraphics();
    lastx = e.x;
    lasty = e.y;
    return true;
  }

  public void mouseDragged(MouseEvent e) {
    if(!containsPointInVisibleRect(e.x,e.y) ||
       viewForMouse(e.x,e.y) != this) {
      wasOutOfBounds = true;
      return;
    }
    if(wasOutOfBounds) return;
    gr.setColor(currentColor);

    if(thickLines) {
      // draw four lines around the center line
      gr.drawLine(lastx-1,lasty, e.x-1, e.y);
      gr.drawLine(lastx+1,lasty, e.x+1, e.y);
      gr.drawLine(lastx, lasty-1, e.x, e.y-1);
      gr.drawLine(lastx, lasty+1, e.x, e.y+1);
    }
    // draw the center line
    gr.drawLine(lastx, lasty, e.x, e.y);

    lastx = e.x;
    lasty = e.y;
  }
```

Dialog Boxes

```
public void mouseUp(MouseEvent e) { gr.dispose(); }

public Parameters options() {
  Parameters p = new Parameters(currentColor,thickLines);
  return p;
}

// ExtendedTarget command
// We need this because ScribbleView will be in the TargetChain.
public boolean canPerformCommand(String command) {
  if(command.equals("setOptions")) return true;
  if(command.equals("clearAll")) return true;
  else return false;
}
}

// a window subclass that contains a ScribbleView
import netscape.application.*;
import netscape.util.*;

public class ScribbleWindow extends InternalWindow{

  ScribbleView scribbleView;
  public ScribbleWindow() {
    scribbleView = new ScribbleView(new Rect(0,0,300,300));
    Size s = windowSizeForContentSize(scribbleView.width(),
                                      scribbleView.height());
    sizeTo(s.width,s.height);
    setTitle("Scribbles");
    addSubview(scribbleView);
    setResizable(true);
    // allow the window to become the document window
    setContainsDocument(true);
  }

  // make the ScribbleView the selected view when
  // the window becomes the document window
  public void didBecomeCurrentDocument() {
    super.didBecomeCurrentDocument();
    scribbleView.setFocusedView();
  }
}

// a simple helper class
import netscape.application.*;
import netscape.util.*;

public class Parameters {
  public Color color;
  public boolean thickLines;

  public Parameters(Color c, boolean thick) {
    color = c;
    thickLines = thick;
  }
}
```

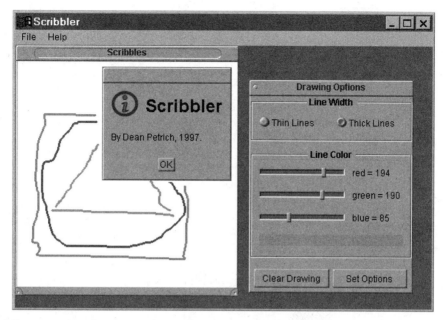

Figure 17-4: A drawing application, with its two dialog boxes

In the previous example, `InternalOptionDialog` operates only on the document window. As an exercise, you could alter the code above so that if more than one `ScribbleWindow` is open, the `InternalOptionDialog` always reflects the current drawing options of the document window: i.e., the `InternalOptionDialog` will have to be updated every time a new window becomes the document window.

CHAPTER 18

Animation and Images

In this chapter we present the IFC classes and interfaces useful for animation: Timer, Image, DrawingSequence, ImageSequence, and DrawingSequenceOwner.

The Timer Class

Java has built-in support for multithreaded applications. However, multithreaded applications are difficult to program and debug, so often it's better to stick with single-threaded applications when possible. The IFC has made this easy by providing a Timer class that eliminates the need for a second thread in certain cases. In particular, IFC animation is normally done with a Timer or a DrawingSequence, which incorporates an internal Timer.

So what does a Timer do? In short, a Timer fires at regular intervals, and every time it does, it notifies its target. Schematically, this is how a Timer works.* When the Timer fires, an Event is placed on the application's event queue. When it's the Event's turn to be processed, the Timer processes it calling the performCommand() method of its target.

The important point is that the Timer uses the application's event queue. That way, the Timer's events are handled by the application's main thread, so you don't need to worry about the synchronization problems that are common with multithreaded applications. As long as the application is able to process the Timer's events in a timely manner, there is no need for a secondary thread.

The most convenient way to create a Timer is to use the following constructor:

```
public Timer(Target target, String command, int delay);
```

---

* In fact, it's slightly more complicated than this because timers are managed by a helper class, TimerQueue. TimerQueue, not Timer, implements Runnable.

The integer *delay* represents the time in milliseconds between `Timer` firings. The *target*, *command*, and *delay* can be set separately using the `setTarget()`, `setCommand()`, and `setDelay()` methods. Table 18-1 lists more `Timer` attributes. Of these, the data attribute is the most important. You can specify the object that's sent to the `Timer`'s target with the `Timer`'s `setData()` method.

Finally, the `start()` and `stop()` methods start and stop the `Timer`.

Table 18-1: Timer Attributes

Attribute	Description
Target	The timer's target.
Command	The `String` that's sent to the timer's target when the timer fires.
Delay	The time in milliseconds between timer firings.
Data	The `Object` sent to the timer's target when the timer fires.
InitialDelay	The time between the call to `start()` and the timer's first firing.
Coalesce	If the timer is set to coalesce its events and there is more than one event from the timer on the event queue, it will process just one and remove the rest.
Repeats	If the timer is set to repeat, it will fire at regular intervals. If not, it will fire only once.

In Example 18-1, we use a `Timer` to perform some simple animation in which two blue circles move around in a periodic (and slightly hypnotic!) way. Figure 18-1 shows one static frame of this animation.

Example 18-1: Animation with Timers

```
import netscape.application.*;
import netscape.util.*;

// a Timer example that performs some simple animation
public class Dots extends Application {
  MovingDots mdots;

  public void init() {
    mdots = new MovingDots(mainRootView().localBounds());
    mainRootView().addSubview(mdots);
  }
}

// a view class that uses a Timer to do some animation
class MovingDots extends View implements Target {
  Button startbutton,stopbutton;
  int x1,y1,x2,y2;
  double time,dt;
  Timer timer;
  double dw,dh;

  public MovingDots(Rect r) {
    super(r);
    setBuffered(true);  // use buffered drawing
    dh = (double) (r.height/2);
    dw = (double) (r.width/2);
```

Example 18-1: Animation with Timers (continued)

```
// (x1,y1) and (x2,y2) are the coordinates of the "dots"
x1 = r.width/2 + r.width/4;
x2 = r.width/2 - r.width/4;
y1 = y2 = r.height/2;

// start at time = 0
time = 0.0;
dt = 0.1;
// create a Timer with 40 milliseconds between firings
timer = new Timer(this,"movedot",40);

// a start button
startbutton = new Button(10,10,50,30);
startbutton.setTitle("Start");
startbutton.setTarget(this);
startbutton.setCommand("start");

// a stop button
stopbutton = new Button(10,50,50,30);
stopbutton.setTitle("Stop");
stopbutton.setTarget(this);
stopbutton.setCommand("stop");

addSubview(startbutton);
addSubview(stopbutton);
}

public void drawView(Graphics g) {
  // draw the background
  g.setColor(Color.cyan);
  g.fillRect(localBounds());
  // draw the two dots as circles with radius 10
  g.setColor(Color.blue);
  g.fillOval(x1,y1,10,10);
  g.fillOval(x2,y2,10,10);
}

public void performCommand(String command, Object anObject) {
  if(command.equals("movedot")) {
    // update the position of the dots
    int x = (int) (dw*Math.cos(3.0*time));
    int y = (int) (dh*Math.sin(2.0*time));
    y1 = bounds.height/2 + y/2;
    x1 = bounds.width/2 + x/2;
    y2 = bounds.height/2 - y/2;
    x2 = bounds.width/2 - x/2;
    // increment time
    time += dt;
    // redraw the dots
    draw();
  }
  if(command.equals("start")){ timer.start(); }
  if(command.equals("stop")){ timer.stop(); }
}
}
```

Timers can be used for purposes other than animation. For instance, the IFC itself uses a timer to implement its blinking cursors in TextField and TextView.

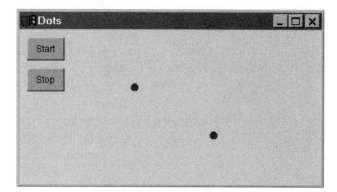

Figure 18-1: An animation with a timer

Simple animation like the one in Example 18-1 is probably better implemented by using a DrawingSequence, which incorporates an internal Timer. We'll learn about the DrawingSequence class shortly.

The Image Class

The Image class is an abstract class used to represent static images, through the Bitmap subclass, and animated images, through the DrawingSequence subclass. Image is useful because many classes in the IFC have built-in support for displaying images. For instance, a Button, ContainerView, or Slider can each display a background image without creating a custom subclass. In general, you won't subclass Image directly, but you'll take advantage of Image's subclasses.

The Image class itself is not very large, and does little more than fix the display style as centered, scaled, or tiled, through the drawCentered(), drawScaled(), drawTiled() or drawWithStyle(int *style*) methods. In the drawWithStyle() method, style can take one of three values, Image.CENTERED, Image.SCALED, or Image.TILED.

Although Image normally isn't subclassed directly, you may want to extend one of Image's subclasses, particularly DrawingSequence. As a consequence, it's helpful to know what Image methods are abstract. They are:

public abstract void drawAt(Graphics, int, int);
　　Draws the Image at the specified coordinates.

public abstract int width();
　　Returns the Image's width.

public abstract int height();
　　Returns the Image's height.

In addition, two other methods should be overridden when applicable:

public String name();
　　Returns the name of the Image. This can be whatever you want; choose something for your convenience!

```
public void drawScaled(Graphics g, int x, int y, int w, int h);
```
> Draws the Image within the Rect given by (x, y, w, h). The draw-Scaled(Graphics, Rect) method calls this method.

Although the name() and drawScaled() methods aren't designated as abstract, and thus it isn't necessary to provide an implementation for them, it's a good idea to do so. For instance, Bitmap, an IFC Image subclass, implements both name() and drawScaled().

Again, normally you won't subclass Image directly, but will use or subclass one of Image's subclasses, Bitmap, DrawingSequence, or ImageSequence. These three classes are covered in detail below.

The Bitmap Class

Bitmap is an Image subclass used for two purposes: displaying picture files such as GIF or JPEG files, and for off-screen drawing. Bitmap is not an abstract class. It provides an implementation for all the abstract methods of Image, so you can use it directly without worrying about subclassing.

Static Images

Bitmap has three static methods for creating bitmaps from image data:

```
public static Bitmap bitmapFromURL(URL);
```
> Returns a Bitmap created from the given URL.

```
public static synchronized Bitmap bitmapNamed(String name,
                                              boolean loadNow);
```
> Creates a Bitmap from the URL *codebase/images/name*, where *codebase* is the directory where the Application resides. If *loadNow* is true, the Bitmap's data is loaded immediately. If not, it's loaded when needed.

```
public static Bitmap bitmapNamed(String name);
```
> Creates a Bitmap from the URL *codebase/images/name*, where *codebase* is the directory where the Application resides. The data is loaded immediately.

Note that the two BitmapNamed methods expect to find the image data in a separate directory named *images*.

To determine whether or not a Bitmap is finished loading its data, you can call the hasLoadedData() method, and you can further check if it's valid by calling the isValid() method. If the Bitmap was created using one of the bitmap-Named() methods, the name() method will return the *name* argument.

Bitmaps are cached by the IFC, which is good for speed but bad for memory. Calling a bitmap's flush() method releases the bitmap's system resources and removes the bitmap from the cache.

Off-Screen Drawing

A Bitmap can also be used for off-screen drawing and therefore it provides a way of implementing flicker-free animation. The IFC's buffered drawing uses an off-screen `Bitmap`, for instance. The advantage of working with the `Bitmap` class directly is that often only a small part of a view needs to be updated in an animation sequence. Updating only this part is called *clipping*. In cases where high-speed drawing is necessary, `View.setBuffered()` is too slow because it buffers the entire view. By creating your own off-screen bitmap and making only incremental changes in it, you can improve drawing performance.

To create a `Bitmap` for off-screen drawing, use the following constructor:

```
public Bitmap(int width, int height);
```

To get a `Graphics` object associated with the `Bitmap`, call the `createGraphics()` method of the `Bitmap`:

```
public Graphics createGraphics();
```

Once you have a `Graphics` object g for a `Bitmap`, you can call all the usual `Graphics` methods in order to draw in the `Bitmap`.

When you're done with the off-screen drawing and want to see the `Bitmap`, you'll need an on-screen `Graphics` object. If you're going to display the `Bitmap` using a `View`'s `drawView()` method, you'll already have a `Graphics` object that represents part of the screen. If not, you can call `View`'s `createGraphics()` method to get an on-screen `Graphics` object for the `View`. (Note that both `Bitmap` and `View` have `createGraphics()` methods!) Either way, once you have an on-screen `Graphics` object *gr*, you can display the bitmap with the `Graphics` object's `draw-BitmapAt()` method:

```
gr.drawBitmapAt(Bitmap b, int x, int y);
```

The `drawBitmapAt()` method displays the `Bitmap` at the coordinates *x* and *y*. `Graphics` also offers the `drawBitmapScaled(Bitmap b, int x, int y, int w, int h)` method, which draws a `Bitmap` in the rectangle given by (*x*,*y*,*w*,*h*). Transferring an off-screen bitmap to the screen is typically very fast, but this depends on the underlying implementation of the Java virtual machine, which is of course platform-dependent.

An Off-Screen Drawing Example

The `Buffered` example, Example 18-2, performs some animation in two separate ways. The `OffScreenRoller` class implements off-screen drawing and clipping directly, while the `Roller` class uses the IFC's built-in double-buffering with `View.setBuffered()`. Both classes portray a circle rolling horizontally across the screen.

`OffScreenRoller` performs its animation using a `Bitmap` in exactly the way it's explained above. `OffScreenRoller` has an internal `Bitmap` that it uses for off-screen drawing, and at each time step, the drawing is first done on a `Graphics` object obtained from the `Bitmap`. Then, a `Graphics` object that has been created from the `View` draws the `Bitmap` with `drawBitmapAt()`. Since this latter `Graphics` object was created from the on-screen `View`, not the `Bitmap`, the `Bitmap` immediately appears on the screen.

The animation in `OffScreenRoller` is fairly simple because the "moving" part is small compared to the size of the whole view. We take advantage of this in

OffScreenRoller and use clipping. Each time we draw on the Bitmap's Graphics, we have to erase the circle in its old position, and redraw the circle in its new position. This is accomplished very efficiently by setting the Graphics' clipping rectangle to be the union of the rectangles defining the old position and the new position, and then calling drawView() with the Bitmap's Graphics as the argument. drawView() will draw only in the clipping rectangle, and leave everything else as is. If you use a clipping rectangle for the Bitmap's Graphics, you need to be sure to use the same (or a smaller) clipping rectangle for the View's Graphics; otherwise, some undrawn areas of the Bitmap will appear in the View.

If you compile and run the Buffered example, you'll see the difference in performance between OffScreenRoller and Roller. On my computer, OffScreenRoller rolls about three times as fast as Roller.

Example 18-2 uses separate threads for its animation, which violates one tenet of IFC application design: since the IFC is not thread safe, Timers, rather than separate threads, should be used whenever possible. However, starting separate threads is the only way to see the difference in speed between the built-in buffered drawing and the custom buffered drawing implemented in OffScreenRoller. To implement thread-safe high-speed animation, combine the drawing technique shown in the OffScreenRoller example with the Timer technique shown in the Dots example.

Example 18-2: Buffered Drawing

```
import netscape.application.*;
import netscape.util.*;

// an example that uses a Bitmap for off-screen drawing
public class Buffered extends Application {
  Roller roller;
  OffScreenRoller osRoller;

  public void init() {
    Rect rect = mainRootView().localBounds();
    roller = new Roller(0,rect.height/2,rect.width,rect.height/2);
    osRoller = new OffScreenRoller(0,0,rect.width,rect.height/2);
    mainRootView().addSubview(roller);
    mainRootView().addSubview(osRoller);
    roller.draw();
    osRoller.draw();
    roller.start();           // start the animation
    osRoller.start();         // start the animation
  }

  public void cleanup() {
    roller.stop();
    osRoller.stop();
  }
}

// a class that does some animation using the View's built-in buffered
// drawing capabilities
class Roller extends View implements Runnable {
```

Example 18-2: Buffered Drawing (continued)

```
  Thread thread;
  int x;
  int angle;
  Rect rect;
  int diam = 30;

  public Roller(int x,int y,int w,int h) {
    super(x,y,w,h);
    setBuffered(true);
    x = diam;
    rect = new Rect(0,0,diam,diam);
  }

  public void start() {
    thread = new Thread(this);
    thread.start();
  }

  public void run() {
    while(true){
      draw();
      x++;                // move the shape
      x = x%width();      // wrap it from right to left
    }
  }

  public void drawView(Graphics g) {
    // draw a black background
    g.setColor(Color.black);
    g.fillRect(localBounds());
    // draw a rolling shape
    angle = -(360/diam)*x;
    rect.setBounds(x,(height()-diam)/2,diam,diam);
    g.setColor(Color.green);
    g.drawOval(rect);
    g.fillArc(rect,angle,90);
    g.fillArc(rect,angle+180,90);
  }

  public void stop() {
    thread.stop();
    thread = null;
  }
}

// a class that performs flicker-free animation by implementing its own
// off-screen drawing with Bitmap
class OffScreenRoller extends View implements Runnable {
  Bitmap bitmap;
  Graphics onscreen,bitmapGraphics;
  Thread thread;
  int x,angle;
  Rect currentRect,oldRect;
  int diam = 30;

  public OffScreenRoller(int x,int y,int w,int h) {
    super(x,y,w,h);
    x = 0;
```

Example 18-2: Buffered Drawing (continued)

```
        currentRect = new Rect(x,(height()-diam)/2,diam,diam);
        oldRect = new Rect(currentRect);
        bitmap = new Bitmap(w,h);
    }

    public void start() {
        onscreen = createGraphics();
        bitmapGraphics = bitmap.createGraphics();
        thread = new Thread(this);
        thread.start();
    }

    public void run() {
        while(true) {
            // compute the current position of the roller
            currentRect.setBounds(x,(height()-diam)/2,diam,diam);

            // compute the clipping rectangle by taking the union
            // with the old position
            Rect clippingRect = Rect.rectFromUnion(currentRect,oldRect);

            // set the clipping rectangle and draw in the bitmap
            // Note the second argument, false.  This clears any previous
            // clipping rectangles from bitmapGraphics.
            bitmapGraphics.setClipRect(clippingRect,false);
            drawView(bitmapGraphics);

            // set the clipping rectangle and draw in the View
            onscreen.setClipRect(clippingRect,false);
            onscreen.drawBitmapAt(bitmap,0,0);

            x++;                    // move the shape
            x = x%width();          // wrap it from right to left
            oldRect.setBounds(currentRect);
        }
    }

    public void drawView(Graphics g) {
        // draw a black background
        g.setColor(Color.black);
        g.fillRect(localBounds());

        // draw a rolling shape
        angle = -(360/diam)*x;
        g.setColor(Color.green);
        g.drawOval(currentRect);
        g.fillArc(currentRect,angle,90);
        g.fillArc(currentRect,angle+180,90);
    }

    public void stop() {
        bitmapGraphics.dispose();   // don't forget to do this!
        onscreen.dispose();         // or this!
        thread.stop();
        thread = null;
    }
}
```

The DrawingSequence Class

DrawingSequence is an abstract subclass of Image that plays a sequence of frames at timed intervals. If you'd like to do some animation where the frames are created "on the fly," you should subclass DrawingSequence. If you already have a sequence of images, and you'd like to play them back as animation, use the Image-Sequence class, a DrawingSequence subclass specifically designed for animating a sequence of pre-existing Image objects. ImageSequence will be covered below.

What You Need to Implement

DrawingSequence subclasses must provide implementations of only three methods:

`public void drawAt(Graphics g, int x, int y);`
> Draws the current frame at *x* and *y*.

`public int width();`
> Returns the width of the Image.

`public int height();`
> Returns the height of the Image.

The implementation of the drawAt() method will depend on the frame number, which can be accessed with the currentFrameNumber() method. After all, if the drawing didn't depend on the current frame number, it wouldn't make sense to call it a drawing sequence!

What You Get for Free

Once you've defined a DrawingSequence subclass by overriding the methods above, you can take advantage of the methods implemented in DrawingSequence.

DrawingSequence has two constructors:

`public DrawingSequence(DrawingSequenceOwner owner);`
> Returns a DrawingSequence with the given *owner*, a frame rate of one frame per millisecond, a current frame number of 0, and a playback mode of FORWARD. A DrawingSequenceOwner controls the DrawingSequence it owns, and we'll cover it in the next section.

`public DrawingSequence();`
> Returns a DrawingSequence. If you use this constructor, you'll have to set the owner yourself.

The playback mode can be set by using the setPlaybackMode() method, and the time between frames can be set with the setFrameRate() method. Table 18-2 lists DrawingSequence's attributes.

Table 18-2: DrawingSequence Attributes

Attribute	Description
CurrentFrameNumber	The current frame number.
FrameCount	The total number of frames in the sequence.

Table 18-2: DrawingSequence Attributes (continued)

Attribute	Description
FrameRate	The time interval between frame updates. Note that this is not a rate; probably this attribute should have been called Delay.
Name	A String that gives the DrawingSequence's name. This is for your convenience, and you can choose any name you want.
Owner	The DrawingSequenceOwner associated with the DrawingSequence. DrawingSequenceOwner is covered below.
PlaybackMode	The playback mode can be FORWARD, FORWARD_LOOP, BACKWARD, BACKWARD_LOOP, or BOUNCE. BOUNCE starts at the first frame, then proceeds forward to the last frame, then backwards to the first frame, then forward to the last frame, etc.
ResetOnStart	Resets the current frame number to the first frame on start().
ResetOnStop	Resets the current frame number to the first frame on stop().

Finally, every DrawingSequence has start() and stop() methods to start and stop their animation.

The DrawingSequenceOwner Interface

Somewhat paradoxically, since DrawingSequence extends Image and not View, a DrawingSequence can't do any drawing on its own! A DrawingSequence's drawing is controlled by a DrawingSequenceOwner, an interface that consists of two methods:

public abstract void drawingSequenceCompleted(DrawingSequence);
  Called after the DrawingSequence is finished.

public abstract void drawingSequenceFrameChanged(DrawingSequence);
  Called after the DrawingSequence's frame has changed.

The logic behind the DrawingSequenceOwner and its drawingSequence-FrameChanged() method is this: every *delay* milliseconds, the DrawingSequence notifies its owner that the frame has changed. When it's notified of a frame change, the DrawingSequenceOwner retrieves the current frame from the DrawingSequence and proceeds to display it. Therefore the implementation of the drawingSequenceFrameChanged() method will normally involve a call to a view's draw() method, which will in turn call the drawAt() method of the DrawingSequence. If this still isn't clear, the next section contains an example that should clarify what should call what when!

A DrawingSequence Example

The application in Example 18-3, SpinnerApp, shows how to create and use a DrawingSequence. The Spinner class extends DrawingSequence and draws a circle with two colored arcs similar to the "rollers" in the `Buffered` example. Starting the sequence causes the circle to rotate. The example shows how to display the `Spinner` directly in the background and on a button. `Buttons` implement `DrawingSequenceOwner`, so having a button display an animated image is simply a matter of calling the button's `setImage()` method.

`SpinnerView` draws the `Spinner` at different locations depending on the frame number. This technique is useful for drawing animation that simulates motion—such as a bird flying, a fish swimming, a slug slithering, and so on. The `Drawing-Sequence` could consist of a sequence of "snapshots" of the bird or fish, and the drawing sequence owner would display each frame at a slightly different location to give the illusion of motion. This is exactly what `SpinnerView` does: each time `draw()` is called, `SpinnerView` positions the `Spinner` according to the current frame number. The technique is quite similar to the technique used in Example 18-2. Figure 18-2 shows a static frame of the animation.

Example 18-3: A DrawingSequence

```
import netscape.application.*;
import netscape.util.*;

// an Application that uses a DrawingSequence
public class SpinnerApp extends Application {
   SpinnerView spinnerview;
   Button spinnerbutton;
   Spinner buttonspinner;

   public void init() {
      Rect rect = mainRootView().bounds();
      // Create a View subclass that acts as a DrawingSequenceOwner.
      // The SpinnerView automatically starts the DrawingSequence.
      spinnerview = new SpinnerView(rect.width/5, rect.height/5,
                                    3*rect.width/5, 3*rect.height/5);
      mainRootView().addSubview(spinnerview);

      // Create a button.  Button implements DrawingSequenceOwner.
      spinnerbutton = new Button(10,10,130,30);
      buttonspinner = new Spinner(spinnerbutton);
      // Set the button's Image and start the playback.
      spinnerbutton.setImage(buttonspinner);
      buttonspinner.setPlaybackMode(DrawingSequence.FORWARD_LOOP);
      // Set the frame rate to 20 milliseconds.
      buttonspinner.setFrameRate(20);
      buttonspinner.start();                  // start the animation
      spinnerbutton.setBuffered(true);
      spinnerbutton.setTitle("Animated Button");

      mainRootView().addSubview(spinnerbutton);
   }
}

class SpinnerView extends View implements DrawingSequenceOwner{
   Spinner spinner;

   public SpinnerView(int x,int y,int w,int h) {
      super(x,y,w,h);
      setBuffered(true);
```

Example 18-3: A DrawingSequence (continued)

```
      spinner = new Spinner(this);       // create the DrawingSequence
      spinner.setFrameRate(50);          // 50 milliseconds between frames
      spinner.setPlaybackMode(DrawingSequence.FORWARD_LOOP);
      spinner.start();                   // start the animation!
  }

  public void drawView(Graphics g) {
    // Get the total number of frames.
    double frameCount = (double) spinner.frameCount();
    // Get the current frame number.
    double currentFrame = (double) spinner.currentFrameNumber();
    // Calculate the DrawingSequence's position in the View based
    // on the total number of frames and the current frame number.
    double phase = 2.0*Math.PI*currentFrame/frameCount;
    double dx = ((double) width())*(1.0 + Math.sin(phase))/10.0;
    double dy = ((double) height())*(1.0 + Math.cos(phase))/10.0;
    Rect rect = new Rect((int) dx, (int) dy, 8*width()/10, 8*height()/10);
    // draw the DrawingSequence at the correct position
    spinner.drawScaled(g,rect);
  }

  public void drawingSequenceCompleted(DrawingSequence ds) {}

  public void drawingSequenceFrameChanged(DrawingSequence ds) {
    draw();                   // call draw() every time the frame changes
  }
}

class Spinner extends DrawingSequence {
  public Spinner(DrawingSequenceOwner dso) {
    super(dso);
    setFrameCount(36);
  }

  // implement DrawingSequence's three abstract methods
  public void drawAt(Graphics g,int x,int y) {
    drawScaled(g,x,y,width(),height());
  }

  public int width() { return 20; }
  public int height() { return 20; }

  // implement the drawScaled() method for convenience.
  public void drawScaled(Graphics g,int x,int y,int w,int h) {
    // draw two circular arcs
    int angle = 5*currentFrameNumber();
    g.setColor(Color.green);
    Rect rect = new Rect(x,y,w,h);
    g.drawOval(rect);
    g.fillArc(rect,angle,90);
    g.fillArc(rect,angle+180,90);
  }
}
```

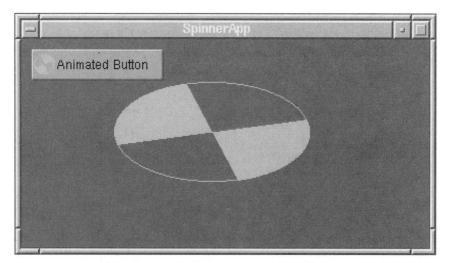

Figure 18-2: The SpinnerApp application

The ImageSequence Class

The ImageSequence class extends the DrawingSequence class, and is used to display a sequence of Image instances. If you can create the images your application will use before the animation begins, you should use an ImageSequence, particularly if the images are complicated. That way, your application won't get bogged down in creating the images a split second before they're drawn on the screen.

An ImageSequence can be created with the following constructor:

```
public ImageSequence(DrawingSequenceOwner d);
```

There are two ways to fix an ImageSequence's set of images. The first is to add images one by one, then play the images. The second is to set the Image-Sequence's *image strip*, a big Image containing *all* the frames, arranged in order from left to right (or top to bottom, if you like). An Image strip is similar in spirit to a movie reel: you specify the height and width of the "frames," and the ImageSequence moves down the image strip, reading the frames one by one. If you set the frame width using the setFrameWidth() method, ImageSequence assumes the image strip is arranged horizontally, and if you set the frame height using the setFrameHeight() method, ImageSequence assumes the image strip is arranged vertically. Figure 18-3 shows a set of eight individual images, and then how they would appear in an image strip.

Once you've fixed the images, using an ImageSequence is exactly the same as using a DrawingSequence. Simply set the playback mode, the frame rate, and start it up! Example 18-4 is some sample code for an ImageView class, which creates an ImageSequence by adding the eight separate GIF files in Figure 18-3.

*Animation
& Images*

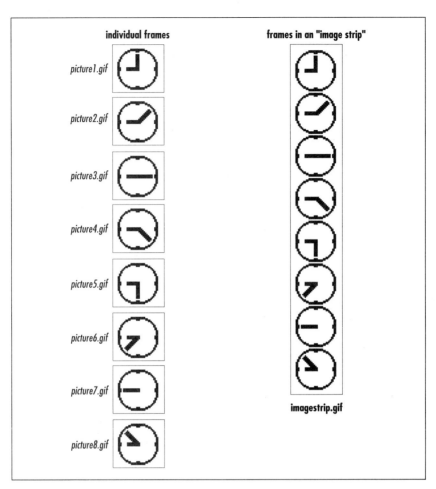

Figure 18-3: Images and an image strip

Example 18-4: A View with an ImageSequence

```
import netscape.application.*;
import netscape.util.*;

public class ImageView extends View implements DrawingSequenceOwner {
  ImageSequence images;

  public ImageView(int x,int y,int w,int h){
    super(x,y,w,h);
    images = new ImageSequence(this);
    setupImages();
    images.setPlaybackMode(DrawingSequence.FORWARD_LOOP);
    images.setFrameRate(100);
  }

  private void setupImages(){
```

Example 18-4: A View with an ImageSequence (continued)

```
    for(int j=1;j<=8;j++){
      images.addImage(Bitmap.bitmapNamed("picture" + j + ".gif"));
    }
  }

  public void drawingSequenceFrameChanged(DrawingSequence d){
    draw();
  }
  public void drawingSequenceCompleted(DrawingSequence d){}
  public void drawView(Graphics g){ images.drawAt(g,0,0); }
  public void start(){ images.start(); }
  public void stop(){ images.stop(); }
}
```

To use the image strip shown in Figure 18-3 rather than the eight separate bitmaps, replace setupImages() with:

```
  private void setupImages(){
      images.setImageStrip(Bitmap.bitmapNamed("imageStrip.gif"));
      images.setFrameHeight(32);    // Or use the height of your own frames
  }
```

CHAPTER 19

Drag-and-Drop

Drag-and-drop user interfaces are very intuitive, and most users find them easy to work with. The IFC provides several classes and interfaces that allow an application to use drag-and-drop *within* an application. For now, Java itself doesn't have any built-in drag-and-drop support—it doesn't take advantage of the underlying system's drag-and-drop functionality—so it's not possible to drag-and-drop between applications. You can look for that in a future release of Java, and you can be sure that future releases of the JFC will take advantage of any native drag-and-drop support offered by Java. Dragging and dropping objects within an application is still very useful, and in this chapter we cover the IFC classes and interfaces for drag-and-drop support.

This chapter assumes you know about MouseEvent and its related View methods; please read Chapter 5, *Drawing in Views*, if you haven't already done so.

Drag-and-Drop Terminology

In an IFC drag-and-drop "session," an Object is dragged from one view, the *source view*, to another, the *destination view*. There are four other objects involved in a drag session in addition to the source and destination views: the Image, the DragSession, the DragDestination, and the DragSource. We'll cover all four of these in more detail below, but for now, we present a brief summary of what each of them do.

The drag session's Image is dragged around the screen when the mouse is moved. The image represents the object that's being dragged, and should be chosen to be something intuitive. For instance, in a drag-and-drop file transfer program, if a file was being dragged, a good image would be a Bitmap displaying the file's name, and if a directory was dragged, a good image would be a Bitmap displaying a picture of a folder, with the directory's name beneath it.

DragSession is an IFC class that manages the drag session. A DragSession is normally created in the source view's mouseDown() or mouseDragged(). The DragSession contains two key pieces of information:

1. The dragged Image

2. The Object that the DragDestination (see below) will receive when the mouse is released

The DragSession notifies the DragDestination when the dragged object is dropped on the destination view. When an object is dropped, the DragDestination decides whether it will *accept* or *reject* the dropped object. In a drag-and-drop file transfer program, for instance, the DragDestination should accept instances of java.io.File, and reject everything else. DragDestination is an interface, but often the destination view itself will implement DragDestination.

Finally, once the DragDestination has accepted or rejected the dropped object, the DragSession notifies the DragSource about the DragDestination's decision. Like DragDestination, DragSource is an interface, but often the source view will implement DragSource.

Figure 19-1 should help clarify drag-and-drop terminology.

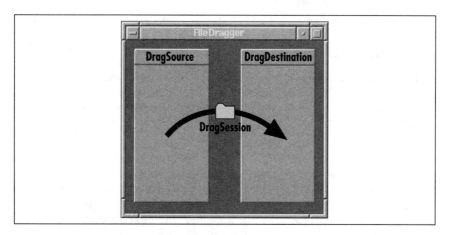

Figure 19-1: Drag-and-drop terminology

As you might have noticed from the above, the DragSession class does all the hard work for you. All you need to do to include drag-and-drop in an IFC application is implement the DragSource and DragDestination interfaces. Now that you've seen an overview of how an IFC drag session works, let's look at DragSource, DragSession, and DragDestination in detail.

Drag Sources

The DragSource interface has three methods:

public void dragWasAccepted(DragSession *dragSession*);
> Notifies the DragSource that the DragSession was accepted by the DragDestination.

public boolean dragWasRejected(DragSession *dragSession*);
> Notifies the DragSource that the DragSession was rejected by the DragDestination. If dragWasRejected() returns false, the DragSession's image will disappear immediately, and if it returns true, the DragSession's image will move back to the source, then disappear.

public View sourceView(DragSession *dragSession*);
> Returns the View that's acting as the source of the DragSession. Normally a View will implement DragSource, and sourceView() will simply return the given view.

The sourceView() method provides information to the DragSession about where the mouse pointer is when the DragSession is created. Keep in mind that the source view does *not* have to be the object implementing the DragSource interface. However, only views are notified about mouse events, and the creation of a DragSession will almost always occur in a particular view's mouseDown() method; this is the view that should be returned by sourceView().

Below we'll see an example that implements DragSource.

The DragSession Class

A drag-and-drop session is initiated when a DragSession is created. Normally the the DragSource will be a View, and the DragSession will be created in the view's mouseDown() or mouseDragged() method. The constructor for DragSession looks like this:

public DragSession(DragSource *source*, Image *image*, int *ix*, int *iy*,
                   int *mx*, int *my*, String *type*, Object *data*);

The *source* is normally the view itself, the *image* is the image that is dragged when the mouse is dragged, *ix* and *iy* represent the initial coordinates for the image, *mx* and *my* are the mouse's coordinates, *type* is a string that you can use to give any information you want about the *data*, and *data* is the object that the DragDestination will be passed if it accepts the drag.

You can retrieve the DragSession's *data* with the data() method, and the DragSession's *type* with the dataType() method.

The *type* string is for your convenience. Normally, a DragDestination will accept or reject a dropped object based on the DragSession's *type*, and possibly its *data*. Two classes, Image and Color, have predefined static strings Image.IMAGE_TYPE and Color.COLOR_TYPE that can be used as the *type* during a drag session. If your application involves dragging and dropping a number of instances of a particular class, you might want to define a similar static string to make it easier to identify instances of the class. As we'll see below, the entire DragSession object is passed to a potential DragDestination. Therefore, if the

DragDestination doesn't recognize the *type* string, it can always decide to accept or reject the dropped object by inspecting the *data* directly.

Drag Destinations

The IFC has a different interface, DragDestination, that must be implemented by objects wishing to receive dropped objects. Here are the DragDestination methods:

public boolean dragDropped(DragSession *dragSession*);

> Called when a dragged object is dropped on the destination view. In drag-Dropped(), you should examine the *dragSession*'s type and/or data and decide whether or not to accept it. Return true if the DragDestination accepts *dragSession*, and false if not.

public boolean dragEntered(DragSession dragSession);

> Called when the mouse enters the destination view. dragEntered() should return true if the DragDestination will accept *dragSession*, and false if not. This method is a good place to put code for custom drag-and-drop behavior; for instance, the DragDestination could have the destination view display itself in a different way. We'll see some examples of that in the "Advanced Drag Sessions" section later in this chapter.

public void dragExited(DragSession *dragSession*);

> Called when the *dragSession* exits the destination view. If dragEntered() initiated any custom drag-and-drop behavior, dragExited() should stop it and return the destination view to its normal state.

public boolean dragMoved(DragSession *dragSession*);

> Called every time the mouse is moved in the destination view. This method should return true if the DragDestination will accept the *dragSession*, and false if not.

Finally, there is one View method you should override if a view is going to be involved in drag-and-drop:

public DragDestination acceptsDrag(DragSession *dragSession*);

The reason for View's acceptsDrag() method is that sometimes the view itself may not be the DragDestination. However, since views are the fundamental object that all IFC graphical user interfaces are built from, it's always a view that objects are dropped on. With acceptsDrag(), the view can pass the dropped object on to the actual DragDestination, if necessary. We'll see an example of this below.

DragSession has one method you might find useful in implementations of DragDestination. The destinationMousePoint() method returns the location of the mouse in the destination view, which allows a DragDestination to accept or reject a DragSession based on where the dragged object was dropped.

An Example: A Drag-and-Drop ListView

Example 19-1 is a ListView subclass with drag-and-drop support. Essentially, it disables ListView's multiple selection feature and replaces it with drag-and-drop.

Note that we create the DragSession in mouseDragged(), not in mouseDown(), and further, we only create it if the mouse has been dragged out of the selected item's rectangle. This way, all ListView features except multiple selection will work as before. Any ListItem can be dragged out of DragListView and any ListItem that is dropped on a DragListView is accepted and added to its list; you should alter this behavior to suit your needs. In fact, if you plan on using DragListView often, you should probably make it an abstract class, and force subclasses to provide a custom implementation for DragDestination, at the least. When a ListItem is dragged out of a DragListView and accepted by another, the ListItem is removed from the source DragListView; in other words, in this example, dragging and dropping "cuts and pastes" rather than "copies." You can also change this behavior as desired.

If you want to experiment with DragListView, you could try writing an application that copies files from one directory to another, where filenames are dragged from one directory listing to another. If you're feeling ambitious, you could build on that and write a drag-and-drop FTP application. Another possibility would be to create a DragListView set of images like circles, rectangles, and ovals, and write a drawing application that allows you to drag-and-drop the shapes onto a drawing area, and subsequently move them around as desired.

Example 19-1: A ListView Subclass with Drag-and-Drop Support

```
import netscape.application.*;
import netscape.util.*;

// a ListView that can have ListItems dragged out of it
public class DragListView extends ListView
                            implements DragSource,DragDestination {
  public DragListView(Rect r) {
    super(r);
    setAllowsMultipleSelection(false);
  }

  public void mouseDragged(MouseEvent e) {
    if(selectedItem() == null) return;
    if(!rectForItem(selectedItem()).contains(e.x,e.y))
      createDragSession(selectedItem(),e.x,e.y);
  }

  protected void createDragSession(ListItem item,int x,int y) {
    // Create an Image based on the ListItem.
    Bitmap bitmap = new Bitmap(item.minWidth(),item.minHeight());
    Graphics gr = bitmap.createGraphics();
    item.drawInRect(gr,new Rect(0,0,item.minWidth(),item.minHeight()));
    gr.dispose();
    // Create a DragSession with the Bitmap and the ListItem.
    DragSession dragSession = new DragSession(this,bitmap,x,y,x,y,
                                        "ListItem",item);
  }

  // a View method related to drag-and-drop
  public DragDestination acceptsDrag(DragSession ds, int x, int y) {
    return this;
  }
```

Example 19-1: A ListView Subclass with Drag-and-Drop Support (continued)

```
// DragSource methods
public void dragWasAccepted(DragSession ds) {
  // If the ListItem was accepted by a DragDestination,
  // remove it from the list.
  removeItem((ListItem) ds.data());
  draw();
}

public boolean dragWasRejected(DragSession ds) {
  return true;
}

public View sourceView(DragSession ds) {
  return this;
}

// DragDestination methods
public boolean dragDropped(DragSession ds) {
  // Reject if 'this' is the source.
  if(ds.source() == this) return false;
  // Reject everything that isn't a ListItem.
  if(!(ds.data() instanceof ListItem)) return false;
  ListItem draggedItem = (ListItem) ds.data();
  // Clone the dragged item.
  ListItem newItem = (ListItem) draggedItem.clone();
  // Add the new ListItem.
  addItem(newItem);
  selectItem(newItem);
  draw();
  return true;
}

public boolean dragEntered(DragSession ds){
  // Reject if 'this' is the source.
  if(ds.source() == this) return false;
  // Accept all ListItems.
  else if(ds.data() instanceof ListItem) return true;
  return false;                   // reject everything else
}

public boolean dragMoved(DragSession ds){
  return dragEntered(ds);
}

public void dragExited(DragSession ds){
  // No special behavior was implemented by dragEntered(),
  // so this method does nothing.
  }
}
```

The DragWell Class

The IFC has two additional classes to simplify drag-and-drop: DragWell and
ColorWell, which extends DragWell. DragWell is a View subclass that implements DragSource, and acts as a source for identical drag sessions. You can set a

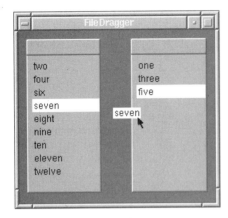

Figure 19-2: Dragging between ListViews

`DragWell`'s data, type, and image, and each drag session originating in the `Drag-Well` results in the same type of object being dragged out. Table 19-1 lists `DragWell`'s attributes.

Table 19-1: DragWell Attributes

Attribute	Description
Border	The `DragWell`'s border
Data	The `Object` that is passed when a `DragDestination` accepts the `DragWell`'s `DragSession`
DataType	A `String` that you can use to specify the data's type
Enabled	Enables or disables the `DragWell`
Image	The `DragSession`'s `Image`

The ColorWell Class

`ColorWell` extends `DragWell` and implements `DragDestination` as well as `DragSource`. If a color is dropped onto a `ColorWell`, it will take on the color that was dropped. If the mouse is clicked in a `ColorWell` and subsequently dragged out, a small swatch of the current color will be dragged out of the `ColorWell`.

A `ColorWell` can also have a target, which is notified when a `Color` is dropped on the `ColorWell`.

Table 19-2 lists `ColorWell`'s attributes.

Table 19-2: ColorWell Attributes

Attribute	Description
Color	The `ColorWell`'s current color.
Command	The `String` that is passed to the target when the `ColorWell` accepts a dropped `Color`.

Table 19-2: ColorWell Attributes (continued)

Attribute	Description
Data	The ColorWell's current Color. No other data types are allowed. To set the data, use setColor() rather than setData().
DataType	The String Color.COLOR_TYPE.
Image	A small swatch of the ColorWell's current color.
Target	The ColorWell's target, notified when the ColorWell accepts a dropped Color.

Advanced Drag Sessions

DragSession, DragSource, and DragDestination offer a great deal of flexibility for creating complicated drag sessions, since a potential DragDestination is notified every time a DragSession enters, exits, or moves over its bounds. This allows you to implement custom behavior. An obvious possibility is to start and stop some animation when a DragSession enters and exits:

```
public boolean dragEntered(DragSession dragSession) {
  if(dragSession.type().equals(acceptableType)) {
    acceptableAnimation.start();
    return true;
  }
  else {
    unacceptableAnimation.start();
    return false;
  }
}
public void dragExited(DragSession dragSession) {
  if(acceptableAnimation.isAnimating()) acceptableAnimation.stop();
  if(unacceptableAnimation.isAnimating()) unacceptableAnimation.stop();
}
```

Animating the source view is also a possibility, too.

DragSession doesn't have a setImage() method, so there's no direct way to change its Image while it's being dragged. You can however, use some trickery to change a DragSession's image: instead of creating a DragSession with a Bitmap, use a DrawingSequence or ImageSequence. Changing the DrawingSequence's frame will change the DragSession's image, and the DragSession's image will be redrawn to reflect the change the next time the mouse moves. Since the mouse is typically moving continuously in a drag-and-drop session, the image should be updated very quickly. Unfortunately, DragSession doesn't implement DrawingSequenceOwner, so there's no way to force the DragSession to update the image immediately.

Part 4

Advanced Topics

CHAPTER 20

TextView

The TextView class is used for editing, displaying, or formatting multiple lines of text. For instance, you might use a TextView in developing a word processing application. TextView is a huge class with over 80 methods and a number of powerful features: support for multiple fonts and colors, support for adding images to the text, built-in HTML formatting, methods for creating your own HTML links within the text, and text filtering. The most important feature of TextView (by far!) is its ability to import HTML, which makes it extremely useful for displaying help files, formatting strings for dialog boxes, and so on. In this chapter we cover TextView from top to bottom, starting with HTML formatting.

Importing HTML

Over the past few years, HTML has become increasingly important because it provides a simple way of formatting text in a platform-independent way. Since HTML is so important, we begin our coverage of TextView with its HTML formatting capabilities. With TextView, HTML can be used in an IFC application *any* time text needs to be formatted. This is one of the most useful features of the entire IFC. Two applications were noted above: first, complete help files can be written in HTML and displayed with TextView, and second, context-sensitive multi-line HTML messages can be generated on the fly by a program and displayed with TextView. For instance, if you'd like to display a formatted message in a dialog box, you could generate a String with your message and the appropriate HTML tags, then import it into a TextView. The TextView will parse the HTML and format your message correctly. Later in this chapter, after we cover other Text-View properties, we'll see how to add links to existing TextView text.

TextView can import HTML 1.0 directly, and with the HTMLParsingRules class, you can specify additional tags and rules as to how TextView should them.

Before we proceed, we need to know what a Range is. A Range is an IFC class that is characterized by two numbers, the *index* and *length*. In the case of a TextView, the first character has index 1, the second character has index 2, and so on. The length is the number of characters, so a Range with index 4 and length 5 would consist of the TextView's fourth through eighth characters, inclusive.

TextView has three methods for importing HTML:

```
public void importHTMLFromURLString(String url);
```
This method imports HTML from a URL String.

```
public void importHTMLInRange(java.io.InputStream inputStream,
                              Range range, java.net.URL URL);
```
This method replaces the text in the *range* with the formatted text generated from the HTML in the *inputStream*. The *URL* is the base URL for the HTML fragment, and as usual, references can be defined with respect to it. *URL* can be null (and often will be, for simple text formatting), but it if is, TextView requires a full HTTP URL for any images in the HTML. importHTMLInRange() throws two exceptions, java.io.IOException and HTMLParsingException.

```
public void importHTMLInRange(java.io.InputStream inputStream,
                              Range range, java.net.URL URL,
                              Hashtable attributes);
```
Same as the above method, but uses *attributes* to determine values for all text attributes left unspecified by the HTML.

All three methods format all the text, highlight all the links, and so on. If you import an HTML file, you should probably make the TextView the content view of a ScrollGroup, because you never know how big the HTML file will be.

As an example of how you could use the importHTMLInRange() method to parse dynamically generated HTML, let's look at a code fragment that formats a "**Hello**, *World!*" message using HTML. It's a three-step process. First, create a String with the message and HTML tags, then create a java.io.StringBufferInputStream, and, finally, pass it to the TextView. Here's the code:

```
String s = "<B> Hello, </B> <I> World! </I>";
java.io.StringBufferInputStream stream = new
java.io.StringBufferInputStream(s);
try{textView.importHTMLInRange(stream,new Range(0,1),null);}
catch(java.io.IOException e){}
catch(HTMLParsingException e){}
```

Notice that we've set the base URL to null since the URL of the HTML fragment is irrelevant.

Unfortunately, TextView can't export HTML directly.

Multiline Labels

If you import an HTML message for display in a dialog box, say, you'll want to make sure the user can't edit the message. TextView can be used as a multiline label, just like `TextField` can be used as a single-line label. To create a multiline label, create the `TextView`, then make the following sequence of calls:

```
textView.setEditable(false);
textView.setSelectable(false);
textView.setTransparent(true);
```

This is essentially the same sequence of calls that `TextField` makes to create a single-line label.

TextView Attributes

Now that we've covered the most important feature of `TextView`, let's take a look at some of the other things `TextView` can do. Since `TextView` can import HTML, you already know about some of its features: multiple fonts, colors, and images. This section provides a more complete overview of `TextView`'s capabilites, and at the end of the section you'll find a table with a listing of many of `TextView`'s properties, each of which can be set or retrieved with the `setProperty()` / `property()` pair of methods (as usual).

`TextView` formats its text according to the text's *attributes*, such as its font and color. To change the attributes of a collection of characters, you'll need to know the range of the characters.

Text Font

`TextView` supports multiple-font text, i.e., different ranges can have different fonts. This allows section headings, for example to be displayed in a bigger font than regular text. If you're writing a text editor using `TextView`, you may want to allow the user to change the current font.

You can change the current font of a `TextView` by calling `setFont()`, of course. Perhaps the simplest way to allow a user to change the font is to show a `FontChooser`. `TextView` is designed to work with the `FontChooser` class—it implements `ExtendedTarget` and responds to the `SET_FONT` command. For this to work, you should make sure that the `TextView` is the first object in the application's `TargetChain` to respond to `SET_FONT`. Normally making the `TextView` the focused view is sufficient.

Text Color

`TextView` also supports multiple text colors. You can set the color with `setText-Color()`, but the simplest way to allow the user to set the text's color is through drag-and-drop: dropping a swatch of color from a `ColorChooser` on the selected text causes the text to take on the swatch's color. Subsequent typing in the region will be in the new color.

Images and TextAttachments

`TextView` can display images among its text, and in fact, images can be dragged and dropped onto a `TextView`. The dropped image replaces any selected text or appears immediately after the text insertion cursor if no text is selected. Below we'll see an example that allows a user to drag-and-drop images from a `DragWell` onto a `TextView`.

When the `TextView` inserts the `Image`, it creates an instance of the `ImageAttachment` class and replaces the text in the selected range with a call to the `replaceRangeWithTextAttachment()` method. `ImageAttachment` is a subclass of the more general `TextAttachment`, an abstract class. You can also create and insert an `ImageAttachment` object programmatically, of course.

If you'd like to include an object other than an `Image` in the text, you'll need to subclass `TextAttachment`. Moreover, if you'd like to be able to drag-and-drop your new `TextAttachment` subclass onto a `TextView`, you'll need to subclass `TextView` and override its `DragDestination` methods, too, because `TextView` accepts only colors and images as dropped objects. To handle a `TextAttachment` subclass called `MyNewTextAttachment` in a `TextView` subclass, you could use an implementation of `dragDropped()` like this:

```
public boolean dragDropped(DragSession dragSession){
   if(dragSession.data() instanceof MyNewTextAttachmentData){
      replaceRangeWithTextAttachment(selectedRange(),
            new MyNewTextAttachment(dragSession.data()));
      return true;
   }
   return super.dragDropped(dragSession);
}
```

Copying, Cutting, and Pasting

Like `TextField`, `TextView` can copy, cut, and paste text from the application's clipboard with the `copy()`, `cut()`, and `paste()` methods.

TextViewOwner

A `TextView` can have a `TextViewOwner`, which is notified when the `TextView`'s text is edited in any way. `TextViewOwner` is an interface, and here are its methods:

```
public void attributesDidChange(TextView textView, Range range);
public void attributesWillChange(TextView textView, Range range);
public void linkWasSelected(TextView textView, Range range,
                     String url);
public void selectionDidChange(TextView textView);
public void textDidChange(TextView textView, Range range);
public void textEditingDidBegin(TextView textView);
public void textEditingDidEnd(TextView textView);
public void textWillChange(TextView textView, Range range);
```

All these methods return void, so unlike `TextFieldOwner`, there's no way to prevent the `TextView` from being edited by returning `false` to `textWill-Change()`. The `linkWasSelected()` method refers to an HTML link. It's the `TextViewOwner`, not the `TextView`, that has the responsibility of loading the new URL when a link is selected. Below we'll cover this aspect of `TextView` and `TextViewOwner` in more detail.

Text Filtering

A `TextView` can employ a `TextFilter`, just like `TextField`. The `TextFilter` intercepts the user's keystrokes and has a chance to process them before they appear on the screen. For more details, see Chapter 11, *TextFields*, and the reference section.

A Summary of TextView's Attributes

Table 20-1 summarizes some of `TextView`'s properties. Don't confuse `TextView`'s attributes with the text attributes described below! As usual, Table 20-1 is to be interpreted as follows: for each Attribute listed in the first row, there is a `setAttribute()` and an `attribute()` method.

Table 20-1: Some TextView Attributes

Attribute	Description
`BackgroundColor`	The `TextView`'s background color.
`Editable`	Allows or prohibits editing.
`Filter`	The `TextView`'s `TextFilter`.
`Font`	The current font.
`Owner`	The `TextView`'s `TextViewOwner`.
`Selectable`	Allows or prohibits the selection of text, either programmatically or with the mouse.
`SelectionColor`	The color of the selected text, if any.
`TextColor`	The current text color.
`Transparent`	If the `TextView` is transparent, the `TextView`'s superview will show through behind the characters.

An Example

Example 20-1 is an application that creates a `FontChooser`, a `ColorChooser`, an `InternalWindow` with a `TextView`, and an `InternalWindow` with a `DragWell` that acts as a source for an `Image`, the results of which are shown in Figure 20-1. To see how a `TextView` works, compile and run this example. Try doing a little typing, then setting the font with the `FontChooser`, and dragging and dropping a color or an image onto the `TextView`.

Example 20-1: Using a TextView

```
import netscape.application.*;
import netscape.util.*;

public class TextTest extends Application {
  TextView tview;
  InternalWindow textWindow,imageWindow;
  DragWell imageWell;

  public void init(){
    // create the window with the TextView
    setupTextWindow();
```

Example 20-1: Using a TextView (continued)

```
    textWindow.setContainsDocument(true);
    tview.setFocusedView();
    makeCurrentDocumentWindow(textWindow);
    // create a window with a DragWell
    setupImageWindow();
    // show the font and color choosers
    mainRootView().showColorChooser();
    mainRootView().showFontChooser();
}

// create a TextView in an InternalWindow
protected void setupTextWindow(){
    // a TextView and a window to put it in
    textWindow = new InternalWindow();
    tview = new TextView(0,0,300,800);

    // put the TextView in a ScrollGroup
    ScrollGroup textGroup = new ScrollGroup(0,0,250,150);
    textGroup.setHasVertScrollBar(true);
    textGroup.setVertScrollBarDisplay(ScrollGroup.AS_NEEDED_DISPLAY);
    textGroup.setHasHorizScrollBar(true);
    textWindow.setResizable(true);

    Size s = textWindow.windowSizeForContentSize(textGroup.width(),
                                                 textGroup.height());

    // add the TextView to the ScrollGroup
    textGroup.setContentView(tview);
    textGroup.scrollView().setBuffered(true);
    textWindow.addSubview(textGroup);
    textWindow.sizeTo(s.width,s.height);     // size the window
    textWindow.moveTo(10,10);
    textWindow.show();                       // show it
}

// create an InternalWindow with a DragWell
protected void setupImageWindow(){
    // create and show the InternalWindow
    imageWindow = new InternalWindow();
    imageWell = new DragWell(0,0,50,50);
    Size s = imageWindow.windowSizeForContentSize(imageWell.width(),
                                                  imageWell.height());
    imageWindow.sizeTo(s.width,s.height);
    imageWindow.addSubview(imageWell);
    imageWindow.center();
    imageWindow.show();

    // create an Image for the DragWell
    Bitmap bitmap = new Bitmap(imageWell.width(),imageWell.height());
    Graphics g = bitmap.createGraphics();
    g.setColor(Color.cyan);
    g.fillRect(0,0,bitmap.width(),bitmap.height());
    g.setColor(Color.black);
    g.fillOval(imageWell.width()/4,imageWell.height()/4,imageWell.width()/2,
               imageWell.height()/2);
    g.dispose();
```

Example 20-1: Using a TextView (continued)

```
    // set the DragWell's data to be the Image
    imageWell.setData(bitmap);
    imageWell.setImage(bitmap);
    imageWell.setDataType(Image.IMAGE_TYPE);
  }
}
```

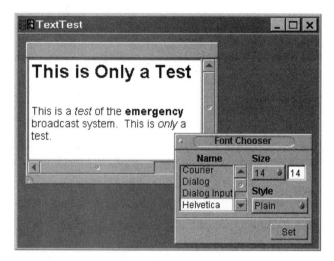

Figure 20-1: A TextView and some windows

Changing Attributes Programmatically

Above we learned how to change text attributes in a `TextView` using a `FontChooser` and `ColorChooser`. Since support for these features is built in, using a `FontChooser` or `ColorChooser` is the simplest way to change text attributes. However, attributes can also be set programmatically using `TextView`'s various `set()` methods. Before we learn how to change `TextView`'s attributes, we need a little more terminology.

A *run* is a `Range` of adjacent characters with identical attributes.

The text's attributes are represented by *keys*, which are constants defined by `TextView`: `FONT_KEY`, `TEXT_COLOR_KEY`, `LINK_KEY`, and so on. There are 11, so I refer you to the reference section for a complete list. Each key is associated with an object, and normally it's fairly obvious what type of object would be associated with a given key. For instance, a `Font` is associated with the `FONT_KEY`, a `Color` is associated with the `TEXT_COLOR_KEY`, and a `String` representing a URL is associated with the `LINK_KEY`. The keys and objects are grouped into a `Hashtable`, an IFC class from the `netscape.util` package.

A `TextView` has a set of default attributes, which can be changed with the `setDefaultAttributes()` or `addDefaultAttribute()` methods. Default attributes are necessary because if no characters appear either before or after a newly typed character, there's no way to determine what its attributes should be! In this case,

`TextView` resorts to the default attributes. When there are characters (or, more precisely, runs) either before or after a new run, `TextView` uses certain rules to determine which attributes the new run should assume. If there are characters before the new run, the new run assumes those attributes in addition to the default attributes. If there are no characters before the new run, `TextView` looks for characters after the new run; if there are any after, the new run assumes those attributes in addition to the default attributes. Finally, if there are no characters either before or after the new run, the new run takes on the default attributes.

Here are four methods you'll need if you'd like to change text attributes:

```
public void addAttributeForRange(String attributeName,
                                 Object attributeValue,
                                 Range range);
```
> Adds an attribute for the *range*. For an example, see the "HTML links" section later in this chapter.

```
public void addAttributesForRange(Hashtable hashtable,
                                  Range range);
```
> Adds multiple attributes for the *range*.

```
public void addDefaultAttribute(String attributeName,
                                Object attributeValue);
```
> Adds a default attribute.

```
public void setAttributesForRange(Hashtable hashtable,
                                  Range range);
```
> Sets the attributes for a *range*. Note this is different than adding an attribute; it sets *all* the attributes.

With the `FontChooser` and `ColorChooser`, you can change the attributes of selected text. If you want to change the attributes of the next character *before* it is typed, use the `addTypingAttributes()` and `setTypingAttributes()` methods. When the user types a key following a call to `addTypingAttributes()` or `setTypingAttributes()`, the new character's attributes are chosen to reflect the new or added attributes, and the typing attributes hashtable is subsequently cleared. Since succeeding characters take their attributes from preceding ones, succeeding characters will be able to take on the same attributes without consulting the typing attributes hashtable. Unfortunately, this procedure doesn't work if there is no text in the `TextView`! In that case, if you'd like to set the text attributes to something other than the default, use the various `set()` methods to set the attributes directly. Finally, note that typing attributes are slightly different from default attributes.

HTML Links

Above we saw how to import HTML, and in this section, as an example of how to work with text attributes, we'll see how to define links inside the text. The following code uses the `addAttributeForRange()` method to turn the fifth through ninth characters into an HTML link:

```
addAttributeForRange(TextView.LINK_KEY, "http://www.ora.com/",
                     new Range(5,5));
```

When `TextView` formats the text, the link will be drawn in the color specified by the `LINK_COLOR_KEY`, and if the `TextView`'s editing has been disabled, when the user clicks the mouse on the link the `TextView` will notify its owner that a link was selected. Remember, it's the `TextViewOwner`, not the `TextView`, that has the responsibility of doing something when the link is pressed. If the `Application` is running as an `Applet` in a browser, the `TextViewOwner`'s method could look something like this:

```
public void linkWasSelected(TextView textView,Range range,String
stringURL){
    java.applet.Applet applet = AWTCompatibility.awtApplet();
    java.applet.AppletContext appletContext;

    if(applet != null) {
      appletContext = applet.getAppletContext();
      if(appletContext != null) {
        try {appletContext.showDocument(new URL(null,stringURL),
                                "_self");}
        catch (MalformedURLException e) {
          Alert.runAlertInternally(Alert.warningImage(),
                             "Bad URL", stringURL +
                             " is invalid","OK",null,null);
        }
      }
    }
}
```

When the link is clicked on, the browser loads the URL, in this case *http:// www.ora.com/*. Depending on the application, it may be more appropriate for the `TextView` itself to import the URL if it's an HTML file.

If you'd like to add a link to somewhere else in the document, you'll need two keys. First, a source link, which looks like any other link:

```
addAttributeForRange(TextView.LINK_KEY, "somewhereImportant",
                    new Range(10,5));
```

And second, something to link to:

```
addAttributeForRange(TextView.LINK_DESTINATION_KEY, "somewhereImportant",
                    new Range(500,1));
```

To get the `TextView` to shift the view from the link to the destination when the user clicks on the link, the implementation of `linkWasSelected()` in the `Text-ViewOwner` could look like this:

```
public void linkWasSelected(TextView textView, Range range,
                      String stringURL) {
  Range destinationRange=textView.runWithLinkDestinationRange(stringURL);
  textView.scrollRangeToVisible(destinationRange);
}
```

If the *textView* is the content view of a `ScrollGroup`, this implementation of `linkWasSelected()` will cause the *textView* to scroll up or down until the destination link is visible.

CHAPTER 21

Archives

An important requirement for a general-purpose class library is that there should be a convenient mechanism for archiving objects, allowing them to outlive the process that created them. (This is often referred to as *object persistence*.) Unfortunately, Java 1.0 itself lacks such a framework, although Java 1.1 has added one. The IFC provides an alternative to Java 1.1's serialization methods, and although Java's serialization is easier to use, the IFC's framework is more flexible: Java 1.1 serialization is based on streams, which means the program must keep track of the order in which objects are written to the stream, while the IFC's object persistence is based on the IFC Archive class, which has methods to write and restore objects based on a *key*, independent of order. An Archive can subsequently be written to a stream in ASCII or binary format.

In this chapter we present the classes and interfaces useful for archiving objects. As we'll see in the next chapter, IFC archives are a crucial component of the IFC Constructor application.

Archiving IFC Objects

Most IFC classes have built-in archiving support, and the ones that don't (e.g., Alert) represent objects that will never need to be archived anyway. IFC archiving is built around the Codable interface, so it's easy to tell if an IFC object has archiving support: just look in the reference section of this book and see if the object's class (or superclass) implements Codable. In this section, we'll learn how to archive and unarchive IFC objects that implement the Codable interface, and in the next section, we'll learn how to implement the Codable interface ourselves.

Writing to an Archive

Information about objects is stored in an instance of the Archive class, and the aptly-named Archiver and Unarchiver classes write to and read from an

Archive. Before we go through the archiving process in detail, let's take a look at some schematic example code that writes to an Archive, then sends the archive itself to System.out:

```
Archive archive = new Archive();
Archiver archiver = new Archiver(archive);
archiver.archiveRootObject(someObject);
archive.writeASCII(System.out, true);
```

As you can see, the steps are:

1. Create an Archive

2. Create an Archiver based on the Archive

3. Archive objects using the Archiver

4. Send the contents of the Archive to an output stream.

The above code is schematic because many of the archiving methods throw exceptions, which we've ignored for simplicity.

Here's the prototype for Archiver's archiveRootObject() method:

```
public void archiveRootObject(Object rootObject)
         throws CodingException;
```

Although archiveRootObject() takes an Object as an argument, *the archiving process will not work unless rootObject implements the Codable interface.* For now, it's not possible to archive an arbitrary Java object directly.

Archive's writeASCII() method takes two arguments and throws two exceptions:

```
public void writeASCII(java.io.OutputStream s, boolean formatted)
         throws CodingException, java.io.IOException;
```

If *formatted* is true, the output is formatted with spaces and indentations, making it simple to read and modify with a text editor; if *formatted* is false, the output is in a more compact form, without the spaces and indentations.

Archive also has a write() method that writes in a binary format, and takes only one argument, the OutputStream, and, strangely, throws only an IOException, and not a CodingException. The binary format is even more compact than the unformatted ASCII, but of course it's impossible to read or edit.

There's one shortcut method that you might find helpful when archiving objects. Archiver has a static method for writing objects to an output stream, which allows you to skip the Archive creation step:

```
public static void writeObject(java.io.OutputStream, Object)
         throws CodingException, java.io.IOException;
```

This method creates its own Archive and uses it to write to the OutputStream directly.

Let's look at an example that writes a single object to an archive, and then to a file. Example 21-1 creates a Label object, archives it, and then saves the archive to a file. It writes the archive in ASCII format, but the commented code shows how to write the archive in binary format.

Example 21-1: Archiving an IFC Object

```
import netscape.application.*;
import netscape.util.*;
import java.io.*;

// an application that archives an IFC object
public class ArchiveWriter extends Application {
  Archive archive;
  Archiver archiver;
  Label label;
  FileOutputStream archiveOutputStream;

  public void init() {
    archive = new Archive();
    archiver = new Archiver(archive);
    label = new Label("An IFC Object",new Font("Helvetica",Font.BOLD,24));
    label.moveTo(10,10);
    mainRootView().addSubview(label);
    try{archiver.archiveRootObject(label);}
    catch(CodingException c) { showExceptionInfo(c); }

    try {
      archiveOutputStream = new FileOutputStream("ASCIIArchive");
      // archiveOutputStream = new FileOutputStream("BinaryArchive");
    }
    catch(IOException i) { showExceptionInfo(i); }

    try { archiver.archive().writeASCII(archiveOutputStream,true); }
    // try { archiver.archive().write(archiveOutputStream); }
    catch(java.io.IOException i) { showExceptionInfo(i); }
    catch(CodingException c) { showExceptionInfo(c); }
  }

  private void showExceptionInfo(Exception e) {
    System.out.println(e.getMessage());
    e.printStackTrace(System.out);
    System.exit(0);
  }
}
```

The code in Example 21-1 creates a file named *ASCIIArchive*. The contents of this file are too long for a full listing, but Example 21-2 shows an excerpt from the file.

Example 21-2: An IFC Archive, Saved in ASCII Format

```
{
    archiveVersion = 1;
    classTables = {
        netscape.application.Color = {
            classNames = [ netscape.application.Color ];
            classVersions = [ 1 ];
            fieldNames = [ r, g, b ];
            fieldTypes = [ byte, byte, byte ];
            instances = {
                Color-0 = { b = 0; g = 0; r = 0;};
                Color-1 = { b = 255; g = 255; r = 255;};
                Color-2 = { b = 192; g = 192; r = 192;};
            };
        };
```

Example 21-2: An IFC Archive, Saved in ASCII Format (continued)

```
netscape.application.Font = {
    classNames = [ netscape.application.Font ];
    classVersions = [ 1 ];
    fieldNames = [ name, style, size ];
    fieldTypes = [ java.lang.String, int, int ];
    instances = {
        Font-0 = { name = Helvetica; size = 24; style = 1;};
    };
};

        . . . // lines omitted here

};
rootInstances = [ Label-0 ];
}
```

Reading from an Archive

Once again, before we look at the details, let's look at some schematic code for unarchiving an ASCII archive:

```
Archive archive = new Archive();
archive.readASCII(System.in);
Unarchiver unarchiver = new Unarchiver(archive);
int rootIds[] = archive.rootIdentifiers();
Object unarchivedObject = unarchiver.unarchiveObject(rootIds[0]);
```

The steps are:

1. Create an `Archive`

2. Read the information from an input stream

3. Create an `Unarchiver`

4. Get the *root identifiers* of the objects in the `Archive`

5. Use the `Unarchiver` to remove elements from the `Archive` according to their root identifier

The prototype for `Archive`'s `readASCII()` method looks like this:

```
public void readASCII(java.io.InputStream)
            throws CodingException, DeserializationException;
```

The `Unarchiver` constructor takes one argument, an `Archive`. To pick out an element in an `Archive`, the `Unarchiver` uses an integer, called a root identifier, as a key. The adjective "root" refers to the fact that it's an object that's been archived directly by a call to an `Archiver`'s `archiveRootObject()`. Typically, since objects generally refer to many other objects, archiving a single root object will involve the archiving of many other objects. However, no matter how many objects get archived by a call to `archiveRootObject()`, exactly one root identifier will be added to the archive's array of root identifiers, and this root identifier will refer to the object that was passed as an argument to `archiveRootObject()`.

The root identifiers are determined by the order in which objects are added to the `Archive`.

Example 21-3 is an example application that reads the archive we created with the ArchiveWriter example. It reads the archive file, extracts a view from it, and displays the view. The result is a window containing a Label that looks just like the window created by Example 21-1, but this example never explicitly creates a Label object.

Example 21-3: An Application That Reads an Archive

```
import netscape.application.*;
import netscape.util.*;
import java.io.*;

// an application that reads the archive from Example 23-1
public class ArchiveReader extends Application {
  Archive archive;
  FileInputStream archiveInputStream;
  View view;

  public void init() {
    archive = new Archive();

    try { archiveInputStream = new FileInputStream("ASCIIArchive"); }
    catch(IOException e) { showExceptionInfo(e); }

    try { archive.readASCII(archiveInputStream); }
    catch(CodingException e) { showExceptionInfo(e); }
    catch(IOException e) { showExceptionInfo(e); }
    catch(DeserializationException e) { showExceptionInfo(e); }

    // commands to restore a binary archive
    /*
    try { archiveInputStream = new FileInputStream("BinaryArchive"); }
    catch(IOException e) { showExceptionInfo(e); }

    try { archive.read(archiveInputStream); }
    catch(IOException e) { showExceptionInfo(e); }
    */

    int[] rootIdentifiers = archive.rootIdentifiers();
    Unarchiver unarchiver = new Unarchiver(archive);

    try { view = (View) unarchiver.unarchiveIdentifier(rootIdentifiers[0]); }
    catch(CodingException e) { showExceptionInfo(e); }

    mainRootView().addSubview(view);
  }

  private void showExceptionInfo(Exception e) {
    System.out.println(e.getMessage());
    e.printStackTrace(System.out);
    System.exit(0);
  }
}
```

Identifying Root Objects

If you read the above carefully, you may have noticed that once we've created an Archive, there's no way of knowing which root identifier corresponds to which object in the archive. A good way to keep track of the correspondence between root identifiers and root objects is to use a Hashtable:

```
Hashtable idTable = new Hashtable();
int id = archiver.archiveRootObject(button1);
idTable.put("first button",id);
id = archiver.archiveRootObject(button2);
idTable.put("second button",id);
```

Notice how we've used human-readable strings, "first button" and "second button," as keys for the root identifiers of the two Java objects button1 and button2.

Finally, after archiving all the other objects, archive the Hashtable with archiver.archiveRootObject(idTable). If the Hashtable is always archived *last*, it can always be unarchived *first*, using the following code:

```
int[] rootIds = archive.rootIdentifiers();
Hashtable table = (Hashtable)
unarchiver.unarchiveIdentifier(rootsIds[rootIds.length-1]);
```

Subsequently, you can retrieve the objects button1 and button2 based on the human-readable strings we entered earlier:

```
int buttonId = (int) table.get("first button");
Button button1 = (Button) unarchiver.unarchiveIdentifier(buttonId);
```

If you use the above Hashtable trick, you can use an Archive as a database, from which you can access an arbitrary object from a human-readable key.

The Codable Interface

Only objects implementing the Codable interface can be archived. As mentioned above, most IFC classes (or their superclasses) implement Codable, and in this section, we'll learn how to implement Codable for other objects. Codable has a number of static strings and four methods. Each of the methods has to be implemented in a specific way, best demonstrated by an example, but here's a brief explanation of each of the four methods:

public abstract void describeClassInfo(ClassInfo *classInfo*);
> In the describeClassInfo() method, you define a set of strings that will be used to identify the class's member variables. The strings, also known as keys, are saved in the ClassInfo object.

public abstract void encode(Encoder *encoder*)
> throws CodingException;
> The encode() method writes the class's member variables to the archive using the *encoder* and the keys defined in describeClassInfo(). Encoder is an interface implemented by Archiver.

public abstract void decode(Decoder *decoder*)
> throws CodingException;
> The decode() method reads in and reconstructs the class's member variables using the *decoder* and the keys defined in describeClassInfo(). Decoder is an interface implemented by Unarchiver.

```
public abstract void finishDecoding();
```
This method is called after decode() has returned and all the class's member variables have been reconstructed. Any special unarchiving requirements should be handled here. For instance, finishDecoding() for a Codable View could call draw(), or a java.lang.Thread could call start(), and so on.

Let's look at Codable's four methods in detail. The first step in implementing Codable is to provide an implementation for describeClassInfo(), which sets up the correspondence between the class's member variables and a set of strings that act as keys. This is done with the ClassInfo's addClass() and addField() methods. Below is some example code for an implementation of describeClass-Info() for a class called ArchivingView:

```
public void describeClassInfo(ClassInfo classInfo){
    super.describeClassInfo(classInfo);
    // Add the class itself to classInfo.
    // ArchivingView is the name of the class 1 is the version number
    classInfo.addClass("ArchivingView",1);
    // Now add member variables. circles is an Object,
    // number is an int, and message is a String.
    classInfo.addField(ArchivingView.CIRCLES,Codable.OBJECT_TYPE);
    classInfo.addField(ArchivingView.NUMBER,Codable.INT_TYPE);
    classInfo.addField(ArchivingView.MESSAGE,Codable.STRING_TYPE);
}
```

The implementation of describeClassInfo() always has three parts, like above. First, call the superclass' describeClassInfo(). Second, add the class itself to the ClassInfo object. As noted in the example comments, addClass() takes a version number. Third, add any member fields that need to be archived. Codable has a number of static strings corresponding to every possible object type that you can use in the addField() method, similar to the way we've used OBJECT_TYPE, INT_TYPE, and STRING_TYPE above. The three strings Archiving-View.CIRCLES, ArchivingView.NUMBER, and ArchivingView.MESSAGE are keys, representing three member variables of the ArchivingView class. It's best to declare the key strings as final static members of the class; for example:

```
private final static String CIRCLES = "circles";
```

We could have left off the class names on ArchivingView.CIRCLES, Archiving-View.NUMBER, and ArchivingView.MESSAGE, but including the class name makes it clear that they are static member variables.

Notice that describeClassInfo() doesn't do any archiving itself, it merely informs the classInfo object what types of member variables will be archived.

The encode() method uses the keys set up by the describeClassInfo() method to write objects to an archive according to their type. The encode() method corresponding to the describeClassInfo() above would probably look something like this:

```
public void encode(Encoder encoder) throws CodingException{
    super.encode(encoder);
    encoder.encodeObject(ArchivingView.CIRCLES,circles);
    encoder.encodeInt(ArchivingView.NUMBER,myNumber);
    encoder.encodeString(ArchivingView.MESSAGE,message);
}
```

The encode( ) method above encodes the three objects we've described in describeClassInfo( ). Here circles is a member Object of ArchivingView, and CIRCLES is its key, as defined in describeClassInfo( ). Similarly, myNumber is a member int with key NUMBER and message is a member String with key MESSAGE.

The decode( ) method decodes the objects encoded by encode( ), using the Decoder's decoding methods. Here's the decode( ) that's the counterpart to the encode( ) above:

```
public void decode(Decoder decoder) throws CodingException{
    super.decode(decoder);
    circles = (Vector) decoder.decodeObject(ArchivingView.CIRCLES);
    myNumber = decoder.decodeInt(ArchivingView.NUMBER);
    message = decoder.decodeString(ArchivingView.MESSAGE);
}
```

Note that when an Object is unarchived with decodeObject( ), it has to be explicitly cast to the correct type. In the decode( ) above, circles is a Vector.

Finally, the finishDecoding( ) method is called after decode( ) has returned. At this point, all the class' member objects have been decoded, and it's up to finishDecoding( ) to take care of any other special decoding requirements. For instance, in the CodableCircleView example below, finishDecoding( ) calls draw( ). (Another possibility would be to use an empty finishDecoding( ) and have the object unarchiving the CodableCircleView call draw( ) after it's decoded.) If another class further up the inheritance hierarchy also implements Codable, you should be sure to call super.finishDecoding( ).

Let's take a look at an example. Example 21-4 shows a class, CodableCircle-View, that is similar to the CircleView class of Chapter 6, *Mouse and Keyboard Events*. If you recall, CircleView has an internal vector of Circle objects. At first glance, it would seem that the programmer would have to worry about archiving each individual circle; in fact, simply archiving the vector is sufficient, because Vector's implementation of Codable takes care of archiving each of its individual elements. We do, however, have to use CodableCircle rather than Circle!

CodableCircleView doesn't extend CircleView because CircleView uses the Circle class, and not the CodableCircle class. Both CodableCircleView and CodableCircle are public classes. Otherwise, the archiving process would not work.

Notice that both CodableCircleView and CodableCircle have an empty constructor. The unarchiver calls the empty constructor in the decoding process, so you should be sure to have an empty constructor in any Codable class. Second, you'll notice the use of finishDecoding( ) in CodableCircleView. Unarchiving the vector of circles doesn't automatically show the circles, so we call draw( ) in finishDecoding( ) in order to display them on the screen.

Example 21-4: Archiving a CircleView

```
import netscape.application.*;
import netscape.util.*;
```

Example 21-4: Archiving a CircleView (continued)

```
// a Codable CircleView  (see Chapter 6)
public class CodableCircleView extends View implements Codable {
  private final static String CIRCLES = "circles";
  Vector circles;
  Color circlecolor;
  int dragnumber;

  // need an empty constructor for Codable
  public CodableCircleView() {
    setBuffered(true);
    circlecolor = Color.blue;
  }

  public CodableCircleView(Rect rect) {
    super(rect);
    circles = new Vector();
    circlecolor = Color.blue;
    setBuffered(true);
  }

  // draw the circles
  public void drawView(Graphics g) {
    g.setColor(circlecolor);
    if(!circles.isEmpty()) {
      CodableCircle circle;
      for(int k=0;k<circles.size();k++) {
        circle = (CodableCircle) circles.elementAt(k);
        g.fillOval(circle.x-circle.r,circle.y-circle.r,2*circle.r,
                   2*circle.r);
      }
    }
  }

  // handle the mouse events
  public boolean mouseDown(MouseEvent e) {
    if(!circles.isEmpty()) {
      CodableCircle circle;
      for(int k = 0;k<circles.size();k++) {
        circle = (CodableCircle) circles.elementAt(k);
        if(circle.isInside(e.x,e.y)) {
          if(e.isMetaKeyDown() || e.clickCount() > 1){
            circles.removeElementAt(k);
            setDirty(true);
            return false;
          }
          else {
            dragnumber = k;
            return true;
          }
        }
      }
    }

    if(e.isMetaKeyDown() || e.clickCount() > 1) return false;
    circles.addElement(new CodableCircle(e.x,e.y));
    dragnumber = circles.size()-1;
    setDirty(true);
    return true;
  }
```

Example 21-4: Archiving a CircleView (continued)

```
public void mouseDragged(MouseEvent e) {
  CodableCircle circle = (CodableCircle) circles.elementAt(dragnumber);
  circle.x = e.x;
  circle.y = e.y;
  setDirty(true);
}

// Codable interface methods

// called by the Unarchiver
public void decode(Decoder decoder) throws CodingException {
  super.decode(decoder);
  circles = (Vector) decoder.decodeObject(CodableCircleView.CIRCLES);
}

// describe the relevant fields to the ClassInfo object
public void describeClassInfo(ClassInfo classInfo) {
  super.describeClassInfo(classInfo);
  classInfo.addClass("CodableCircleView",1);
  classInfo.addField(CodableCircleView.CIRCLES,Codable.OBJECT_TYPE);
}

// called by the Archiver
public void encode(Encoder encoder) throws CodingException {
  super.encode(encoder);
  encoder.encodeObject(CodableCircleView.CIRCLES,circles);
}

// called after unarchiving is finished
// Here, we just call draw().
public void finishDecoding(){ draw();}
}

// a Codable class representing a circle.
import netscape.application.*;
import netscape.util.*;

public class CodableCircle implements Codable {
  private final static String X = "x";
  private final static String Y = "y";
  public int x,y;
  public int r=10;

  public CodableCircle() {}

  public CodableCircle(int x, int y) {
    this.x = x;
    this.y = y;
  }

  public boolean isInside(int a,int b) {
    if(((x-a)*(x-a) + (y-b)*(y-b)) <= r*r)
      return true;
    else return false;
  }

  public void decode(Decoder decoder) throws CodingException {
    x = decoder.decodeInt(CodableCircle.X);
```

Example 21-4: Archiving a CircleView (continued)

```
    y = decoder.decodeInt(CodableCircle.Y);
  }

  public void describeClassInfo(ClassInfo classInfo) {
    classInfo.addClass("CodableCircle",1);
    classInfo.addField(CodableCircle.X,INT_TYPE);
    classInfo.addField(CodableCircle.Y,INT_TYPE);
  }

  public void encode(Encoder encoder) throws CodingException {
    encoder.encodeInt(CodableCircle.X,x);
    encoder.encodeInt(CodableCircle.Y,y);
  }

  public void finishDecoding(){}
}
```

CHAPTER 22

Constructor and Plan Files

Netscape's Constructor is an IFC application designed to aid in rapid GUI development. It has a "build mode" with an intuitive drag-and-drop user interface for creating complex view hierarchies, as well as a "wire mode" for specifying Targets for GUI components that issue commands. For instance, in the build mode a programmer could drag a button into the view hierarchy construction area, and in the wire mode, the programmer could specify that the application receive a given command when the button is pressed.

Constructor doesn't generate Java code, but instead generates a *plan file* that is an Archive. The process of reading and creating an IFC view hierarchy from a plan file is very similar to the unarchiving process covered in Chapter 21, *Archives*. The classes of the netscape.constructor package are used to work with plan files created by Constructor.

The plan file, which can be in either ASCII or binary format, contains enough information to reconstruct the objects in a view hierarchy. The Plan class is used to create the corresponding Java objects. The Plan constructor takes a plan file as argument and constructs Java objects representing the plan file's view hierarchy. The calling application can then ask the Plan object to return references to its objects, either one at a time or all at once, displaying the plan file's entire view hierarchy in a Window or View. Ultimately, then, starting with a plan file, we can construct real Java objects and attach them to existing objects in our application.

The major complication in this process is that we need to make sure that all the objects in the plan file that require targets are matched up with existing targets in the application. Constructor does this with a class called TargetProxy, which we'll see later in this chapter.

Loading a Plan File

Loading a plan file without target proxies is a simple matter indeed. Use the following constructor:

```
public Plan(String planFile);
```

The *planFile* is the name of the plan file, expected to be in the same directory as the application.

A Plan object contains references to real Java objects, one for each object in the plan file's view hierarchy. There are several ways to connect these references to objects within the application itself. Here are the two main ones:

- Put the Plan's entire view hierarchy into an ExternalWindow, InternalWindow, or View. For example:

```
ExternalWindow eWindow = myPlan.externalWindowWith-Contents();
```

- Extract the objects one at a time. For example:

```
Button button1 = (Button) myPlan.componentNamed-("button1");
```

The second technique is possible because Constructor allows a programmer to name each object in a hierarchy with a String. Using the name, we can recover the corresponding object in the Plan. As you can see, in the code snippet above, we've assumed that one of the buttons in the Constructor document is named "button1," and based on the String "button1", we've been able to recover the Button itself from myPlan.

Here is a list of a few of the methods you might use:

```
public Object componentNamed(String name);
```
Returns the Object with the given *name*. The *name* must be specified by the programmer in Constructor.

```
public ExternalWindow externalWindowWithContents();
```
Returns an ExternalWindow containing the Plan's entire view hierarchy.

```
public InternalWindow internalWindowWithContents();
```
Returns an InternalWindow containing the Plan's entire view hierarchy.

```
public View viewWithContents();
```
Returns a View containing the Plan's entire view hierarchy.

Making Multiple Copies of Objects

The Plan constructor reads in the contents of a plan file, and then calls the unarchiveObjects() method to actually create the objects described in the file. If you want to make another copy of those objects, you can call unarchiveObjects() explicitly yourself. For example, to create identical InternalWindows we could use:

```
Plan myPlan = new Plan("myPlanFile");
InternalWindow iWindow1 = myPlan.internalWindowWithContents();
myPlan.unarchiveObjects();
InternalWindow iWindow2 = myPlan.internalWindowWithContents();
```

To remove the Plan's references to existing objects, call its releaseObjects() method.

Target Proxies

With Constructor, a programmer creates a view hierarchy by selecting GUI components and dragging them onto the Constructor's document. If a GUI component requires a Target other than one of the other components, Constructor allows a programmer to add a special object called a *target proxy* as a stand-in for the real target. If a target proxy is necessary, in Constructor we give the target proxy a name (a String), and we specify which commands the target proxy should respond to. When the corresponding plan file is loaded into an application, we must connect the target proxy to an existing Target within the application. If there is only one target proxy in the plan, we can use the following constructor for the Plan object:

```
public Plan(String planFile, Target realTarget);
```

In other words, we pass in the existing Target as an argument, and the Plan constructor will automatically identify the plan's target proxy with the object *realTarget*.

More often, a plan file will have multiple target proxies. In this case, a Hashtable connecting the names of the target proxies to real targets must be created and passed to the Plan constructor. For example, if we had two target proxies named "targetProxy1" and "targetProxy2", we could use the following code:

```
Hashtable hash = new Hashtable();
hash.put("targetProxy1", target1);
hash.put("targetProxy2", target2);
Plan myPlan = new Plan("planFile",hash);
```

Above, target1 and target2 must be existing objects implementing the Target interface.

The unarchiveObjects() method, discussed above in its simplest form, also comes in two other varieties, one for the single target proxy case, and one for the multiple target proxy case.

A Short Example

The code in Example 22-1 shows the whole process of loading a plan file with two target proxies into an ExternalWindow. The two target proxies are called "target1" and "target2"; using the Hashtable hash, we connect the target proxies to two existing Targets, existingTarget1 and existingTarget2. Finally, we load the plan file's view hierarchy into an ExternalWindow and show it.

Example 22-1: Code to Load a Plan File

```
try {
  Hashtable hash = new Hashtable();
  hash.put("target1",existingTarget1);
  hash.put("target2",existingTarget2);
  plan = new Plan("constructorTest.plana",hash);
  ExternalWindow eWin = plan.externalWindowWithContents();
```

Example 22-1: Code to Load a Plan File (continued)

```
  eWin.moveTo(100,100);
  eWin.show( );
}
catch(java.io.IOException e) {}
```

Part 5

IFC Reference

How to Use This Quick Reference

The quick-reference section that follows packs a lot of information into a small space. This introduction explains how to get the most out of that information. It explains how the quick reference is organized and how to read the individual entries.

Finding a Quick Reference Entry

The following chapters each document one package of the Netscape IFC API. The packages are listed alphabetically: `netscape.application`, `netscape.constructor`, and `netscape.util`. Each chapter begins with an overview of the package, including a hierarchy diagram for the classes and interfaces in the package. Within each chapter, the classes and interfaces of a package are themselves listed alphabetically.

If you know the name of a class, but not of the package that it is a part of, or if you know the name of a method or field, but do not know what class defines it, use the *Class, Method, and Field Index* at the end of the quick reference section to find the information you need.

Reading a Quick Reference Entry

Each class and interface has its own entry in this quick reference. These quick-reference entries document the class or interface as described below. Because the information in each entry is quite dense, the descriptions of it that follow are somewhat complicated. I recommend that you flip through the following chapters as you read to find examples of each of the features described.

Name

Each quick reference entry has a title that is the name of the class or interface it documents.

Description

The class name is followed by a short description of the most important features of the class. This description may be anywhere from a couple of sentences to several paragraphs long.

Synopsis

The description is always followed by a synopsis of the class or interface. This is a listing that looks like a Java class definition, except that method bodies and field initializers are omitted. This synopsis contains the following information:

Class Modifiers

The synopsis begins with a list of class modifiers. All classes and interfaces in this quick reference are `public`; some are also declared `abstract` or `final`.

Class or Interface

If the modifiers are followed by the `class` keyword, it is a class that is being documented. If they are followed by the `interface` keyword, it is an interface that is being documented.

Class Name

The name of the class or interface follows the `class` or `interface` keyword. It is highlighted in bold.

Superclass

The superclass of the class follows the `extends` keywords.

Interfaces

The list of interfaces that the class implements, if any, follows the `implements` keyword.

Members

The constructors, fields, and methods defined by the class or interface form the bulk of the synopsis. All `public` and `protected` members are listed. They are divided into the following categories, and listed alphabetically by name within each category. Each category begins with a comment to break the synopsis listing into logical sections. The categories, in the order listed, are:

1. Public constructors

2. Protected constructors

3. Constants

4. Class variables

5. Public instance variables

6. Protected instance variables

7. Class methods

---

8. Public instance methods

9. Protected instance methods

Member Modifiers

The modifiers for each member are listed. These provide important information about how the members are used. The modifiers you may find listed are: `public`, `protected`, `static`, `abstract`, `final`, `synchronized`, `native`, and `transient`.

Member Type

The listing for a member may include a type. The types of fields and constants are shown, as are the return types of methods. Constructors do not have return types in Java.

Member Name

The name of each class member is in bold, for easy scanning.

Parameters

The synopsis for a method or constructor includes the type and name of each parameter that it takes. The parameter names are shown in italic to indicate that they are not to be used literally. Any class or interface in the `netscape.application`, `netscape.constructor`, or `netscape.util` packages are listed in short form, without their package name. The same is true of classes, like `String` and `Object`, from the `java.lang` package. A class or interface from any other package is listed with its full name. This prevents ambiguity, especially since a number of IFC classes have the same name as `java.awt` classes.

Exceptions

The exceptions that may be thrown by a method or constructor follow the `throws` keyword in the synopsis.

Inheritance

The synopsis for a method may be followed by a comment that includes a class or interface name. If a method is followed by a `// Overrides` comment, the method overrides a method by the same name in the specified superclass. If a method synopsis is followed by a `// Defines` comment, the method provides the definition of an abstract method of the specified superclass. Finally, if a method synopsis is followed by a `// From` comment, the method implements a method from the named interface (which is implemented by the class or a superclass).

Undocumented Members

Some field and method synopses are followed by the comment `// Undocumented`. These are members that you may want to know about, but which you should typically never use. These methods are marked `@private` in documentation comments in the IFC source code, and are not listed in the IFC documentation. Most of these undocumented members would have been made `private`, except for the need to allow access to them from other IFC packages. Others would be documented except that the features they represent are not fully functional in the current version of the IFC. In the `netscape.constructor` package, there are quite a few methods marked "Undocumented" because they are intended for use only by the Constructor application, and not by IFC programmers. Undocumented fields and methods are not an official part of the IFC API. Netscape reserves the right remove them or change them in future releases. Thus, you should treat them as if they were `private` and never use them.

There is an exception, however. Some methods are incorrectly or misleadingly marked "Undocumented." If a class implements an interface, for example, then the methods of that interface cannot be private or subject to change. It may never make sense to call these methods, but at least it is safe to do so. Similarly, some methods that override a method in the superclass were marked `@private` and left undocumented to conceal the fact that the method was overridden. But just because a method overrides another and is "Undocumented" doesn't mean that it cannot be used. Thus, if you see the `// Undocumented` comment following a `// From`, `// Overrides` or `// Defines` comment, you know that the method, while undocumented in the Netscape documentation, is still safe to use.

Cross References

The synopsis section is followed by a number of optional "cross reference" sections that indicate other, related classes that may be of interest:

Hierarchy
> This section lists all of the superclasses of the class, as well as any interfaces implemented by those superclasses. It may also list any interfaces extended by an interface. This section only appears when it provides information that is not available from the `extends` and `implements` clauses of the class synopsis. In the hierarchy listing, arrows indicate superclass to subclass relationships, while the interfaces implemented by a class follow the class name in parentheses. This information can be useful, for example, to determine whether a class implements `Codable` or `Cloneable` somewhere up its superclass hierarchy.

Extended By
> This section lists all direct subclasses of this class, or any interfaces that extend this interface, which tells you that there are more specific classes or interfaces to look at.

Implemented By
> This section lists all of the classes that directly implement this interface, which is useful when you know that you want to use the interface but you don't know what implementations of it are available.

Passed To
> This section lists all of the methods and constructors that are passed an object of this type as an argument, which is useful when you have an object of a given type and want to figure out what you can do with it.

Returned By
> This section lists all of the methods (but not constructors) that return an object of this type, which is useful when you know that you want to work with an object of this type, but don't know how to obtain one.

Type Of
> This section lists all of the fields and constants that are of this type, which can help you figure out how to obtain an object of this type.

Thrown By

For exception and error classes, this section lists all of the methods and constructors that throw exceptions of this type. This material helps you figure out when a given exception or error may be thrown. Note, however, that this section is based on the exception types listed in the `throws` clauses of methods and constructors. Subclasses of `RuntimeException` do not have to be listed in `throws` clauses, so it is not possible to generate a complete cross reference of methods that throw these types of "unchecked" exceptions.

CHAPTER 23

The netscape.application Package

The netscape.application package is the core of the IFC; it contains nearly all of the important IFC classes. These classes can be loosely grouped into three categories:

View classes

The View class and all of its subclasses form the basis for developing GUIs with the IFC. This category also includes View-related classes, such as layout managers, borders, and choosers. Figure 23-1 shows a class hierarchy for these classes.

Graphics classes

These classes include Graphics, Color, Font, and others used for displaying graphics or playing sounds. Most of these classes are simple wrappers around classes from the core java.awt package. See Figure 23-2.

Application services and miscellaneous classes

These classes include the very important Application class, classes that define the event-handling framework for IFC applications, and classes that provide "application services," such as support for drag-and-drop and HTML parsing. See Figure 23-3.

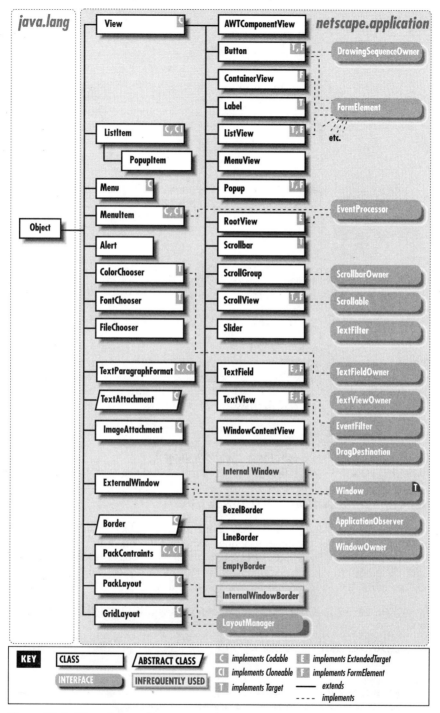

Figure 23-1: View classes of netscape.application

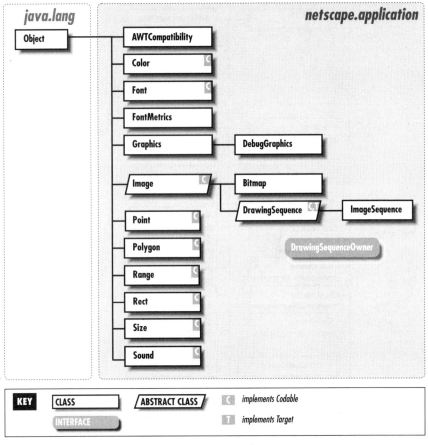

Figure 23-2: Graphics classes of netscape.application

netscape.application.AWTCompatibility

This class defines static methods that return the AWT object used internally by many IFC objects. For example, it defines a method to obtain the java.awt.Font object encapsulated by a netscape.application.Font object. awtApplet() is a similar method, but takes no argument. It returns the underlying AWT Applet object that the IFC Application is being run in, if any.

To include an AWT Component in an IFC application, use the AWTComponentView class.

```
public class AWTCompatibility extends Object {
// No Constructor
// Class Methods
    public static java.applet.Applet awtApplet();
    public static java.applet.AudioClip awtAudioClipForSound(Sound sound);
    public static java.awt.Color awtColorForColor(Color color);
    public static java.awt.FileDialog awtFileDialogForFileChooser(FileChooser fileChooser);
    public static java.awt.Font awtFontForFont(Font font);
    public static java.awt.FontMetrics awtFontMetricsForFontMetrics(FontMetrics fontMetrics);
```

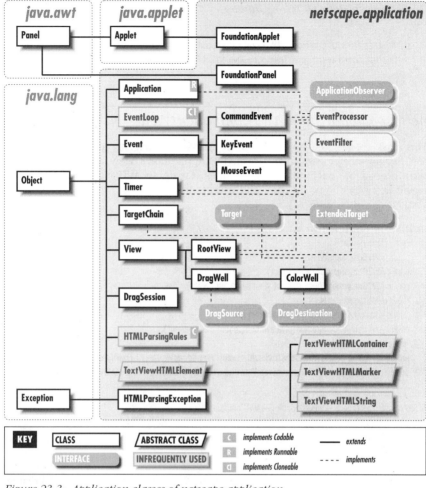

Figure 23-3: Application classes of netscape.application

```
public static java.awt.Frame awtFrameForRootView(RootView rootView);
public static java.awt.Graphics awtGraphicsForGraphics(Graphics g);
public static java.awt.Image awtImageForBitmap(Bitmap bitmap);
public static java.awt.image.ImageProducer awtImageProducerForBitmap(Bitmap bitmap);
public static java.awt.MenuBar awtMenuBarForMenu(Menu menu);
public static java.awt.Menu awtMenuForMenu(Menu menu);
public static java.awt.MenuItem awtMenuItemForMenuItem(MenuItem menuItem);
public static java.awt.Panel awtPanelForRootView(RootView rootView);
public static java.awt.Toolkit awtToolkit();
public static java.awt.Window awtWindowForExternalWindow(ExternalWindow window);
public static Bitmap bitmapForAWTImage(java.awt.Image awtImage);
public static Bitmap bitmapForAWTImageProducer(java.awt.image.ImageProducer producer);
public static Color colorForAWTColor(java.awt.Color awtColor);
public static Font fontForAWTFont(java.awt.Font awtFont);
public static FontMetrics fontMetricsForAWTFontMetrics(java.awt.FontMetrics awtFontMetrics);
```

→

```
        public static Graphics graphicsForAWTGraphics(java.awt.Graphics g);
        public static Sound soundForAWTAudioClip(java.applet.AudioClip clip);
}
```

netscape.application.AWTComponentView

This class creates a View that contains an AWT Component, and thus allows an AWT component to be added to an IFC application's view hierarchy. The IFC takes care of the necessary event handling. Create an AWTComponentView as you would any other View subclass, and use setAWTComponent() to specify the AWT Component it should display.

```
public class AWTComponentView extends View {
    // Public Constructors
        public AWTComponentView();
        public AWTComponentView(Rect rect);
        public AWTComponentView(int x, int y, int width, int height);
    // Public Instance Methods
        public java.awt.Component awtComponent();
        public void setAWTComponent(java.awt.Component aComponent);
    // Protected Instance Methods
        protected void ancestorWasAddedToViewHierarchy(View addedView);  // Overrides View
        protected void ancestorWillRemoveFromViewHierarchy(View removedView);  // Overrides View
}
```

Hierarchy: Object→View(Codable)→AWTComponentView

netscape.application.Alert

This class defines static convenience methods that create and display modal dialog boxes to the user. runAlertExternally() displays a dialog in an ExternalWindow, and runAlertInternally() displays a dialog in an InternalWindow. The arguments to these methods specify an optional image, a title, a message, and labels for up to three buttons. One or both of the last two arguments may be omitted if fewer than three buttons are needed. The return value of these methods will be one of the three constants defined by the class; this value specifies which of the three buttons the user clicked to dismiss the dialog.

Any Image may be passed to the runAlert...() methods, but notificationImage(), questionImage(), and warningImage() return standard Image objects suitable for common dialog types.

```
public class Alert extends Object {
    // No Constructor
    // Constants
        public static final int DEFAULT_OPTION;
        public static final int SECOND_OPTION;
        public static final int THIRD_OPTION;
    // Class Methods
        public static Image notificationImage();
```

```
        public static Image questionImage();
        public static int runAlertExternally(String title, String message, String defaultOption,
                                    String secondOption, String thirdOption);
        public static int runAlertExternally(Image image, String title, String message, String defaultOption,
                                    String secondOption, String thirdOption);
        public static int runAlertInternally(String title, String message, String defaultOption,
                                    String secondOption, String thirdOption);
        public static int runAlertInternally(Image image, String title, String message, String defaultOption,
                                    String secondOption, String thirdOption);
        public static Image warningImage();
}
```

---

netscape.application.Application

This class is the superclass of all IFC programs. A program written as a subclass of `Application` can be run as an applet through a trivial subclass of `FoundationApplet`, and can be run as a standalone application with the addition of a short `main()` method that creates and sets up a window for the `Application` to display itself in.

The `init()` method of an `Application` is called to allow the program to initialize itself. For example, this is typically where the program's GUI will be created. You should override this method in your `Application` subclass. The `cleanup()` method the counterpart of `init()`; it is called just before the `Application` stops running, and should free any system resources that have been allocated. If you override `init()`, be sure to invoke `super.init()`, and if you override `cleanup()`, you must invoke `super.cleanup()`. Between the calls to `init()` and `cleanup()`, the `Application` processes events, and it is the responses to these events that constitute the main body of the application.

The static `Application.application()` method returns the current `Application` instance. That is, it returns the `Application` instance for the current thread.

The `run()` method is what starts an `Application` going. It invokes `init()`, runs an `EventLoop`, and then calls `cleanup()`. When an `Application` is run as an applet, this method is automatically called. When run as a standalone application, it must be called explicitly. `setMainRootView()` specifies the `RootView` within which the `Application` should display itself. Again, this is set automatically when an `Application` is run by a `FoundationApplet`, but must be set explicitly when an `Application` is run from the command line as a standalone program. At its simplest, the code to run an `Application` standalone looks something like this:

```
public static void main(String args[]) {
    Application app = new MyApplication();
    ExternalWindow mainWindow = new ExternalWindow();
    size = mainWindow.windowSizeForContentSize(400, 400);
    mainWindow.sizeTo(size.width, size.height);
    app.setMainRootView(mainWindow.rootView());
    mainWindow.show();
    app.run();
    System.exit(0);
}
```

→

Application.releaseName() is another static method that returns the version of the IFC. The current version returns the string "IFC 1.1".

The static methods clipboardText() and setClipboardText() provide a simple interface to the system clipboard when the IFC is running in a Java 1.1 environment. clipboardText() returns the current clipboard contents as a string (if possible). It is used to implement **Paste** commands. setClipboardText() sets the system clipboard contents to the specified string; it is used to implement **Cut** commands.

setKeyboardUIEnabled() specifies whether the Application should allow keyboard traversal between views. The default is true. You may only call this method from the init() method of your Application subclass.

There are a number of other Application methods of interest: stopRunning() is the polite way to quit an Application. The addObserver() method allows you to specify an ApplicationObserver object that will be notified if the Application (running as an applet) should pause or resume. isApplet() determines whether an Application is running as an applet or not. If an Application is running as an applet, parameterNamed() calls the Applet.getParameter() method to look up the value of a named parameter. The keyDown() and keyUp() methods are invoked when key events occur and there are no views that have the keyboard focus. You can override these methods to catch these stray events. makeCurrentDocumentWindow() makes the specified Window the current "document window" for the application. This means that the window has a special place in the TargetChain.

```
public class Application extends Object implements Runnable, EventProcessor {
    // Public Constructors
        public Application();
        public Application(java.applet.Applet applet);
    // Constants
        public static final int BOTTOM_LEFT_POSITION;
        public static final int BOTTOM_RIGHT_POSITION;
        public static final int TOP_LEFT_POSITION;
        public static final int TOP_RIGHT_POSITION;
    // Class Methods
        public static Application application();
        public static String clipboardText();
        public static String releaseName();
        public static void setClipboardText(String text);
    // Public Instance Methods
        public void addObserver(ApplicationObserver observer);
        public java.applet.Applet applet();  // Undocumented
        public AppletResources appletResources();  // Undocumented
        public void appletStarted();
        public void appletStopped();
        public void chooseNextCurrentDocumentWindow(Window aWindow);
        public void cleanup();
        public java.net.URL codeBase();
        public Window currentDocumentWindow();
        public void didProcessEvent(Event anEvent);
```

```
        public EventLoop eventLoop( );
        public Vector externalWindows( );
        public void init( );
        public boolean isApplet( );
        public boolean isKeyboardUIEnabled( );
        public boolean isPaused( );
        public boolean isRunning( );
        public void keyDown(KeyEvent event);
        public void keyUp(KeyEvent event);
        public Point keyboardArrowHotSpot(int position);
        public Image keyboardArrowImage(int position);
        public Point keyboardArrowLocation(View aView, int position);
        public int keyboardArrowPosition(View aView);
        public RootView mainRootView( );
        public void makeCurrentDocumentWindow(Window aWindow);
        public View modalView( );
        public String parameterNamed(String name);
        public void performCommandAndWait(Target target, String command, Object data);
        public void performCommandLater(Target target, String command, Object data, boolean ignorePrevious);
        public void performCommandLater(Target target, String command, Object data);
        public void processEvent(Event event);  // From EventProcessor
        public void removeObserver(ApplicationObserver observer);
        public Vector rootViews( );
        public void run( );  // From Runnable
        public void setKeyboardUIEnabled(boolean aFlag);
        public void setMainRootView(RootView view);
        public void stopRunning( );
        public void willProcessEvent(Event anEvent);
    // Protected Instance Methods
        protected FoundationApplet createApplet( );
}
```

Passed To: ApplicationObserver.applicationDidPause(), ApplicationObserver.applicationDidResume(),
ApplicationObserver.applicationDidStart(), ApplicationObserver.applicationDidStop(),
ApplicationObserver.currentDocumentDidChange(), ApplicationObserver.focusDidChange(),
ExternalWindow.applicationDidPause(), ExternalWindow.applicationDidResume(),
ExternalWindow.applicationDidStart(), ExternalWindow.applicationDidStop(),
ExternalWindow.currentDocumentDidChange(), ExternalWindow.focusDidChange(),
FoundationApplet.setApplication()

Returned By: Application.application(), FoundationApplet.application(),
FoundationApplet.pushIFCContext()

---

netscape.application.ApplicationObserver

This interface is implemented by objects that want to receive notification when the
application changes state. An ApplicationObserver must be registered by calling
the addObserver() method of the Application object. The applicationDid-
Pause() and applicationDidResume() methods are somewhat misleadingly
named; they are invoked when the applet containing the Application becomes

→

invisible or visible again—i.e., they correspond to the stop() and start() methods of java.applet.Applet.

```
public abstract interface ApplicationObserver {
  // Public Instance Methods
    public abstract void applicationDidPause(Application application);
    public abstract void applicationDidResume(Application application);
    public abstract void applicationDidStart(Application application);
    public abstract void applicationDidStop(Application application);
    public abstract void currentDocumentDidChange(Application application, Window document);
    public abstract void focusDidChange(Application application, View focusedView);
}
```

Implemented By: ExternalWindow

Passed To: Application.addObserver(), Application.removeObserver()

---

netscape.application.BezelBorder

This class is used to draw raised, lowered, or grooved borders around IFC GUI components. The constructors allow you to create BezelBorder instances of various types (using the constants defined by the class) using specified colors, but it is more common and more efficient to use the five static . . . Bezel() methods to return reusable BezelBorder objects of the five possible types using the standard background colors.

The four static draw. . .() methods are conveniences for drawing bezels anywhere in your own code.

```
public class BezelBorder extends Border {
  // Public Constructors
    public BezelBorder();
    public BezelBorder(int type);
    public BezelBorder(int type, Color baseColor);
    public BezelBorder(int type, Color baseColor, Color lighterColor, Color darkerColor);
  // Constants
    public static final int GROOVED;
    public static final int LOWERED;
    public static final int LOWERED_BUTTON;
    public static final int RAISED;
    public static final int RAISED_BUTTON;
  // Class Methods
    public static void drawBezel(Graphics g, int x, int y, int width, int height, Color baseColor, Color lighterColor,
                     Color darkerColor, Color blackColor, boolean raised);
    public static void drawGroovedBezel(Graphics g, int x, int y, int width, int height,
                     Color lighterColor, Color darkerColor);
    public static void drawLoweredButtonBezel(Graphics g, int x, int y, int width, int height);
    public static void drawRaisedButtonBezel(Graphics g, int x, int y, int width, int height);
    public static Border groovedBezel();
    public static Border loweredBezel();
    public static Border loweredButtonBezel();
    public static Border raisedBezel();
```

```
        public static Border raisedButtonBezel( );
    // Public Instance Methods
        public int bottomMargin( ); // Defines Border
        public void decode(Decoder decoder) throws CodingException; // Overrides Border
        public void describeClassInfo(ClassInfo info); // Overrides Border
        public void drawInRect(Graphics g, int x, int y, int width, int height); // Defines Border
        public void encode(Encoder encoder) throws CodingException; // Overrides Border
        public void finishDecoding( ) throws CodingException; // Overrides Border
        public int leftMargin( ); // Defines Border
        public int rightMargin( ); // Defines Border
        public int topMargin( ); // Defines Border
        public int type( );
}
```

Hierarchy: Object→Border(Codable)→BezelBorder

---

netscape.application.Bitmap

A `Bitmap` is a kind of `Image` that represents a rectangular region of pixels. When you create a `Bitmap` with one of the constructors, you get an empty `Bitmap` suitable for off-screen drawing. Use `createGraphics( )` to obtain a `Graphics` object that you can use to draw into such a `Bitmap`.

More commonly, however, you will create a `Bitmap` using one of the static methods. These methods load image data from a GIF or JPEG file specified by URL or by name. Image files loaded with `bitmapNamed( )` are loaded from the *images/* subdirectory of the directory from which the `Application` was loaded. The optional *startLoading* argument specifies whether the image file should start loading right away or only once the `Bitmap` is actually used. The default is `true`, which means that the `Bitmap` should be loaded right away. The optional *cache* argument specifies whether the named image should be cached in memory for rapid access later. The default is `true`.

Because large images can be time consuming to load, especially over the network, you can specify that a `Bitmap` should be loaded incrementally by passing `true` to `setLoadsIncrementally( )`. A `Bitmap` that is being loaded incrementally will draw whatever data is available instead of waiting for all data to become available before drawing. Also, when a `Bitmap` is loading incrementally, it will notify its "update target" by sending its "update command" whenever more data is loaded.

Call `flush( )` when a `Bitmap` will no longer be used. This frees up cached image data and system resources associated with the `Bitmap`.

The remaining `Bitmap` methods are mainly overridden versions of `Image` methods.

```
public class Bitmap extends Image {
    // Public Constructors
        public Bitmap( );
        public Bitmap(int width, int height);
        public Bitmap(int[] pixels, int width, int height);
        public Bitmap(int[] pixels, int width, int height, int offset, int scanSize);
    // Class Methods
        public static Bitmap bitmapFromURL(java.net.URL url);
        public static synchronized Bitmap bitmapNamed(String bitmapName, boolean startLoading, boolean cache);
```

→

```
        public static Bitmap bitmapNamed(String bitmapName, boolean startLoading);
        public static Bitmap bitmapNamed(String bitmapName);
// Public Instance Methods
        public Graphics createGraphics();
        public void decode(Decoder decoder) throws CodingException;  // Overrides Image
        public void describeClassInfo(ClassInfo info);  // Overrides Image
        public void drawAt(Graphics g, int x, int y);  // Defines Image
        public void drawScaled(Graphics g, int x, int y, int width, int height);  // Overrides Image
        public void drawTiled(Graphics g, int x, int y, int width, int height);  // Overrides Image. Undocumented
        public void encode(Encoder encoder) throws CodingException;  // Overrides Image
        public void flush();
        public boolean grabPixels(int[] pixels);
        public boolean grabPixels(int[] pixels, int x, int y, int width, int height, int offset, int scanSize);
        public boolean hasLoadedData();
        public int height();  // Defines Image
        public Image imageWithName(String name);  // Overrides Image. Undocumented
        public boolean isTransparent();  // Overrides Image
        public boolean isValid();
        public void loadData();
        public boolean loadsIncrementally();
        public String name();  // Overrides Image
        public void setLoadsIncrementally(boolean flag);
        public void setTransparent(boolean transparent);
        public synchronized void setUpdateCommand(String command);
        public synchronized void setUpdateTarget(Target aTarget);
        public String toString();  // Overrides Object
        public synchronized String updateCommand();
        public synchronized Rect updateRect();
        public synchronized Target updateTarget();
        public int width();  // Defines Image
}
```

Hierarchy: Object→Image(Codable)→Bitmap

Passed To: AWTCompatibility.awtImageForBitmap(), AWTCompatibility.awtImageProducerForBitmap(), DebugGraphics(), DebugGraphics.drawBitmapAt(), DebugGraphics.drawBitmapScaled(), Graphics(), Graphics.drawBitmapAt(), Graphics.drawBitmapScaled()

Returned By: AWTCompatibility.bitmapForAWTImage(), AWTCompatibility.bitmapForAWTImageProducer(), Bitmap.bitmapFromURL(), Bitmap.bitmapNamed(), Graphics.buffer(), View.createBuffer(), View.drawingBuffer()

---

netscape.application.Border

Border is an abstract subclass that represents a border for a GUI component. Sub-classes must implement each of the five abstract methods. The . . . Border() methods return the number of pixels required for each edge of the border, and the drawInRect() method should draw the border entirely within those specified margins.

```
public abstract class Border extends Object implements Codable {
    // Default Constructor: public Border()
```

```
// Public Instance Methods
    public abstract int bottomMargin( );
    public void computeInteriorRect(int x, int y, int width, int height, Rect interiorRect);
    public void computeInteriorRect(Rect rect, Rect interiorRect);
    public void decode(Decoder decoder) throws CodingException; // From Codable
    public void describeClassInfo(ClassInfo info); // From Codable
    public abstract void drawInRect(Graphics g, int x, int y, int width, int height);
    public void drawInRect(Graphics g, Rect rect);
    public void encode(Encoder encoder) throws CodingException; // From Codable
    public void finishDecoding( ) throws CodingException; // From Codable
    public int heightMargin( );
    public Rect interiorRect(int x, int y, int width, int height);
    public Rect interiorRect(Rect rect);
    public abstract int leftMargin( );
    public abstract int rightMargin( );
    public abstract int topMargin( );
    public int widthMargin( );
}
```

Extended By: BezelBorder, EmptyBorder, InternalWindowBorder, LineBorder

Passed To: Button.setLoweredBorder(), Button.setRaisedBorder(), ContainerView.setBorder(), DragWell.setBorder(), InternalWindow.setBorder(), Menu.setBorder(), Popup.setBorder(), ScrollGroup.setBorder(), Slider.setBorder(), TextField.setBorder()

Returned By: BezelBorder.groovedBezel(), BezelBorder.loweredBezel(), BezelBorder.loweredButtonBezel(), BezelBorder.raisedBezel(), BezelBorder.raisedButtonBezel(), Button.loweredBorder(), Button.raisedBorder(), ContainerView.border(), DragWell.border(), EmptyBorder.emptyBorder(), InternalWindow.border(), LineBorder.blackLine(), LineBorder.grayLine(), Menu.border(), MenuView.border(), Popup.border(), ScrollGroup.border(), Slider.border(), TextField.border()

netscape.application.Button

This is a very versatile class that implements push buttons, "continuous buttons" (push buttons with auto repeat), check boxes, and radio buttons. It is also a very flexible class with quite a few adjustable properties, including the text, images, borders, and sounds to be displayed (or played) by the button.

Because the Button class is so flexible, it is easiest to create buttons using the three static methods, which produce Button objects in commonly used configurations. createCheckButton() and createRadioButton(), for example, create Button objects with default check box and radio box images.

When a Button is clicked, it notifies its target by calling its performCommand() method. Button implements the Target interface itself. When sent the SEND_COMMAND command, it will notify its own target, just as if the button had been clicked.

Unlike the AWT Button class, the IFC Button can display an Image (which may even be an animation) as well as text, and can even display a different image when clicked. setImage() and setAltImage() specify the images to display, and setImagePosition() specifies where to display it in relation to the button's textual label. Legal values are the IMAGE_ constants.

→

```
public class Button extends View implements Target, DrawingSequenceOwner, FormElement {
// Public Constructors
    public Button();
    public Button(Rect rect);
    public Button(int x, int y, int width, int height);
// Constants
    public static final int CONTINUOUS_TYPE;
    public static final int PUSH_TYPE;
    public static final int RADIO_TYPE;
    public static final int TOGGLE_TYPE;
    public static final int IMAGE_ABOVE;
    public static final int IMAGE_BELOW;
    public static final int IMAGE_BENEATH;
    public static final int IMAGE_ON_LEFT;
    public static final int IMAGE_ON_RIGHT;
    public static final String CLICK;
    public static final String SELECT_NEXT_RADIO_BUTTON;
    public static final String SELECT_PREVIOUS_RADIO_BUTTON;
    public static final String SEND_COMMAND;
// Class Methods
    public static Button createCheckButton(int x, int y, int width, int height);
    public static Button createPushButton(int x, int y, int width, int height);
    public static Button createRadioButton(int x, int y, int width, int height);
// Public Instance Methods
    public Image altImage();
    public String altTitle();
    public boolean canBecomeSelectedView();  // Overrides View
    public void click();
    public int clickCount();
    public String command();
    public void decode(Decoder decoder) throws CodingException;  // Overrides View
    public void describeClassInfo(ClassInfo info);  // Overrides View
    public Color disabledTitleColor();
    public void drawView(Graphics g);  // Overrides View
    public void drawViewBackground(Graphics g, Rect interiorRect, boolean drawDownState);
    public void drawViewInterior(Graphics g, String title, Image image, Rect interiorRect);
    public void drawViewTitleInRect(Graphics g, String title, Font titleFont, Rect textBounds, int justification);
    public void drawingSequenceCompleted(DrawingSequence aSequence);  // From DrawingSequenceOwner
    public void drawingSequenceFrameChanged(DrawingSequence aSequence);  // From
                                                                        // DrawingSequenceOwner
    public void encode(Encoder encoder) throws CodingException;  // Overrides View
    public Font font();
    public String formElementText();  // From FormElement
    public Image image();
    public Size imageAreaSize();
    public int imagePosition();
    public boolean isBordered();
    public boolean isEnabled();
    public boolean isTransparent();  // Overrides View
    public Border loweredBorder();
```

```
        public Color loweredColor( );
        public Size minSize( );  // Overrides View
        public boolean mouseDown(MouseEvent event);  // Overrides View
        public Sound mouseDownSound( );
        public void mouseDragged(MouseEvent event);  // Overrides View
        public void mouseUp(MouseEvent event);  // Overrides View
        public Sound mouseUpSound( );
        public void performCommand(String command, Object data);  // From Target
        public Border raisedBorder( );
        public Color raisedColor( );
        public int repeatDelay( );
        public void sendCommand( );
        public void setAltImage(Image anImage);
        public void setAltTitle(String aString);
        public void setBordered(boolean flag);
        public void setCommand(String command);
        public void setDisabledTitleColor(Color aColor);
        public void setEnabled(boolean enabled);
        public void setFont(Font aFont);
        public void setImage(Image anImage);
        public void setImagePosition(int aPosition);
        public void setLoweredBorder(Border border);
        public void setLoweredColor(Color aColor);
        public void setMouseDownSound(Sound aSound);
        public void setMouseUpSound(Sound aSound);
        public void setRaisedBorder(Border border);
        public void setRaisedColor(Color aColor);
        public void setRepeatDelay(int milliseconds);
        public void setState(boolean newState);
        public void setTarget(Target aTarget);
        public void setTitle(String aString);
        public void setTitleColor(Color aColor);
        public void setTransparent(boolean flag);
        public void setType(int buttonType);
        public boolean state( );
        public Target target( );
        public String title( );
        public Color titleColor( );
        public int type( );
// Protected Instance Methods
        protected void ancestorWasAddedToViewHierarchy(View aView);  // Overrides View
        protected boolean isHighlighted( );
        protected void setHighlighted(boolean highlighted);
}
```

Hierarchy: Object→View(Codable)→Button(Target, DrawingSequenceOwner, FormElement)

Passed To: ScrollBar.setDecreaseButton(), ScrollBar.setIncreaseButton()

Returned By: Button.createCheckButton(), Button.createPushButton(), Button.createRadioButton(), InternalWindow.createCloseButton(), ScrollBar.decreaseButton(), ScrollBar.increaseButton()

netscape.application.Color

This class represents a color as a set of red, green, and blue components between 0 and 255 or between 0.0 and 1.0. The various constants are predefined Color objects, and you can create custom colors with the various Color() constructors. The COLOR_TYPE constant is for use with the IFC drag-and-drop mechanism.

This class is very similar to java.awt.Color, but has additional methods to support IFC archiving.

```
public class Color extends Object implements Codable {
// Public Constructors
    public Color();
    public Color(int red, int green, int blue);
    public Color(int rgb);
    public Color(float red, float green, float blue);
// Constants
    public static final String COLOR_TYPE;
    public static final Color black, blue, cyan, darkGray, gray;
    public static final Color green, lightGray, magenta, orange, pink;
    public static final Color red, white, yellow;
// Class Methods
    public static Color colorForHSB(float hue, float saturation, float brightness);
    public static int rgbForHSB(float hue, float saturation, float brightness);
// Public Instance Methods
    public int blue();
    public Color darkerColor();
    public void decode(Decoder decoder) throws CodingException; // From Codable
    public void describeClassInfo(ClassInfo info); // From Codable
    public void encode(Encoder encoder) throws CodingException; // From Codable
    public boolean equals(Object anObject); // Overrides Object
    public void finishDecoding() throws CodingException; // From Codable
    public int green();
    public int hashCode(); // Overrides Object
    public Color lighterColor();
    public int red();
    public int rgb();
    public String toString(); // Overrides Object
}
```

Passed To: many methods

Returned By: many methods

Type Of: Color.black, Color.blue, Color.cyan, Color.darkGray, Color.gray, Color.green, Color.lightGray, Color.magenta, Color.orange, Color.pink, Color.red, Color.white, Color.yellow

netscape.application.ColorChooser

The ColorChooser class lets the user select a Color. ColorChooser is designed to work with the IFC's drag-and-drop framework, so colors can be dragged out of or dropped on to a ColorChooser. You can also use the color() method to query the currently set color.

ColorChooser creates views, but is not itself a subclass of View. Use contentView() to obtain the View (and its subviews) created by the ColorChooser. If you create your own ColorChooser() you must add the resulting View to your view hierarchy, or place it in a window with setWindow(). Instead, it is more common to use the showColorChooser() method of the RootView class to display a predefined ColorChooser dialog box.

```
public class ColorChooser extends Object implements Target, TextFieldOwner {
    // Public Constructor
        public ColorChooser();
    // Public Instance Methods
        public Color color();
        public View contentView();
        public void hide();
        public void performCommand(String command, Object data);  // From Target
        public void setColor(Color aColor);
        public void setWindow(Window aWindow);
        public void show();
        public void textEditingDidBegin(TextField textField);  // From TextFieldOwner
        public void textEditingDidEnd(TextField textField, int endCondition,
                                    boolean contentsChanged);  // From TextFieldOwner
        public boolean textEditingWillEnd(TextField textField, int endCondition,
                                    boolean contentsChanged);  // From TextFieldOwner
        public void textWasModified(TextField textField);  // From TextFieldOwner
        public Window window();
}
```

Returned By: RootView.colorChooser()

netscape.application.ColorWell

ColorWell is a DragWell subclass that acts as a source and sink for dragged colors: a small swatch of the ColorWell's current color can be dragged out of the ColorWell and dropped on other objects, and, similarly, if a Color is dropped on a ColorWell, the ColorWell takes on the dropped color. When a Color is dropped on a ColorWell, the well sends the specified command to the specified target, passing itself as the second argument to the target's performCommand method.

```
public class ColorWell extends DragWell implements DragDestination, Target {
    // Public Constructors
        public ColorWell();
        public ColorWell(Rect rect);
        public ColorWell(int x, int y, int width, int height);
    // Constants
        public static final String SHOW_COLOR_CHOOSER;
    // Public Instance Methods
        public DragDestination acceptsDrag(DragSession session, int x, int y);  // Overrides View
        public boolean canBecomeSelectedView();  // Overrides View
        public Color color();
        public String command();
        public String dataType();  // Overrides DragWell
        public void decode(Decoder decoder) throws CodingException;  // Overrides DragWell
```

→

```
        public void describeClassInfo(ClassInfo info);  // Overrides DragWell
        public boolean dragDropped(DragSession session);  // From DragDestination
        public boolean dragEntered(DragSession session);  // From DragDestination
        public void dragExited(DragSession session);  // From DragDestination
        public boolean dragMoved(DragSession session);  // From DragDestination
        public void drawView(Graphics g);  // Overrides DragWell
        public void encode(Encoder encoder) throws CodingException;  // Overrides DragWell
        public Image image();  // Overrides DragWell
        public boolean mouseDown(MouseEvent event);  // Overrides DragWell
        public void mouseDragged(MouseEvent event);  // Overrides View
        public void mouseUp(MouseEvent event);  // Overrides View
        public void performCommand(String command, Object data);  // From Target
        public void sendCommand();
        public void setColor(Color aColor);
        public void setCommand(String command);
        public void setData(Object anObject);  // Overrides DragWell
        public void setDataType(String dataType);  // Overrides DragWell
        public void setImage(Image image);  // Overrides DragWell
        public void setTarget(Target aTarget);
        public Target target();
}
```

Hierarchy: Object→View(Codable)→DragWell(DragSource)→ColorWell(DragDestination, Target)

---

netscape.application.CommandEvent

CommandEvent is used as a support class for the IFC's callback framework. A CommandEvent has target, command, and data, fields and when a CommandEvent is processed, the target's performCommand() method is called with the given command and data. Applications do not generally need to use this class.

```
public class CommandEvent extends Event implements EventProcessor {
    // Public Constructors
        public CommandEvent();
        public CommandEvent(Target target, String command, Object data);
    // Public Instance Methods
        public String command();
        public Object data();
        public void processEvent(Event event);  // From EventProcessor
        public void setCommand(String command);
        public void setData(Object data);
        public void setTarget(Target target);
        public Target target();
}
```

Hierarchy: Object→Event(Cloneable)→CommandEvent(EventProcessor)

netscape.application.ContainerView

ContainerView is a View subclass that can display a border, title, and background color or image. ContainerView is useful for grouping objects in complex graphical user interfaces. The various set...() methods set the title, border, image, and related properties. setImageDisplayStyle() should be passed one of the CENTERED, TILED, or SCALED constants defined by the Image class.

```
public class ContainerView extends View implements FormElement {
    // Public Constructors
        public ContainerView();
        public ContainerView(Rect rect);
        public ContainerView(int x, int y, int width, int height);
    // Public Instance Methods
        public Color backgroundColor();
        public Border border();
        public void decode(Decoder decoder) throws CodingException;  // Overrides View
        public void describeClassInfo(ClassInfo info);  // Overrides View
        public void drawSubviews(Graphics g);  // Overrides View
        public void drawView(Graphics g);  // Overrides View
        public void drawViewBackground(Graphics g);
        public void drawViewBorder(Graphics g);
        public void encode(Encoder encoder) throws CodingException;  // Overrides View
        public void finishDecoding() throws CodingException;  // Overrides View
        public String formElementText();  // From FormElement
        public Image image();
        public int imageDisplayStyle();
        public Rect interiorRect();
        public boolean isTransparent();  // Overrides View
        public void layoutView(int deltaX, int deltaY);  // Overrides View
        public Size minSize();  // Overrides View
        public void setBackgroundColor(Color aColor);
        public void setBorder(Border newBorder);
        public void setImage(Image anImage);
        public void setImageDisplayStyle(int aStyle);
        public void setTitle(String aString);
        public void setTitleColor(Color aColor);
        public void setTitleFont(Font aFont);
        public void setTransparent(boolean flag);
        public String title();
        public Color titleColor();
        public Font titleFont();
}
```

Hierarchy: Object→View(Codable)→ContainerView(FormElement)

netscape.application.DebugGraphics

DebugGraphics is a Graphics subclass helpful in debugging graphics. You rarely create a DebugGraphics object yourself; instead, you call the setGraphicsDebugOptions() method of the View that needs to be debugged, passing the constant DebugGraphics.NONE_OPTION to turn off debugging, or passing a bitwise OR

→

of the remaining three _OPTION constants. LOG_OPTION specifies that graphics operations should be logged to an output stream. FLASH_OPTION specifies that all graphics operations should flash several times. BUFFERED_OPTION specifies that all drawing operations performed in off-screen buffers should be displayed in a special on-screen window. The static methods of DebugGraphics allow you to specify the output stream for graphics logging, and to specify several parameters for FLASH_OPTION debugging.

```
public class DebugGraphics extends Graphics {
// Public Constructors
    public DebugGraphics(View view);
    public DebugGraphics(Bitmap aBitmap);
// Constants
    public static final int BUFFERED_OPTION;
    public static final int FLASH_OPTION;
    public static final int LOG_OPTION;
    public static final int NONE_OPTION;
// Class Methods
    public static Color flashColor();
    public static int flashCount();
    public static int flashTime();
    public static java.io.PrintStream logStream();
    public static void setFlashColor(Color flashColor);
    public static void setFlashCount(int flashCount);
    public static void setFlashTime(int flashTime);
    public static void setLogStream(java.io.PrintStream stream);
// Public Instance Methods
    public int debug();
    public int debugOptions();  // Overrides Graphics
    public void drawArc(int x, int y, int width, int height, int startAngle, int arcAngle);  // Overrides Graphics
    public void drawBitmapAt(Bitmap bitmap, int x, int y);  // Overrides Graphics
    public void drawBitmapScaled(Bitmap bitmap, int x, int y, int width, int height);  // Overrides Graphics
    public void drawBytes(byte[] data, int offset, int length, int x, int y);  // Overrides Graphics
    public void drawChars(char[] data, int offset, int length, int x, int y);  // Overrides Graphics
    public void drawLine(int x1, int y1, int x2, int y2);  // Overrides Graphics
    public void drawOval(int x, int y, int width, int height);  // Overrides Graphics
    public void drawPoint(int x, int y);  // Overrides Graphics
    public void drawPolygon(int[] xPoints, int[] yPoints, int nPoints);  // Overrides Graphics
    public void drawRect(int x, int y, int width, int height);  // Overrides Graphics
    public void drawRoundedRect(int x, int y, int width, int height, int arcWidth,
                            int arcHeight);  // Overrides Graphics
    public void drawString(String aString, int x, int y);  // Overrides Graphics
    public void fillArc(int x, int y, int width, int height, int startAngle, int arcAngle);  // Overrides Graphics
    public void fillOval(int x, int y, int width, int height);  // Overrides Graphics
    public void fillPolygon(int[] xPoints, int[] yPoints, int nPoints);  // Overrides Graphics
    public void fillRect(int x, int y, int width, int height);  // Overrides Graphics
    public void fillRoundedRect(int x, int y, int width, int height, int arcWidth,
                            int arcHeight);  // Overrides Graphics
    public void popState();  // Overrides Graphics
    public void pushState();  // Overrides Graphics
    public void setClipRect(Rect rect, boolean intersect);  // Overrides Graphics
```

```
    public void setColor(Color aColor);  // Overrides Graphics
    public void setDebugOptions(int debugOptions);  // Overrides Graphics
    public void setFont(Font aFont);  // Overrides Graphics
    public void setPaintMode();  // Overrides Graphics
    public void setXORMode(Color aColor);  // Overrides Graphics
    public void translate(int x, int y);  // Overrides Graphics
}
```

Hierarchy: Object→Graphics→DebugGraphics

---

netscape.application.DragDestination

This interface is implemented by objects that want to be able to receive dragged objects through the drag-and-drop mechanism. The methods defined here are invoked by a DragSession object at various stages of the drag-and-drop data transfer. The methods that return a boolean value should return true if the destination object accepts or would accept the dragged data.

```
public abstract interface DragDestination {
    // Public Instance Methods
    public abstract boolean dragDropped(DragSession session);
    public abstract boolean dragEntered(DragSession session);
    public abstract void dragExited(DragSession session);
    public abstract boolean dragMoved(DragSession session);
}
```

Implemented By: ColorWell, TextView

Returned By: ColorWell.acceptsDrag(), DragSession.destination(), ScrollView.acceptsDrag(), TextView.acceptsDrag(), View.acceptsDrag()

---

netscape.application.DragSession

This class is used by the IFC drag-and-drop mechanism to maintain the state of a "drag" in progress. A DragSession is typically created in the mouseDown() method of the View that serves as the DragSource. The DragSession constructor is passed all the information necessary to initiate a drag. The arguments are the DragSource object, the Image to drag, the initial coordinates of the upper-left corner of the image in the DragSource, the coordinates of the mouse click that started the drag, a String that identifies the type of the data to be transferred, and an arbitrary object that contains that data. The constant strings Image.IMAGE_TYPE and Color.COLOR_TYPE are standard data type strings for use when dragging images and colors. For other data types, you should define some other string.

The DragSource object calls the DragSession() constructor to initiate a drag-and-drop interaction. This DragSession object will later be passed to the DragDestination, which can call DragSession methods to determine the data being transferred, the type of that data, and other information about the "drag."

→

```
public class DragSession extends Object {
    // Public Constructors
        public DragSession(DragSource source, Image image, int initialX, int initialY, int mouseDownX,
                        int mouseDownY, String dataType, Object data,
                        boolean createDragView); // Undocumented
        public DragSession(DragSource source, Image image, int initialX, int initialY, int mouseDownX,
                        int mouseDownY, String dataType, Object data);
    // Constants
        public static final int ALT_MASK;
        public static final int CONTROL_MASK;
        public static final int META_MASK;
        public static final int SHIFT_MASK;
    // Public Instance Methods
        public Rect absoluteBounds();
        public Point absoluteMousePoint();
        public Object data();
        public String dataType();
        public DragDestination destination();
        public Rect destinationBounds();
        public boolean destinationIsAccepting(); // Undocumented
        public Point destinationMousePoint();
        public View destinationView();
        public int dragModifiers();
        public boolean isAltKeyDown();
        public boolean isControlKeyDown();
        public boolean isMetaKeyDown();
        public boolean isShiftKeyDown();
        public void mouseDragged(MouseEvent event); // Undocumented
        public void mouseUp(MouseEvent event); // Undocumented
        public void setData(Object data);
        public void setDataType(String dataType);
        public DragSource source();
}
```

Passed To: ColorWell.acceptsDrag(), ColorWell.dragDropped(), ColorWell.dragEntered(),
ColorWell.dragExited(), ColorWell.dragMoved(), DragDestination.dragDropped(), DragDestination.dragEntered(),
DragDestination.dragExited(), DragDestination.dragMoved(), DragSource.dragWasAccepted(),
DragSource.dragWasRejected(), DragSource.sourceView(), DragWell.dragWasAccepted(),
DragWell.dragWasRejected(), DragWell.sourceView(), ScrollView.acceptsDrag(), TextView.acceptsDrag(),
TextView.dragDropped(), TextView.dragEntered(), TextView.dragExited(), TextView.dragMoved(), View.acceptsDrag()

---

netscape.application.DragSource

This interface is implemented by objects that want to be able to originate data
transfer through the drag-and-drop mechanism. sourceView() should return the
view from which the data was dragged. dragWasAccepted() provides notification
when a drop is successful. dragWasRejected() provides notification when a drop
is unsuccessful; it should return true to specify that the DragSession image
should animate back to the source view.

```
public abstract interface DragSource {
  // Public Instance Methods
      public abstract void dragWasAccepted(DragSession session);
      public abstract boolean dragWasRejected(DragSession session);
      public abstract View sourceView(DragSession session);
}
```

Implemented By: DragWell

Passed To: DragSession()

Returned By: DragSession.source()

netscape.application.DragWell

A DragWell is a View that acts as a source for dragged objects; when the user clicks on a DragWell, it creates a DragSession object to initiate a drag.

setData() sets the data that is to be transferred from the DragWell, and setData-Type() sets the type of that data. setImage() specifies the image displayed by the DragWell and the DragSession that it initiates.

```
public class DragWell extends View implements DragSource {
  // Public Constructors
      public DragWell();
      public DragWell(Rect rect);
      public DragWell(int x, int y, int width, int height);
  // Public Instance Methods
      public Border border();
      public Object data();
      public String dataType();
      public void decode(Decoder decoder) throws CodingException; // Overrides View
      public void describeClassInfo(ClassInfo info); // Overrides View
      public void dragWasAccepted(DragSession session); // From DragSource
      public boolean dragWasRejected(DragSession session); // From DragSource
      public void drawView(Graphics g); // Overrides View
      public void encode(Encoder encoder) throws CodingException; // Overrides View
      public Image image();
      public boolean isEnabled();
      public boolean isTransparent(); // Overrides View
      public boolean mouseDown(MouseEvent event); // Overrides View
      public void setBorder(Border newBorder);
      public void setData(Object anObject);
      public void setDataType(String dataType);
      public void setEnabled(boolean flag);
      public void setImage(Image anImage);
      public View sourceView(DragSession session); // From DragSource
}
```

Hierarchy: Object→View(Codable)→DragWell(DragSource)

Extended By: ColorWell

netscape.application.DrawingSequence

DrawingSequence is an abstract Image subclass useful for animation. A DrawingSequence must be used in conjunction with a DrawingSequenceOwner, which is typically a View. For example, the Button class implements DrawingSequenceOwner so that it can display animations as well as static images.

A DrawingSequence has an internal Timer, and every time the timer fires, the DrawingSequence notifies its owner that its frame has changed. The owner will normally respond by calling the DrawingSequence's drawAt() method, which should draw the current frame at the given location.

To animate a sequence of Image objects, use the ImageSequence class, a DrawingSequence subclass. To perform animations involving drawn graphics, create a custom subclass of DrawingSequence and override the drawAt() method. This method should call currentFrameNumber() to determine what frame of the animation to draw.

```
public abstract class DrawingSequence extends Image implements Target, Codable {
// Public Constructors
    public DrawingSequence();
    public DrawingSequence(DrawingSequenceOwner owner);
// Constants
    public static final int BACKWARD;
    public static final int BACKWARD_LOOP;
    public static final int BOUNCE;
    public static final int FORWARD;
    public static final int FORWARD_LOOP;
    public static final String NEXT_FRAME;
    public static final String START;
    public static final String STOP;
// Public Instance Methods
    public int currentFrameNumber();
    public void decode(Decoder decoder) throws CodingException; // Overrides Image
    public void describeClassInfo(ClassInfo info); // Overrides Image
    public boolean doesLoop();
    public boolean doesResetOnStart();
    public boolean doesResetOnStop();
    public abstract void drawAt(Graphics g, int x, int y); // Defines Image
    public void encode(Encoder encoder) throws CodingException; // Overrides Image
    public void finishDecoding() throws CodingException; // Overrides Image
    public int frameCount();
    public int frameRate();
    public abstract int height(); // Defines Image
    public boolean isAnimating();
    public String name(); // Overrides Image
    public boolean nextFrame();
    public DrawingSequenceOwner owner();
    public void performCommand(String command, Object data); // From Target
    public int playbackMode();
    public void reset();
    public void setCurrentFrameNumber(int anInt);
    public void setFrameCount(int count);
```

```
        public void setFrameRate(int milliseconds);
        public void setName(String aName);
        public void setOwner(DrawingSequenceOwner anObject);
        public void setPlaybackMode(int mode);
        public void setResetOnStart(boolean flag);
        public void setResetOnStop(boolean flag);
        public void start();
        public void stop();
        public abstract int width();  // Defines Image
}
```

Hierarchy: Object→Image(Codable)→DrawingSequence(Target, Codable)

Extended By: ImageSequence

Passed To: Button.drawingSequenceCompleted(), Button.drawingSequenceFrameChanged(), DrawingSequenceOwner.drawingSequenceCompleted(), DrawingSequenceOwner.drawingSequenceFrameChanged()

---

netscape.application.DrawingSequenceOwner

This interface is implemented by objects that are interested in being notified when a DrawingSequence displays a new frame or reaches its last frame. A DrawingSequenceOwner must be registered with a DrawingSequence by passing it to either the DrawingSequence() constructor or to setOwner().

```
public abstract interface DrawingSequenceOwner {
    // Public Instance Methods
        public abstract void drawingSequenceCompleted(DrawingSequence aSequence);
        public abstract void drawingSequenceFrameChanged(DrawingSequence aSequence);
}
```

Implemented By: Button

Passed To: DrawingSequence(), DrawingSequence.setOwner(), ImageSequence()

Returned By: DrawingSequence.owner()

---

netscape.application.EmptyBorder

EmptyBorder is a Border subclass that implements a zero-width "empty" border. The static emptyBorder() method returns a predefined instance of this class, which is useful as a default "null border" for custom Views. Only view implementors will ever need to use this class.

```
public class EmptyBorder extends Border {
    // Public Constructor
        public EmptyBorder();
    // Class Methods
        public static Border emptyBorder();
    // Public Instance Methods
        public int bottomMargin();  // Defines Border
        public void decode(Decoder decoder) throws CodingException;  // Overrides Border
        public void drawInRect(Graphics g, int x, int y, int width, int height);  // Defines Border
        public int leftMargin();  // Defines Border
```

→

```
      public int rightMargin( ); // Defines Border
      public int topMargin( ); // Defines Border
}
```

Hierarchy: Object→Border(Codable)→EmptyBorder

---

netscape.application.Event

Event is the base class for all IFC events. Typical IFC programs only need to use the KeyEvent and MouseEvent subclasses, which represent key presses, mouse clicks, and other keyboard and mouse input events generated by the user.

A program that wants to handle some special type of event through the IFC's event-handling mechanism can create a custom subclass of Event. When a custom event is created, you must call setProcessor( ) to specify the EventProcessor object that will handle the event when it reaches the front of the event queue. See EventLoop for information on adding events to the event queue.

```
public class Event extends Object implements Cloneable {
   // Public Constructors
      public Event( );
      public Event(long timeStamp);
   // Public Instance Methods
      public Object clone( ); // Overrides Object
      public EventProcessor processor( );
      public void setProcessor(EventProcessor aProcessor);
      public void setTimeStamp(long timeStamp);
      public void setType(int aType);
      public long timeStamp( );
      public int type( );
}
```

Extended By: CommandEvent, KeyEvent, MouseEvent

Passed To: Application.didProcessEvent(), Application.processEvent(), Application.willProcessEvent(), CommandEvent.processEvent(), EventLoop.addEvent(), EventLoop.addEventAndWait(), EventLoop.processEvent(), EventLoop.removeEvent(), EventProcessor.processEvent(), MenuItem.processEvent(), RootView.processEvent(), Timer.processEvent()

Returned By: EventLoop.getNextEvent(), EventLoop.peekNextEvent()

---

netscape.application.EventFilter

This simple interface is implemented by objects interested in filtering events. When an EventFilter object is passed to the filterEvents( ) method of an EventLoop, the filterEvents( ) method of the EventFilter is passed a Vector of Event objects, which it should examine and modify as desired. An EventFilter may add, remove, or reorder events in the Vector. filterEvents( ) should complete promptly and not call any View methods, as this can lead to deadlock.

```
public abstract interface EventFilter {
   // Public Instance Methods
      public abstract Object filterEvents(Vector events);
}
```

Implemented By: TextView, Timer

Passed To: EventLoop.filterEvents()

---

netscape.application.EventLoop

The EventLoop class implements the main loop of any IFC Application. Every Application has an internal EventLoop object that maintains a queue of Event objects awaiting processing. The run() method of this EventLoop extracts Event objects one at a time from the queue by calling getNextEvent() and processes them by passing them to processEvent(). Everything an IFC program does is a direct or indirect response to an event, and so the EventLoop and its run() method sit at the core of all IFC programs.

Most events in an IFC program are KeyEvent and MouseEvent objects. A separate thread runs in every IFC program to receive native AWT events, convert them to IFC event objects, and place them asynchronously on the IFC event queue.

You never need to create your own EventLoop object; instead you can call the eventLoop() method of the Application object to obtain the application's EventLoop instance.

Some applications may want to use the advanced event-processing features of the EventLoop. You can add a synthetic keyboard or mouse event, or add a custom event type to the event queue with addEvent(), and you can remove an event with removeEvent(). peekNextEvent() allows you to take a look at the next event in the queue without removing it. filterEvents() passes the entire event queue (a Vector) to an EventFilter object that can modify it as desired. Finally, the processEvent() method invokes the willProcessEvent() method of the Application object before processing the event, and invokes didProcessEvent() after processing the event. You can override these methods in your Application subclass to allow pre- and post-processing of events.

```
public class EventLoop extends Object implements Runnable {
   // Public Constructor
      public EventLoop();
   // Public Instance Methods
      public void addEvent(Event anEvent);
      public void addEventAndWait(Event event);
      public Object filterEvents(EventFilter filter);
      public Event getNextEvent();
      public synchronized boolean isRunning();
      public Event peekNextEvent();
      public void processEvent(Event nextEvent);
      public void removeEvent(Event anEvent);
      public void run(); // From Runnable
      public synchronized void stopRunning();
      public synchronized String toString(); // Overrides Object
}
```

→

Passed To: Timer()

Returned By: Application.eventLoop(), Timer.eventLoop()

---

netscape.application.EventProcessor

This simple interface is implemented by an object interested in dispatching and processing events removed from an EventLoop. The processEvent() method should process the event in some appropriate way. You never typically need to use this interface. If you want to provide custom event processing for certain events, you can use the setProcessor() method to specify special EventProcessor objects for them.

```
public abstract interface EventProcessor {
    // Public Instance Methods
        public abstract void processEvent(Event event);
}
```

Implemented By: Application, CommandEvent, MenuItem, RootView, Timer

Passed To: Event.setProcessor()

Returned By: Event.processor()

---

netscape.application.ExtendedTarget

This interface extends the Target interface and allows an implementing object to declare the commands it can support. canPerformCommand() should return true if the ExtendedTarget interface is able to perform the specified command. The constant strings are commonly used command strings, or commands that are used internally by the IFC.

```
public abstract interface ExtendedTarget extends Target {
    // Constants
        public static final String COPY;
        public static final String CUT;
        public static final String NEW_FONT_SELECTION;
        public static final String PASTE;
        public static final String SET_FONT;
        public static final String SHOW_COLOR_CHOOSER;
        public static final String SHOW_FONT_CHOOSER;
    // Public Instance Methods
        public abstract boolean canPerformCommand(String command);
}
```

Implemented By: Plan, RootView, TargetChain, TextField, TextView

Passed To: TargetChain.addTarget(), TargetChain.removeTarget()

netscape.application.ExternalWindow

The `ExternalWindow` class represents a native, platform-dependent window. It implements the `Window` interface, and therefore implements many of the same methods as `InternalWindow`. The optional argument to the `ExternalWindow()` constructor specifies whether the window should have a titlebar and other decorations or not. It should be `Window.TITLE_TYPE` or `Window.BLANK_TYPE`. Use `moveTo()` and `sizeTo()` to set the position and size of an ExternalWindow. Use `windowSizeForContentSize()` to determine the window size required to accommodate a desired content size. Finally, use `show()` to make an `ExternalWindow` visible, or `showModally()` to make it visible and modal. (A modal window blocks input to all other windows until it is dismissed.)

Each `ExternalWindow` has its own automatically created `RootView`, which can be obtained with `rootView()`. As a shortcut, views can be added to the `RootView` with the `addSubview()` method of the `ExternalWindow` object.

The `hide()` method removes the window from the screen but does not destroy it; calling the `show()` method of a hidden window causes the window to reappear. On the other hand, the `dispose()` method destroys the window. Since an `ExternalWindow` uses system resources, `dispose()` should always be called to free up those resources when the application is finished with the `ExternalWindow`.

An `ExternalWindow` can have a `WindowOwner` object that is notified when the window's state changes. A window's owner is notified when the window is moved, resized, or closed, for example.

```
public class ExternalWindow extends Object implements Window, ApplicationObserver {
    // Public Constructors
        public ExternalWindow();
        public ExternalWindow(int windowType);
    // Public Instance Methods
        public void addSubview(View aView); // From Window
        public void applicationDidPause(Application application); // From ApplicationObserver
        public void applicationDidResume(Application application); // From ApplicationObserver
        public void applicationDidStart(Application application); // From ApplicationObserver
        public void applicationDidStop(Application application); // From ApplicationObserver
        public Rect bounds(); // From Window
        public void center(); // From Window
        public boolean containsDocument(); // From Window
        public Size contentSize(); // From Window
        public void currentDocumentDidChange(Application application,
                                        Window document); // From ApplicationObserver
        public void didBecomeCurrentDocument(); // From Window
        public void didResignCurrentDocument(); // From Window
        public void dispose();
        public void focusDidChange(Application application, View focusedView); // From ApplicationObserver
        public void hide(); // From Window
        public boolean hidesWhenPaused();
        public boolean isCurrentDocument(); // From Window
        public boolean isResizable(); // From Window
        public boolean isVisible(); // From Window
        public Menu menu();
```

$\rightarrow$

```
        public MenuView menuView( );  // From Window
        public Size minSize( );  // From Window
        public void moveBy(int deltaX, int deltaY);  // From Window
        public void moveTo(int x, int y);  // From Window
        public void moveToBack( );  // From Window
        public void moveToFront( );  // From Window
        public WindowOwner owner( );  // From Window
        public FoundationPanel panel( );
        public void performCommand(String command, Object data);  // From Target
        public RootView rootView( );
        public void setBounds(int x, int y, int width, int height);  // From Window
        public void setBounds(Rect newBounds);  // From Window
        public void setContainsDocument(boolean containsDocument);  // From Window
        public void setHidesWhenPaused(boolean flag);
        public void setMenu(Menu aMenu);
        public void setMenuView(MenuView aMenuView);  // From Window
        public void setMinSize(int width, int height);  // From Window
        public void setOwner(WindowOwner wOwner);  // From Window
        public void setResizable(boolean flag);  // From Window
        public void setTitle(String aTitle);  // From Window
        public void show( );  // From Window
        public void showModally( );  // From Window
        public void sizeBy(int deltaWidth, int deltaHeight);  // From Window
        public void sizeTo(int width, int height);  // From Window
        public String title( );  // From Window
        public View viewForMouse(int x, int y);  // From Window
        public Size windowSizeForContentSize(int width, int height);  // From Window
 // Protected Instance Methods
        protected FoundationDialog createDialog( );
        protected FoundationFrame createFrame( );
        protected FoundationPanel createPanel( );
        protected FoundationWindow createWindow( );  // Undocumented
}
```

Hierarchy: Object→ExternalWindow(Window(Target), ApplicationObserver)

Passed To: AWTCompatibility.awtWindowForExternalWindow()

Returned By: Plan.externalWindowWithContents(), PlanLoader.putPlanInExternalWindow(),
RootView.externalWindow()

---

netscape.application.FileChooser

A FileChooser is a modal dialog box for choosing a file. A FileChooser can be
created in one of two types: LOAD_TYPE or SAVE_TYPE. You can set initial values to
be displayed in the FileChooser with setDirectory() and setFile(). Display a
FileChooser by calling showModally(). This method will not return until the user
has selected a file and dismissed the dialog (you do not have to call hide()

yourself). Once showModally() has returned, you can call file() and direc-
tory() to obtain the filename and directory that the user selected.

```
public class FileChooser extends Object {
    // Public Constructor
        public FileChooser(RootView rootView, String title, int type);
    // Constants
        public static final int LOAD_TYPE;
        public static final int SAVE_TYPE;
    // Public Instance Methods
        public String directory();
        public String file();
        public java.io.FilenameFilter filenameFilter();
        public void setDirectory(String directory);
        public void setFile(String filePath);
        public void setFilenameFilter(java.io.FilenameFilter aFilter);
        public void setTitle(String title);
        public void showModally();
        public String title();
        public int type();
}
```

Passed To: AWTCompatibility.awtFileDialogForFileChooser()

---

netscape.application.Font

The Font class represents a font; it is a wrapper around the java.awt.Font class
and has methods to support the IFC archiving mechanism. You create a Font by
specifying a font name, a style, and a point size. In Java 1.1, valid font names are
Serif, SansSerif, MonoSpaced, Dialog, and DialogInput. Valid styles are PLAIN,
BOLD, ITALIC, and BOLD+ITALIC. The static method fontNamed() supports caching
and is therefore somewhat more efficient than the Font() constructor.
fontMetrics() returns a FontMetrics object that allows you to query the size of
the font and measure the width of strings drawn using the font.

```
public class Font extends Object implements Codable {
    // Public Constructors
        public Font();
        public Font(String name, int style, int size);
    // Constants
        public static final int BOLD;
        public static final int ITALIC;
        public static final int PLAIN;
    // Class Methods
        public static Font defaultFont();
        public static synchronized Font fontNamed(String fontName, int style, int size);
        public static Font fontNamed(String aString);
    // Public Instance Methods
        public void decode(Decoder decoder) throws CodingException; // From Codable
        public void describeClassInfo(ClassInfo info); // From Codable
        public void encode(Encoder encoder) throws CodingException; // From Codable
```

```
      public String family( );
      public void finishDecoding( ) throws CodingException; // From Codable
      public FontMetrics fontMetrics( );
      public boolean isBold( );
      public boolean isItalic( );
      public boolean isPlain( );
      public String name( );
      public int size( );
      public int style( );
      public String toString( ); // Overrides Object
}
```

Passed To: AWTCompatibility.awtFontForFont(), Button.drawViewTitleInRect(), Button.setFont(), ContainerView.setTitleFont(), DebugGraphics.setFont(), FontChooser.setFont(), FontMetrics(), Graphics.setFont(), Label(), Label.setFont(), ListItem.drawStringInRect(), ListItem.setFont(), MenuItem.drawStringInRect(), MenuItem.setFont(), TextField.createLabel(), TextField.setFont(), TextView.setFont()

Returned By: AWTCompatibility.fontForAWTFont(), Button.font(), ContainerView.titleFont(), Font.defaultFont(), Font.fontNamed(), FontChooser.font(), FontMetrics.font(), Graphics.font(), InternalWindow.font(), Label.font(), ListItem.font(), MenuItem.font(), TextField.font(), TextView.font(), TextViewHTMLElement.fontFromAttributes()

---

netscape.application.FontChooser

A FontChooser is an object that creates a View hierarchy that allows the user to select a font. The contentView() method returns the root of that View hierarchy. You can place the FontChooser View hierarchy into your own hierarchy explicitly, or you can call setWindow() to have the FontChooser place itself in a Window object you specify. Rather than creating and displaying a FontChooser explicitly yourself, it is more common to call the showFontChooser() method of the Root-View object of your Application object or of an ExternalWindow. This method displays the FontChooser in a modeless dialog box. The FontChooser displays a Set button. When the user clicks this button, the FontChooser sends a SET_FONT command to the application's target chain, passing the currently selected font as the data object to the performCommand() method.

```
public class FontChooser extends Object implements Target {
// Public Constructor
      public FontChooser( );
// Public Instance Methods
      public View contentView( );
      public Font font( );
      public void hide( );
      public void performCommand(String command, Object data); // From Target
      public void setFont(Font aFont);
      public void setWindow(Window aWindow);
```

```
        public void show( );
        public Window window( );
}
```

netscape.application.FontMetrics

The FontMetrics class allows a programmer to query the size of a font and to measure the width of strings drawn with the font. You obtain a FontMetrics object by calling the fontMetrics() method of the desired Font. height(), ascent(), and descent() return information about the vertical dimension of a font. charWidth() and stringWidth() return the width of a character or of a string drawn using the font.

```
public class FontMetrics extends Object {
    // Public Constructors
        public FontMetrics( );
        public FontMetrics(Font aFont);
    // Public Instance Methods
        public int ascent( );
        public int bytesWidth(byte[] data, int offset, int length);
        public int charHeight( );
        public int charWidth(int aChar);
        public int charWidth(char aChar);
        public int charsWidth(char[] data, int offset, int length);
        public int descent( );
        public Font font( );
        public int height( );
        public int leading( );
        public int maxAdvance( );
        public int maxAscent( );
        public int maxDescent( );
        public int stringHeight( );
        public Size stringSize(String aString);
        public int stringWidth(String aString);
        public String toString( );  // Overrides Object
        public int[ ] widthsArray( );
        public int widthsArrayBase( );
}
```

netscape.
application

Passed To: AWTCompatibility.awtFontMetricsForFontMetrics()

Returned By: AWTCompatibility.fontMetricsForAWTFontMetrics(), Font.fontMetrics()

netscape.application.FormElement

This interface defines a single method used by views that accept user input (possibly as part of an input "form") to return a text representation of the user's input. This interface could be used, for example, to write a method that would automatically extract the user's input from an arbitrary View hierarchy.

→

```
public abstract interface FormElement {
 // Public Instance Methods
    public abstract String formElementText( );
}
```

Implemented By: Button, ContainerView, ListView, Popup, Slider, TextField, TextView

---

netscape.application.FoundationApplet

This class adds IFC extensions to the standard Java Applet class. Most importantly, it reads the applet parameter (specified by the <PARAM> tag) named "Application-Class," and loads and runs an Application class with that name. In order for FoundationApplet to load an Application class specified by name, you must provide a subclass that defines a simple classForName( ) method that works around limitations in the Java ClassLoader API. Thus, to create an applet with the IFC, you must define an Application class, and also a trivial subclass of FoundationApplet. The following subclass is suitable for any IFC applet. It is the same code that appears in the NetscapeApplet class used in most IFC example programs.

```
import netscape.application.*;
public class AppLoader extends FoundationApplet {
    public Class classForName(String className)
                 throws ClassNotFoundException {
        return Class.forName(className);
    }
}
```

Other than defining a trivial subclass of this class you never need to use the FoundationApplet directly. Your Application class interacts with it automatically.

```
public class FoundationApplet extends java.applet.Applet implements Runnable {
 // Public Constructor
    public FoundationApplet( );
 // Public Instance Methods
    public Application application( );
    public Class classForName(String className) throws ClassNotFoundException;
    public void destroy( );  // Overrides Applet
    public void init( );  // Overrides Applet
    public void layout( );  // Overrides Container
    public void paint(java.awt.Graphics g);  // Overrides Component. Undocumented
    public FoundationPanel panel( );
    public void popIFCContext( );
    public Application pushIFCContext( );
    public void run( );  // From Runnable
    public void setApplication(Application application);
    public void start( );  // Overrides Applet
    public void stop( );  // Overrides Applet
 // Protected Instance Methods
    protected FoundationPanel createPanel( );
}
```

Returned By: Application.createApplet()

---

netscape.application.FoundationPanel

This class is a subclass of java.awt.Panel that supports the IFC View model. It is a bridge that connects the IFC with the AWT. All Application and RootView objects contain a FoundationPanel. You should never need to use this class directly; instead use Application and RootView.

```
public class FoundationPanel extends java.awt.Panel {
    // Public Constructors
        public FoundationPanel();
        public FoundationPanel(int width, int height);
    // Public Instance Methods
        public boolean gotFocus(java.awt.Event evt, Object what); // Overrides Component
        public boolean keyDown(java.awt.Event evt, int key); // Overrides Component
        public boolean keyUp(java.awt.Event evt, int key); // Overrides Component
        public void layout(); // Overrides Container. Undocumented
        public synchronized boolean lostFocus(java.awt.Event evt, Object what); // Overrides Component
        public boolean mouseDown(java.awt.Event evt, int x, int y); // Overrides Component
        public boolean mouseDrag(java.awt.Event evt, int x, int y); // Overrides Component
        public boolean mouseEnter(java.awt.Event evt, int x, int y); // Overrides Component
        public boolean mouseExit(java.awt.Event evt, int x, int y); // Overrides Component
        public boolean mouseMove(java.awt.Event evt, int x, int y); // Overrides Component
        public boolean mouseUp(java.awt.Event evt, int x, int y); // Overrides Component
        public void paint(java.awt.Graphics g); // Overrides Component
        public void printAll(java.awt.Graphics g); // Overrides Component. Undocumented
        public void reshape(int x, int y, int width, int height); // Overrides Component
        public void resize(int width, int height); // Overrides Component
        public RootView rootView();
        public void setCursor(int cursor); // Undocumented
        public void setRootView(RootView rootView);
        public void update(java.awt.Graphics g); // Overrides Component
}
```

Hierarchy: Object→Component(ImageObserver, MenuContainer, Serializable)→Container→
Panel→FoundationPanel

Returned By: ExternalWindow.createPanel(), ExternalWindow.panel(), FoundationApplet.createPanel(), FoundationApplet.panel(), RootView.panel()

---

netscape.application.Graphics

This class provides methods for line and text drawing, and also serves as a "graphics context," storing information such as a color, a font, and a region in which drawing is to be done. The pushState() method saves the current graphics state, and popState() restored the most recently pushed state. While you can create a Graphics object, you typically just use the one passed to the drawView() method of a View object. If you do create your own Graphics object, you should be sure

→

to call its dispose() method when you no longer need it. This will free up system resources associated with it. This class is very similar to java.awt.Graphics.

```
public class Graphics extends Object {
  // Public Constructors
     public Graphics(View view);
     public Graphics(Bitmap aBitmap);
  // Constants
     public static final int CENTERED;
     public static final int LEFT_JUSTIFIED;
     public static final int RIGHT_JUSTIFIED;
  // Public Instance Methods
     public Bitmap buffer();
     public void clearClipRect();
     public Rect clipRect();
     public Color color();
     public int debugOptions();
     public void dispose();
     public void drawArc(Rect aRect, int startAngle, int arcAngle);
     public void drawArc(int x, int y, int width, int height, int startAngle, int arcAngle);
     public void drawBitmapAt(Bitmap bitmap, int x, int y);
     public void drawBitmapScaled(Bitmap bitmap, int x, int y, int width, int height);
     public void drawBytes(byte[] data, int offset, int length, int x, int y);
     public void drawChars(char[] data, int offset, int length, int x, int y);
     public void drawLine(int x1, int y1, int x2, int y2);
     public void drawOval(Rect aRect);
     public void drawOval(int x, int y, int width, int height);
     public void drawPoint(int x, int y);
     public void drawPolygon(int[] xPoints, int[] yPoints, int nPoints);
     public void drawPolygon(Polygon polygon);
     public void drawRect(Rect aRect);
     public void drawRect(int x, int y, int width, int height);
     public void drawRoundedRect(Rect aRect, int arcWidth, int arcHeight);
     public void drawRoundedRect(int x, int y, int width, int height, int arcWidth, int arcHeight);
     public void drawString(String aString, int x, int y);
     public void drawStringInRect(String aString, int x, int y, int width, int height, int justification);
     public void drawStringInRect(String aString, Rect aRect, int justification);
     public void fillArc(Rect aRect, int startAngle, int arcAngle);
     public void fillArc(int x, int y, int width, int height, int startAngle, int arcAngle);
     public void fillOval(Rect aRect);
     public void fillOval(int x, int y, int width, int height);
     public void fillPolygon(int[] xPoints, int[] yPoints, int nPoints);
     public void fillPolygon(Polygon polygon);
     public void fillRect(Rect aRect);
     public void fillRect(int x, int y, int width, int height);
     public void fillRoundedRect(Rect aRect, int arcWidth, int arcHeight);
     public void fillRoundedRect(int x, int y, int width, int height, int arcWidth, int arcHeight);
     public Font font();
     public boolean isDrawingBuffer();
     public void popState();
     public void pushState();
```

```
    public void setClipRect(Rect rect, boolean intersect);
    public void setClipRect(Rect rect);
    public void setColor(Color aColor);
    public void setDebugOptions(int debugOptions);
    public void setFont(Font aFont);
    public void setPaintMode();
    public void setXORMode(Color aColor);
    public void sync();
    public String toString();  // Overrides Object
    public void translate(int x, int y);
    public Point translation();
    public int xTranslation();
    public int yTranslation();
}
```

Extended By: DebugGraphics

Passed To: many methods, including various drawView() methods

Returned By: AWTCompatibility.graphicsForAWTGraphics(), Bitmap.createGraphics(),
View.createGraphics()

---

netscape.application.GridLayout

This LayoutManager subclass makes all child views the same size, and arranges
them into a grid with the specified number of rows and columns, and with the
specified horizontal and vertical "gaps" between those rows and columns. If either
the number of rows or columns is left unspecified, then the grid will grow to arbitrary size in that dimension, while the other dimension remains as specified. If neither dimension is specified, then the GridLayout will use a square grid that most
closely fits the number of child views.

```
public class GridLayout extends Object implements LayoutManager, Codable {
// Public Constructors
    public GridLayout();
    public GridLayout(int numRows, int numCols);
    public GridLayout(int numRows, int numCols, int horizGap, int vertGap, int flow);
// Constants
    public static final int FLOW_ACROSS;
    public static final int FLOW_DOWN;
// Public Instance Methods
    public void addSubview(View aView);  // From LayoutManager
    public int columnCount();
    public void decode(Decoder decoder) throws CodingException;  // From Codable
    public void describeClassInfo(ClassInfo info);  // From Codable
    public void encode(Encoder encoder) throws CodingException;  // From Codable
    public void finishDecoding() throws CodingException;  // From Codable
    public int flowDirection();
    public Size gridSize(View aView);
    public int horizGap();
    public void layoutView(View aView, int deltaWidth, int deltaHeight);  // From LayoutManager
    public void removeSubview(View aView);  // From LayoutManager
    public int rowCount();
    public void setColumnCount(int numCols);
```

$\rightarrow$

netscape.application.GridLayout

←

```
    public void setFlowDirection(int flow);
    public void setHorizGap(int gap);
    public void setRowCount(int numRows);
    public void setVertGap(int gap);
    public int vertGap();
}
```

netscape.application.HTMLParsingException

This exception signals that an exception, typically a syntax error, occurred while parsing HTML. The `lineNumber()` method returns the line number at which the exception occurred.

```
public class HTMLParsingException extends Exception {
  // Public Constructor
    public HTMLParsingException(String string, int lineNumber);
  // Public Instance Methods
    public int lineNumber();
}
```

Hierarchy: Object→Throwable(Serializable)→Exception→HTMLParsingException

Thrown By: TextView.importHTMLInRange()

netscape.application.HTMLParsingRules

This class stores rules for parsing HTML. You can use it to extend the HTML parsing capabilities of the `TextView` class. By default, `TextView` can parse HTML 1.0. For every HTML tag (or "marker") you wish to parse, you specify parsing rules by providing values for a number of "keys." The class defines a number of constants that serve as these keys. Each tag is represented by a subclass of `TextViewHTMLElement`, and the name of this subclass is specified as the value of the REPRESENTA-TION_KEY key.

```
public class HTMLParsingRules extends Object implements Codable {
  // Public Constructor
    public HTMLParsingRules();
  // Constants
    public static final String BEGIN_TERMINATION_MARKERS_KEY;
    public static final String COMMENT_MARKER_KEY;
    public static final String END_TERMINATION_MARKERS_KEY;
    public static final String IS_CONTAINER_KEY;
    public static final String REPRESENTATION_KEY;
    public static final String SHOULD_IGNORE_END_KEY;
    public static final String SHOULD_RETAIN_FORMATTING_KEY;
    public static final String STRING_MARKER_KEY;
  // Public Instance Methods
    public String classNameForComment();
    public String classNameForMarker(String aMarker);
    public String classNameForString();
```

```
    public void decode(Decoder decoder) throws CodingException; // From Codable
    public String defaultContainerClassName();
    public String defaultMarkerClassName();
    public void describeClassInfo(ClassInfo info); // From Codable
    public void encode(Encoder encoder) throws CodingException; // From Codable
    public void finishDecoding() throws CodingException; // From Codable
    public Hashtable rulesForMarker(String aMarker);
    public void setClassNameForComment(String className);
    public void setClassNameForMarker(String className, String aMarker);
    public void setDefaultContainerClassName(String aClassName);
    public void setDefaultMarkerClassName(String aClassName);
    public void setRuleForMarker(String rule, Object value, String marker);
    public void setRulesForMarker(Hashtable markerRules, String marker);
    public void setStringClassName(String className);
}
```

Passed To: TextView.setHTMLParsingRules()

Returned By: TextView.htmlParsingRules()

---

netscape.application.Image

This abstract class represents an object with a width and height that knows how to draw itself. `Bitmap` and `DrawingSequence` are concrete subclasses. The non-abstract methods of `Image` allow you to draw images in several ways. `Image` objects are commonly used to customize the appearance of various `View` objects.

Note that the IFC `Image` class is substantially different from the `java.awt.Image` class, which is actually closer to the IFC `Bitmap` class.

```
public abstract class Image extends Object implements Codable {
    // Default Constructor: public Image()
    // Constants
        public static final int CENTERED;
        public static final String IMAGE_TYPE;
        public static final int SCALED;
        public static final int TILED;
    // Class Methods
        public static Image imageNamed(String name); // Undocumented
    // Public Instance Methods
        public void decode(Decoder decoder) throws CodingException; // From Codable
        public void describeClassInfo(ClassInfo info); // From Codable
        public abstract void drawAt(Graphics g, int x, int y);
        public void drawCentered(Graphics g, int x, int y, int width, int height);
        public void drawCentered(Graphics g, Rect rect);
        public void drawScaled(Graphics g, int x, int y, int width, int height);
        public void drawScaled(Graphics g, Rect rect);
        public void drawTiled(Graphics g, int x, int y, int width, int height);
        public void drawTiled(Graphics g, Rect rect);
        public void drawWithStyle(Graphics g, int x, int y, int width, int height, int style);
        public void drawWithStyle(Graphics g, Rect rect, int style);
        public void encode(Encoder encoder) throws CodingException; // From Codable
        public void finishDecoding() throws CodingException; // From Codable
        public abstract int height();
```

→

```
        public Image imageWithName(String name); // Undocumented
        public boolean isTransparent();
        public String name();
        public abstract int width();
}
```

Extended By: Bitmap, DrawingSequence

Passed To: Alert.runAlertExternally(), Alert.runAlertInternally(), Button.drawViewInterior(), Button.setAltImage(), Button.setImage(), ColorWell.setImage(), ContainerView.setImage(), DragSession(), DragWell.setImage(), ImageAttachment(), ImageAttachment.setImage(), ImageSequence.addImage(), ImageSequence.removeImage(), ImageSequence.setImageStrip(), ListItem.setImage(), ListItem.setSelectedImage(), MenuItem.setCheckedImage(), MenuItem.setImage(), MenuItem.setSelectedImage(), MenuItem.setUncheckedImage(), Popup.setPopupImage(), RootView.setImage(), ScrollBar.setKnobImage(), Slider.setImage(), Slider.setKnobImage()

Returned By: Alert.notificationImage(), Alert.questionImage(), Alert.warningImage(), Application.keyboardArrowImage(), Bitmap.imageWithName(), Button.altImage(), Button.image(), ColorWell.image(), ContainerView.image(), DragWell.image(), Image.imageNamed(), Image.imageWithName(), ImageAttachment.image(), ImageSequence.currentImage(), ImageSequence.imageStrip(), ListItem.image(), ListItem.selectedImage(), MenuItem.checkedImage(), MenuItem.image(), MenuItem.selectedImage(), MenuItem.uncheckedImage(), Popup.popupImage(), RootView.image(), ScrollBar.knobImage(), Slider.image(), Slider.knobImage()

---

netscape.application.ImageAttachment

This class is a `TextAttachment` that displays a specified `Image` object within a `TextView` object. `TextView` defines methods for inserting attachments into the flow of text to be displayed. Instead of manipulating `ImageAttachment` objects directly, it is usually easier to have the `TextView` parse and display HTML formatted text containing `<IMG>` tags.

```
public class ImageAttachment extends TextAttachment implements Codable {
    // Public Constructors
        public ImageAttachment();
        public ImageAttachment(Image anImage);
    // Public Instance Methods
        public void decode(Decoder decoder) throws CodingException; // Overrides TextAttachment
        public void describeClassInfo(ClassInfo info); // Overrides TextAttachment
        public void drawInRect(Graphics g, Rect boundsRect); // Overrides TextAttachment
        public void encode(Encoder encoder) throws CodingException; // Overrides TextAttachment
        public void finishDecoding() throws CodingException; // Overrides TextAttachment
        public int height(); // Overrides TextAttachment
        public Image image();
        public void setImage(Image anImage);
        public int width(); // Overrides TextAttachment
}
```

Hierarchy: Object→TextAttachment(Codable)→ImageAttachment(Codable)

netscape.application.ImageSequence

This subclass of DrawingSequence animates a number of Image objects. You can specify the objects to animate in three ways. addImage() allows you to add individual Image objects one at a time. addImagesFromName() loads a series of numbered images that share the same base name. Or you can call setImageStrip() to specify a single image that consists of a strip of individual animation "frames" to be extracted and displayed. Call setFrameWidth() or setFrameHeight() to specify the size and orientation of the strip of frames.

```
public class ImageSequence extends DrawingSequence {
// Public Constructors
     public ImageSequence();
     public ImageSequence(DrawingSequenceOwner owner);
// Public Instance Methods
     public void addImage(Image anImage);
     public void addImagesFromName(String firstImageName, int count);
     public Image currentImage();
     public void decode(Decoder decoder) throws CodingException;  // Overrides DrawingSequence
     public void describeClassInfo(ClassInfo info);  // Overrides DrawingSequence
     public void drawAt(Graphics g, int x, int y);  // Defines DrawingSequence
     public void drawScaled(Graphics g, int x, int y, int width, int height);  // Overrides Image
     public void encode(Encoder encoder) throws CodingException;  // Overrides DrawingSequence
     public int frameHeight();
     public int frameWidth();
     public int height();  // Defines DrawingSequence
     public int imageCount();
     public Image imageStrip();
     public Vector images();
     public Size maxSize();
     public void removeAllImages();
     public void removeImage(Image anImage);
     public void setCurrentImageNumber(int imageNumber);
     public void setFrameHeight(int pixels);
     public void setFrameWidth(int pixels);
     public void setImageStrip(Image anImage);
     public int width();  // Defines DrawingSequence
}
```

Hierarchy: Object→Image(Codable)→DrawingSequence(Target, Codable)→ImageSequence

---

netscape.application.InternalWindow

InternalWindow is a View that looks and behaves much like a regular top-level window, but appears within a top-level window or applet. InternalWindow implements the Window interface, and therefore defines many of the same methods as the ExternalWindow class. Call show() to make an InternalWindow visible, and call hide() to make it disappear.

```
public class InternalWindow extends View implements Window {
// Public Constructors
     public InternalWindow();
```

→

```
    public InternalWindow(Rect rect);
    public InternalWindow(int x, int y, int width, int height);
    public InternalWindow(int type, int x, int y, int width, int height);
// Constants
    public static final int DEFAULT_LAYER;
    public static final int DRAG_LAYER;
    public static final int IGNORE_WINDOW_CLIPVIEW_LAYER; // Undocumented
    public static final int MODAL_LAYER;
    public static final int PALETTE_LAYER;
    public static final int POPUP_LAYER;
// Public Instance Methods
    public void addSubview(View aView); // Overrides View
    public void addSubviewToWindow(View aView);
    public Border border();
    public boolean canBecomeDocument();
    public boolean canBecomeMain();
    public boolean canBecomeSelectedView(); // Overrides View
    public void center(); // From Window
    public boolean containsDocument(); // From Window
    public Size contentSize(); // From Window
    public WindowContentView contentView();
    public void decode(Decoder decoder) throws CodingException; // Overrides View
    public View defaultSelectedView();
    public void describeClassInfo(ClassInfo info); // Overrides View
    public void didBecomeCurrentDocument(); // From Window
    public void didBecomeMain();
    public void didResignCurrentDocument(); // From Window
    public void didResignMain();
    public void draw(Graphics g, Rect clipRect); // Overrides View
    public void drawBottomBorder();
    public void drawTitleBar();
    public void drawView(Graphics g); // Overrides View
    public void encode(Encoder encoder) throws CodingException; // Overrides View
    public void finishDecoding() throws CodingException; // Overrides View
    public View focusedView();
    public Font font(); // Undocumented
    public void hide(); // From Window
    public boolean hidesSubviewsFromKeyboard(); // Overrides View
    public boolean isCloseable();
    public boolean isCurrentDocument(); // From Window
    public boolean isMain();
    public boolean isPointInBorder(int x, int y);
    public boolean isResizable(); // From Window
    public boolean isTransparent(); // Overrides View
    public boolean isVisible(); // From Window
    public int layer();
    public void layoutParts();
    public MenuView menuView(); // From Window
    public Size minSize(); // Overrides View
    public boolean mouseDown(MouseEvent event); // Overrides View
    public void mouseDragged(MouseEvent event); // Overrides View
```

```
    public void mouseUp(MouseEvent event); // Overrides View
    public void moveToBack(); // From Window
    public void moveToFront(); // From Window
    public boolean onscreenAtStartup(); // Undocumented
    public WindowOwner owner(); // From Window
    public void performCommand(String command, Object data); // From Target
    public void scrollRectToVisible(Rect aRect); // Overrides View. Undocumented
    public boolean scrollsToVisible(); // Undocumented
    public void setBorder(Border border);
    public void setBounds(int x, int y, int width, int height); // Overrides View
    public void setCanBecomeDocument(boolean containsDocument);
    public void setCanBecomeMain(boolean flag);
    public void setCloseable(boolean flag);
    public void setContainsDocument(boolean containsDocument); // From Window
    public void setDefaultSelectedView(View aView);
    public void setFocusedView(View view); // Overrides View
    public void setLayer(int windowLayer);
    public void setMenuView(MenuView aMenuView); // From Window
    public void setOnscreenAtStartup(boolean flag); // Undocumented
    public void setOwner(WindowOwner anObject); // From Window
    public void setResizable(boolean flag); // From Window
    public void setRootView(RootView rView);
    public void setScrollsToVisible(boolean flag); // Undocumented
    public void setTitle(String aString); // From Window
    public void setTransparent(boolean flag);
    public void setType(int windowType);
    public void show(); // From Window
    public void showBehind(InternalWindow aWindow);
    public void showInFrontOf(InternalWindow aWindow);
    public void showModally(); // From Window
    public void subviewDidResize();
    public String title(); // From Window
    public String toString(); // Overrides View
    public int type();
    public View viewForMouse(int x, int y); // Overrides View
    public InternalWindow window(); // Overrides View
    public Size windowSizeForContentSize(int width, int height); // From Window
// Protected Instance Methods
    protected Button createCloseButton();
    protected void willMoveTo(Point newPoint);
}
```

Hierarchy: Object→View(Codable)→InternalWindow(Window(Target))

Passed To: InternalWindow.showBehind(), InternalWindow.showInFrontOf(), InternalWindowBorder(),
InternalWindowBorder.setWindow(), RootView.redrawTransparentWindows()

Returned By: InternalWindow.window(), InternalWindowBorder.window(),
MenuView.createMenuWindow(), Plan.internalWindowWithContents(), PlanLoader.putPlanInInternalWindow(),
RootView.mainWindow(), View.window()

netscape.application.InternalWindowBorder

This class is a type of Border used to draw the title bar and resize handles of an InternalWindow. You do not typically need to use this class directly in your applications.

```
public class InternalWindowBorder extends Border {
    // Public Constructors
        public InternalWindowBorder();
        public InternalWindowBorder(InternalWindow aWindow);
    // Public Instance Methods
        public int bottomMargin(); // Defines Border
        public void decode(Decoder decoder) throws CodingException; // Overrides Border
        public void describeClassInfo(ClassInfo info); // Overrides Border
        public void drawBottomBorder(Graphics g, int x, int y, int width, int height);
        public void drawInRect(Graphics g, int x, int y, int width, int height); // Defines Border
        public void drawLeftBorder(Graphics g, int x, int y, int width, int height);
        public void drawRightBorder(Graphics g, int x, int y, int width, int height);
        public void drawTitleBar(Graphics g, int x, int y, int width, int height);
        public void encode(Encoder encoder) throws CodingException; // Overrides Border
        public int leftMargin(); // Defines Border
        public int resizePartWidth();
        public int rightMargin(); // Defines Border
        public void setWindow(InternalWindow aWindow);
        public int topMargin(); // Defines Border
        public InternalWindow window();
}
```

Hierarchy: Object→Border(Codable)→InternalWindowBorder

---

netscape.application.KeyEvent

This class represents a key press or key release event. The inherited type field specifies the type; it is the constant KEY_DOWN or KEY_UP. The key field specifies the key that was pressed. It is either the ASCII code of the key, or a function key represented by one of the constants ending in _KEY. The modifiers field specifies the modifier keys in effect when the key event occurred. It is a bit mask of the constants that end in _MASK. Various methods provide alternative ways to test for particular keys and modifiers.

```
public class KeyEvent extends Event {
    // Public Constructors
        public KeyEvent();
        public KeyEvent(long timeStamp, int key, int modifiers, boolean down);
    // Key Constants
        public static final int BACKSPACE_KEY;
        public static final int DELETE_KEY;
        public static final int RETURN_KEY;
        public static final int TAB_KEY;
        public static final int ESCAPE_KEY;
        public static final int DOWN_ARROW_KEY, LEFT_ARROW_KEY;
        public static final int RIGHT_ARROW_KEY, UP_ARROW_KEY;
```

```
        public static final int PAGE_DOWN_KEY, PAGE_UP_KEY;
        public static final int END_KEY, HOME_KEY;
        public static final int F1_KEY, F2_KEY, F3_KEY, F4_KEY;
        public static final int F5_KEY, F6_KEY, F7_KEY, F8_KEY;
        public static final int  F9_KEY, F10_KEY, F11_KEY, F12_KEY;
    // Modifier Constants
        public static final int ALT_MASK;
        public static final int CONTROL_MASK;
        public static final int META_MASK;
        public static final int SHIFT_MASK;
        public static final int NO_MODIFIERS_MASK;
    // Event Type Constants
        public static final int KEY_DOWN;
        public static final int KEY_UP;
    // Public Instance Variables
        public int key;
        public int modifiers;
    // Public Instance Methods
        public boolean isAltKeyDown();
        public boolean isArrowKey();
        public boolean isBackTabKey();
        public boolean isBackspaceKey();
        public boolean isControlKeyDown();
        public boolean isDeleteKey();
        public boolean isDownArrowKey();
        public boolean isEndKey();
        public boolean isEscapeKey();
        public int isFunctionKey();
        public boolean isHomeKey();
        public boolean isLeftArrowKey();
        public boolean isMetaKeyDown();
        public boolean isPageDownKey();
        public boolean isPageUpKey();
        public boolean isPrintableKey();
        public boolean isReturnKey();
        public boolean isRightArrowKey();
        public boolean isShiftKeyDown();
        public boolean isTabKey();
        public boolean isUpArrowKey();
        public RootView rootView();
        public void setRootView(RootView rootView);
        public String toString(); // Overrides Object
}
```

Hierarchy: Object→Event(Cloneable)→KeyEvent

Passed To: Application.keyDown(), Application.keyUp(), Menu.handleCommandKeyEvent(), TextField.keyDown(), TextFilter.acceptsEvent(), TextView.keyDown(), View.keyDown(), View.keyUp()

netscape.application.Label

Label is a View that displays a single line of static text, typically to indicate the purpose of particular parts of an interface. setTitle() specifies the text to be displayed, and setFont() specifies the font to be used. Label uses a TextField internally to display the text.

If you pass a character to setCommandKey(), then that letter will be underlined in the label, and the specified command string will be sent to the specified target when the user presses the corresponding key on the keyboard.

```
public class Label extends View implements Target {
    // Public Constructors
        public Label();
        public Label(String title, Font aFont);
    // Public Instance Methods
        public Color color();
        public String command();
        public int commandKey();
        public void decode(Decoder decoder) throws CodingException;  // Overrides View
        public void describeClassInfo(ClassInfo info);  // Overrides View
        public void didSizeBy(int deltaWidth, int deltaHeight);  // Overrides View
        public void drawView(Graphics g);  // Overrides View
        public void encode(Encoder encoder) throws CodingException;  // Overrides View
        public Font font();
        public boolean isTransparent();  // Overrides View
        public int justification();
        public Size minSize();  // Overrides View
        public void performCommand(String command, Object data);  // From Target. Undocumented
        public void setColor(Color aColor);
        public void setCommand(String aCommand);
        public void setCommandKey(int aKey);
        public void setFont(Font aFont);
        public void setJustification(int aJustification);
        public void setTarget(Target aTarget);
        public void setTitle(String aTitle);
        public Target target();
        public String title();
        public Rect underlineRect();
}
```

Hierarchy: Object→View(Codable)→Label(Target)

netscape.application.LayoutManager

This interface defines the methods necessary to provide layout management for the children of a View. Once a LayoutManager is specified for a view by calling setLayoutManager(), the view will invoke the various LayoutManager methods at the appropriate times. addSubview() and removeSubview() are invoked when a subview is added to or removed from the view under management. layoutView()

is invoked when the size of the view changes; it should calculate and set the size and position of all subviews.

```
public abstract interface LayoutManager {
    // Public Instance Methods
        public abstract void addSubview(View aView);
        public abstract void layoutView(View aView, int deltaWidth, int deltaHeight);
        public abstract void removeSubview(View aView);
}
```

Implemented By: GridLayout, PackLayout

Passed To: View.setLayoutManager()

Returned By: View.layoutManager()

netscape.application.LineBorder

This class is a kind of Border that draws a line, one pixel wide, in the specified color around a view. The static methods grayLine() and blackLine() return predefined LineBorder objects that draw gray and black lines.

```
public class LineBorder extends Border {
    // Public Constructors
        public LineBorder();
        public LineBorder(Color borderColor);
    // Class Methods
        public static Border blackLine();
        public static Border grayLine();
    // Public Instance Methods
        public int bottomMargin(); // Defines Border
        public Color color();
        public void decode(Decoder decoder) throws CodingException; // Overrides Border
        public void describeClassInfo(ClassInfo info); // Overrides Border
        public void drawInRect(Graphics g, int x, int y, int width, int height); // Defines Border
        public void encode(Encoder encoder) throws CodingException; // Overrides Border
        public void finishDecoding() throws CodingException; // Overrides Border
        public int leftMargin(); // Defines Border
        public int rightMargin(); // Defines Border
        public void setColor(Color aColor);
        public int topMargin(); // Defines Border
}
```

Hierarchy: Object→Border(Codable)→LineBorder

netscape.application.ListItem

A ListItem is a single item that appears within a ListView object. setTitle() specifies the text to appear in the item, and setCommand() specifies the command to be sent by the ListView when the ListItem is selected. Other methods allow you to specify a font for the ListItem, and the colors and images to display in the

$\rightarrow$

ListItem in its selected and unselected states. setData() allows you to associate an arbitrary object with a ListItem.

```
public class ListItem extends Object implements Cloneable, Codable {
// Public Constructor
     public ListItem();
// Public Instance Methods
     public Object clone(); // Overrides Object
     public String command();
     public Object data();
     public void decode(Decoder decoder) throws CodingException; // From Codable
     public void describeClassInfo(ClassInfo info); // From Codable
     public void drawInRect(Graphics g, Rect boundsRect);
     public void encode(Encoder encoder) throws CodingException; // From Codable
     public void finishDecoding() throws CodingException; // From Codable
     public Font font();
     public Image image();
     public boolean isEnabled();
     public boolean isSelected();
     public boolean isTransparent();
     public ListView listView();
     public int minHeight();
     public int minWidth();
     public Color selectedColor();
     public Image selectedImage();
     public void setCommand(String newCommand);
     public void setData(Object data);
     public void setEnabled(boolean flag);
     public void setFont(Font aFont);
     public void setImage(Image anImage);
     public void setSelected(boolean flag);
     public void setSelectedColor(Color color);
     public void setSelectedImage(Image anImage);
     public void setTextColor(Color color);
     public void setTitle(String aString);
     public Color textColor();
     public String title();
// Protected Instance Methods
     protected void drawBackground(Graphics g, Rect boundsRect);
     protected void drawStringInRect(Graphics g, String title, Font titleFont, Rect textBounds, int justification);
}
```

Extended By: PopupItem

Passed To: ListView.addItem(), ListView.deselectItem(), ListView.indexOfItem(), ListView.insertItemAt(), ListView.rectForItem(), ListView.removeItem(), ListView.scrollItemToVisible(), ListView.selectItem(), ListView.selectOnly(), ListView.setPrototypeItem(), Popup.selectItem(), Popup.setPrototypeItem()

Returned By: ListView.addItem(), ListView.insertItemAt(), ListView.itemAt(), ListView.itemForPoint(), ListView.prototypeItem(), ListView.selectedItem(), Popup.addItem(), Popup.itemAt(), Popup.prototypeItem(), Popup.selectedItem()

netscape.application.ListView

This class is a `View` that displays a single column of selectable `ListItem` objects. It is often placed inside a `ScrollView` so that the column of `ListItem`s can scroll. `setCommand()` specifies the command string to be sent when a `ListItem` without a command string of its own is selected. `setDoubleCommand()` specifies a command string to be sent when an item is double-clicked.

After adding or removing `ListItem` objects to a `ListView`, you must call `sizeToMinSize()` to force the `ListView` to adjust its size to accommodate its new list of items

```
public class ListView extends View implements Target, FormElement {
    // Public Constructors
        public ListView();
        public ListView(Rect rect);
        public ListView(int x, int y, int width, int height);
    // Class Variables
        public static String SELECT_NEXT_ITEM;
        public static String SELECT_PREVIOUS_ITEM;
    // Public Instance Methods
        public ListItem addItem();
        public ListItem addItem(ListItem item);
        public boolean allowsEmptySelection();
        public boolean allowsMultipleSelection();
        public Color backgroundColor();
        public boolean canBecomeSelectedView();  // Overrides View
        public String command();
        public int count();
        public void decode(Decoder decoder) throws CodingException;  // Overrides View
        public void describeClassInfo(ClassInfo info);  // Overrides View
        public void deselectItem(ListItem item);
        public String doubleCommand();
        public void drawItemAt(int index);
        public void drawView(Graphics g);  // Overrides View
        public void drawViewBackground(Graphics g, int x, int y, int width, int height);
        public void encode(Encoder encoder) throws CodingException;  // Overrides View
        public String formElementText();  // From FormElement
        public int indexOfItem(ListItem item);
        public ListItem insertItemAt(ListItem item, int index);
        public ListItem insertItemAt(int index);
        public boolean isEnabled();
        public boolean isTransparent();  // Overrides View
        public ListItem itemAt(int index);
        public ListItem itemForPoint(int x, int y);
        public int minItemHeight();
        public int minItemWidth();
        public Size minSize();  // Overrides View
        public boolean mouseDown(MouseEvent event);  // Overrides View
        public void mouseDragged(MouseEvent event);  // Overrides View
        public void mouseUp(MouseEvent event);  // Overrides View
        public boolean multipleItemsSelected();
```

$\rightarrow$

```
         public void performCommand(String aCommand, Object anObject); // From Target
         public ListItem prototypeItem( );
         public Rect rectForItem(ListItem item);
         public Rect rectForItemAt(int index);
         public void removeAllItems( );
         public void removeItem(ListItem item);
         public void removeItemAt(int index);
         public int rowHeight( );
         public void scrollItemAtToVisible(int index);
         public void scrollItemToVisible(ListItem item);
         public void selectItem(ListItem item);
         public void selectItemAt(int index);
         public void selectOnly(ListItem item);
         public int selectedIndex( );
         public ListItem selectedItem( );
         public Vector selectedItems( );
         public void sendCommand( );
         public void sendDoubleCommand( );
         public void setAllowsEmptySelection(boolean flag);
         public void setAllowsMultipleSelection(boolean flag);
         public void setBackgroundColor(Color color);
         public void setCommand(String newCommand);
         public void setDoubleCommand(String newCommand);
         public void setEnabled(boolean flag);
         public void setPrototypeItem(ListItem item);
         public void setRowHeight(int height);
         public void setTarget(Target newTarget);
         public void setTracksMouseOutsideBounds(boolean flag);
         public void setTransparent(boolean flag);
         public Target target( );
         public boolean tracksMouseOutsideBounds( );
         public boolean wantsAutoscrollEvents( ); // Overrides View
}
```

Hierarchy: Object→View(Codable)→ListView(Target, FormElement)

Passed To: Popup.setPopupList()

Returned By: ListItem.listView(), Popup.popupList()

---

netscape.application.Menu

This class has several important purposes in the IFC menuing system. It represents either a menu bar (if true is passed to the constructor) or a menu pane (if false is passed to the constructor). The MenuItem class is used to add items to a menu bar or menu pane. A Menu object that represents a menu bar may be added directly to an ExternalWindow, in which case it will use native AWT menus, or it can be added to a MenuView object, which can then be added to either an InternalWindow or ExternalWindow. In this latter case, the menu is implemented as an IFC View and does not use native menus. Note that the IFC does not support true

---

popup menus. (The Popup class represents a dropdown or option menu rather than an actual popup menu.)

Use one of the addItem() methods to automatically create a MenuItem object and add it to a Menu. Note that you may optionally specify a keyboard shortcut and menu item position, and may also optionally specify whether a menu item should be a toggle button. Use addItemWithSubmenu() to automatically create a MenuItem that displays a submenu when selected. This method returns the created MenuItem object; use its submenu() method to obtain the Menu object that the newly created MenuItem displays.

Use setPrototypeItem() to specify a MenuItem to be used as the prototype for all menu items automatically created by the addItem() methods. This prototype item will be cloned to create new items, thereby copying its default font, color, and other property values.

```
public class Menu extends Object implements Codable {
// Public Constructors
    public Menu();
    public Menu(boolean isTopLevel);
// Public Instance Methods
    public MenuItem addItem(String title, String command, Target target);
    public MenuItem addItem(String title, String command, Target target, boolean isCheckbox);
    public MenuItem addItem(String title, char key, String command, Target target);
    public MenuItem addItem(String title, char key, String command, Target target, boolean isCheckbox);
    public MenuItem addItemAt(String title, char key, String command, Target target,
                                        boolean isCheckbox, int index);
    public void addItemAt(MenuItem menuItem, int index);
    public MenuItem addItemWithSubmenu(String title);
    public MenuItem addSeparator();
    public Color backgroundColor();
    public Border border();
    public void decode(Decoder decoder) throws CodingException; // From Codable
    public void describeClassInfo(ClassInfo info); // From Codable
    public void encode(Encoder encoder) throws CodingException; // From Codable
    public void finishDecoding() throws CodingException; // From Codable
    public boolean handleCommandKeyEvent(KeyEvent event);
    public int indexOfItem(MenuItem item);
    public boolean isTransparent();
    public MenuItem itemAt(int index);
    public int itemCount();
    public void performCommand(String command, Object data);
    public MenuItem prototypeItem();
    public void removeItem(MenuItem menuItem);
    public void removeItemAt(int index);
    public void replaceItem(MenuItem item, MenuItem newItem);
    public void replaceItemAt(int index, MenuItem menuItem);
    public void setBackgroundColor(Color color);
    public void setBorder(Border aBorder);
    public void setPrototypeItem(MenuItem prototype);
    public void setTransparent(boolean flag);
// Protected Instance Methods
    protected Menu createMenuAsSubmenu();
}
```

netscape.
application

→

Passed To: AWTCompatibility.awtMenuBarForMenu(), AWTCompatibility.awtMenuForMenu(), ExternalWindow.setMenu(), MenuItem.setSubmenu(), MenuItem.setSupermenu(), MenuView(), MenuView.createMenuView(), MenuView.setMenu()

Returned By: ExternalWindow.menu(), Menu.createMenuAsSubmenu(), MenuItem.submenu(), MenuItem.supermenu(), MenuView.menu()

netscape.application.MenuItem

This class represents a single item in a Menu. You do not typically create MenuItem objects directly, but instead create them with the addItem() or addItemWithSubmenu() methods of the Menu class. If you want to set color, font, or other properties or otherwise manipulate an individual MenuItem, use the itemAt() method of Menu to retrieve the desired MenuItem object.

```
public class MenuItem extends Object implements Codable, Cloneable, EventProcessor {
  // Public Constructors
    public MenuItem();
    public MenuItem(String title, String command, Target target);
    public MenuItem(String title, char key, String command, Target target);
    public MenuItem(String title, String command, Target target, boolean isCheckbox);
    public MenuItem(String title, char key, String command, Target target, boolean isCheckbox);
  // Public Instance Methods
    public Image checkedImage();
    public Object clone();                                    // Overrides Object
    public String command();
    public char commandKey();
    public Object data();
    public void decode(Decoder decoder) throws CodingException;     // From Codable
    public void describeClassInfo(ClassInfo info);                  // From Codable
    public Color disabledColor();
    public void drawInRect(Graphics g, Rect boundsRect, boolean showsArrow);
    public void encode(Encoder encoder) throws CodingException;     // From Codable
    public void finishDecoding() throws CodingException;            // From Codable
    public Font font();
    public boolean hasSubmenu();
    public Image image();
    public boolean isEnabled();
    public boolean isSelected();
    public boolean isSeparator();
    public int minHeight();
    public int minWidth();
    public void processEvent(Event event);                          // From EventProcessor
    public void requestDraw();
    public Color selectedColor();
    public Image selectedImage();
    public Color selectedTextColor();
    public void sendCommand();
    public void setCheckedImage(Image theImage);
    public void setCommand(String newCommand);
```

```
        public void setCommandKey(char key);
        public void setData(Object data);
        public void setDisabledColor(Color color);
        public void setEnabled(boolean isEnabled);
        public void setFont(Font aFont);
        public void setImage(Image theImage);
        public void setSelected(boolean isSelected);
        public void setSelectedColor(Color color);
        public void setSelectedImage(Image theImage);
        public void setSelectedTextColor(Color color);
        public void setSeparator(boolean isSeparator);
        public void setState(boolean aState);
        public void setSubmenu(Menu aMenu);
        public void setSupermenu(Menu aMenu);
        public void setTarget(Target aTarget);
        public void setTextColor(Color color);
        public void setTitle(String aString);
        public void setUncheckedImage(Image theImage);
        public boolean state();
        public Menu submenu();
        public Menu supermenu();
        public Target target();
        public Color textColor();
        public String title();
        public Image uncheckedImage();
    // Protected Instance Methods
        protected void drawBackground(Graphics g, Rect boundsRect);
        protected void drawSeparator(Graphics g, Rect boundsRect);
        protected void drawStringInRect(Graphics g, String title, Font titleFont, Rect textBounds, int justification);
}
```

Passed To: AWTCompatibility.awtMenuItemForMenuItem(), Menu.addItemAt(), Menu.indexOfItem(), Menu.removeItem(), Menu.replaceItem(), Menu.replaceItemAt(), Menu.setPrototypeItem(), MenuView.selectItem()

Returned By: Menu.addItem(), Menu.addItemAt(), Menu.addItemWithSubmenu(), Menu.addSeparator(), Menu.itemAt(), Menu.prototypeItem(), MenuView.itemForPoint(), MenuView.selectedItem()

netscape.application.MenuView

This class displays the contents of a Menu object as a View. By enclosing a Menu object in a MenuView, you can display the menu within either an InternalWindow or an ExternalWindow using the IFC menuing system. Without a MenuView, a Menu can only be displayed in an ExternalWindow using the native AWT menuing system.

You typically create a MenuView by passing the desired Menu object to its constructor. You display a MenuView in an InternalWindow or ExternalWindow by passing it to the window's setMenuView() method.

```
public class MenuView extends View {
    // Public Constructors
        public MenuView();
        public MenuView(Menu aMenu);
        public MenuView(int x, int y, int width, int height);
```

$\rightarrow$

```
    public MenuView(int x, int y, int width, int height, Menu aMenu);
    public MenuView(int x, int y, int width, int height, Menu aMenu, MenuView anOwner);
// Constants
    public static final int HORIZONTAL;
    public static final int VERTICAL;
// Public Instance Variables
    public MenuView child;
    public MenuView owner;
// Public Instance Methods
    public Color backgroundColor();
    public Border border();
    public void decode(Decoder decoder) throws CodingException;  // Overrides View
    public void describeClassInfo(ClassInfo info);  // Overrides View
    public void deselectItem();
    public void drawItemAt(int index);
    public void drawView(Graphics g);  // Overrides View
    public void encode(Encoder encoder) throws CodingException;  // Overrides View
    public void finishDecoding() throws CodingException;  // Overrides View
    public void hide();
    public Rect interiorRect();
    public boolean isTransparent();  // Overrides View
    public boolean isVisible();
    public MenuItem itemForPoint(int x, int y);
    public int itemHeight();
    public Menu menu();
    public int minItemHeight();
    public int minItemWidth();
    public Size minSize();  // Overrides View
    public boolean mouseDown(MouseEvent event);  // Overrides View
    public void mouseDragged(MouseEvent event);  // Overrides View
    public void mouseEntered(MouseEvent event);  // Overrides View
    public void mouseExited(MouseEvent event);  // Overrides View
    public void mouseMoved(MouseEvent event);  // Overrides View
    public void mouseUp(MouseEvent event);  // Overrides View
    public MenuView owner();
    public Rect rectForItemAt(int index);
    public void selectItem(MenuItem item);
    public int selectedIndex();
    public MenuItem selectedItem();
    public void setItemHeight(int height);
    public void setMenu(Menu theMenu);
    public void setOwner(MenuView menuView);
    public void setTransparent(boolean flag);
    public void setType(int aType);
    public void show(RootView rootView, MouseEvent event);
    public int type();
    public boolean wantsAutoscrollEvents();  // Overrides View
// Protected Instance Methods
    protected MenuView createMenuView(Menu theMenu);
    protected InternalWindow createMenuWindow();
}
```

Passed To: ExternalWindow.setMenuView(), InternalWindow.setMenuView(), MenuView(), MenuView.setOwner(), Window.setMenuView()

Returned By: ExternalWindow.menuView(), InternalWindow.menuView(), MenuView.createMenuView(), MenuView.owner(), Window.menuView()

Type Of: MenuView.child, MenuView.owner

---

netscape.application.MouseEvent

This subclass of Event represents an IFC mouse event. The inherited type field specifies the type of event; its value is one of the MOUSE_ constants. The x and y fields specify the coordinates of the mouse relative to the View in which the event occurred. Various methods allow you to check whether modifier keys were pressed when the event occurred. clickCount() returns the number of times that the mouse was clicked (without moving). It will return 2 for double-clicks.

```
public class MouseEvent extends Event {
// Public Constructors
    public MouseEvent();
    public MouseEvent(long timeStamp, int type, int x, int y, int modifiers);
// Constants
    public static final int MOUSE_DOWN;
    public static final int MOUSE_DRAGGED;
    public static final int MOUSE_ENTERED;
    public static final int MOUSE_EXITED;
    public static final int MOUSE_MOVED;
    public static final int MOUSE_UP;
// Public Instance Variables
    public int x;
    public int y;
// Public Instance Methods
    public int clickCount();
    public boolean isAltKeyDown();
    public boolean isControlKeyDown();
    public boolean isMetaKeyDown();
    public boolean isShiftKeyDown();
    public int modifiers();
    public RootView rootView();
    public void setClickCount(int count);
    public void setModifiers(int modifiers);
    public void setRootView(RootView rootView);
    public String toString(); // Overrides Object
}
```

Hierarchy: Object→Event(Cloneable)→MouseEvent

Passed To: many methods, including various mouseDown(), mouseDragged(), and mouseUp() methods

Returned By: View.convertEventToView()

netscape.application.PackConstraints

This class stores the "constraints" that tell the PackLayout layout manager how to lay out a subview of the View that it manages. You may specify constraints by passing them to the constructor, or by setting them individually through the various methods. The ANCHOR_ constants are values for the anchor constraint, and the SIDE_ constants are values for the side constraint.

```
public class PackConstraints extends Object implements Codable, Cloneable {
// Public Constructors
    public PackConstraints();
    public PackConstraints(int anchor, boolean expand, boolean fillX, boolean fillY, int iPadX, int iPadY,
                           int padX, int padY, int side);
// Constants
    public static final int ANCHOR_CENTER;
    public static final int ANCHOR_EAST;
    public static final int ANCHOR_NORTH;
    public static final int ANCHOR_NORTHEAST;
    public static final int ANCHOR_NORTHWEST;
    public static final int ANCHOR_SOUTH;
    public static final int ANCHOR_SOUTHEAST;
    public static final int ANCHOR_SOUTHWEST;
    public static final int ANCHOR_WEST;
    public static final int SIDE_BOTTOM;
    public static final int SIDE_LEFT;
    public static final int SIDE_RIGHT;
    public static final int SIDE_TOP;
// Public Instance Methods
    public int anchor();
    public Object clone();  // Overrides Object
    public void decode(Decoder decoder) throws CodingException;  // From Codable
    public void describeClassInfo(ClassInfo info);  // From Codable
    public void encode(Encoder encoder) throws CodingException;  // From Codable
    public boolean expand();
    public boolean fillX();
    public boolean fillY();
    public void finishDecoding() throws CodingException;  // From Codable
    public int internalPadX();
    public int internalPadY();
    public int padX();
    public int padY();
    public void setAnchor(int value);
    public void setExpand(boolean value);
    public void setFillX(boolean value);
    public void setFillY(boolean value);
    public void setInternalPadX(int value);
    public void setInternalPadY(int value);
    public void setPadX(int value);
    public void setPadY(int value);
    public void setSide(int value);
    public int side();
}
```

netscape.application.PackLayout

This class implements the LayoutManager interface and arranges the subviews of the View it manages according to constraints specified in a PackConstraints object for each subview. The layout algorithm it uses is a complex one and is described, along with the meaning of each of the constraints, in Chapter 15, *Layout Managers*. When using the PackLayout, you must explicitly call the layoutView() method of the View being managed after subviews are added or removed from it. When doing this, specify both arguments as 0.

```
public class PackLayout extends Object implements LayoutManager, Codable {
// Public Constructor
    public PackLayout( );
// Public Instance Methods
    public void addSubview(View aView); // From LayoutManager
    public PackConstraints constraintsFor(View aView);
    public void decode(Decoder decoder) throws CodingException; // From Codable
    public PackConstraints defaultConstraints( );
    public void describeClassInfo(ClassInfo info); // From Codable
    public void encode(Encoder encoder) throws CodingException; // From Codable
    public void finishDecoding( ) throws CodingException; // From Codable
    public void layoutView(View aView, int deltaWidth, int deltaHeight); // From LayoutManager
    public Size preferredLayoutSize(View target);
    public void removeSubview(View aView); // From LayoutManager
    public void setConstraints(View aView, PackConstraints constraints);
    public void setDefaultConstraints(PackConstraints constraints);
}
```

netscape.application.Point

This trivial class represents a two-dimensional point, with x and y coordinates. It is similar to the java.awt.Point class, but has methods to support IFC archiving.

```
public class Point extends Object implements Codable {
// Public Constructors
    public Point( );
    public Point(int x, int y);
    public Point(Point templatePoint);
// Public Instance Variables
    public int x;
    public int y;
// Public Instance Methods
    public void decode(Decoder decoder) throws CodingException; // From Codable
    public void describeClassInfo(ClassInfo info); // From Codable
    public void encode(Encoder encoder) throws CodingException; // From Codable
    public boolean equals(Object anObject); // Overrides Object
    public void finishDecoding( ) throws CodingException; // From Codable
    public int hashCode( ); // Overrides Object
```

$\rightarrow$

```
       public void moveBy(int deltaX, int deltaY);
       public void moveTo(int x, int y);
       public String toString();  // Overrides Object
}
```

Passed To: InternalWindow.willMoveTo(), Point(), Polygon.containsPoint(), Rect.contains(), View.convertPointToView(), View.convertToView()

Returned By: Application.keyboardArrowHotSpot(), Application.keyboardArrowLocation(), DragSession.absoluteMousePoint(), DragSession.destinationMousePoint(), Graphics.translation(), RootView.mousePoint(), View.convertPointToView(), View.convertToView()

netscape.application.Polygon

This simple class represents a polygon as arrays of x and y coordinates. The vertices of the polygon may be passed to the constructor, or specified individually with the addPoint() method. This class is similar to the java.awt.Polygon class, but has methods to support IFC archiving.

```
public class Polygon extends Object implements Codable {
    // Public Constructors
       public Polygon();
       public Polygon(int[] xPoints, int[] yPoints, int numPoints);
    // Public Instance Variables
       public int numPoints;
       public int[] xPoints;
       public int[] yPoints;
    // Public Instance Methods
       public void addPoint(int x, int y);
       public Rect boundingRect();
       public boolean containsPoint(int x, int y);
       public boolean containsPoint(Point aPoint);
       public void decode(Decoder decoder) throws CodingException;  // From Codable
       public void describeClassInfo(ClassInfo info);  // From Codable
       public void encode(Encoder encoder) throws CodingException;  // From Codable
       public void finishDecoding() throws CodingException;  // From Codable
       public void moveBy(int deltaX, int deltaY);
}
```

Passed To: Graphics.drawPolygon(), Graphics.fillPolygon()

netscape.application.Popup

This View subclass implements a "dropdown menu" or "option menu." It normally looks something like a button, but when clicked on it pops up a window that contains a ListView with various PopupItem objects. The addItem() method is the easiest way to add items to a Popup, but you can also use popupList() to obtain the internal ListView and add items directly to it. setCommand() specifies a command string for the Popup. This string is used when a list item that does not have its own command string is selected. Use `setPopupImage()` to customize the image displayed next to the currently selected item.

```
public class Popup extends View implements Target, FormElement {
// Public Constructors
    public Popup();
    public Popup(Rect rect);
    public Popup(int x, int y, int width, int height);
// Constants
    public static final String POPUP;
    public static final String SELECT_NEXT_ITEM;
    public static final String SELECT_PREVIOUS_ITEM;
// Public Instance Methods
    public ListItem addItem(String title, String command);
    public Border border();
    public boolean canBecomeSelectedView();  // Overrides View
    public String command();
    public int count();
    public void decode(Decoder decoder) throws CodingException;  // Overrides View
    public void describeClassInfo(ClassInfo info);  // Overrides View
    public void drawView(Graphics g);  // Overrides View
    public void encode(Encoder encoder) throws CodingException;  // Overrides View
    public String formElementText();  // From FormElement
    public void hidePopupIfNeeded();  // Undocumented
    public boolean isEnabled();
    public boolean isTransparent();  // Overrides View
    public ListItem itemAt(int index);
    public Size minSize();  // Overrides View
    public boolean mouseDown(MouseEvent event);  // Overrides View
    public void performCommand(String command, Object data);  // From Target
    public Image popupImage();
    public ListView popupList();
    public Window popupWindow();
    public ListItem prototypeItem();
    public void removeAllItems();
    public void removeItem(String title);
    public void removeItemAt(int index);
    public void selectItem(ListItem item);
    public void selectItemAt(int index);
    public int selectedIndex();
    public ListItem selectedItem();
    public void sendCommand();
    public void setBorder(Border aBorder);
    public void setCommand(String newCommand);
    public void setEnabled(boolean flag);
    public void setPopupImage(Image anImage);
    public void setPopupList(ListView list);
    public void setPopupWindow(Window window);
    public void setPrototypeItem(ListItem item);
    public void setTarget(Target newTarget);
    public boolean showingPopupForKeyboard();  // Undocumented
    public Target target();
```

$\rightarrow$

```
    // Protected Instance Methods
        protected void ancestorWillRemoveFromViewHierarchy(View view); // Overrides View
        protected void layoutPopupWindow();
        protected void showPopupWindow(MouseEvent event);
}
```

Hierarchy: Object→View(Codable)→Popup(Target, FormElement)

Passed To: PopupItem.setPopup()

Returned By: PopupItem.popup()

netscape.application.PopupItem

This subclass of ListItem is used in the ListView maintained by a Popup. It differs from a ListItem in that it displays a special image if the PopupItem is the currently selected one in the Popup. This image can be set with the setPopupImage() method of Popup.

```
public class PopupItem extends ListItem {
    // Public Constructor
        public PopupItem();
    // Public Instance Methods
        public void decode(Decoder decoder) throws CodingException; // Overrides ListItem
        public void describeClassInfo(ClassInfo info); // Overrides ListItem
        public void drawInRect(Graphics g, Rect boundsRect); // Overrides ListItem
        public void encode(Encoder encoder) throws CodingException; // Overrides ListItem
        public Popup popup();
        public void setPopup(Popup aPopup);
}
```

Hierarchy: Object→ListItem(Cloneable, Codable)→PopupItem

netscape.application.Range

A Range represents a set of contiguous integers specified as a starting position, or "index," and a length. The index and length fields store this index and length. It is typically used with the TextView to represent a subset of the displayed text. The various methods perform unions and intersections on ranges, and test whether an integer or Range is within another Range.

```
public class Range extends Object implements Codable {
    // Public Constructors
        public Range();
        public Range(int index, int length);
        public Range(Range templateRange);
    // Public Instance Variables
        public int index;
        public int length;
    // Class Methods
        public static Range nullRange();
```

```
        public static Range rangeFromIndices(int index1, int index2);
        public static Range rangeFromIntersection(Range range1, Range range2);
        public static Range rangeFromUnion(Range range1, Range range2);
   // Public Instance Methods
        public boolean contains(int anIndex);
        public void decode(Decoder decoder) throws CodingException;  // From Codable
        public void describeClassInfo(ClassInfo info);  // From Codable
        public void encode(Encoder encoder) throws CodingException;  // From Codable
        public boolean equals(Object anObject);  // Overrides Object
        public void finishDecoding() throws CodingException;  // From Codable
        public int index();
        public void intersectWith(Range aRange);
        public void intersectWith(int anIndex, int aLength);
        public boolean intersects(Range aRange);
        public boolean intersects(int anIndex, int aLength);
        public boolean isEmpty();
        public boolean isNullRange();
        public int lastIndex();
        public int length();
        public String toString();  // Overrides Object
        public void unionWith(Range aRange);
        public void unionWith(int anIndex, int aLength);
}
```

Passed To: Range(), Range.intersects(), Range.intersectWith(), Range.rangeFromIntersection(), Range.rangeFromUnion(), Range.unionWith(), TextField.replaceRangeWithString(), TextField.selectRange(), TextField.stringForRange(), TextView.addAttributeForRange(), TextView.addAttributesForRange(), TextView.importHTMLInRange(), TextView.insertHTMLElementsInRange(), TextView.paragraphsForRange(), TextView.rectsForRange(), TextView.removeAttributeForRange(), TextView.replaceRangeWithString(), TextView.replaceRangeWithTextAttachment(), TextView.runsForRange(), TextView.scrollRangeToVisible(), TextView.selectRange(), TextView.setAttributesForRange(), TextView.stringForRange(), TextViewOwner.attributesDidChange(), TextViewOwner.attributesWillChange(), TextViewOwner.linkWasSelected(), TextViewOwner.textDidChange(), TextViewOwner.textWillChange()

Returned By: Range.nullRange(), Range.rangeFromIndices(), Range.rangeFromIntersection(), Range.rangeFromUnion(), TextField.selectedRange(), TextView.appendString(), TextView.paragraphForIndex(), TextView.paragraphForPoint(), TextView.runForIndex(), TextView.runForPoint(), TextView.runWithLinkDestinationNamed(), TextView.selectedRange()

---

netscape.application.Rect

This class represents a rectangle, specified as the x and y coordinates of the upper-left corner, and a width and height. These values are stored in the x, y, width, and height fields. The various methods perform intersections and unions on Rect objects, and test whether points are inside of a Rect. Rect is similar to java.awt.Rectangle, but defines methods to support IFC archiving.

```
public class Rect extends Object implements Codable {
   // Public Constructors
        public Rect();
        public Rect(int x, int y, int width, int height);
        public Rect(Rect templateRect);
```

→

```
// Public Instance Variables
    public int height;
    public int width;
    public int x;
    public int y;
// Class Methods
    public static boolean contains(int x, int y, int width, int height, int pointX, int pointY);
    public static Rect rectFromIntersection(Rect rect1, Rect rect2);
    public static Rect rectFromUnion(Rect rect1, Rect rect2);
// Public Instance Methods
    public void computeDisunionRects(Rect aRect, Vector rects);
    public boolean contains(int x, int y);
    public boolean contains(Point aPoint);
    public boolean contains(Rect aRect);
    public void decode(Decoder decoder) throws CodingException; // From Codable
    public void describeClassInfo(ClassInfo info); // From Codable
    public void encode(Encoder encoder) throws CodingException; // From Codable
    public boolean equals(Object anObject); // Overrides Object
    public void finishDecoding() throws CodingException; // From Codable
    public void growBy(int deltaX, int deltaY);
    public int hashCode(); // Overrides Object
    public void intersectWith(int x, int y, int width, int height);
    public void intersectWith(Rect aRect);
    public Rect intersectionRect(Rect aRect);
    public boolean intersects(int x, int y, int width, int height);
    public boolean intersects(Rect aRect);
    public boolean isEmpty();
    public int maxX();
    public int maxY();
    public int midX();
    public int midY();
    public void moveBy(int deltaX, int deltaY);
    public void moveTo(int x, int y);
    public void setBounds(int x, int y, int width, int height);
    public void setBounds(Rect rect);
    public void setCoordinates(int x1, int y1, int x2, int y2);
    public void sizeBy(int deltaWidth, int deltaHeight);
    public void sizeTo(int width, int height);
    public String toString(); // Overrides Object
    public Rect unionRect(Rect aRect);
    public void unionWith(int x, int y, int width, int height);
    public void unionWith(Rect aRect);
}
```

Passed To: AWTComponentView(), many methods

Returned By: many methods

Type Of: View.bounds

This View subclass serves as the top or "root" of the view hierarchy. Each applet and ExternalWindow has an automatically created RootView. RootView displays nothing except a background color or background image, which you can specify with setColor() or setImage().

```
public class RootView extends View implements EventProcessor, ExtendedTarget {
// Public Constructors
     public RootView();
     public RootView(Rect rect);
     public RootView(int x, int y, int width, int height);
// Public Instance Methods
     public boolean canBecomeSelectedView(); // Overrides View
     public boolean canDraw(); // Overrides View. Undocumented
     public boolean canPerformCommand(String command); // From ExtendedTarget
     public Color color();
     public ColorChooser colorChooser();
     public int cursor();
     public View defaultSelectedView();
     public void draw(Graphics g, Rect aRect); // Overrides View
     public synchronized void drawDirtyViews();
     public void drawView(Graphics g); // Overrides View
     public ExternalWindow externalWindow();
     public View focusedView();
     public FontChooser fontChooser();
     public Image image();
     public int imageDisplayStyle();
     public Vector internalWindows();
     public boolean isTransparent(); // Overrides View
     public boolean isVisible();
     public InternalWindow mainWindow();
     public boolean mouseDown(MouseEvent event); // Overrides View
     public Point mousePoint();
     public boolean mouseStillDown(); // Undocumented
     public View mouseView();
     public FoundationPanel panel();
     public void performCommand(String command, Object data); // From Target
     public void processEvent(Event event); // From EventProcessor
     public void redraw(Rect aRect);
     public boolean redrawAll(); // Undocumented
     public void redrawTransparentWindows(Rect clipRect,
                                     InternalWindow aboveWindow); // Undocumented
     public void redrawTransparentWindows(Graphics g, Rect clipRect,
                                     InternalWindow aboveWindow); // Undocumented
     public void removeOverrideCursor();
     public synchronized void resetDirtyViews();
     public RootView rootView(); // Overrides View
     public void selectView(View newSelectedView, boolean abortCurrentEditing);
     public void selectViewAfter(View aView);
     public void selectViewBefore(View aView);
     public void setColor(Color aColor);
```

$\rightarrow$

```
        public void setDefaultSelectedView(View aView);
        public void setFocusedView(View view); // Overrides View
        public void setImage(Image anImage);
        public void setImageDisplayStyle(int aStyle);
        public void setMouseView(View aView);
        public void setOverrideCursor(int cursorIdent);
        public void setRedrawAll(boolean flag); // Undocumented
        public void setWindowClipView(View aView); // Undocumented
        public void showColorChooser();
        public void showFontChooser();
        public void subviewDidMove(View aView); // Overrides View. Undocumented
        public void subviewDidResize(View aView); // Overrides View. Undocumented
        public void updateCursor();
        public void updateCursorLater();
        public boolean viewExcludedFromModalSession(View aView);
        public View viewForMouse(int x, int y); // Overrides View
        public View windowClipView(); // Undocumented
}
```

Hierarchy: Object→View(Codable)→RootView(EventProcessor, ExtendedTarget(Target))

Passed To: Application.setMainRootView(), AWTCompatibility.awtFrameForRootView(), AWTCompatibility.awtPanelForRootView(), FileChooser(), FoundationPanel.setRootView(), InternalWindow.setRootView(), KeyEvent.setRootView(), MenuView.show(), MouseEvent.setRootView()

Returned By: Application.mainRootView(), ExternalWindow.rootView(), FoundationPanel.rootView(), KeyEvent.rootView(), MouseEvent.rootView(), RootView.rootView(), View.rootView()

---

netscape.application.ScrollBar

This class is a View that implements a graphical scrollbar. You must connect it to an object that implements the Scrollable interface by calling setScrollable-Object(). It is often easier to use a ScrollGroup instead.

ScrollBar does not have a target and command; rather, it notifies its Scrollable object of any scrolling. ScrollBar does define the Target interface itself, however, and can respond to the commands specified by the SCROLL_ class constants.

```
public class ScrollBar extends View implements Target {
    // Public Constructors
        public ScrollBar();
        public ScrollBar(Rect rect);
        public ScrollBar(int x, int y, int width, int height);
        public ScrollBar(int x, int y, int width, int height, int theAxis);
    // Constants
        public static final int DEFAULT_HEIGHT; // Undocumented
        public static final int DEFAULT_LINE_INCREMENT;
        public static final float DEFAULT_PAGE_SIZE;
        public static final int DEFAULT_WIDTH; // Undocumented
        public static final String SCROLL_LINE_BACKWARD;
        public static final String SCROLL_LINE_FORWARD;
        public static final String SCROLL_PAGE_BACKWARD;
```

```
        public static final String SCROLL_PAGE_FORWARD;
        public static final String UPDATE;
// Public Instance Methods
    public void addParts();
    public int axis();
    public void decode(Decoder decoder) throws CodingException;  // Overrides View
    public Button decreaseButton();
    public void describeClassInfo(ClassInfo info);  // Overrides View
    public void didSizeBy(int deltaWidth, int deltaHeight);  // Overrides View
    public void drawScrollTray();
    public void drawView(Graphics g);  // Overrides View
    public void drawViewKnobInRect(Graphics g, Rect rect);
    public void encode(Encoder encoder) throws CodingException;  // Overrides View
    public boolean hidesSubviewsFromKeyboard();  // Overrides View
    public Button increaseButton();
    public Rect interiorRect();
    public boolean isActive();
    public boolean isEnabled();
    public boolean isTransparent();  // Overrides View
    public Image knobImage();
    public int knobLength();
    public Rect knobRect();
    public int lineIncrement();
    public int minKnobLength();
    public Size minSize();  // Overrides View
    public boolean mouseDown(MouseEvent event);  // Overrides View
    public void mouseDragged(MouseEvent event);  // Overrides View
    public void mouseUp(MouseEvent event);  // Overrides View
    public float pageSizeAsPercent();
    public void performCommand(String command, Object data);  // From Target
    public void removeParts();
    public ScrollBarOwner scrollBarOwner();
    public void scrollLineBackward();
    public void scrollLineForward();
    public void scrollPageBackward();
    public void scrollPageForward();
    public float scrollPercent();
    public void scrollToCurrentPosition();
    public int scrollTrayLength();
    public Rect scrollTrayRect();
    public int scrollValue();
    public Scrollable scrollableObject();
    public void setActive(boolean value);
    public void setDecreaseButton(Button aButton);
    public void setEnabled(boolean value);
    public void setIncreaseButton(Button aButton);
    public void setKnobImage(Image anImage);
    public void setKnobLength(int newKnobLength);
    public void setLineIncrement(int value);
    public void setPageSizeAsPercent(float value);
    public void setScrollBarOwner(ScrollBarOwner owner);
```

→

```
        public void setScrollPercent(float value);
        public void setScrollableObject(Scrollable aScrollableView);
}
```

Hierarchy: Object→View(Codable)→ScrollBar(Target)

Passed To: ScrollBarOwner.scrollBarDidBecomeActive(), ScrollBarOwner.scrollBarDidBecomeInactive(),
ScrollBarOwner.scrollBarWasDisabled(), ScrollBarOwner.scrollBarWasEnabled(),
ScrollGroup.scrollBarDidBecomeActive(), ScrollGroup.scrollBarDidBecomeInactive(),
ScrollGroup.scrollBarWasDisabled(), ScrollGroup.scrollBarWasEnabled()

Returned By: ScrollGroup.createScrollBar(), ScrollGroup.horizScrollBar(), ScrollGroup.vertScrollBar()

---

netscape.application.ScrollBarOwner

This interface should be implemented by objects that want to be notified of
changes to a scrollbar's state. When registered by calling the setScrollBar-
Owner() method of a ScrollBar, the methods defined by this interface will be
invoked when appropriate changes occur on the scrollbar. Notice that these methods are invoked for changes in the state of the ScrollBar, not when the scrollbar
scrolls. Methods of the Scrollable interface are notified when scrolling occurs.

```
public abstract interface ScrollBarOwner {
  // Public Instance Methods
        public abstract void scrollBarDidBecomeActive(ScrollBar aScrollBar);
        public abstract void scrollBarDidBecomeInactive(ScrollBar aScrollBar);
        public abstract void scrollBarWasDisabled(ScrollBar aScrollBar);
        public abstract void scrollBarWasEnabled(ScrollBar aScrollBar);
}
```

Implemented By: ScrollGroup

Passed To: ScrollBar.setScrollBarOwner()

Returned By: ScrollBar.scrollBarOwner()

---

netscape.application.ScrollGroup

This class combines a ScrollView object with vertical and/or horizontal scrollbars.
It is the most common and easiest way to perform simple scrolling of one large
View within a smaller area. Use setContentView() to specify the View to be
scrolled within the automatically created ScrollView object. Call setHasHor-
izScrollBar() and setHasVertScrollBar() to specify whether the ScrollGroup
should create and display horizontal and vertical ScrollBar objects on the bottom
and right of the ScrollView. Use setHorizScrollBarDisplay() and set-
VertScrollBarDisplay() to specify the "display policy" for the scrollbars. The
argument to these methods should be one of the constants defined by this class.

```
public class ScrollGroup extends View implements ScrollBarOwner {
  // Public Constructors
        public ScrollGroup();
        public ScrollGroup(Rect rect);
```

```
        public ScrollGroup(int x, int y, int width, int height);
    // Constants
        public static final int ALWAYS_DISPLAY;
        public static final int AS_NEEDED_DISPLAY;
        public static final int NEVER_DISPLAY;
    // Public Instance Methods
        public Border border();
        public View contentView();
        public void decode(Decoder decoder) throws CodingException; // Overrides View
        public void describeClassInfo(ClassInfo info); // Overrides View
        public void drawContents();
        public void drawSubviews(Graphics g); // Overrides View. Undocumented
        public void drawView(Graphics g); // Overrides View
        public void encode(Encoder encoder) throws CodingException; // Overrides View
        public boolean hasHorizScrollBar();
        public boolean hasVertScrollBar();
        public ScrollBar horizScrollBar();
        public int horizScrollBarDisplay();
        public boolean horizScrollBarIsVisible();
        public boolean isTransparent(); // Overrides View
        public void layoutView(int x, int y); // Overrides View
        public Size minSize(); // Overrides View
        public void scrollBarDidBecomeActive(ScrollBar aScrollBar); // From ScrollBarOwner
        public void scrollBarDidBecomeInactive(ScrollBar aScrollBar); // From ScrollBarOwner
        public void scrollBarWasDisabled(ScrollBar aScrollBar); // From ScrollBarOwner
        public void scrollBarWasEnabled(ScrollBar aScrollBar); // From ScrollBarOwner
        public ScrollView scrollView();
        public void setBackgroundColor(Color aColor);
        public void setBorder(Border newBorder);
        public void setContentView(View aView);
        public void setCornerColor(Color aColor); // Undocumented
        public void setHasHorizScrollBar(boolean flag);
        public void setHasVertScrollBar(boolean flag);
        public void setHorizScrollBarDisplay(int flag);
        public void setVertScrollBarDisplay(int flag);
        public ScrollBar vertScrollBar();
        public int vertScrollBarDisplay();
        public boolean vertScrollBarIsVisible();
    // Protected Instance Methods
        protected ScrollBar createScrollBar(boolean horizontal);
        protected ScrollView createScrollView();
}
```

Hierarchy: Object→View(Codable)→ScrollGroup(ScrollBarOwner)

---

netscape.application.ScrollView

This is a class that implements the Scrollable interface and can be used to display and scroll a portion of a larger View within its (usually smaller) bounds. Use setContentView() to specify the View that is to be scrolled and displayed within those bounds. Note that ScrollView does not create any ScrollBar objects—you

→

netscape.application.ScrollView   273

must create and manage those yourself, or use the `ScrollGroup` class, which handles this for you automatically.

```
public class ScrollView extends View implements Scrollable {
  // Public Constructors
      public ScrollView();
      public ScrollView(Rect rect);
      public ScrollView(int x, int y, int width, int height);
  // Public Instance Methods
      public DragDestination acceptsDrag(DragSession session, int x, int y); // Overrides View
      public void addScrollBar(Target aScrollBar);
      public void addSubview(View aView); // Overrides View
      public Color backgroundColor();
      public void computeVisibleRect(Rect aRect); // Overrides View
      public View contentView();
      public int cursorForPoint(int x, int y); // Overrides View
      public void decode(Decoder decoder) throws CodingException; // Overrides View
      public void describeClassInfo(ClassInfo info); // Overrides View
      public void didSizeBy(int deltaWidth, int deltaHeight); // Overrides View
      public void drawSubviews(Graphics g); // Overrides View
      public void drawView(Graphics g); // Overrides View
      public void encode(Encoder encoder) throws CodingException; // Overrides View
      public boolean isTransparent(); // Overrides View
      public int lengthOfContentViewForAxis(int axis); // From Scrollable
      public int lengthOfScrollViewForAxis(int axis); // From Scrollable
      public boolean mouseDown(MouseEvent event); // Overrides View
      public int positionOfContentViewForAxis(int axis); // From Scrollable
      public void removeScrollBar(Target aScrollBar);
      public boolean scrollBarUpdatesEnabled();
      public void scrollBy(int deltaX, int deltaY); // From Scrollable
      public void scrollRectToVisible(Rect contentRect); // Overrides View
      public void scrollTo(int x, int y); // From Scrollable
      public void setBackgroundColor(Color aColor);
      public void setContentView(View aView);
      public void setScrollBarUpdatesEnabled(boolean flag);
      public void setTransparent(boolean flag);
      public void subviewDidResize(View aSubview); // Overrides View
      public void updateScrollBars();
}
```

Hierarchy: Object→View(Codable)→ScrollView(Scrollable)

Returned By: ScrollGroup.createScrollView(), ScrollGroup.scrollView()

---

netscape.application.Scrollable

This interface defines the methods required for an object that is to be controlled by a `ScrollBar`. `ScrollView` is one such item that is commonly used. `scrollBy()` is called to cause a relative scroll. `scrollTo()` is called to cause an absolute scroll. `lengthOfContentViewForAxis()` should return the full size of the object being scrolled in either the horizontal or vertical dimension, according to the argument, which will be one of the constants defined by the class. Similarly, `lengthOf-ScrollViewForAxis()` should return the length of the visible portion of the object being scrolled—this will serve as the length of the `ScrollBar` "knob." Finally, `positionOfContentViewForAxis()` should return the current position of the object in the specified dimension. Somewhat counterintuitively, this is usually a negative number indicating the position of the origin of the content view relative to the origin of the scroll view.

```
public abstract interface Scrollable {
    // Constants
        public static final int HORIZONTAL;
        public static final int VERTICAL;
    // Public Instance Methods
        public abstract int lengthOfContentViewForAxis(int axis);
        public abstract int lengthOfScrollViewForAxis(int axis);
        public abstract int positionOfContentViewForAxis(int axis);
        public abstract void scrollBy(int deltaX, int deltaY);
        public abstract void scrollTo(int x, int y);
}
```

Implemented By: ScrollView

Passed To: ScrollBar.setScrollableObject()

Returned By: ScrollBar.scrollableObject()

---

netscape.application.Size

This simple class represents an integer width and height of something. The `width` and `height` fields contain the obvious values. This class is similar to the `java.awt.Dimension` class, but has methods to support IFC archiving.

```
public class Size extends Object implements Codable {
    // Public Constructors
        public Size();
        public Size(int width, int height);
        public Size(Size templateSize);
    // Public Instance Variables
        public int height;
        public int width;
    // Public Instance Methods
        public void decode(Decoder decoder) throws CodingException; // From Codable
        public void describeClassInfo(ClassInfo info); // From Codable
        public void encode(Encoder encoder) throws CodingException; // From Codable
        public boolean equals(Object anObject); // Overrides Object
        public void finishDecoding() throws CodingException; // From Codable
        public int hashCode(); // Overrides Object
        public boolean isEmpty();
        public void sizeBy(int deltaWidth, int deltaHeight);
        public void sizeTo(int width, int height);
        public String toString(); // Overrides Object
        public void union(Size aSize);
}
```

Passed To: Plan.setSize(), Size(), Size.union(), WindowOwner.windowWillSizeBy()

Returned By: Button.imageAreaSize(), Button.minSize(), ContainerView.minSize(), ExternalWindow.contentSize(), ExternalWindow.minSize(), ExternalWindow.windowSizeForContentSize(), FontMetrics.stringSize(), GridLayout.gridSize(), ImageSequence.maxSize(), InternalWindow.contentSize(), InternalWindow.minSize(), InternalWindow.windowSizeForContentSize(), Label.minSize(), ListView.minSize(), MenuView.minSize(), PackLayout.preferredLayoutSize(), Plan.size(), Popup.minSize(), ScrollBar.minSize(), ScrollGroup.minSize(), Slider.minSize(), TextField.minSize(), View.minSize(), Window.contentSize(), Window.minSize(), Window.windowSizeForContentSize()

---

netscape.application.Slider

This class is a View that is similar to a ScrollBar except that it does not have buttons at either end. setLimits() specifies the minimum and maximum values represented by the Slider, and setValue() specifies the current value (i.e., the position of the "knob" displayed by the Slider.) setIncrementResolution() specifies how many divisions the slider's range should be divided into for the purposes of keyboard navigation of the Slider.

When the user drags the knob, the Slider sends its command string to its target. The receiving target can call the Slider's value() method to determine the current position. Slider implements the Target interface itself, and can accept commands to increase or decrease its value. The constants defined by the class provide the command strings for these actions.

```
public class Slider extends View implements Target, FormElement {
    // Public Constructors
        public Slider();
        public Slider(Rect rect);
        public Slider(int x, int y, int width, int height);
    // Constants
        public static final String DECREASE_VALUE;
        public static final String INCREASE_VALUE;
    // Public Instance Methods
        public Color backgroundColor();
        public Border border();
        public boolean canBecomeSelectedView();  // Overrides View
        public String command();
        public void decode(Decoder decoder) throws CodingException;  // Overrides View
        public void describeClassInfo(ClassInfo info);  // Overrides View
        public void didSizeBy(int deltaWidth, int deltaHeight);  // Overrides View
        public void drawView(Graphics g);  // Overrides View
        public void drawViewGroove(Graphics g);
        public void drawViewKnob(Graphics g);
        public void encode(Encoder encoder) throws CodingException;  // Overrides View
        public String formElementText();  // From FormElement
        public int grooveHeight();
        public Image image();
        public int imageDisplayStyle();
        public int incrementResolution();
        public boolean isEnabled();
        public int knobHeight();
        public Image knobImage();
```

```
    public Rect knobRect( );
    public int knobWidth( );
    public int maxValue( );
    public Size minSize( ); // Overrides View
    public int minValue( );
    public boolean mouseDown(MouseEvent event); // Overrides View
    public void mouseDragged(MouseEvent event); // Overrides View
    public void performCommand(String command, Object data); // From Target
    public void sendCommand( );
    public void setBackgroundColor(Color aColor);
    public void setBorder(Border newBorder);
    public void setCommand(String command);
    public void setEnabled(boolean enabled);
    public void setGrooveHeight(int anInt);
    public void setImage(Image anImage);
    public void setImageDisplayStyle(int aStyle);
    public void setIncrementResolution(int aValue);
    public void setKnobHeight(int anInt);
    public void setKnobImage(Image anImage);
    public void setLimits(int minValue, int maxValue);
    public void setTarget(Target aTarget);
    public void setValue(int aValue);
    public Target target( );
    public int value( );
}
```

Hierarchy: Object→View(Codable)→Slider(Target, FormElement)

---

netscape.application.Sound

This class represents a sound that can be played. play( ) plays the sound and stop( ) stops it. setLoops( ) specifies whether the sound should loop repeatedly or be played only once. You create a Sound with one of the two static methods. soundFromURL( ) loads a sound file from the specified URL. soundNamed( ) looks for a named sound file in (or beneath) the *sounds/* directory relative to the application's code base. Sound is a wrapper around the java.applet.AudioClip class and will therefore only play sounds that are encoded in an 8 bit, µlaw, 8000 Hz, one-channel, Sun *.au* file.

```
public class Sound extends Object implements Codable {
  // Public Constructor
    public Sound( );
  // Class Methods
    public static Sound soundFromURL(java.net.URL url);
    public static synchronized Sound soundNamed(String soundName);
  // Public Instance Methods
    public void decode(Decoder decoder) throws CodingException; // From Codable
    public void describeClassInfo(ClassInfo info); // From Codable
    public boolean doesLoop( );
    public void encode(Encoder encoder) throws CodingException; // From Codable
    public void finishDecoding( ) throws CodingException; // From Codable
    public String name( );
    public void play( );
```

→

```
        public void setLoops(boolean flag);
        public void stop( );
        public String toString( );  // Overrides Object
}
```

Passed To: AWTCompatibility.awtAudioClipForSound(), Button.setMouseDownSound(),
Button.setMouseUpSound()

Returned By: AWTCompatibility.soundForAWTAudioClip(), Button.mouseDownSound(),
Button.mouseUpSound(), Sound.soundFromURL(), Sound.soundNamed()

---

netscape.application.Target

This interface defines a method that an object should implement if it wants to be
able to receive requests to perform commands. The performCommand( ) method of
a Target object is invoked by some other object under certain well-defined condi-
tions. For example, the Button object may have a Target object and a command
string specified for it, and it will pass the command string to the performCom-
mand( ) method of the target object when the user clicks on the button.

```
public abstract interface Target {
  // Public Instance Methods
      public abstract void performCommand(String command, Object data);
}
```

Extended By: ExtendedTarget, Window

Implemented By: Button, ColorChooser, ColorWell, DrawingSequence, FontChooser, Label, ListView,
PlanLoader, Popup, Script, ScrollBar, Slider, TargetProxy, ViewProxy

Passed To: Application.performCommandAndWait(), Application.performCommandLater(),
Bitmap.setUpdateTarget(), Button.setTarget(), ColorWell.setTarget(), CommandEvent(),
CommandEvent.setTarget(), Label.setTarget(), ListView.setTarget(), Menu.addItem(), Menu.addItemAt(),
MenuItem(), MenuItem.setTarget(), Plan(), Plan.createPlan(), Plan.unarchiveObjects(), Popup.setTarget(),
ScrollView.addScrollBar(), ScrollView.removeScrollBar(), Slider.setTarget(),
TargetProxy.setAttributesToReplacingTarget(), TextField.setContentsChangedCommandAndTarget(),
TextField.setTarget(), Timer(), Timer.setTarget()

Returned By: Bitmap.updateTarget(), Button.target(), ColorWell.target(), CommandEvent.target(),
Label.target(), ListView.target(), MenuItem.target(), Popup.target(), Slider.target(),
TargetChain.targetForCommand(), TextField.contentsChangedTarget(), TextField.target(), Timer.target()

---

netscape.application.TargetChain

This class is an ExtendedTarget that searches a number of standard places to find
a Target to perform a specified command. Use the static applicationChain( )
method to obtain a TargetChain instance. Use addTarget( ) to add additional
ExtendedTarget objects to the list of targets, either at the beginning or at the end
of the standard list.

A `TargetChain` is useful for context-sensitive commands, such as **Cut** or **Paste**, that should operate on the current `View` in the current `Window`. Using an application's `TargetChain` object in place of a standard static `Target` enables this sort of context-sensitive command.

```
public class TargetChain extends Object implements ExtendedTarget {
    // No Constructor
    // Class Methods
        public static TargetChain applicationChain();
    // Public Instance Methods
        public synchronized void addTarget(ExtendedTarget target, boolean atFront);
        public boolean canPerformCommand(String command); // From ExtendedTarget
        public void performCommand(String command, Object data); // From Target
        public synchronized void removeTarget(ExtendedTarget target);
        public synchronized Target targetForCommand(String command);
}
```

Hierarchy: Object→TargetChain(ExtendedTarget(Target))

Returned By: TargetChain.applicationChain()

---

netscape.application.TextAttachment

This abstract class serves as the superclass for any object that is to be embedded ("attached") within the text displayed in a `TextView`. `ImageAttachment` is its only concrete subclass among the standard IFC classes. To implement a new type of text attachment, you must subclass `TextAttachment`, providing definitions of several important methods. The `width()` and `height()` methods should return the width and height of the attachment, and `drawInRect()` should draw the attachment in the specified `Rect` using the specified `Graphics` object. Other `TextAttachment` methods are invoked to notify the attachment of events or of changes in its visibility or other state. These methods may be optionally implemented if the attachment needs this notification. For example, an attachment type that supports drag-and-drop will implement the `mouseDown()` and `mouseDragged()` methods.

```
public abstract class TextAttachment extends Object implements Codable {
    // Default Constructor: public TextAttachment()
    // Public Instance Methods
        public void TextAttachment();
        public void boundsDidChange(Rect newBounds);
        public void decode(Decoder decoder) throws CodingException; // From Codable
        public void describeClassInfo(ClassInfo info); // From Codable
        public void drawInRect(Graphics g, Rect boundsRect);
        public void encode(Encoder encoder) throws CodingException; // From Codable
        public void finishDecoding() throws CodingException; // From Codable
        public int height();
        public boolean mouseDown(MouseEvent event);
        public void mouseDragged(MouseEvent event);
        public void mouseUp(MouseEvent event);
        public TextView owner();
        public void setHeight(int height);
        public void setOwner(TextView aTextView);
        public void setWidth(int width);
```

→

```
        public int width( );
        public void willBecomeInvisible( );
        public void willBecomeVisibleWithBounds(Rect bounds);
}
```

Extended By: ImageAttachment

Passed To: TextView.replaceRangeWithTextAttachment()

---

netscape.application.TextField

This View displays a single line of single-font text and optionally allows the user to edit it. setStringValue() sets the string to be displayed and replaceRangeWith-String() modifies a portion of that value. stringValue() returns the (possibly edited) text displayed in a TextField, stringForRange() returns a specified substring of the value, and intValue() returns the text as an integer, or returns 0 if the text is not a valid number.

TextField performs three different types of notification when events occur. set-Target() and setCommand() specify a target and command pair to notify when the user strikes the **Return** key or edits the displayed value and then ends the edit by tabbing out of the TextField or otherwise moving focus away from the Text-Field. The setContentsChangedCommandAndTarget() method specifies a separate target and command to notify whenever any change edit occurs in the TextField. Finally, the TextField also provides notification to a TextFieldOwner object specified with the setOwner() method. The notifications provided to the owner are more detailed than those provided to the two targets. A TextField can also have a TextFilter object registered with setFilter(). The TextFilter is notified of every KeyEvent that occurs in the TextField and therefore the opportunity to accept, reject, or modify every keystroke that occurs.

The TextField allows the user to select text. Various methods test whether text is selected, return the selected region, and set the selected region. A number of other methods set the value of other TextField properties. Notably, setTab-Field() and setBacktabField() specify other TextField objects that should receive keyboard focus when the user tabs out of the current one.

```
public class TextField extends View implements ExtendedTarget, FormElement {
    // Public Constructors
        public TextField( );
        public TextField(Rect rect);
        public TextField(int x, int y, int width, int height);
    // Constants
        public static final String SELECT_TEXT;
    // Class Variables
        public static char ANY_CHARACTER;
    // Class Methods
      # public static TextField createLabel(String string, Font font);
        public static TextField createLabel(String string);
    // Public Instance Methods
        public Color backgroundColor( );
        public TextField backtabField( );
```

public int **baseline**( );
public Border **border**( );
public boolean **canBecomeSelectedView**( ); // *Overrides View*
public boolean **canPerformCommand**(String *command*); // *From ExtendedTarget*
public void **cancelEditing**( );
public Color **caretColor**( );
public int **charCount**( );
public int **charNumberForPoint**(int *x*);
public String **command**( );
public void **completeEditing**( );
public String **contentsChangedCommand**( );
public Target **contentsChangedTarget**( );
public void **copy**( );
public int **cursorForPoint**(int *x*, int *y*); // *Overrides View*
public void **cut**( );
public void **decode**(Decoder *decoder*) throws CodingException; // *Overrides View*
public void **describeClassInfo**(ClassInfo *info*); // *Overrides View*
public void **drawInterior**( );
public void **drawView**(Graphics *g*); // *Overrides View*
public void **drawViewBorder**(Graphics *g*);
public void **drawViewInterior**(Graphics *g*, Rect *interiorRect*);
public void **drawViewStringAt**(Graphics *g*, String *aString*, int *x*, int *y*);
public char **drawableCharacter**( );
public boolean **drawsDropShadow**( );
public void **encode**(Encoder *encoder*) throws CodingException; // *Overrides View*
public TextFilter **filter**( );
public void **finishDecoding**( ) throws CodingException; // *Overrides View*
public Font **font**( );
public String **formElementText**( ); // *From FormElement*
public boolean **hasInsertionPoint**( );
public boolean **hasSelection**( );
public int **intValue**( );
public boolean **isBeingEdited**( );
public boolean **isEditable**( );
public boolean **isEmpty**( );
public boolean **isScrollable**( );
public boolean **isSelectable**( );
public boolean **isTransparent**( ); // *Overrides View*
public int **justification**( );
public void **keyDown**(KeyEvent *event*); // *Overrides View*
public int **leftIndent**( );
public Size **minSize**( ); // *Overrides View*
public boolean **mouseDown**(MouseEvent *event*); // *Overrides View*
public void **mouseDragged**(MouseEvent *event*); // *Overrides View*
public void **mouseUp**(MouseEvent *event*); // *Overrides View*
public View **nextSelectableView**( ); // *Overrides View*
public TextFieldOwner **owner**( );
public void **paste**( );
public void **pauseFocus**( ); // *Overrides View*
public void **performCommand**(String *command*, Object *data*); // *From Target*
public View **previousSelectableView**( ); // *Overrides View*
public void **replaceRangeWithString**(Range *aRange*, String *aString*);
public void **resumeFocus**( ); // *Overrides View*

$\rightarrow$

```
        public int rightIndent();
        public void selectRange(Range aRange);
        public void selectText();
        public Range selectedRange();
        public String selectedStringValue();
        public Color selectionColor();
        public void setBackgroundColor(Color aColor);
        public void setBacktabField(TextField aTextField);
        public void setBorder(Border newBorder);
        public void setCaretColor(Color aColor);
        public void setCommand(String aCommand);
        public void setContentsChangedCommandAndTarget(String aCommand, Target aTarget);
        public void setDrawableCharacter(char aChar);
        public void setDrawsDropShadow(boolean flag);
        public void setEditable(boolean aFlag);
        public void setFilter(TextFilter aFilter);
        public void setFocusedView();  // Overrides View
        public void setFont(Font aFont);
        public void setInsertionPoint(int position);
        public void setIntValue(int anInt);
        public void setJustification(int aJustification);
        public void setOwner(TextFieldOwner owner);
        public void setScrollable(boolean value);
        public void setSelectable(boolean flag);
        public void setSelectionColor(Color aColor);
        public void setStringValue(String aString);
        public void setTabField(TextField aTextField);
        public void setTarget(Target aTarget);
        public void setTextColor(Color aColor);
        public void setTransparent(boolean flag);
        public void setWrapsContents(boolean flag);
        public void startFocus();  // Overrides View
        public void stopFocus();  // Overrides View
        public String stringForRange(Range aRange);
        public String stringValue();
        public TextField tabField();
        public Target target();
        public Color textColor();
        public boolean wantsAutoscrollEvents();  // Overrides View
        public void willBecomeSelected();  // Overrides View
        public boolean wrapsContents();
        public int xPositionOfCharacter(int charNumber);
  // Protected Instance Methods
        protected void selectRange(int start, int stop);
}
```

Hierarchy: Object→View(Codable)→TextField(ExtendedTarget(Target), FormElement)

Passed To: ColorChooser.textEditingDidBegin(), ColorChooser.textEditingDidEnd(), ColorChooser.textEditingWillEnd(), ColorChooser.textWasModified(), TextField.setBacktabField(),

TextField.setTabField(), TextFieldOwner.textEditingDidBegin(), TextFieldOwner.textEditingDidEnd(), TextFieldOwner.textEditingWillEnd(), TextFieldOwner.textWasModified()

Returned By: TextField.backtabField(), TextField.createLabel(), TextField.tabField()

---

netscape.application.TextFieldOwner

This interface defines the methods that an object must implement if it wants to receive detailed notifications from a TextField. textEditingDidBegin() is called when a TextField first receives keyboard focus. textWasModified() is called when the user edits the text. textEditingWillEnd() is called just before the TextField gives up keyboard focus. The second argument specifies why it is giving up focus, and is one of the constants defined by the interface. The third argument specifies if any changes have been made to the displayed text. This method may return false to prevent editing from ending as a result of the **Tab** or **Return** keys. Finally, textEditingDidEnd() is called just after the TextField has given up keyboard focus. Its arguments are the same as textEditingWillEnd() except that it cannot prevent editing from ending.

```
public abstract interface TextFieldOwner {
// Constants
    public static final int BACKTAB_KEY;
    public static final int LOST_FOCUS;
    public static final int RESIGNED_FOCUS;
    public static final int RETURN_KEY;
    public static final int TAB_KEY;
// Public Instance Methods
    public abstract void textEditingDidBegin(TextField textField);
    public abstract void textEditingDidEnd(TextField textField, int endCondition, boolean contentsChanged);
    public abstract boolean textEditingWillEnd(TextField textField, int endCondition, boolean contentsChanged);
    public abstract void textWasModified(TextField textField);
}
```

Implemented By: ColorChooser

Passed To: TextField.setOwner()

Returned By: TextField.owner()

---

netscape.application.TextFilter

This interface defines the acceptsEvent() method required by any object that needs to filter user keystrokes that occur over TextField or TextView objects. The acceptsEvent() method is passed the KeyEvent corresponding to every keystroke the user makes. To accept an event as-is, acceptsEvent() should simply return true. To reject the keystroke, it should return false. To modify the keystroke, it should insert one or more alternative KeyEvent objects into the specified Vector object and return false.

For efficiency, acceptsEvent() must return quickly, and to prevent deadlock, it is not allowed to call methods of other View objects.

$\rightarrow$

```
public abstract interface TextFilter {
  // Public Instance Methods
      public abstract boolean acceptsEvent(Object textObject, KeyEvent event, Vector events);
}
```

Passed To: TextField.setFilter(), TextView.setFilter()

Returned By: TextField.filter(), TextView.filter()

---

netscape.application.TextParagraphFormat

This class specifies the justification, margins, indent, line spacing, and tab stops for a region of text in a TextView object. These formatting attributes are applied to text in a TextView with the addAttributeForRange() method.

```
public class TextParagraphFormat extends Object implements Cloneable, Codable {
  // Public Constructor
      public TextParagraphFormat();
  // Public Instance Methods
      public void addTabPosition(int position);
      public void clearAllTabPositions();
      public Object clone(); // Overrides Object
      public void decode(Decoder decoder) throws CodingException; // From Codable
      public void describeClassInfo(ClassInfo info); // From Codable
      public void encode(Encoder encoder) throws CodingException; // From Codable
      public void finishDecoding() throws CodingException; // From Codable
      public int justification();
      public int leftIndent();
      public int leftMargin();
      public int lineSpacing();
      public int positionForTab(int tabNumber);
      public int rightMargin();
      public void setJustification(int justification);
      public void setLeftIndent(int indent);
      public void setLeftMargin(int leftMargin);
      public void setLineSpacing(int spacing);
      public void setRightMargin(int rightMargin);
      public void setTabPositions(int[] tabArray);
      public void setWrapsUnderFirstCharacter(boolean flag);
      public int[] tabPositions();
      public String toString(); // Overrides Object
      public boolean wrapsUnderFirstCharacter(); // Undocumented
}
```

---

netscape.application.TextView

This class supports the display and editing of multiline, multi-font text, which may include inline images, links, and other "attachments." While it can be used as the core of a simple formatted-text editor, it is more commonly used to allow the user

---

to enter multiline, single-font unformatted text, and for the display of static multi-font formatted text, such as help files. TextView includes a simple, extensible HTML parser that can parse all of the tags defined by HTML 1.0 by default. Use importHTMLFromURLString() or importHTMLInRange() to parse HTML and display the resulting formatted text in a TextView. Additional HTML parsing rules may be specified with setHTMLParsingRules().

When the user edits text displayed in a TextView, the TextView performs notification by calling methods of a TextViewOwner object registered with the setOwner() method. A program can filter user input by registering a TextFilter object with setFilter(). Note that TextView does not support target and command notification as most simpler views do.

A program can have explicit control over the formatted text by specifying "attributes" for the text. The TextView supports a default set of attributes, a set of attributes for characters typed by the user, and also allows attributes to be applied to specified ranges of the text. An attribute consists of an attribute name, which is one of the _KEY constants defined by the class, and an attribute value, which is an Object of appropriate type. For example, the PARAGRAPH_FORMAT_KEY attribute must be paired with a TextParagraphFormat object. You may specify individual attributes by passing both name and value to a method, or you may specify multiple attributes at once by passing a Hashtable of name/value pairs. To include a text attachment (such as an image) in the flow of text, specify an attribute with the name TEXT_ATTACHMENT_KEY and with a value which is some subclass of TextAttachment.

The TextView class is a large and complex one, and it supports a number of other methods. These methods specify other TextView properties, manipulate the selected region of text, and perform text replacement, among other things. There are also a number of useful methods that perform a kind of "unit conversion." One method, for example, returns the index of the character closest to a given pixel position, and another returns the Range of the paragraph that contains a specified character position.

```
public class TextView extends View implements ExtendedTarget, EventFilter, DragDestination, FormElement {
// Public Constructors
    public TextView();
    public TextView(Rect rect);
    public TextView(int x, int y, int width, int height);
// Constants
    public static final String CARET_COLOR_KEY;
    public static final String FONT_KEY;
    public static final String LINK_COLOR_KEY;
    public static final String LINK_DESTINATION_KEY;
    public static final String LINK_KEY;
    public static final String PARAGRAPH_FORMAT_KEY;
    public static final String PRESSED_LINK_COLOR_KEY;
    public static final String TEXT_ATTACHMENT_BASELINE_OFFSET_KEY;
    public static final String TEXT_ATTACHMENT_KEY;
    public static final String TEXT_ATTACHMENT_STRING;
    public static final String TEXT_COLOR_KEY;
// Class Methods
    public static String stringWithoutCarriageReturns(String aString);
```

→

// *Public Instance Methods*
    public DragDestination **acceptsDrag**(DragSession *session*, int *x*, int *y*); // *Overrides View*
    public void **addAttributeForRange**(String *attribute*, Object *value*, Range *range*);
    public void **addAttributesForRange**(Hashtable *attributes*, Range *range*);
    public void **addDefaultAttribute**(String *attribute*, Object *value*);
    public void **addTypingAttribute**(String *key*, Object *value*);
    public Range **appendString**(String *aString*);
    public Hashtable **attributesAtIndex**(int *anIndex*);
    public Color **backgroundColor**();
    public java.net.URL **baseURL**();
    public boolean **canBecomeSelectedView**(); // *Overrides View*
    public boolean **canPerformCommand**(String *command*); // *From ExtendedTarget*
    public Color **caretColor**();
    public void **copy**();
    public int **cursorForPoint**(int *x*, int *y*); // *Overrides View*
    public void **cut**();
    public void **decode**(Decoder *decoder*) throws CodingException; // *Overrides View*
    public Hashtable **defaultAttributes**();
    public void **describeClassInfo**(ClassInfo *info*); // *Overrides View*
    public void **didMoveBy**(int *deltaX*, int *deltaY*); // *Overrides View*
    public void **didSizeBy**(int *dw*, int *dh*); // *Overrides View*
    public void **disableResizing**();
    public boolean **dragDropped**(DragSession *session*); // *From DragDestination*
    public boolean **dragEntered**(DragSession *session*); // *From DragDestination*
    public void **dragExited**(DragSession *session*); // *From DragDestination*
    public boolean **dragMoved**(DragSession *session*); // *From DragDestination*
    public void **drawView**(Graphics *g*); // *Overrides View*
    public void **enableResizing**();
    public void **encode**(Encoder *encoder*) throws CodingException; // *Overrides View*
    public TextFilter **filter**();
    public Object **filterEvents**(Vector *events*); // *From EventFilter*
    public void **finishDecoding**() throws CodingException; // *Overrides View*
    public Font **font**();
    public String **formElementText**(); // *From FormElement*
    public boolean **hasSelection**();
    public HTMLParsingRules **htmlParsingRules**();
    public void **importHTMLFromURLString**(String *urlString*);
    public void **importHTMLInRange**(java.io.InputStream *inputStream*, Range *aRange*, java.net.URL *baseURL*)
        throws java.io.IOException, HTMLParsingException;
    public void **importHTMLInRange**(java.io.InputStream *inputStream*, Range *aRange*, java.net.URL *baseURL*,
        Hashtable *attributes*)
        throws java.io.IOException, HTMLParsingException;
    public int **indexForPoint**(int *x*, int *y*);
    public void **insertHTMLElementsInRange**(Vector *components*, Range *aRange*, Hashtable *attributes*);
    public boolean **isEditable**();
    public boolean **isResizingEnabled**();
    public boolean **isSelectable**();
    public boolean **isTransparent**(); // *Overrides View*
    public void **keyDown**(KeyEvent *event*); // *Overrides View*
    public int **length**();
    public int **lineCount**();

```
public boolean mouseDown(MouseEvent event);  // Overrides View
public void mouseDragged(MouseEvent event);  // Overrides View
public void mouseUp(MouseEvent event);  // Overrides View
public TextViewOwner owner();
public Range paragraphForIndex(int anIndex);
public Range paragraphForPoint(int x, int y);
public Vector paragraphsForRange(Range aRange);
public void paste();
public void pauseFocus();  // Overrides View
public void performCommand(String command, Object data);  // From Target
public Vector rectsForRange(Range aRange);
public void removeAttributeForRange(String attribute, Range r);
public void replaceRangeWithString(Range r, String aString);
public void replaceRangeWithTextAttachment(Range r, TextAttachment aTextAttachment);
public void resumeFocus();  // Overrides View
public Range runForIndex(int anIndex);
public Range runForPoint(int x, int y);
public Range runWithLinkDestinationNamed(String aName);
public Vector runsForRange(Range aRange);
public void scrollRangeToVisible(Range aRange);
public void selectRange(Range aRange);
public Range selectedRange();
public Color selectionColor();
public void setAttributesForRange(Hashtable attributes, Range r);
public void setBackgroundColor(Color aColor);
public void setCaretColor(Color aColor);
public void setDefaultAttributes(Hashtable attributes);
public void setEditable(boolean flag);
public void setFilter(TextFilter aFilter);
public void setFont(Font aFont);
public void setHTMLParsingRules(HTMLParsingRules newRules);
public void setOwner(TextViewOwner owner);
public void setSelectable(boolean flag);
public void setSelectionColor(Color aColor);
public void setString(String textString);
public void setTextColor(Color aColor);
public void setTransparent(boolean flag);
public void setTypingAttributes(Hashtable attr);
public void setUseSingleFont(boolean flag);
public void sizeBy(int deltaWidth, int deltaHeight);  // Overrides View
public void sizeToMinSize();  // Overrides View
public void startFocus();  // Overrides View
public void stopFocus();  // Overrides View
public String string();
public String stringForRange(Range r);
public Color textColor();
public String toString();  // Overrides View
public Hashtable typingAttributes();
public boolean usesSingleFont();
public boolean wantsAutoscrollEvents();  // Overrides View
public void willBecomeSelected();  // Overrides View
}
```

Hierarchy: Object→View(Codable)→TextView(ExtendedTarget(Target), EventFilter, DragDestination, FormElement)

Passed To: TextAttachment.setOwner(), TextViewHTMLContainer.attributesForContents(), TextViewHTMLContainer.attributesForPrefix(), TextViewHTMLContainer.attributesForSuffix(), TextViewHTMLElement.fontFromAttributes(), TextViewHTMLMarker.attributesForMarker(), TextViewHTMLMarker.attributesForPrefix(), TextViewHTMLMarker.attributesForSuffix(), TextViewOwner.attributesDidChange(), TextViewOwner.attributesWillChange(), TextViewOwner.linkWasSelected(), TextViewOwner.selectionDidChange(), TextViewOwner.textDidChange(), TextViewOwner.textEditingDidBegin(), TextViewOwner.textEditingDidEnd(), TextViewOwner.textWillChange()

Returned By: TextAttachment.owner()

---

netscape.application.TextViewHTMLContainer

This class defines methods that specify how an HTML container tag is to be converted into text and text attributes. To add support for parsing HTML container tags, such as <FONT> and </FONT>, you must define a custom subclass of this class and specify the name of that subclass in an HTMLParsingRules object.

```
public abstract class TextViewHTMLContainer extends TextViewHTMLElement {
    // Default Constructor: public TextViewHTMLContainer()
    // Public Instance Methods
        public boolean appliesAttributesToChildren();
        public Hashtable attributes();
        public Hashtable attributesForContents(Hashtable context, Hashtable initialAttributes, TextView textView);
        public Hashtable attributesForPrefix(Hashtable context, Hashtable initialAttributes, TextView textView);
        public Hashtable attributesForSuffix(Hashtable context, Hashtable initialAttributes, TextView textView);
        public Object[] children();
        public Vector childrenVector();
        public void cleanupContext(Hashtable context);
        public String marker();
        public String prefix(Hashtable context, char lastChar);
        public void setAttributes(String attr); // Overrides TextViewHTMLElement. Undocumented
        public void setChildren(Object[] children); // Overrides TextViewHTMLElement. Undocumented
        public void setMarker(String aString); // Overrides TextViewHTMLElement. Undocumented
        public void setString(String aString); // Overrides TextViewHTMLElement. Undocumented
        public void setupContext(Hashtable context);
        public String string(Hashtable context); // Defines TextViewHTMLElement
        public String suffix(Hashtable context, char lastChar);
        public String toString(); // Overrides Object
}
```

Hierarchy: Object→TextViewHTMLElement(HTMLElement)→TextViewHTMLContainer

---

netscape.application.TextViewHTMLElement

To extend the HTML parsing capabilities of a TextView, an HTMLParsingRules object must be provided to specify how HTML tags will be parsed. For each new tag to be parsed, the HTMLParsingRules object will specify a subclass (typically a custom subclass) TextViewHTMLElement. These subclasses do not perform parsing themselves, but instead control the conversion of the HTML element into a text string and a set of text attributes.

TextViewHTMLElement has three concrete subclasses: TextViewHTMLContainer, TextViewHTMLMarker, and TextViewHTMLString. You should always subclass one of these classes instead of subclassing TextViewHTMLElement directly.

```
public abstract class TextViewHTMLElement extends Object implements HTMLElement {
    // Default Constructor: public TextViewHTMLElement( )
    // Public Instance Methods
        public Font fontFromAttributes(Hashtable attr, TextView textView );
        public Hashtable hashtableForHTMLAttributes(String attr );
        public void setAttributes(String attributes );   // From HTMLElement. Undocumented
        public void setChildren(Object[] child );   // From HTMLElement. Undocumented
        public void setMarker(String aString );   // From HTMLElement. Undocumented
        public void setString(String aString );   // From HTMLElement. Undocumented
        public abstract String string(Hashtable context );
}
```

Extended By: TextViewHTMLContainer, TextViewHTMLMarker, TextViewHTMLString

---

netscape.application.TextViewHTMLMarker

This class defines methods that specify how an HTML tag that is not a container is converted into text and text attributes (including, perhaps, text attachments). To add support for parsing HTML "marker" tags, create a custom subclass of this class, and specify the name of that subclass in the HTMLParsingRules object.

```
public abstract class TextViewHTMLMarker extends TextViewHTMLElement {
    // Default Constructor: public TextViewHTMLMarker( )
    // Public Instance Methods
        public Hashtable attributes( );
        public Hashtable attributesForMarker(Hashtable context, Hashtable initialAttributes, TextView textView );
        public Hashtable attributesForPrefix(Hashtable context, Hashtable initialAttributes, TextView textView );
        public Hashtable attributesForSuffix(Hashtable context, Hashtable initialAttributes, TextView textView );
        public String marker( );
        public String prefix(Hashtable context, char lastChar );
        public void setAttributes(String attr );   // Overrides TextViewHTMLElement. Undocumented
        public void setChildren(Object[] child );   // Overrides TextViewHTMLElement. Undocumented
        public void setMarker(String aString );   // Overrides TextViewHTMLElement. Undocumented
        public void setString(String aString );   // Overrides TextViewHTMLElement. Undocumented
        public abstract String string(Hashtable context );   // Defines TextViewHTMLElement
        public String suffix(Hashtable context, char lastChar );
        public String toString( );   // Overrides Object
}
```

Hierarchy: Object→TextViewHTMLElement(HTMLElement)→TextViewHTMLMarker

---

netscape.application.TextViewHTMLString

This class defines the methods that specify how HTML strings are converted to strings for display in a TextView. When extending the HTML parsing capabilities of the TextView you do not usually need to subclass this class. If you do need to

→

subclass it, you should specify the name of the subclass in the `HTMLParsingRules` object.

```
public class TextViewHTMLString extends TextViewHTMLElement {
    // Default Constructor: public TextViewHTMLString()
    // Public Instance Methods
        public void setAttributes(String attributes);  // Overrides TextViewHTMLElement. Undocumented
        public void setChildren(Object[] child);  // Overrides TextViewHTMLElement. Undocumented
        public void setMarker(String aString);  // Overrides TextViewHTMLElement. Undocumented
        public void setString(String aString);  // Overrides TextViewHTMLElement. Undocumented
        public String string(Hashtable context);  // Defines TextViewHTMLElement
        public String string();
        public String toString();  // Overrides Object
}
```

Hierarchy: Object→TextViewHTMLElement(HTMLElement)→TextViewHTMLString

---

netscape.application.TextViewOwner

This interface defines the methods that an object must implement to receive notification of a variety of events from a `TextView` object. When a `TextViewOwner` is passed to the `setOwner()` method of a `TextView`, its various methods are invoked before and after text or attributes change, when the user selects text, when a link is selected, and when the `TextView` gains or loses focus. Focus changes are reported through the somewhat misleadingly named `textEditingDidBegin()` (focus gained) and `textEditingDidEnd()` (focus lost).

```
public abstract interface TextViewOwner {
    // Public Instance Methods
        public abstract void attributesDidChange(TextView textView, Range aRange);
        public abstract void attributesWillChange(TextView textView, Range aRange);
        public abstract void linkWasSelected(TextView sender, Range linkRange, String stringURL);
        public abstract void selectionDidChange(TextView textView);
        public abstract void textDidChange(TextView textView, Range aRange);
        public abstract void textEditingDidBegin(TextView textView);
        public abstract void textEditingDidEnd(TextView textView);
        public abstract void textWillChange(TextView textView, Range aRange);
}
```

Passed To: TextView.setOwner()

Returned By: TextView.owner()

---

netscape.application.Timer

A `Timer` object repeatedly passes the specified command string and data object to the specified target with a specified delay between invocations of the target's `performCommand()` method. To start a `Timer`, call its `start()` method, and to stop it, call `stop()`.

The Timer class has other options besides its target, command, data, and delay. setInitialDelay() specifies the delay between the call to start() and the first performCommand() call. setRepeats() allows you to specify that a Timer should not "repeat"; that is, it should invoke performCommand() once and stop. setCoalesce() specifies whether the Timer should coalesce multiple pending calls to performCommand() into a single call or not. This situation only arises when a short delay is specified, or when the computer is fairly busy.

```
public class Timer extends Object implements EventProcessor, EventFilter {
    // Public Constructors
        public Timer(EventLoop eventLoop, Target target, String command, int delay);
        public Timer(Target target, String command, int delay);
    // Public Instance Methods
        public String command();
        public Object data();
        public int delay();
        public boolean doesCoalesce();
        public EventLoop eventLoop();
        public Object filterEvents(Vector events);  // From EventFilter
        public int initialDelay();
        public boolean isRunning();
        public void processEvent(Event event);  // From EventProcessor
        public boolean repeats();
        public void setCoalesce(boolean flag);
        public void setCommand(String command);
        public void setData(Object data);
        public void setDelay(int delay);
        public void setInitialDelay(int initialDelay);
        public void setRepeats(boolean flag);
        public void setTarget(Target target);
        public void start();
        public void stop();
        public Target target();
        public long timeStamp();
        public String toString();  // Overrides Object
}
```

netscape.application.View

This class is the superclass of all GUI components in the IFC, and has methods shared by all views. addSubview() adds a subview to a view. Counterintuitively, you should use removeFromSuperview() to remove a view from its superview, instead of using removeSubview(). superview() returns a view's parent, and subviews() returns a Vector of all children of a view. descendsFrom() determines whether the current view is a descendent of another. isInViewHierarchy() determines whether a view has been added to the view hierarchy of the application.

setBounds() sets the position and size of a view within its superview, and bounds() returns the current position and size as do x(), y(), width(), and height(). setMinSize() specifies a minimum size for a view that cannot compute its own preferred size based on other properties, such as the amount of space required to display a specified string in a specified font. Call layoutView() to set

→

the size and position of the subviews of a view. Call setLayoutManager() to specify a LayoutManager object to perform this layout for the view. If a view is contained in a view without a layout manager, you may want to call setHorizResizeInstruction() and setVertResizeInstruction() to specify how the view's size and position should change when its parent is resized. The possible instruction values are the _CAN_CHANGE constants defined by this class. You can use setAutoResizeSubviews() to specify whether a view automatically calls layoutView() to update the size and position of its children when it is resized.

Calling draw() causes a view to redraw itself immediately. Alternatively, passing true to setDirty() causes the IFC to redraw the view asynchronously after the current event is processed. Similarly, passing a Rect to addDirtyRect() causes the IFC to asynchronously redraw a specified region of a view. Passing true to setBuffered() specifies that the view should be drawn using automatic double-buffering, which can reduce flickering for some complex or frequently redrawn views. To temporarily disable drawing of a View, for example, when making a number of changes to the properties of a view, call disableDrawing(). To resume normal drawing call reenableDrawing().

Call setFocusedView() to tell a view to take the keyboard focus. To assign a keyboard shortcut for a view, use setCommandForKey(). The *when* argument of this method should be one of the constants WHEN_SELECTED, WHEN_IN_MAIN_WINDOW, or ALWAYS.

The methods described above are ones you may want to use with any View object. Many of the remaining methods of the View class, however, are methods that you may want to override when you are defining your own custom views. The drawView() method is one of the most important of these methods. It draws the contents of the view.

Also important are keyDown(), keyUp(), mouseDown(), mouseDragged(), and related methods that are invoked when the user generates a keyboard or mouse event. By default these methods do nothing; they ignore the event and do *not* pass it on to the containing superview. You should override these methods to respond to the events as necessary for your custom view. There are a number of similar methods that notify your view that something has changed. For example: startFocus(), stopFocus(), pauseFocus(), resumeFocus(), willBecomeSelected() and willBecomeUnselected(). The didSizeBy() and didMoveBy() methods notify a view when it has been resized or moved. If you override these methods you should be sure to invoke the superclass definition of the method, which performs the actual move or resize.

Other methods that you may want to override in a custom view are methods that the IFC infrastructure calls to obtain information about the behavior of your custom view. minSize() is one of the most important of these; it plays an important role in layout management. minSize() should return the minimum size specified by setMinSize(), if any has been specified, or otherwise return the preferred size of the view—i.e., return the amount of space the view needs to display itself effectively.

isTransparent() specifies whether a view may have any transparent regions. If your view is totally opaque, you should override this method to return false. Override wantsAutoscrollEvents() to return true if your view wants to receive mouse-dragged events even when the mouse has been dragged outside of the bounds of the view. Override `wantsMouseEventCoalescing()` to return `false` if it is important that your view receive every single mouse drag or motion event that is generated, rather than having multiple events combined into a single one. `can-BecomeSelectedView()`, `nextSelectableView()`, `previousSelectableView()`, and `hidesSubviewsFromKeyboard()` provide keyboard navigation information about the view. Override these methods as necessary.

public class **View** extends Object implements Codable {
  // *Public Constructors*
    public **View**( );
    public **View**(Rect *rect*);
    public **View**(int *x*, int *y*, int *width*, int *height*);
  // *Cursor Constants*
    public static final int **ARROW_CURSOR**;
    public static final int **CROSSHAIR_CURSOR**;
    public static final int **HAND_CURSOR**;
    public static final int **MOVE_CURSOR**;
    public static final int **TEXT_CURSOR**;
    public static final int **WAIT_CURSOR**;
    public static final int **E_RESIZE_CURSOR, NE_RESIZE_CURSOR**;
    public static final int **NW_RESIZE_CURSOR, N_RESIZE_CURSOR**;
    public static final int **SE_RESIZE_CURSOR, SW_RESIZE_CURSOR**;
    public static final int **S_RESIZE_CURSOR, W_RESIZE_CURSOR**;

  // *Resize Instruction Constants*
    public static final int **CENTER_HORIZ, CENTER_VERT**;
    public static final int **LEFT_MARGIN_CAN_CHANGE**;
    public static final int **RIGHT_MARGIN_CAN_CHANGE**;
    public static final int **WIDTH_CAN_CHANGE**;
    public static final int **BOTTOM_MARGIN_CAN_CHANGE**;
    public static final int **TOP_MARGIN_CAN_CHANGE**;
    public static final int **HEIGHT_CAN_CHANGE**;
  // *Other Constants*
    public static final int **ALWAYS**;
    public static final int **WHEN_IN_MAIN_WINDOW**;
    public static final int **WHEN_SELECTED**;
  // *Public Instance Variables*
    public Rect **bounds**;
  // *Public Instance Methods*
    public DragDestination **acceptsDrag**(DragSession *session*, int *x*, int *y*);
    public void **addDirtyRect**(Rect *rect*);
    public void **addSubview**(View *aView*);
    public Rect **bounds**( );
    public boolean **canBecomeSelectedView**( );
    public boolean **canDraw**( );
    public void **computeVisibleRect**(Rect *visibleRect*);
    public boolean **containsPoint**(int *x*, int *y*);
    public boolean **containsPointInVisibleRect**(int *x*, int *y*);
    public MouseEvent **convertEventToView**(View *otherView*, MouseEvent *sourceEvent*);
    public void **convertPointToView**(View *otherView*, Point *sourcePoint*, Point *destPoint*);
    public Point **convertPointToView**(View *otherView*, Point *sourcePoint*);
    public void **convertRectToView**(View *otherView*, Rect *sourceRect*, Rect *destRect*);

$\rightarrow$

```
public Rect convertRectToView(View otherView, Rect sourceRect);
public void convertToView(View otherView, int x, int y, Point destPoint);
public Point convertToView(View otherView, int x, int y);
public Graphics createGraphics();
public int cursorForPoint(int x, int y);
public void decode(Decoder decoder) throws CodingException;  // From Codable
public boolean descendsFrom(View aView);
public void describeClassInfo(ClassInfo info);  // From Codable
public void didMoveBy(int deltaX, int deltaY);
public void didSizeBy(int deltaWidth, int deltaHeight);
public void disableDrawing();
public boolean doesAutoResizeSubviews();
public void draw(Graphics g, Rect clipRect);
public void draw(Rect clipRect);
public void draw();
public void drawSubviews(Graphics g);
public void drawView(Graphics g);
public Bitmap drawingBuffer();
public void encode(Encoder encoder) throws CodingException;  // From Codable
public void finishDecoding() throws CodingException;  // From Codable
public int graphicsDebugOptions();
public int height();
public boolean hidesSubviewsFromKeyboard();
public int horizResizeInstruction();
public void invalidateKeyboardSelectionOrder();
public boolean isBuffered();
public boolean isDirty();
public boolean isDrawingEnabled();
public boolean isInViewHierarchy();
public boolean isTransparent();
public void keyDown(KeyEvent event);
public void keyUp(KeyEvent event);
public Rect keyboardRect();
public LayoutManager layoutManager();
public void layoutView(int deltaWidth, int deltaHeight);
public Rect localBounds();
public Size minSize();
public boolean mouseDown(MouseEvent event);
public void mouseDragged(MouseEvent event);
public void mouseEntered(MouseEvent event);
public void mouseExited(MouseEvent event);
public void mouseMoved(MouseEvent event);
public void mouseUp(MouseEvent event);
public void moveBy(int deltaX, int deltaY);
public void moveTo(int x, int y);
public View nextSelectableView();
public void pauseFocus();
public Vector peersForSubview(View subview);  // Undocumented
public View previousSelectableView();
public void reenableDrawing();
public void removeAllCommandsForKeys();
```

```
    public void removeCommandForKey(int aKey);
    public void removeFromSuperview();
    public void resumeFocus();
    public RootView rootView();
    public void scrollRectToVisible(Rect aRect);
    public void setAutoResizeSubviews(boolean flag);
    public void setBounds(Rect rect);
    public void setBounds(int x, int y, int width, int height);
    public void setBuffered(boolean flag);
    public void setCommandForKey(String aCommand, Object cmdData, int key, int modifiers, int when);
    public void setCommandForKey(String aCommand, int aKey, int when);
    public void setDirty(boolean flag);
    public void setFocusedView();
    public void setGraphicsDebugOptions(int debugOptions);
    public void setHorizResizeInstruction(int instruction);
    public void setLayoutManager(LayoutManager value);
    public void setMinSize(int width, int height);
    public void setVertResizeInstruction(int instruction);
    public void sizeBy(int deltaWidth, int deltaHeight);
    public void sizeTo(int width, int height);
    public void sizeToMinSize();
    public void startFocus();
    public void stopFocus();
    public void subviewDidMove(View aSubview);
    public void subviewDidResize(View aSubview);
    public Vector subviews();
    public View superview();
    public String toString();  // Overrides Object
    public int vertResizeInstruction();
    public View viewForMouse(int x, int y);
    public boolean wantsAutoscrollEvents();
    public boolean wantsMouseEventCoalescing();
    public int width();
    public void willBecomeSelected();
    public void willBecomeUnselected();
    public InternalWindow window();
    public int x();
    public int y();
 // Protected Instance Methods
    protected void ancestorWasAddedToViewHierarchy(View addedView);
    protected void ancestorWillRemoveFromViewHierarchy(View removedView);
    protected Bitmap createBuffer();
    protected void removeSubview(View aView);
}
```

Extended By: AWTComponentView, Button, ContainerView, DragWell, InternalWindow, Label, ListView, MenuView, Popup, RootView, ScrollBar, ScrollGroup, ScrollView, Slider, TextField, TextView, ViewProxy, WindowContentView

Passed To: Application.keyboardArrowLocation(), Application.keyboardArrowPosition(), ApplicationObserver.focusDidChange(), AWTComponentView.ancestorWasAddedToViewHierarchy(), AWTComponentView.ancestorWillRemoveFromViewHierarchy(), Button.ancestorWasAddedToViewHierarchy(), DebugGraphics(), ExternalWindow.addSubview(), ExternalWindow.focusDidChange(), Graphics(), GridLayout.addSubview(), GridLayout.gridSize(), GridLayout.layoutView(), GridLayout.removeSubview(),

InternalWindow.addSubview(), InternalWindow.addSubviewToWindow(), InternalWindow.setDefaultSelectedView(),
InternalWindow.setFocusedView(), LayoutManager.addSubview(), LayoutManager.layoutView(),
LayoutManager.removeSubview(), PackLayout.addSubview(), PackLayout.constraintsFor(),
PackLayout.layoutView(), PackLayout.preferredLayoutSize(), PackLayout.removeSubview(),
PackLayout.setConstraints(), Plan.addContentsToView(), Popup.ancestorWillRemoveFromViewHierarchy(),
RootView.selectView(), RootView.selectViewAfter(), RootView.selectViewBefore(),
RootView.setDefaultSelectedView(), RootView.setFocusedView(), RootView.setMouseView(),
RootView.setWindowClipView(), RootView.subviewDidMove(), RootView.subviewDidResize(),
RootView.viewExcludedFromModalSession(), ScrollGroup.setContentView(), ScrollView.addSubview(),
ScrollView.setContentView(), ScrollView.subviewDidResize(), View.addSubview(),
View.ancestorWasAddedToViewHierarchy(), View.ancestorWillRemoveFromViewHierarchy(),
View.convertEventToView(), View.convertPointToView(), View.convertRectToView(), View.convertToView(),
View.descendsFrom(), View.peersForSubview(), View.removeSubview(), View.subviewDidMove(),
View.subviewDidResize(), ViewProxy.setAttributesToReplacingView(), Window.addSubview()

Returned By: Application.modalView(), ColorChooser.contentView(), DragSession.destinationView(),
DragSource.sourceView(), DragWell.sourceView(), ExternalWindow.viewForMouse(), FontChooser.contentView(),
InternalWindow.defaultSelectedView(), InternalWindow.focusedView(), InternalWindow.viewForMouse(),
Plan.viewWithContents(), RootView.defaultSelectedView(), RootView.focusedView(), RootView.mouseView(),
RootView.viewForMouse(), RootView.windowClipView(), ScrollGroup.contentView(), ScrollView.contentView(),
TextField.nextSelectableView(), TextField.previousSelectableView(), View.nextSelectableView(),
View.previousSelectableView(), View.superview(), View.viewForMouse(), Window.viewForMouse()

---

netscape.application.Window

This interface defines the methods shared by both InternalWindow and ExternalWindow. Methods of particular interest are setTitle(), which specifies the text
to appear in the window's title bar; show() and hide(), which pop up and pop
down a window; showModally(), which shows a window and blocks input to all
other windows until it is dismissed; and windowSizeForContentSize(), which
returns the size a window must be to have a display area of the specified size.

```
public abstract interface Window extends Target {
    // Constants
        public static final int BLANK_TYPE;
        public static final String HIDE;
        public static final String SHOW;
        public static final int TITLE_TYPE;
    // Public Instance Methods
        public abstract void addSubview(View aView);
        public abstract Rect bounds();
        public abstract void center();
        public abstract boolean containsDocument();
        public abstract Size contentSize();
        public abstract void didBecomeCurrentDocument();
        public abstract void didResignCurrentDocument();
        public abstract void hide();
        public abstract boolean isCurrentDocument();
        public abstract boolean isResizable();
        public abstract boolean isVisible();
        public abstract MenuView menuView();
        public abstract Size minSize();
        public abstract void moveBy(int deltaX, int deltaY);
```

```
        public abstract void moveTo(int x, int y);
        public abstract void moveToBack();
        public abstract void moveToFront();
        public abstract WindowOwner owner();
        public abstract void setBounds(int x, int y, int width, int height);
        public abstract void setBounds(Rect newBounds);
        public abstract void setContainsDocument(boolean containsDocument);
        public abstract void setMenuView(MenuView aMenuView);
        public abstract void setMinSize(int width, int height);
        public abstract void setOwner(WindowOwner anObject);
        public abstract void setResizable(boolean flag);
        public abstract void setTitle(String aString);
        public abstract void show();
        public abstract void showModally();
        public abstract void sizeBy(int deltaWidth, int deltaHeight);
        public abstract void sizeTo(int width, int height);
        public abstract String title();
        public abstract View viewForMouse(int x, int y);
        public abstract Size windowSizeForContentSize(int width, int height);
}
```

Implemented By: ExternalWindow, InternalWindow

Passed To: Application.chooseNextCurrentDocumentWindow(),
Application.makeCurrentDocumentWindow(), ApplicationObserver.currentDocumentDidChange(),
ColorChooser.setWindow(), ExternalWindow.currentDocumentDidChange(), FontChooser.setWindow(),
Popup.setPopupWindow(), WindowOwner.windowDidBecomeMain(), WindowOwner.windowDidHide(),
WindowOwner.windowDidResignMain(), WindowOwner.windowDidShow(), WindowOwner.windowWillHide(),
WindowOwner.windowWillShow(), WindowOwner.windowWillSizeBy()

Returned By: Application.currentDocumentWindow(), ColorChooser.window(), FontChooser.window(),
Popup.popupWindow()

---

netscape.application.WindowContentView

This class is a View used by InternalWindow objects to hold their contents. Use
the contentView() method of an InternalWindow to obtain a WindowContentView
object. You do not often need to use this class.

```
public class WindowContentView extends View {
    // Public Constructors
        public WindowContentView();
        public WindowContentView(Rect rect);
        public WindowContentView(int x, int y, int width, int height);
    // Public Instance Methods
        public Color backgroundColor();
        public void decode(Decoder decoder) throws CodingException; // Overrides View
        public void describeClassInfo(ClassInfo info); // Overrides View
        public void drawView(Graphics g); // Overrides View
        public void encode(Encoder encoder) throws CodingException; // Overrides View
        public boolean isTransparent(); // Overrides View
        public void setBackgroundColor(Color aColor);
```

→

```
      public void setColor(Color aColor);
      public void setTransparent(boolean flag);
}
```

Hierarchy: Object→View(Codable)→WindowContentView

Returned By: InternalWindow.contentView()

---

netscape.application.WindowOwner

This interface defines methods that an object must implement to receive notification of a variety of events from an InternalWindow or an ExternalWindow. A WindowOwner object must be registered with a Window by passing it to the window's setOwner() method. Notice that the windowWillHide() and windowWillShow() methods return boolean values. These methods can prevent a window from being hidden or shown by returning false.

```
public abstract interface WindowOwner {
   // Public Instance Methods
      public abstract void windowDidBecomeMain(Window aWindow);
      public abstract void windowDidHide(Window aWindow);
      public abstract void windowDidResignMain(Window aWindow);
      public abstract void windowDidShow(Window aWindow);
      public abstract boolean windowWillHide(Window aWindow);
      public abstract boolean windowWillShow(Window aWindow);
      public abstract void windowWillSizeBy(Window aWindow, Size deltaSize);
}
```

Passed To: ExternalWindow.setOwner(), InternalWindow.setOwner(), Window.setOwner()

Returned By: ExternalWindow.owner(), InternalWindow.owner(), Window.owner()

CHAPTER 24

The netscape.constructor Package

The netscape.constructor package contains only five classes and one interface. They are all related to the use of the Constructor GUI builder application with IFC programs. The Plan class is by far the most frequently used. Figure 24-1 shows the class hierarchy of this package.

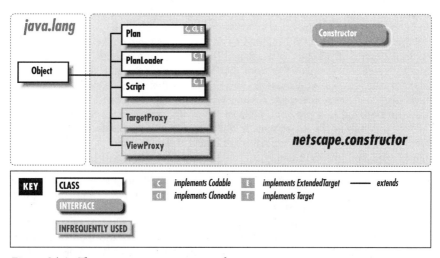

Figure 24-1: The netscape.constructor package

netscape.constructor.Constructor

Custom views may need to implement slightly different behavior when they are used within Constructor than they do when running in a standalone IFC program. This interface allows custom View classes to test whether they are running inside

→

of the Constructor application. When running within Constructor, the following Java expression will evaluate to `true`:

```
Application.application() instanceof netscape.constructor.Constructor
```

If the code is running standalone, the expression will evaluate to `false`.

The `inConstructionMode()` method of this interface enables code running within the Constructor application to determine what mode Constructor is running in. If this method returns `true`, then Constructor is in "build" or "wire" mode. Otherwise, Constructor is in "test" mode. When in "test" mode, a custom view should behave as if it was in a standalone application.

```
public abstract interface Constructor {
   // Public Instance Methods
      public abstract boolean inConstructionMode();
}
```

---

netscape.constructor.Plan

This is the most important and commonly used class in the `netscape.construc-tor` package. It allows an IFC program to read in a *.plan* file created by the Constructor application and recreate the View hierarchy described by that file.

The `Plan()` constructors are passed a URL that refers to a *.plan* file (which should actually have the extension *.plana* for an ASCII encoding and *.planb* for a binary encoding). They read the contents of the named file into an IFC archive, and then call the `unarchiveObjects()` method to unarchive, or recreate the views and other objects described in the plan file. (The `Plan()` constructor that takes an InputStream reads a plan file from that stream, but does not automatically call `unarchiveObjects()`; you must do so yourself in this case.) Once these objects have been recreated, there are several ways to obtain references to them so that they can be used in a program. `componentNamed()` returns a given named object. (Names can optionally be assigned to views and other objects in Constructor.) `nameToComponent()` returns a `Hashtable` object that maps names to objects for all named objects in the plan file.

While it is often useful to obtain references to individual objects by name, you sometimes simply want to extract the entire `View` hierarchy from a plan file. `externalWindowWithContents()`, `internalWindowWithContents()`, and `viewWithContents()` do this. They create an `ExternalWindow`, `InternalWindow`, and `ContainerView`, respectively, set its size appropriately, and then place all of the top-level views into it. The result is a window that is ready to be displayed, or a `View` hierarchy that is ready to be added to an interface somewhere. Finally, you can also add the views described in a plan file to a `View` of your own by calling `addContentsToView()`. You may want to call the `size()` method of the `Plan` first to determine the appropriate size of your `View` object.

Plan files not only contain `View` hierarchies; they also allow `Target` objects to be specified for views. Sometimes these targets are other views within the plan file, and there is no difficulty specifying them. Often, however, a `View` must refer to a `Target` that is outside the scope of the plan file or of Constructor. In this case, the

---

user of Constructor will create one or more `TargetProxy` objects to represent the desired targets. When the plan file is loaded, you must specify the actual `Target` object or objects to be used in place of these proxies. When there is only a single `TargetProxy` in use, you can simply pass the desired `Target` object to the `Plan()` constructor. When there is more than one `TargetProxy`, you must create a `Hashtable` that maps proxy names to actual `Target` objects and pass this `Hashtable` to the `Plan` constructor.

Once you have loaded a plan file, and extracted all the object references you need from it, you can call `releaseObjects()` to allow the plan file to forget about those objects, freeing up memory for garbage collection. If you want to create another copy of the objects described in a plan file (for example, if you want multiple copies of a dialog box described by a plan file) you can call `unarchiveObjects()` to create another copy of the archived objects. When you do this, note that you may need to pass a `Target` or `Hashtable` of `Target` objects as described above.

```
public class Plan extends Object implements ExtendedTarget, Codable, Cloneable {
// Public Constructors
    public Plan(); // Undocumented
    public Plan(String url) throws java.io.IOException;
    public Plan(String url, Hashtable targets) throws java.io.IOException;
    public Plan(String url, Target target) throws java.io.IOException;
    public Plan(java.io.InputStream stream, int formatOfStream) throws java.io.IOException;
// Constants
    public static final String ALL_COMPONENTS_KEY; // Undocumented
    public static final String ASCII_FILE_EXTENSION;
    public static final int ASCII_TYPE;
    public static final String BACKGROUND_COLOR_KEY; // Undocumented
    public static final String BINARY_FILE_EXTENSION;
    public static final int BINARY_TYPE;
    public static final int CURRENT_VERSION_NUMBER; // Undocumented
    public static final String DOCUMENT_SIZE_KEY; // Undocumented
    public static final String NAME_TO_COMPONENT_KEY; // Undocumented
    public static final String OBJECT_TO_BOUNDS_KEY; // Undocumented
    public static final String ROOT_COMPONENTS_KEY; // Undocumented
    public static final int UNKNOWN_TYPE; // Undocumented
    public static final String VERSION_NUMBER_KEY; // Undocumented
// Class Methods
    public static Plan createPlan(String url);
    public static Plan createPlan(String url, Hashtable targets);
    public static Plan createPlan(String url, Target target);
    public static Plan createPlan(java.io.InputStream stream, int formatOfStream);
// Public Instance Methods
    public void addContentsToView(View aView);
    public Archive archiveData(); // Undocumented
    public int archiveFormat(); // Undocumented
    public void archiveObjectsToArchiveData(); // Undocumented
    public Color backgroundColor();
    public Rect boundingRect();
    public boolean canPerformCommand(String command); // From ExtendedTarget. Undocumented
    public Object clone(); // Overrides Object. Undocumented
    public Object componentNamed(String name);
    public Vector components();
```

$\rightarrow$

public void **decode**(Decoder *decoder*) throws CodingException; // *From Codable. Undocumented*
public void **describeClassInfo**(ClassInfo *info*); // *From Codable. Undocumented*
public void **encode**(Encoder *encoder*) throws CodingException; // *From Codable. Undocumented*
public ExternalWindow **externalWindowWithContents**( );
public void **finishDecoding**( ) throws CodingException; // *From Codable. Undocumented*
public boolean **hasValidObjects**( ); // *Undocumented*
public InternalWindow **internalWindowWithContents**( );
public boolean **isValidArchive**( ); // *Undocumented*
public void **moveBy**(int *x*, int *y*);
public Hashtable **nameToComponent**( );
public Hashtable **objectToBounds**( );
public void **performCommand**(String *command*, Object *object*); // *From Target. Undocumented*
public void **releaseObjects**( );
public Vector **rootComponents**( );
public boolean **save**( ); // *Undocumented*
public boolean **saveToStream**(java.io.OutputStream *stream*, int *format*); // *Undocumented*
public void **setArchiveData**(Archive *archive*); // *Undocumented*
public void **setArchiveFormat**(int *format*); // *Undocumented*
public void **setBackgroundColor**(Color *color*); // *Undocumented*
public void **setComponents**(Vector *vector*); // *Undocumented*
public void **setNameToComponent**(Hashtable *table*); // *Undocumented*
public void **setObjectToBounds**(Hashtable *table*); // *Undocumented*
public void **setRootComponents**(Vector *vector*); // *Undocumented*
public void **setSize**(Size *size*); // *Undocumented*
public void **setSize**(int *width*, int *height*); // *Undocumented*
public void **setTargetProxyManager**(TargetProxyManager *manager*); // *Undocumented*
public void **setURL**(String *url*); // *Undocumented*
public void **setValidArchive**(boolean *value*); // *Undocumented*
public void **setValidObjects**(boolean *value*); // *Undocumented*
public void **setVersionNumber**(int *version*); // *Undocumented*
public Size **size**( );
public void **sizeToFit**( );
public TargetProxyManager **targetProxyManager**( ); // *Undocumented*
public boolean **unarchiveObjects**(Hashtable *targets*);
public boolean **unarchiveObjects**(Target *target*);
public boolean **unarchiveObjects**( );
public String **url**( );
public int **versionNumber**( ); // *Undocumented*
public View **viewWithContents**( );
// *Protected Instance Methods*
protected int **archiveFormatOf**(String *url*); // *Undocumented*
protected Archive **archiveFromStream**(java.io.InputStream *stream*, int *format*)
            throws java.io.IOException; // *Undocumented*
protected void **archiveTo**(Archive *archive*); // *Undocumented*
protected boolean **constructorComponentWasView**(Object *object*); // *Undocumented*
protected void **decodeBETADocumentInformation**(Hashtable *info*); // *Undocumented*
protected void **decodeDocumentInformation**(Hashtable *info*); // *Undocumented*
protected void **encodeDocumentInformation**(Hashtable *hashtable*); // *Undocumented*
protected void **finishUnarchiving**( ); // *Undocumented*
protected void **initFrom**(java.io.InputStream *stream*, int *formatOfStream*)
            throws java.io.IOException; // *Undocumented*

```
        protected java.io.InputStream streamFromURL(String url) throws java.io.IOException; // Undocumented
        protected boolean unarchiveFrom(Archive archive, Hashtable proxies); // Undocumented
}
```

Hierarchy: Object→Plan(ExtendedTarget(Target), Codable, Cloneable)

Passed To: PlanLoader.setPlan()

Returned By: Plan.createPlan(), PlanLoader.plan()

netscape.constructor.PlanLoader

This class is a kind of Target which, when sent the command CREATE_PLAN, will load the plan file specified by the URL passed to the constructor or setPlanURL() method. Once it loads the plan file, it places the View hierarchy of that file into an InternalWindow or an ExternalWindow (the default) depending on the value passed to setLoadInExternalWindow(). Finally, the PlanLoader displays the window. Thus, the PlanLoader is a convenience class that makes it possible to create and display a dialog box or other View hierarchy with a single command.

Note that despite the optional *isRelative* argument to the Plan() constructor, the URL you specify must be an absolute URL. The *isRelative* argument is non-functional.

```
public class PlanLoader extends Object implements Target, Codable {
// Public Constructors
    public PlanLoader();
    public PlanLoader(String planURL);
    public PlanLoader(String planURL, boolean isRelative);
// Constants
    public static final String CREATE_PLAN;
// Class Methods
    public static void hideWindows(); // Undocumented
    public static boolean rememberWindows(); // Undocumented
    public static void setRememberWindows(boolean value); // Undocumented
    public static void showWindows(); // Undocumented
    public static Vector windowVector(); // Undocumented
// Public Instance Methods
    public void createPlan(); // Undocumented
    public void decode(Decoder decoder) throws CodingException; // From Codable. Undocumented
    public void describeClassInfo(ClassInfo info); // From Codable. Undocumented
    public void encode(Encoder encoder) throws CodingException; // From Codable. Undocumented
    public void finishDecoding() throws CodingException; // From Codable. Undocumented
    public String fullURL(); // Undocumented
    public boolean isRelativeURL(); // Undocumented
    public boolean loadInExternalWindow();
    public void loadPlan(); // Undocumented
    public void performCommand(String command, Object object); // From Target
    public Plan plan();
    public String planURL();
    public ExternalWindow putPlanInExternalWindow();
    public InternalWindow putPlanInInternalWindow();
    public void setLoadInExternalWindow(boolean value);
    public void setPlan(Plan aPlan);
```

→

```
    public void setPlanURL(String urlString);
    public void setRelativeURL(boolean value); // Undocumented
}
```

---

netscape.constructor.Script

This class is a kind of `Target` that runs a specified string of JavaScript code when the `RUN_COMMAND` command is sent to it, or when its `run()` method is called. The JavaScript code to be run may be passed to the constructor or set with `setScriptText()`.

If the JavaScript code needs to make use of Java variables, then these variables must first be inserted into the JavaScript environment. You can do this by creating a `Hashtable` that maps variable name strings to Java objects, and by passing this `hashtable` to `setNamedObjects()`. Before running the script, the `Script` object will associate the Java objects with their assigned names in the JavaScript environment, so that the script can access them. When the script finishes running, these name/value associations are removed from the JavaScript environment.

When a `Script` object finishes running its script, it uses its optionally specified target/command pair to send out a notification.

```
public class Script extends Object implements Target, Codable {
  // Public Constructors
    public Script();
    public Script(String scriptText);
  // Constants
    public static final String RUN_COMMAND;
  // Public Instance Methods
    public String command();
    public void decode(Decoder decoder) throws CodingException; // From Codable. Undocumented
    public void describeClassInfo(ClassInfo info); // From Codable. Undocumented
    public void encode(Encoder encoder) throws CodingException; // From Codable. Undocumented
    public void finishDecoding() throws CodingException; // From Codable. Undocumented
    public synchronized boolean isRunning();
    public boolean isUsingLiveConnect(); // Undocumented
    public Hashtable namedObjects();
    public void performCommand(String command, Object anObject); // From Target
    public boolean removeNames(Hashtable nameTable); // Undocumented
    public void run();
    public String scriptText();
    public void setCommand(String command);
    public void setNamedObjects(Hashtable names);
    public boolean setNames(Hashtable nameTable); // Undocumented
    public void setScriptText(String scriptText);
    public void setTarget(Target aTarget);
    public void setUsingLiveConnect(boolean value); // Undocumented
    public Target target();
}
```

netscape.constructor.TargetProxy

The TargetProxy class acts as a surrogate Target object that allows views in Constructor to refer to targets that are outside of the scope of Constructor. When a view hierarchy is created with the Plan objects, any TargetProxy objects in that hierarchy are typically replaced with actual Target objects that were passed to the Plan constructor.

Although TargetProxy objects are replaced by their corresponding actual Target objects, the original TargetProxy object can still be extracted by name from the Plan object. The only reason to do this is to call the commands() method of the TargetProxy to obtain a Vector of the commands that the corresponding Target object must support. This is not a common thing to do, and most applications will never use TargetProxy.

```
public class TargetProxy extends Object implements Target, Codable {
    // Public Constructors
        public TargetProxy();
        public TargetProxy(TargetProxyManager targetProxyManager); // Undocumented
    // Constants
        public static final int APPLICATION_TYPE;
        public static final int CUSTOM_TYPE;
        public static final int TARGET_CHAIN_TYPE;
    // Public Instance Methods
        public Vector commands();
        public void decode(Decoder decoder) throws CodingException; // From Codable. Undocumented
        public void describeClassInfo(ClassInfo info); // From Codable. Undocumented
        public void encode(Encoder encoder) throws CodingException; // From Codable. Undocumented
        public void finishDecoding() throws CodingException; // From Codable. Undocumented
        public String name();
        public void performCommand(String command, Object anObject); // From Target
        public void setAttributesToReplacingTarget(Target realTarget);
        public void setCommands(Vector newCommands); // Undocumented
        public void setName(String value);
        public void setTargetProxyManager(TargetProxyManager tpManager); // Undocumented
        public void setType(int value);
        public TargetProxyManager targetProxyManager(); // Undocumented
        public int type();
}
```

netscape.constructor.ViewProxy

This class is a View used within Constructor to represent some other View that is not available on a Constructor "tray" and so cannot be added directly to the view hierarchy. setViewClassName() specifies the class name of the actual View for which the ViewProxy is a surrogate. When the Constructor plan file is loaded into an IFC application (through the Plan class), the ViewProxy will be replaced with an instance of the named class.

Applications never need to use ViewProxy directly.

→

public class **ViewProxy** extends View implements Target, Codable {
  // *Public Constructors*
    public **ViewProxy**( ); // *Undocumented*
    public **ViewProxy**(int *x*, int *y*, int *width*, int *height*);
  // *Constants*
    public static final String **CLASS_NAME_KEY**;
    public static final String **COMMANDS_KEY**;
    public static final String **VIEWPROXY_CLASS_NAME**;
  // *Public Instance Methods*
    public String[ ] **commands**( );
    public void **decode**(Decoder *decoder*) throws CodingException; // *Overrides View. Undocumented*
    public void **describeClassInfo**(ClassInfo *info*); // *Overrides View. Undocumented*
    public void **drawView**(Graphics *g*); // *Overrides View. Undocumented*
    public void **encode**(Encoder *encoder*) throws CodingException; // *Overrides View. Undocumented*
    public void **finishDecoding**( ) throws CodingException; // *Overrides View. Undocumented*
    public boolean **isTransparent**( ); // *Overrides View. Undocumented*
    public void **performCommand**(String *command*, Object *object*); // *From Target. Undocumented*
    public void **setAttributesToReplacingView**(View *realView*);
    public void **setCommands**(String[ ] *values*);
    public void **setViewClassName**(String *viewName*);
    public String **viewClassName**( );
}

Hierarchy: Object→View(Codable)→ViewProxy(Target, Codable)

CHAPTER 25

The netscape.util Package

The netscape.util package contains utility classes and interfaces for use with the IFC. Most of the classes and interfaces in this package are part of the IFC archiving mechanism, but the class also contains useful datatypes (Hashtable and Vector and their companion interface Enumeration) and a sorting utility (Comparable and Sort). Figure 25-1 shows the class hierarchy for this package.

---

netscape.util.Archive

This class stores object data. Objects are written to an archive with an Archiver, and read from an archive with an Unarchiver. A number of the Archive methods allow you to manipulate object data directly, but you never need to do this; it is always easier to use Archiver and Unarchiver.

Once object data has been stored in an Archive it can be written to a stream with write() or writeASCII(). write() outputs the data in binary format, and write-ASCII() outputs the data in text format. If the second argument to writeASCII() is true, it will output formatted ASCII that is easy to read and edit. Similarly, binary object data may be read from an input stream into an Archive with read(), and object data in text form may be read with readASCII().

```
public class Archive extends Object {
    // Public Constructor
        public Archive();
    // Constants
        public static final int ARCHIVE_MAGIC; // Undocumented
    // Public Instance Variables
        public boolean performanceDebug; // Undocumented
    // Public Instance Methods
        public void addClassTable(ClassTable table);
        public void addRootIdentifier(int id);
        public ClassTable classTableForIdentifier(int id);
        public ClassTable classTableForName(String className);
```

→

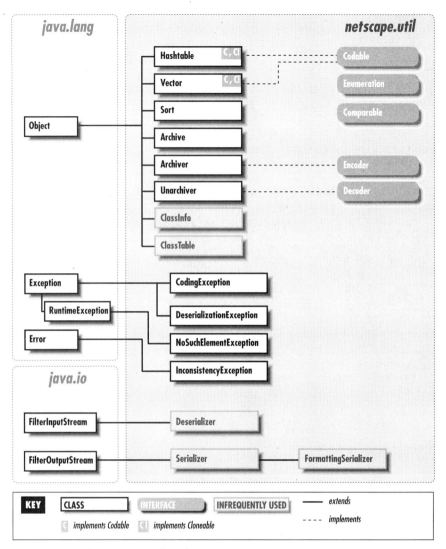

Figure 25-1: The netscape.util package

netscape.util.Archive

←

```
        public int identifierCount( );
        public int mapIdentifier(ClassTable table, int row);
        public void read(java.io.InputStream inputStream) throws java.io.IOException;
        public void readASCII(java.io.InputStream inputStream)
                throws CodingException, DeserializationException, java.io.IOException;
        public boolean removeRootIdentifier(int id);
        public int[] rootIdentifiers( );
        public int rowForIdentifier(int id);
        public void write(java.io.OutputStream outputStream) throws java.io.IOException;
        public void writeASCII(java.io.OutputStream outputStream, boolean formatted)
                throws CodingException, java.io.IOException;
}
```

Passed To: Archiver(), ClassTable(), Plan.archiveTo(), Plan.setArchiveData(), Plan.unarchiveFrom(), Unarchiver()

Returned By: Archiver.archive(), ClassTable.archive(), Plan.archiveData(), Plan.archiveFromStream(), Unarchiver.archive()

netscape.util.Archiver

This class allows object data to be written into an Archive. When you create an Archiver, you must specify the Archive object that it will write to. To archive an object, call archiveRootObject(), which will archive the specified object and recursively archive all the objects it refers to.

The static writeObject() method is a convenience method useful when you want write only a single root object into an Archive and then output the contents of the Archive to an output stream in binary format. This method automatically creates the required Archive object, writes the specified object to that Archive, and then outputs the contents of the Archive to the specified string. writeObject() is intended for use with the corresponding static shortcut method Unarchiver.readObject().

The various encode methods of this class are the methods required by the Encoder interface. When an object is being archived with the Archiver, its encode() method will be called with the Archiver specified as its Encoder argument. That encode() method will use the various Encoder methods to write the value of its fields into the Archive.

```
public class Archiver extends Object implements Encoder {
    // Public Constructor
        public Archiver(Archive archive);
    // Class Methods
        public static void writeObject(java.io.OutputStream outputStream, Object root)
                        throws java.io.IOException, CodingException;
    // Public Instance Methods
        public Archive archive();
        public void archiveRootObject(Object root) throws CodingException;
        public void encodeBoolean(String key, boolean value) throws CodingException; // From Encoder
        public void encodeBooleanArray(String key, boolean[] value, int offset, int length)
                throws CodingException; // From Encoder
        public void encodeByte(String key, byte value) throws CodingException; // From Encoder
        public void encodeByteArray(String key, byte[] value, int offset, int length)
                throws CodingException; // From Encoder
        public void encodeChar(String key, char value) throws CodingException; // From Encoder
        public void encodeCharArray(String key, char[] value, int offset, int length)
                throws CodingException; // From Encoder
        public void encodeDouble(String key, double value) throws CodingException; // From Encoder
        public void encodeDoubleArray(String key, double[] value, int offset, int length)
                throws CodingException; // From Encoder
        public void encodeFloat(String key, float value) throws CodingException; // From Encoder
        public void encodeFloatArray(String key, float[] value, int offset, int length)
                throws CodingException; // From Encoder
        public void encodeInt(String key, int value) throws CodingException; // From Encoder
```

$\rightarrow$

```
        public void encodeIntArray(String key, int[] value, int offset, int length)
                throws CodingException;  // From Encoder
        public void encodeLong(String key, long value) throws CodingException;  // From Encoder
        public void encodeLongArray(String key, long[] value, int offset, int length)
                throws CodingException;  // From Encoder
        public void encodeObject(String key, Object value) throws CodingException;  // From Encoder
        public void encodeObjectArray(String key, Object[] value, int offset, int length)
                throws CodingException;  // From Encoder
        public void encodeShort(String key, short value) throws CodingException;  // From Encoder
        public void encodeShortArray(String key, short[] value, int offset, int length)
                throws CodingException;  // From Encoder
        public void encodeString(String key, String value) throws CodingException;  // From Encoder
        public void encodeStringArray(String key, String[] value, int offset, int length)
                throws CodingException;  // From Encoder
}
```

netscape.util.ClassInfo

This class stores archiving information about a class: the class name, version, and the name and type of each of its persistent fields. A ClassInfo object is passed to the describeClassInfo() method of any Codable object. This method must call addClass() to specify the class name and version number, and then it must call addField() repeatedly to specify the name and types of each of its fields. The valid field types are the _TYPE constants defined by the Codable interface.

addClass() and addField() are the only ClassInfo methods most programs need to use. The remaining methods are internal to the archiving mechanisms.

```
public class ClassInfo extends Object {
    // Public Constructor
        public ClassInfo(String className);
    // Public Instance Methods
        public void addClass(String className, int version);
        public void addField(String fieldName, byte fieldType);
        public int classCount();
        public String className();
        public String[] classNames();
        public int[] classVersions();
        public int fieldCapacityFor(int cap);
        public int fieldCount();
        public String[] fieldNames();
        public byte[] fieldTypes();
    // Protected Instance Methods
        protected void ensureClassCapacity(int cap);
        protected void ensureFieldCapacity(int cap);
}
```

Passed To: the describeClassInfo() methods of various Codable classes

netscape.util.ClassTable

This class is used internally by the Archive class to store data for any number of instances of a single class. You never need to use this class directly in your programs.

```
public class ClassTable extends Object {
// Public Constructors
    public ClassTable(Archive archive);
    public ClassTable(Archive archive, ClassInfo classInfo);
// Public Instance Methods
    public Archive archive();
    public boolean[] booleanArrayAt(int row, int column);
    public boolean booleanAt(int row, int column);
    public byte[] byteArrayAt(int row, int column);
    public byte byteAt(int row, int column);
    public char[] charArrayAt(int row, int column);
    public char charAt(int row, int column);
    public String className();
    public String[] classNames();
    public int columnForField(String key);
    public double[] doubleArrayAt(int row, int column);
    public double doubleAt(int row, int column);
    public float[] floatArrayAt(int row, int column);
    public float floatAt(int row, int column);
    public int[] identifierArrayAt(int row, int column);
    public int identifierAt(int row, int column);
    public int[] intArrayAt(int row, int column);
    public int intAt(int row, int column);
    public long[] longArrayAt(int row, int column);
    public long longAt(int row, int column);
    public int newIdentifier();
    public void readData(java.io.InputStream inputStream) throws java.io.IOException;
    public void readInfo(java.io.InputStream inputStream) throws java.io.IOException;
    public int rowCount();
    public int rowForIdentifier(int id);
    public void setBooleanArrayAt(int row, int column, boolean[] value);
    public void setBooleanAt(int row, int column, boolean value);
    public void setByteArrayAt(int row, int column, byte[] value);
    public void setByteAt(int row, int column, byte value);
    public void setCharArrayAt(int row, int column, char[] value);
    public void setCharAt(int row, int column, char value);
    public void setDoubleArrayAt(int row, int column, double[] value);
    public void setDoubleAt(int row, int column, double value);
    public void setFloatArrayAt(int row, int column, float[] value);
    public void setFloatAt(int row, int column, float value);
    public void setIdentifierArrayAt(int row, int column, int[] value);
    public void setIdentifierAt(int row, int column, int value);
    public void setIntArrayAt(int row, int column, int[] value);
    public void setIntAt(int row, int column, int value);
    public void setLongArrayAt(int row, int column, long[] value);
    public void setLongAt(int row, int column, long value);
```

$\rightarrow$

```
        public void setShortArrayAt(int row, int column, short[] value);
        public void setShortAt(int row, int column, short value);
        public void setStringArrayAt(int row, int column, String[] value);
        public void setStringAt(int row, int column, String value);
        public short[] shortArrayAt(int row, int column);
        public short shortAt(int row, int column);
        public String[] stringArrayAt(int row, int column);
        public String stringAt(int row, int column);
        public int versionForClassName(String className);
        public void writeData(java.io.OutputStream outputStream) throws java.io.IOException;
        public void writeInfo(java.io.OutputStream outputStream) throws java.io.IOException;
}
```

Passed To: Archive.addClassTable(), Archive.mapIdentifier()

Returned By: Archive.classTableForIdentifier(), Archive.classTableForName()

---

netscape.util.Codable

This interface defines the methods required by any object that needs to support IFC-style archiving and unarchiving. It also defines constants used to specify the type of the fields of a class.

The `describeClassInfo()` method is called once for each class involved in archiving and unarchiving. It must call the `addClass()` and `addField()` methods of the specified `ClassInfo` object to specify the class name, version number, and the name and type of all of its persistent fields.

`encode()` is called to archive an object. It should use the various `Encoder` methods to output the value of each of its fields. `decode()` is called to unarchive an object, and it should use the methods of the specified `Decoder` to read in the value of each of its fields. This method may also set initial values for non-persistent fields that were not decoded. Finally, `finishDecoding()` is invoked when an object has been fully decoded; it can be used to perform any additional initialization required for the object.

If the superclass of a `Codable` class is also `Codable`, then each of the `Codable` methods should first invoke the corresponding method in the superclass. For successful unarchiving, every `Codable` object must have a constructor that expects no arguments.

```
public abstract interface Codable {
// Constants
        public static final byte BOOLEAN_TYPE, BOOLEAN_ARRAY_TYPE;
        public static final byte BYTE_TYPE, BYTE_ARRAY_TYPE;
        public static final byte CHAR_TYPE, CHAR_ARRAY_TYPE;
        public static final byte DOUBLE_TYPE, DOUBLE_ARRAY_TYPE;
        public static final byte FLOAT_TYPE, FLOAT_ARRAY_TYPE;
        public static final byte INT_TYPE, INT_ARRAY_TYPE;
        public static final byte LONG_TYPE, LONG_ARRAY_TYPE;
        public static final byte OBJECT_TYPE, OBJECT_ARRAY_TYPE;
        public static final byte SHORT_TYPE, SHORT_ARRAY_TYPE;
```

public static final byte **STRING_TYPE, STRING_ARRAY_TYPE**;
// *Public Instance Methods*
    public abstract void **decode**(Decoder *decoder*) throws CodingException;
    public abstract void **describeClassInfo**(ClassInfo *info*);
    public abstract void **encode**(Encoder *encoder*) throws CodingException;
    public abstract void **finishDecoding**() throws CodingException;
}

Implemented By: Border, Color, DrawingSequence, Font, GridLayout, Hashtable, HTMLParsingRules, Image, ImageAttachment, ListItem, Menu, MenuItem, PackConstraints, PackLayout, Plan, PlanLoader, Point, Polygon, Range, Rect, Script, Size, Sound, TargetProxy, TextAttachment, TextParagraphFormat, Vector, View, ViewProxy

---

netscape.util.CodingException

This exception signals that an error occurred during the encoding of an object into an Archive or the decoding of the object from an Archive.

public class **CodingException** extends Exception {
// *Public Constructors*
    public **CodingException**();
    public **CodingException**(String *string*);
}

Hierarchy: Object→Throwable(Serializable)→Exception→CodingException

Thrown By: many methods, including the encode(), decode(), and finishDecoding() methods of various Codable classes

---

netscape.util.Comparable

This interface defines the compareTo() method that a class must implement if it wants to allow instances to be sorted by the Sort.sort() or Vector.sort() methods. compareTo() should return –1 if the this object is less than the object passed as an argument (i.e., if this should appear before the object in a sorted ascending list). compareTo() should return 0 if the two objects are equal or are equivalent for sorting purposes, and can appear in any order. Finally, compareTo() should return 1 if the this object is greater than or comes after the argument object.

public abstract interface **Comparable** {
// *Public Instance Methods*
    public abstract int **compareTo**(Object *other*);
}

---

netscape.util.Decoder

This interface defines the methods that an object invokes to read the value of its named fields from an Archive. There is one Decoder method for each possible field type. The Unarchiver object implements this interface.

→

The `replaceObject()` method is an advanced feature that is not commonly required. It allows a class to provide an entirely new object, which should replace the object being unarchived.

```
public abstract interface Decoder {
  // Public Instance Methods
     public abstract boolean decodeBoolean(String key) throws CodingException;
     public abstract boolean[] decodeBooleanArray(String key) throws CodingException;
     public abstract byte decodeByte(String key) throws CodingException;
     public abstract byte[] decodeByteArray(String key) throws CodingException;
     public abstract char decodeChar(String key) throws CodingException;
     public abstract char[] decodeCharArray(String key) throws CodingException;
     public abstract double decodeDouble(String key) throws CodingException;
     public abstract double[] decodeDoubleArray(String key) throws CodingException;
     public abstract float decodeFloat(String key) throws CodingException;
     public abstract float[] decodeFloatArray(String key) throws CodingException;
     public abstract int decodeInt(String key) throws CodingException;
     public abstract int[] decodeIntArray(String key) throws CodingException;
     public abstract long decodeLong(String key) throws CodingException;
     public abstract long[] decodeLongArray(String key) throws CodingException;
     public abstract Object decodeObject(String key) throws CodingException;
     public abstract Object[] decodeObjectArray(String key) throws CodingException;
     public abstract short decodeShort(String key) throws CodingException;
     public abstract short[] decodeShortArray(String key) throws CodingException;
     public abstract String decodeString(String key) throws CodingException;
     public abstract String[] decodeStringArray(String key) throws CodingException;
     public abstract void replaceObject(Object replacement) throws CodingException;
     public abstract int versionForClassName(String className) throws CodingException;
}
```

Implemented By: Unarchiver

Passed To: BezelBorder.decode(), Bitmap.decode(), Border.decode(), Button.decode(), Codable.decode(), Color.decode(), ColorWell.decode(), ContainerView.decode(), DragWell.decode(), DrawingSequence.decode(), EmptyBorder.decode(), Font.decode(), GridLayout.decode(), Hashtable.decode(), HTMLParsingRules.decode(), Image.decode(), ImageAttachment.decode(), ImageSequence.decode(), InternalWindow.decode(), InternalWindowBorder.decode(), Label.decode(), LineBorder.decode(), ListItem.decode(), ListView.decode(), Menu.decode(), MenuItem.decode(), MenuView.decode(), PackConstraints.decode(), PackLayout.decode(), Plan.decode(), PlanLoader.decode(), Point.decode(), Polygon.decode(), Popup.decode(), PopupItem.decode(), Range.decode(), Rect.decode(), ScrollBar.decode(), ScrollGroup.decode(), ScrollView.decode(), Size.decode(), Slider.decode(), Sound.decode(), TargetProxy.decode(), TextAttachment.decode(), TextField.decode(), TextParagraphFormat.decode(), TextView.decode(), Vector.decode(), View.decode(), ViewProxy.decode(), WindowContentView.decode()

---

netscape.util.DeserializationException

This exception signals that an error occurred during deserialization of a `Vector`, `Hashtable`, or other data structure from its ASCII format. The `lineNumber()` method returns the line number at which the error occurred.

```
public class DeserializationException extends Exception {
   // Public Constructor
      public DeserializationException(String string, int lineNumber);
   // Public Instance Methods
      public int lineNumber();
}
```

Hierarchy: Object→Throwable(Serializable)→Exception→DeserializationException

Thrown By: Archive.readASCII(), Deserializer.readObject()

netscape.util.Deserializer

This input stream type is used internally by Archive.readASCII() to read a text representation of an Archive. You never need to use this class explicitly in the unarchiving process. You may occasionally find it useful, however to deserialize textual representations of Vector and Hashtable objects written with a Serializer or FormattingSerializer stream. Note that Deserializer can only deserialize vectors and hashtables when all elements or key/value pairs are strings.

```
public class Deserializer extends java.io.FilterInputStream {
   // Public Constructor
      public Deserializer(java.io.InputStream inputStream);
   // Class Methods
      public static Object deserializeObject(String serialization);
      public static Object readObject(java.io.InputStream inputStream);
   // Public Instance Methods
      public Object readObject() throws java.io.IOException, DeserializationException;
}
```

Hierarchy: Object→InputStream→FilterInputStream→Deserializer

netscape.util.Encoder

This interface defines the methods that an object invokes to write the value of its named fields to an Archive. There is one Encoder method for each possible field type. The Archiver object implements this interface.

```
public abstract interface Encoder {
   // Public Instance Methods
      public abstract void encodeBoolean(String key, boolean value) throws CodingException;
      public abstract void encodeBooleanArray(String key, boolean[] value, int offset, int length)
                     throws CodingException;
      public abstract void encodeByte(String key, byte value) throws CodingException;
      public abstract void encodeByteArray(String key, byte[] value, int offset, int length) throws CodingException;
      public abstract void encodeChar(String key, char value) throws CodingException;
      public abstract void encodeCharArray(String key, char[] value, int offset, int length) throws CodingException;
      public abstract void encodeDouble(String key, double value) throws CodingException;
      public abstract void encodeDoubleArray(String key, double[] value, int offset, int length)
                     throws CodingException;
      public abstract void encodeFloat(String key, float value) throws CodingException;
      public abstract void encodeFloatArray(String key, float[] value, int offset, int length)
                     throws CodingException;
```

$\rightarrow$

```
        public abstract void encodeInt(String key, int value) throws CodingException;
        public abstract void encodeIntArray(String key, int[] value, int offset, int length) throws CodingException;
        public abstract void encodeLong(String key, long value) throws CodingException;
        public abstract void encodeLongArray(String key, long[] value, int offset, int length)
                throws CodingException;
        public abstract void encodeObject(String key, Object value)
                throws CodingException;
        public abstract void encodeObjectArray(String key, Object[] value, int offset, int length)
                throws CodingException;
        public abstract void encodeShort(String key, short value)
                throws CodingException;
        public abstract void encodeShortArray(String key, short[] value, int offset, int length)
                throws CodingException;
        public abstract void encodeString(String key, String value) throws CodingException;
        public abstract void encodeStringArray(String key, String[] value, int offset, int length)
                throws CodingException;
}
```

Implemented By: Archiver

Passed To: BezelBorder.encode(), Bitmap.encode(), Border.encode(), Button.encode(), Codable.encode(), Color.encode(), ColorWell.encode(), ContainerView.encode(), DragWell.encode(), DrawingSequence.encode(), Font.encode(), GridLayout.encode(), Hashtable.encode(), HTMLParsingRules.encode(), Image.encode(), ImageAttachment.encode(), ImageSequence.encode(), InternalWindow.encode(), InternalWindowBorder.encode(), Label.encode(), LineBorder.encode(), ListItem.encode(), ListView.encode(), Menu.encode(), MenuItem.encode(), MenuView.encode(), PackConstraints.encode(), PackLayout.encode(), Plan.encode(), PlanLoader.encode(), Point.encode(), Polygon.encode(), Popup.encode(), PopupItem.encode(), Range.encode(), Rect.encode(), ScrollBar.encode(), ScrollGroup.encode(), ScrollView.encode(), Size.encode(), Slider.encode(), Sound.encode(), TargetProxy.encode(), TextAttachment.encode(), TextField.encode(), TextParagraphFormat.encode(), TextView.encode(), Vector.encode(), View.encode(), ViewProxy.encode(), WindowContentView.encode()

---

netscape.util.Enumeration

This interface defines the methods necessary to enumerate a set of values, such as the values contained in a vector or hashtable data structure. To use an Enumeration object, you use its two methods in a loop: hasMoreElements() returns true if there are more values to be enumerated, and can be used to determine whether the loop should continue. Within a loop, a call to nextElement() returns a value from the enumeration. An Enumeration makes no guarantees about the order in which the values are returned. You can only iterate through an Enumeration once; there are no methods to back up or start over at the beginning.

Vector and Hashtable define methods that return internal objects that implement the Enumeration interface.

This interface is identical to java.util.Enumeration.

```
public abstract interface Enumeration {
    // Public Instance Methods
        public abstract boolean hasMoreElements();
```

```
    public abstract Object nextElement( );
}
```

Returned By: Hashtable.elements(), Hashtable.keys(), Vector.elements()

netscape.util.FormattingSerializer

This subclass of Serializer produces formatted output that is more easily human-readable than the output of Serializer. It is used internally by the Archive.writeASCII() method when formatted text output is requested. You never need to use it explicitly in your programs.

```
public class FormattingSerializer extends Serializer {
  // Public Constructor
      public FormattingSerializer(java.io.OutputStream outputStream);
  // Class Methods
      public static byte[] formatBytes(byte[] input);
      public static String serializeObject(Object anObject);
      public static boolean writeObject(java.io.OutputStream outputStream, Object anObject);
  // Public Instance Methods
      public int indentationLength( );
      public void setIndentationLength(int numberOfSpaces);
      public void writeComment(String aComment, boolean cStyle) throws java.io.IOException;
      public void writeObject(Object anObject) throws java.io.IOException;  // Overrides Serializer
}
```

Hierarchy: Object→OutputStream→FilterOutputStream→Serializer→FormattingSerializer

netscape.util.Hashtable

This class implements a Hashtable data structure to efficiently associate arbitrary key objects with arbitrary value objects. put() associates a value with a key. get() retrieves the value associated with a key. remove() removes a key and its value from the hashtable. keys() and elements() return Enumeration objects that allow you to iterate through the keys and values stored in the hashtable. Other methods return the lists of keys and values as vectors or arrays.

This class is very similar to and has all the public methods of java.util.Hashtable. It also has additional convenience methods, and methods to support IFC archiving. An important difference between the two classes is that the methods of netscape.util.Hashtable are not synchronized, which increases efficiency but means that instances of this class must not be used by more than one thread.

```
public class Hashtable extends Object implements Cloneable, Codable {
  // Public Constructors
      public Hashtable( );
      public Hashtable(int initialCapacity);
  // Public Instance Methods
      public void clear( );
      public Object clone( );  // Overrides Object
      public boolean contains(Object element);
      public boolean containsKey(Object key);
      public int count( );
```

→

```
        public void decode(Decoder decoder) throws CodingException;  // From Codable
        public void describeClassInfo(ClassInfo info);  // From Codable
        public Enumeration elements();
        public Object[] elementsArray();
        public Vector elementsVector();
        public void encode(Encoder encoder) throws CodingException;  // From Codable
        public void finishDecoding() throws CodingException;  // From Codable
        public Object get(Object key);
        public boolean isEmpty();
        public Enumeration keys();
        public Object[] keysArray();
        public Vector keysVector();
        public Object put(Object key, Object element);
        public Object remove(Object key);
        public int size();
        public String toString();  // Overrides Object
}
```

Passed To: HTMLParsingRules.setRulesForMarker(), Plan(), Plan.createPlan(), Plan.decodeBETADocumentInformation(), Plan.decodeDocumentInformation(), Plan.encodeDocumentInformation(), Plan.setNameToComponent(), Plan.setObjectToBounds(), Plan.unarchiveFrom(), Plan.unarchiveObjects(), TextView.addAttributesForRange(), TextView.importHTMLInRange(), TextView.insertHTMLElementsInRange(), TextView.setAttributesForRange(), TextView.setDefaultAttributes(), TextView.setTypingAttributes(), TextViewHTMLContainer.attributesForContents(), TextViewHTMLContainer.attributesForPrefix(), TextViewHTMLContainer.attributesForSuffix(), TextViewHTMLContainer.cleanupContext(), TextViewHTMLContainer.prefix(), TextViewHTMLContainer.setupContext(), TextViewHTMLContainer.string(), TextViewHTMLContainer.suffix(), TextViewHTMLElement.fontFromAttributes(), TextViewHTMLElement.string(), TextViewHTMLMarker.attributesForMarker(), TextViewHTMLMarker.attributesForPrefix(), TextViewHTMLMarker.attributesForSuffix(), TextViewHTMLMarker.prefix(), TextViewHTMLMarker.string(), TextViewHTMLMarker.suffix(), TextViewHTMLString.string()

Returned By: HTMLParsingRules.rulesForMarker(), Plan.nameToComponent(), Plan.objectToBounds(), TextView.attributesAtIndex(), TextView.defaultAttributes(), TextView.typingAttributes(), TextViewHTMLContainer.attributes(), TextViewHTMLContainer.attributesForContents(), TextViewHTMLContainer.attributesForPrefix(), TextViewHTMLContainer.attributesForSuffix(), TextViewHTMLElement.hashtableForHTMLAttributes(), TextViewHTMLMarker.attributes(), TextViewHTMLMarker.attributesForMarker(), TextViewHTMLMarker.attributesForPrefix(), TextViewHTMLMarker.attributesForSuffix()

---

netscape.util.InconsistencyException

Despite its name, this class is a type of Error, not an Exception. It indicates that the IFC has detected invalid data or an inconsistent state. It is typically thrown when your program calls an IFC method with an invalid argument. It may also be thrown when an internal error occurs within an IFC class.

```
public class InconsistencyException extends Error {
    // Public Constructors
        public InconsistencyException();
```

```
    public InconsistencyException(String s);
}
```

Hierarchy: Object→Throwable(Serializable)→Error→InconsistencyException

netscape.util.NoSuchElementException

This exception signals that an Enumeration is empty or has no more elements to enumerate. This exception is identical to java.util.NoSuchElementException.

```
public class NoSuchElementException extends RuntimeException {
    // Public Constructors
        public NoSuchElementException();
        public NoSuchElementException(String s);
}
```

Hierarchy: Object→Throwable(Serializable)→Exception→RuntimeException→NoSuchElementException

netscape.util.Serializer

This output stream is used internally by Archive.writeASCII() to output the contents of an Archive in text format. Although you never need to use it explicitly in the archiving process, you may occasionally find it helpful to output a textual representation of a Vector or Hashtable object that can be read back in with a Deserializer. In order for deserialization to work, the elements of the Vector or the key/value pairs in the Hashtable must all be strings.

```
public class Serializer extends java.io.FilterOutputStream {
    // Public Constructor
        public Serializer(java.io.OutputStream outputStream);
    // Class Methods
        public static String serializeObject(Object anObject);
        public static boolean writeObject(java.io.OutputStream outputStream, Object anObject);
    // Public Instance Methods
        public void flush() throws java.io.IOException; // Overrides FilterOutputStream
        public void writeObject(Object anObject) throws java.io.IOException;
}
```

Hierarchy: Object→OutputStream→FilterOutputStream→Serializer

Extended By: FormattingSerializer

netscape.util.Sort

This class defines two static methods that efficiently sort strings and Comparable objects. sort() sorts the specified elements of the first array into ascending or descending order, and also reorders the second array in the same way. The specified elements of the array must all be String objects or implement the Comparable interface, and they all must be of the same type. sortStrings() sorts the specified elements of the specified array (which must all be strings) into ascending or descending order. If *ignoreCase* is true, then the sort will be case-insensitive.

→

```
public class Sort extends Object {
  // No Constructor
  // Class Methods
    public static void sort(Object[] array, Object[] other, int begin, int count, boolean ascending);
    public static void sortStrings(Object[] strings, int begin, int count, boolean ascending, boolean ignoreCase);
}
```

---

netscape.util.Unarchiver

This class allows object data to be read from an Archive. When you create an Unarchiver, you must specify the Archive object that it will read from. To unarchive an object, call unarchiveIdentifier(), specifying an integer that identifies the object to be unarchived. This integer should be an element of the array returned by the rootIdentifiers() method of the Archive being read. unarchiveIdentifier() reads the specified root object and recursively reads all objects it refers to. It returns the unarchived object as an Object; you are responsible for casting it to its actual type.

The static readObject() method is a convenient shortcut that is useful when you want to read the contents of a binary archive that contains only a single root object. This method automatically creates the required Archive object, reads binary data from the specified stream into the Archive, and then creates an Unarchiver to read the archived object from the Archive. readObject() is intended for use with the corresponding static shortcut method Archiver.writeObject().

The various decode methods of this class are the methods required by the Decoder interface. When an object is being unarchived with the Unarchiver, its decode() method will be called with the Unarchiver passed as its Decoder argument. That decode() method will use the various Decoder methods to read the values of its fields from the Archive.

```
public class Unarchiver extends Object implements Decoder {
  // Public Constructor
    public Unarchiver(Archive archive);
  // Class Methods
    public static Object readObject(java.io.InputStream inputStream)
                    throws java.io.IOException, CodingException;
  // Public Instance Methods
    public Archive archive();
    public boolean decodeBoolean(String key) throws CodingException;  // From Decoder
    public boolean[] decodeBooleanArray(String key) throws CodingException;  // From Decoder
    public byte decodeByte(String key) throws CodingException;  // From Decoder
    public byte[] decodeByteArray(String key) throws CodingException;  // From Decoder
    public char decodeChar(String key) throws CodingException;  // From Decoder
    public char[] decodeCharArray(String key) throws CodingException;  // From Decoder
    public double decodeDouble(String key) throws CodingException;  // From Decoder
    public double[] decodeDoubleArray(String key) throws CodingException;  // From Decoder
    public float decodeFloat(String key) throws CodingException;  // From Decoder
    public float[] decodeFloatArray(String key) throws CodingException;  // From Decoder
    public int decodeInt(String key) throws CodingException;  // From Decoder
```

```
        public int[] decodeIntArray(String key) throws CodingException; // From Decoder
        public long decodeLong(String key) throws CodingException; // From Decoder
        public long[] decodeLongArray(String key) throws CodingException; // From Decoder
        public Object decodeObject(String key) throws CodingException; // From Decoder
        public Object[] decodeObjectArray(String key) throws CodingException; // From Decoder
        public short decodeShort(String key) throws CodingException; // From Decoder
        public short[] decodeShortArray(String key) throws CodingException; // From Decoder
        public String decodeString(String key) throws CodingException; // From Decoder
        public String[] decodeStringArray(String key) throws CodingException; // From Decoder
        public void replaceObject(Object replacement) throws CodingException; // From Decoder
        public Object unarchiveIdentifier(int identifier) throws CodingException;
        public int versionForClassName(String className) throws CodingException; // From Decoder
    // Protected Instance Methods
        protected Class classForName(String className) throws CodingException;
}
```

netscape.util.Vector

This class implements an array of objects that grows in size as necessary. It is useful when you need to keep track of a number of objects but do not know in
advance how many there will be. There are a number of methods for storing
objects in and removing objects from a Vector. Other methods search for a given
object within a Vector. sort() sorts the elements of a Vector, assuming all elements are strings or Comparable objects.

This class is very similar to and duplicates almost all the public methods of
java.util.Vector. It also has a number of additional convenience methods, and
methods to support IFC archiving. An important difference between the two
classes is that the methods of netscape.util.Vector are not synchronized, which
increases efficiency but means that instances of this class must not be used by
more than one thread without explicit synchronization. Another difference is that
netscape.util.Vector does not allow null to be added as an element.

```
public class Vector extends Object implements Cloneable, Codable {
    // Public Constructors
        public Vector();
        public Vector(int initialCapacity);
    // Public Instance Methods
        public void addElement(Object element);
        public void addElementIfAbsent(Object element);
        public void addElements(Vector aVector);
        public void addElementsIfAbsent(Vector aVector);
        public int capacity();
        public Object clone(); // Overrides Object
        public boolean contains(Object element);
        public boolean containsIdentical(Object element);
        public void copyInto(Object[] anArray);
        public int count();
        public void decode(Decoder decoder) throws CodingException; // From Codable
        public void describeClassInfo(ClassInfo info); // From Codable
        public Object[] elementArray();
        public Object elementAt(int index);
```

$\rightarrow$

```
        public Enumeration elements( );
        public Enumeration elements(int index);
        public void encode(Encoder encoder) throws CodingException;  // From Codable
        public void ensureCapacity(int minCapacity);
        public void finishDecoding( ) throws CodingException;  // From Codable
        public Object firstElement( );
        public int indexOf(Object element);
        public int indexOf(Object element, int index);
        public int indexOfIdentical(Object element, int index);
        public int indexOfIdentical(Object element);
        public boolean insertElementAfter(Object element, Object existingElement);
        public void insertElementAt(Object element, int index);
        public boolean insertElementBefore(Object element, Object existingElement);
        public boolean isEmpty( );
        public Object lastElement( );
        public int lastIndexOf(Object element);
        public int lastIndexOf(Object element, int index);
        public void removeAll(Object element);
        public void removeAllElements( );
        public boolean removeElement(Object element);
        public Object removeElementAt(int index);
        public boolean removeElementIdentical(Object element);
        public Object removeFirstElement( );
        public Object removeLastElement( );
        public Object replaceElementAt(int index, Object element);
        public void setElementAt(Object element, int index);
        public int size( );
        public void sort(boolean ascending);
        public void sortStrings(boolean ascending, boolean ignoreCase);
        public String toString( );  // Overrides Object
        public void trimToSize( );
}
```

Passed To: EventFilter.filterEvents(), Plan.setComponents(), Plan.setRootComponents(),
Rect.computeDisunionRects(), TargetProxy.setCommands(), TextFilter.acceptsEvent(), TextView.filterEvents(),
TextView.insertHTMLElementsInRange(), Timer.filterEvents(), Vector.addElements(), Vector.addElementsIfAbsent()

Returned By: Application.externalWindows(), Application.rootViews(), Hashtable.elementsVector(),
Hashtable.keysVector(), ImageSequence.images(), ListView.selectedItems(), Plan.components(),
Plan.rootComponents(), PlanLoader.windowVector(), RootView.internalWindows(), TargetProxy.commands(),
TextView.paragraphsForRange(), TextView.rectsForRange(), TextView.runsForRange(),
TextViewHTMLContainer.childrenVector(), View.peersForSubview(), View.subviews()

Class, Method, and Field Index

The following index allows you to look up a class or interface and find out what package it is defined in. It also allows you to look up a method or field and find out what class it is defined in. Use it when you want to look up a class but don't know its package, or want to look up a method but don't know its class.

ANCHOR_NORTH: PackConstraints
ANCHOR_NORTHEAST: PackConstraints
ANCHOR_NORTHWEST: PackConstraints
ANCHOR_SOUTH: PackConstraints
ANCHOR_SOUTHEAST: PackConstraints
ANCHOR_SOUTHWEST: PackConstraints
ANCHOR_WEST: PackConstraints
ANY_CHARACTER: TextField
appendString(): TextView
applet(): Application
appletResources(): Application
appletStarted(): Application
appletStopped(): Application
Application: netscape.application
application(): Application, FoundationApplet
APPLICATION_TYPE: TargetProxy
applicationChain(): TargetChain
applicationDidPause(): ApplicationObserver, ExternalWindow
applicationDidResume(): ApplicationObserver, ExternalWindow
applicationDidStart(): ApplicationObserver, ExternalWindow
applicationDidStop(): ApplicationObserver, ExternalWindow
ApplicationObserver: netscape.application
appliesAttributesToChildren(): TextViewHTMLContainer
Archive: netscape.util
archive(): Archiver, ClassTable, Unarchiver
ARCHIVE_MAGIC: Archive
archiveData(): Plan
archiveFormat(): Plan
archiveFormatOf(): Plan
archiveFromStream(): Plan
archiveObjectsToArchiveData(): Plan
Archiver: netscape.util
archiveRootObject(): Archiver
archiveTo(): Plan
ARROW_CURSOR: View
AS_NEEDED_DISPLAY: ScrollGroup
ascent(): FontMetrics
ASCII_FILE_EXTENSION: Plan
ASCII_TYPE: Plan
attributes(): TextViewHTMLContainer, TextViewHTMLMarker
attributesAtIndex(): TextView
attributesDidChange(): TextViewOwner
attributesForContents(): TextViewHTMLContainer
attributesForMarker(): TextViewHTMLMarker
attributesForPrefix(): TextViewHTMLContainer, TextViewHTMLMarker

attributesForSuffix(): TextViewHTMLContainer, TextViewHTMLMarker
attributesWillChange(): TextViewOwner
awtApplet(): AWTCompatibility
awtAudioClipForSound(): AWTCompatibility
awtColorForColor(): AWTCompatibility
AWTCompatibility: netscape.application
awtComponent(): AWTComponentView
AWTComponentView: netscape.application
awtFileDialogForFileChooser(): AWTCompatibility
awtFontForFont(): AWTCompatibility
awtFontMetricsForFontMetrics(): AWTCompatibility
awtFrameForRootView(): AWTCompatibility
awtGraphicsForGraphics(): AWTCompatibility
awtImageForBitmap(): AWTCompatibility
awtImageProducerForBitmap(): AWTCompatibility
awtMenuBarForMenu(): AWTCompatibility
awtMenuForMenu(): AWTCompatibility
awtMenuItemForMenuItem(): AWTCompatibility
awtPanelForRootView(): AWTCompatibility
awtToolkit(): AWTCompatibility
awtWindowForExternalWindow(): AWTCompatibility
axis(): ScrollBar

B

BACKGROUND_COLOR_KEY: Plan
backgroundColor(): ContainerView, ListView, Menu, MenuView, Plan, ScrollView, Slider, TextField, TextView, WindowContentView
BACKSPACE_KEY: KeyEvent
BACKTAB_KEY: TextFieldOwner
backtabField(): TextField
BACKWARD: DrawingSequence
BACKWARD_LOOP: DrawingSequence
baseline(): TextField
baseURL(): TextView
BEGIN_TERMINATION_MARKERS_KEY: HTMLParsingRules
BezelBorder: netscape.application
BINARY_FILE_EXTENSION: Plan
BINARY_TYPE: Plan
Bitmap: netscape.application
bitmapForAWTImage(): AWTCompatibility
bitmapForAWTImageProducer(): AWTCompatibility
bitmapFromURL(): Bitmap
bitmapNamed(): Bitmap
black: Color
blackLine(): LineBorder
BLANK_TYPE: Window
blue: Color
blue(): Color

BOLD: Font
BOOLEAN_ARRAY_TYPE: Codable
BOOLEAN_TYPE: Codable
booleanArrayAt(): ClassTable
booleanAt(): ClassTable
Border: netscape.application
border(): ContainerView, DragWell, InternalWindow, Menu, MenuView, Popup, ScrollGroup, Slider, TextField
BOTTOM_LEFT_POSITION: Application
BOTTOM_MARGIN_CAN_CHANGE: View
BOTTOM_RIGHT_POSITION: Application
bottomMargin(): BezelBorder, Border, EmptyBorder, InternalWindowBorder, LineBorder
BOUNCE: DrawingSequence
boundingRect(): Plan, Polygon
bounds: View
bounds(): ExternalWindow, View, Window
boundsDidChange(): TextAttachment
buffer(): Graphics
BUFFERED_OPTION: DebugGraphics
Button: netscape.application
BYTE_ARRAY_TYPE: Codable
BYTE_TYPE: Codable
byteArrayAt(): ClassTable
byteAt(): ClassTable
bytesWidth(): FontMetrics

C

canBecomeDocument(): InternalWindow
canBecomeMain(): InternalWindow
canBecomeSelectedView(): Button, ColorWell, InternalWindow, ListView, Popup, RootView, Slider, TextField, TextView, View
cancelEditing(): TextField
canDraw(): RootView, View
canPerformCommand(): ExtendedTarget, Plan, Root-View, TargetChain, TextField, TextView
capacity(): Vector
CARET_COLOR_KEY: TextView
caretColor(): TextField, TextView
center(): ExternalWindow, InternalWindow, Window
CENTER_HORIZ: View
CENTER_VERT: View
CENTERED: Graphics, Image
CHAR_ARRAY_TYPE: Codable
CHAR_TYPE: Codable
charArrayAt(): ClassTable
charAt(): ClassTable
charCount(): TextField
charHeight(): FontMetrics

charNumberForPoint(): TextField
charsWidth(): FontMetrics
charWidth(): FontMetrics
checkedImage(): MenuItem
child: MenuView
children(): TextViewHTMLContainer
childrenVector(): TextViewHTMLContainer
chooseNextCurrentDocumentWindow(): Application
CLASS_NAME_KEY: ViewProxy
classCount(): ClassInfo
classForName(): FoundationApplet, Unarchiver
ClassInfo: netscape.util
className(): ClassInfo, ClassTable
classNameForComment(): HTMLParsingRules
classNameForMarker(): HTMLParsingRules
classNameForString(): HTMLParsingRules
classNames(): ClassInfo, ClassTable
ClassTable: netscape.util
classTableForIdentifier(): Archive
classTableForName(): Archive
classVersions(): ClassInfo
cleanup(): Application
cleanupContext(): TextViewHTMLContainer
clear(): Hashtable
clearAllTabPositions(): TextParagraphFormat
clearClipRect(): Graphics
CLICK: Button
click(): Button
clickCount(): Button, MouseEvent
clipboardText(): Application
clipRect(): Graphics
clone(): Event, Hashtable, ListItem, MenuItem, PackConstraints, Plan, TextParagraphFormat, Vector
Codable: netscape.util
codeBase(): Application
CodingException: netscape.util
Color: netscape.application
color(): ColorChooser, ColorWell, Graphics, Label, LineBorder, RootView
COLOR_TYPE: Color
ColorChooser: netscape.application
colorChooser(): RootView
colorForAWTColor(): AWTCompatibility
colorForHSB(): Color
ColorWell: netscape.application
columnCount(): GridLayout
columnForField(): ClassTable
command(): Button, ColorWell, CommandEvent, Label, ListItem, ListView, MenuItem, Popup, Script, Slider, TextField, Timer
CommandEvent: netscape.application
commandKey(): Label, MenuItem

commands(): TargetProxy, ViewProxy
COMMANDS_KEY: ViewProxy
COMMENT_MARKER_KEY: HTMLParsingRules
Comparable: netscape.util
compareTo(): Comparable
completeEditing(): TextField
componentNamed(): Plan
components(): Plan
computeDisunionRects(): Rect
computeInteriorRect(): Border
computeVisibleRect(): ScrollView, View
constraintsFor(): PackLayout
Constructor: netscape.constructor
constructorComponentWasView(): Plan
ContainerView: netscape.application
contains(): Hashtable, Range, Rect, Vector
containsDocument(): ExternalWindow, Internal-
Window, Window
containsIdentical(): Vector
containsKey(): Hashtable
containsPoint(): Polygon, View
containsPointInVisibleRect(): View
contentsChangedCommand(): TextField
contentsChangedTarget(): TextField
contentSize(): ExternalWindow, InternalWindow,
Window
contentView(): ColorChooser, FontChooser, Internal-
Window, ScrollGroup, ScrollView
CONTINUOUS_TYPE: Button
CONTROL_MASK: DragSession, KeyEvent
convertEventToView(): View
convertPointToView(): View
convertRectToView(): View
convertToView(): View
COPY: ExtendedTarget
copy(): TextField, TextView
copyInto(): Vector
count(): Hashtable, ListView, Popup, Vector
CREATE_PLAN: PlanLoader
createApplet(): Application
createBuffer(): View
createCheckButton(): Button
createCloseButton(): InternalWindow
createDialog(): ExternalWindow
createFrame(): ExternalWindow
createGraphics(): Bitmap, View
createLabel(): TextField
createMenuAsSubmenu(): Menu
createMenuView(): MenuView
createMenuWindow(): MenuView
createPanel(): ExternalWindow, FoundationApplet
createPlan(): Plan, PlanLoader
createPushButton(): Button

createRadioButton(): Button
createScrollBar(): ScrollGroup
createScrollView(): ScrollGroup
createWindow(): ExternalWindow
CROSSHAIR_CURSOR: View
CURRENT_VERSION_NUMBER: Plan
currentDocumentDidChange(): ApplicationObserver,
ExternalWindow
currentDocumentWindow(): Application
currentFrameNumber(): DrawingSequence
currentImage(): ImageSequence
cursor(): RootView
cursorForPoint(): ScrollView, TextField, TextView,
View
CUSTOM_TYPE: TargetProxy
CUT: ExtendedTarget
cut(): TextField, TextView
cyan: Color

D

darkerColor(): Color
darkGray: Color
data(): CommandEvent, DragSession, DragWell, List-
Item, MenuItem, Timer
dataType(): ColorWell, DragSession, DragWell
debug(): DebugGraphics
DebugGraphics: netscape.application
debugOptions(): DebugGraphics, Graphics
decode(): BezelBorder, Bitmap, Border, Button, Cod-
able, Color, ColorWell, ContainerView, DragWell,
DrawingSequence, EmptyBorder, Font, Grid-
Layout, Hashtable, HTMLParsingRules, Image,
ImageAttachment, ImageSequence, Internal-
Window, InternalWindowBorder, Label, Line-
Border, ListItem, ListView, Menu, MenuItem,
MenuView, PackConstraints, PackLayout, Plan,
PlanLoader, Point, Polygon, Popup, PopupItem,
Range, Rect, Script, ScrollBar, ScrollGroup,
ScrollView, Size, Slider, Sound, TargetProxy, Text-
Attachment, TextField, TextParagraphFormat,
TextView, Vector, View, ViewProxy, Window-
ContentView
decodeBETADocumentInformation(): Plan
decodeBoolean(): Decoder, Unarchiver
decodeBooleanArray(): Decoder, Unarchiver
decodeByte(): Decoder, Unarchiver
decodeByteArray(): Decoder, Unarchiver
decodeChar(): Decoder, Unarchiver
decodeCharArray(): Decoder, Unarchiver
decodeDocumentInformation(): Plan
decodeDouble(): Decoder, Unarchiver

decodeDoubleArray(): Decoder, Unarchiver
decodeFloat(): Decoder, Unarchiver
decodeFloatArray(): Decoder, Unarchiver
decodeInt(): Decoder, Unarchiver
decodeIntArray(): Decoder, Unarchiver
decodeLong(): Decoder, Unarchiver
decodeLongArray(): Decoder, Unarchiver
decodeObject(): Decoder, Unarchiver
decodeObjectArray(): Decoder, Unarchiver
Decoder: netscape.util
decodeShort(): Decoder, Unarchiver
decodeShortArray(): Decoder, Unarchiver
decodeString(): Decoder, Unarchiver
decodeStringArray(): Decoder, Unarchiver
DECREASE_VALUE: Slider
decreaseButton(): ScrollBar
DEFAULT_HEIGHT: ScrollBar
DEFAULT_LAYER: InternalWindow
DEFAULT_LINE_INCREMENT: ScrollBar .
DEFAULT_OPTION: Alert
DEFAULT_PAGE_SIZE: ScrollBar
DEFAULT_WIDTH: ScrollBar
defaultAttributes(): TextView
defaultConstraints(): PackLayout
defaultContainerClassName(): HTMLParsingRules
defaultFont(): Font
defaultMarkerClassName(): HTMLParsingRules
defaultSelectedView(): InternalWindow, RootView
delay(): Timer
DELETE_KEY: KeyEvent
descendsFrom(): View
descent(): FontMetrics
describeClassInfo(): BezelBorder, Bitmap, Border,
    Button, Codable, Color, ColorWell, ContainerView,
    DragWell, DrawingSequence, Font, GridLayout,
    Hashtable, HTMLParsingRules, Image, Image-
    Attachment, ImageSequence, InternalWindow,
    InternalWindowBorder, Label, LineBorder, List-
    Item, ListView, Menu, MenuItem, MenuView,
    PackConstraints, PackLayout, Plan, PlanLoader,
    Point, Polygon, Popup, PopupItem, Range, Rect,
    Script, ScrollBar, ScrollGroup, ScrollView, Size,
    Slider, Sound, TargetProxy, TextAttachment, Text-
    Field, TextParagraphFormat, TextView, Vector,
    View, ViewProxy, WindowContentView
deselectItem(): ListView, MenuView
DeserializationException: netscape.util
deserializeObject(): Deserializer
Deserializer: netscape.util
destination(): DragSession
destinationBounds(): DragSession
destinationIsAccepting(): DragSession
destinationMousePoint(): DragSession

destinationView(): DragSession
destroy(): FoundationApplet
didBecomeCurrentDocument(): ExternalWindow,
    InternalWindow, Window
didBecomeMain(): InternalWindow
didMoveBy(): TextView, View
didProcessEvent(): Application
didResignCurrentDocument(): ExternalWindow,
    InternalWindow, Window
didResignMain(): InternalWindow
didSizeBy(): Label, ScrollBar, ScrollView, Slider,
    TextView, View
directory(): FileChooser
disabledColor(): MenuItem
disableDrawing(): View
disabledTitleColor(): Button
disableResizing(): TextView
dispose(): ExternalWindow, Graphics
DOCUMENT_SIZE_KEY: Plan
doesAutoResizeSubviews(): View
doesCoalesce(): Timer
doesLoop(): DrawingSequence, Sound
doesResetOnStart(): DrawingSequence
doesResetOnStop(): DrawingSequence
DOUBLE_ARRAY_TYPE: Codable
DOUBLE_TYPE: Codable
doubleArrayAt(): ClassTable
doubleAt(): ClassTable
doubleCommand(): ListView
DOWN_ARROW_KEY: KeyEvent
DRAG_LAYER: InternalWindow
DragDestination: netscape.application
dragDropped(): ColorWell, DragDestination, Text-
    View
dragEntered(): ColorWell, DragDestination, TextView
dragExited(): ColorWell, DragDestination, TextView
dragModifiers(): DragSession
dragMoved(): ColorWell, DragDestination, TextView
DragSession: netscape.application
DragSource: netscape.application
dragWasAccepted(): DragSource, DragWell
dragWasRejected(): DragSource, DragWell
DragWell: netscape.application
draw(): InternalWindow, RootView, View
drawableCharacter(): TextField
drawArc(): DebugGraphics, Graphics
drawAt(): Bitmap, DrawingSequence, Image, Image-
    Sequence
drawBackground(): ListItem, MenuItem
drawBezel(): BezelBorder
drawBitmapAt(): DebugGraphics, Graphics
drawBitmapScaled(): DebugGraphics, Graphics

drawBottomBorder(): InternalWindow, Internal-WindowBorder

drawBytes(): DebugGraphics, Graphics

drawCentered(): Image

drawChars(): DebugGraphics, Graphics

drawContents(): ScrollGroup

drawDirtyViews(): RootView

drawGroovedBezel(): BezelBorder

drawingBuffer(): View

DrawingSequence: netscape.application

drawingSequenceCompleted(): Button, DrawingSequenceOwner

drawingSequenceFrameChanged(): Button, DrawingSequenceOwner

DrawingSequenceOwner: netscape.application

drawInRect(): BezelBorder, Border, EmptyBorder, ImageAttachment, InternalWindowBorder, LineBorder, ListItem, MenuItem, PopupItem, TextAttachment

drawInterior(): TextField

drawItemAt(): ListView, MenuView

drawLeftBorder(): InternalWindowBorder

drawLine(): DebugGraphics, Graphics

drawLoweredButtonBezel(): BezelBorder

drawOval(): DebugGraphics, Graphics

drawPoint(): DebugGraphics, Graphics

drawPolygon(): DebugGraphics, Graphics

drawRaisedButtonBezel(): BezelBorder

drawRect(): DebugGraphics, Graphics

drawRightBorder(): InternalWindowBorder

drawRoundedRect(): DebugGraphics, Graphics

drawScaled(): Bitmap, Image, ImageSequence

drawScrollTray(): ScrollBar

drawsDropShadow(): TextField

drawSeparator(): MenuItem

drawString(): DebugGraphics, Graphics

drawStringInRect(): Graphics, ListItem, MenuItem

drawSubviews(): ContainerView, ScrollGroup, ScrollView, View

drawTiled(): Bitmap, Image

drawTitleBar(): InternalWindow, InternalWindowBorder

drawView(): Button, ColorWell, ContainerView, DragWell, InternalWindow, Label, ListView, MenuView, Popup, RootView, ScrollBar, ScrollGroup, ScrollView, Slider, TextField, TextView, View, ViewProxy, WindowContentView

drawViewBackground(): Button, ContainerView, ListView

drawViewBorder(): ContainerView, TextField

drawViewGroove(): Slider

drawViewInterior(): Button, TextField

drawViewKnob(): Slider

drawViewKnobInRect(): ScrollBar

drawViewStringAt(): TextField

drawViewTitleInRect(): Button

drawWithStyle(): Image

E

E_RESIZE_CURSOR: View

elementArray(): Vector

elementAt(): Vector

elements(): Hashtable, Vector

elementsArray(): Hashtable

elementsVector(): Hashtable

EmptyBorder: netscape.application

emptyBorder(): EmptyBorder

enableResizing(): TextView

encode(): BezelBorder, Bitmap, Border, Button, Codable, Color, ColorWell, ContainerView, DragWell, DrawingSequence, Font, GridLayout, Hashtable, HTMLParsingRules, Image, ImageAttachment, ImageSequence, InternalWindow, InternalWindowBorder, Label, LineBorder, ListItem, ListView, Menu, MenuItem, MenuView, PackConstraints, PackLayout, Plan, PlanLoader, Point, Polygon, Popup, PopupItem, Range, Rect, Script, ScrollBar, ScrollGroup, ScrollView, Size, Slider, Sound, TargetProxy, TextAttachment, TextField, TextParagraphFormat, TextView, Vector, View, ViewProxy, WindowContentView

encodeBoolean(): Archiver, Encoder

encodeBooleanArray(): Archiver, Encoder

encodeByte(): Archiver, Encoder

encodeByteArray(): Archiver, Encoder

encodeChar(): Archiver, Encoder

encodeCharArray(): Archiver, Encoder

encodeDocumentInformation(): Plan

encodeDouble(): Archiver, Encoder

encodeDoubleArray(): Archiver, Encoder

encodeFloat(): Archiver, Encoder

encodeFloatArray(): Archiver, Encoder

encodeInt(): Archiver, Encoder

encodeIntArray(): Archiver, Encoder

encodeLong(): Archiver, Encoder

encodeLongArray(): Archiver, Encoder

encodeObject(): Archiver, Encoder

encodeObjectArray(): Archiver, Encoder

Encoder: netscape.util

encodeShort(): Archiver, Encoder

encodeShortArray(): Archiver, Encoder

encodeString(): Archiver, Encoder

encodeStringArray(): Archiver, Encoder

END_KEY: KeyEvent

END_TERMINATION_MARKERS_KEY: HTMLParsing-Rules
ensureCapacity(): Vector
ensureClassCapacity(): ClassInfo
ensureFieldCapacity(): ClassInfo
Enumeration: netscape.util
equals(): Color, Point, Range, Rect, Size
ESCAPE_KEY: KeyEvent
Event: netscape.application
EventFilter: netscape.application
EventLoop: netscape.application
eventLoop(): Application, Timer
EventProcessor: netscape.application
expand(): PackConstraints
ExtendedTarget: netscape.application
ExternalWindow: netscape.application
externalWindow(): RootView
externalWindows(): Application
externalWindowWithContents(): Plan

F

F1_KEY: KeyEvent
F2_KEY: KeyEvent
F3_KEY: KeyEvent
F4_KEY: KeyEvent
F5_KEY: KeyEvent
F6_KEY: KeyEvent
F7_KEY: KeyEvent
F8_KEY: KeyEvent
F9_KEY: KeyEvent
F10_KEY: KeyEvent
F11_KEY: KeyEvent
F12_KEY: KeyEvent
family(): Font
fieldCapacityFor(): ClassInfo
fieldCount(): ClassInfo
fieldNames(): ClassInfo
fieldTypes(): ClassInfo
file(): FileChooser
FileChooser: netscape.application
filenameFilter(): FileChooser
fillArc(): DebugGraphics, Graphics
fillOval(): DebugGraphics, Graphics
fillPolygon(): DebugGraphics, Graphics
fillRect(): DebugGraphics, Graphics
fillRoundedRect(): DebugGraphics, Graphics
fillX(): PackConstraints
fillY(): PackConstraints
filter(): TextField, TextView
filterEvents(): EventFilter, EventLoop, TextView, Timer

finishDecoding(): BezelBorder, Border, Codable, Color, ContainerView, DrawingSequence, Font, GridLayout, Hashtable, HTMLParsingRules, Image, ImageAttachment, InternalWindow, LineBorder, ListItem, Menu, MenuItem, MenuView, PackConstraints, PackLayout, Plan, PlanLoader, Point, Polygon, Range, Rect, Script, Size, Sound, TargetProxy, TextAttachment, TextField, TextParagraphFormat, TextView, Vector, View, ViewProxy
finishUnarchiving(): Plan
firstElement(): Vector
FLASH_OPTION: DebugGraphics
flashColor(): DebugGraphics
flashCount(): DebugGraphics
flashTime(): DebugGraphics
FLOAT_ARRAY_TYPE: Codable
FLOAT_TYPE: Codable
floatArrayAt(): ClassTable
floatAt(): ClassTable
FLOW_ACROSS: GridLayout
FLOW_DOWN: GridLayout
flowDirection(): GridLayout
flush(): Bitmap, Serializer
focusDidChange(): ApplicationObserver, ExternalWindow
focusedView(): InternalWindow, RootView
Font: netscape.application
font(): Button, FontChooser, FontMetrics, Graphics, InternalWindow, Label, ListItem, MenuItem, TextField, TextView
FONT_KEY: TextView
FontChooser: netscape.application
fontChooser(): RootView
fontForAWTFont(): AWTCompatibility
fontFromAttributes(): TextViewHTMLElement
FontMetrics: netscape.application
fontMetrics(): Font
fontMetricsForAWTFontMetrics(): AWTCompatibility
fontNamed(): Font
formatBytes(): FormattingSerializer
FormattingSerializer: netscape.util
FormElement: netscape.application
formElementText(): Button, ContainerView, FormElement, ListView, Popup, Slider, TextField, TextView
FORWARD: DrawingSequence
FORWARD_LOOP: DrawingSequence
FoundationApplet: netscape.application
FoundationPanel: netscape.application
frameCount(): DrawingSequence
frameHeight(): ImageSequence
frameRate(): DrawingSequence

frameWidth(): ImageSequence
fullURL(): PlanLoader

G

get(): Hashtable
getNextEvent(): EventLoop
gotFocus(): FoundationPanel
grabPixels(): Bitmap
Graphics: netscape.application
graphicsDebugOptions(): View
graphicsForAWTGraphics(): AWTCompatibility
gray: Color
grayLine(): LineBorder
green: Color
green(): Color
GridLayout: netscape.application
gridSize(): GridLayout
GROOVED: BezelBorder
groovedBezel(): BezelBorder
grooveHeight(): Slider
growBy(): Rect

H

HAND_CURSOR: View
handleCommandKeyEvent(): Menu
hashCode(): Color, Point, Rect, Size
hasHorizScrollBar(): ScrollGroup
Hashtable: netscape.util
hashtableForHTMLAttributes(): TextViewHTML-Element
hasInsertionPoint(): TextField
hasLoadedData(): Bitmap
hasMoreElements(): Enumeration
hasSelection(): TextField, TextView
hasSubmenu(): MenuItem
hasValidObjects(): Plan
hasVertScrollBar(): ScrollGroup
height: Rect, Size
height(): Bitmap, DrawingSequence, FontMetrics, Image, ImageAttachment, ImageSequence, Text-Attachment, View
HEIGHT_CAN_CHANGE: View
heightMargin(): Border
HIDE: Window
hide(): ColorChooser, ExternalWindow, FontChooser, InternalWindow, MenuView, Window
hidePopupIfNeeded(): Popup
hidesSubviewsFromKeyboard(): InternalWindow, ScrollBar, View

hidesWhenPaused(): ExternalWindow
hideWindows(): PlanLoader
HOME_KEY: KeyEvent
horizGap(): GridLayout
HORIZONTAL: MenuView, Scrollable
horizResizeInstruction(): View
horizScrollBar(): ScrollGroup
horizScrollBarDisplay(): ScrollGroup
horizScrollBarIsVisible(): ScrollGroup
HTMLParsingException: netscape.application
HTMLParsingRules: netscape.application
htmlParsingRules(): TextView

I

identifierArrayAt(): ClassTable
identifierAt(): ClassTable
identifierCount(): Archive
IGNORE_WINDOW_CLIPVIEW_LAYER: Internal-Window
Image: netscape.application
image(): Button, ColorWell, ContainerView, DragWell, ImageAttachment, ListItem, MenuItem, RootView, Slider
IMAGE_ABOVE: Button
IMAGE_BELOW: Button
IMAGE_BENEATH: Button
IMAGE_ON_LEFT: Button
IMAGE_ON_RIGHT: Button
IMAGE_TYPE: Image
imageAreaSize(): Button
ImageAttachment: netscape.application
imageCount(): ImageSequence
imageDisplayStyle(): ContainerView, RootView, Slider
imageNamed(): Image
imagePosition(): Button
images(): ImageSequence
ImageSequence: netscape.application
imageStrip(): ImageSequence
imageWithName(): Bitmap, Image
importHTMLFromURLString(): TextView
importHTMLInRange(): TextView
InconsistencyException: netscape.util
inConstructionMode(): Constructor
INCREASE_VALUE: Slider
increaseButton(): ScrollBar
incrementResolution(): Slider
indentationLength(): FormattingSerializer
index: Range
index(): Range
indexForPoint(): TextView

indexOf(): Vector
indexOfIdentical(): Vector
indexOfItem(): ListView, Menu
init(): Application, FoundationApplet
initFrom(): Plan
initialDelay(): Timer
insertElementAfter(): Vector
insertElementAt(): Vector
insertElementBefore(): Vector
insertHTMLElementsInRange(): TextView
insertItemAt(): ListView
INT_ARRAY_TYPE: Codable
INT_TYPE: Codable
intArrayAt(): ClassTable
intAt(): ClassTable
interiorRect(): Border, ContainerView, MenuView, ScrollBar
internalPadX(): PackConstraints
internalPadY(): PackConstraints
InternalWindow: netscape.application
InternalWindowBorder: netscape.application
internalWindows(): RootView
internalWindowWithContents(): Plan
intersectionRect(): Rect
intersects(): Range, Rect
intersectWith(): Range, Rect
intValue(): TextField
invalidateKeyboardSelectionOrder(): View
IS_CONTAINER_KEY: HTMLParsingRules
isActive(): ScrollBar
isAltKeyDown(): DragSession, KeyEvent, MouseEvent
isAnimating(): DrawingSequence
isApplet(): Application
isArrowKey(): KeyEvent
isBackspaceKey(): KeyEvent
isBackTabKey(): KeyEvent
isBeingEdited(): TextField
isBold(): Font
isBordered(): Button
isBuffered(): View
isCloseable(): InternalWindow
isControlKeyDown(): DragSession, KeyEvent, MouseEvent
isCurrentDocument(): ExternalWindow, Internal-Window, Window
isDeleteKey(): KeyEvent
isDirty(): View
isDownArrowKey(): KeyEvent
isDrawingBuffer(): Graphics
isDrawingEnabled(): View
isEditable(): TextField, TextView
isEmpty(): Hashtable, Range, Rect, Size, TextField, Vector

isEnabled(): Button, DragWell, ListItem, ListView, MenuItem, Popup, ScrollBar, Slider
isEndKey(): KeyEvent
isEscapeKey(): KeyEvent
isFunctionKey(): KeyEvent
isHighlighted(): Button
isHomeKey(): KeyEvent
isInViewHierarchy(): View
isItalic(): Font
isKeyboardUIEnabled(): Application
isLeftArrowKey(): KeyEvent
isMain(): InternalWindow
isMetaKeyDown(): DragSession, KeyEvent, Mouse-Event
isNullRange(): Range
isPageDownKey(): KeyEvent
isPageUpKey(): KeyEvent
isPaused(): Application
isPlain(): Font
isPointInBorder(): InternalWindow
isPrintableKey(): KeyEvent
isRelativeURL(): PlanLoader
isResizable(): ExternalWindow, InternalWindow, Win-dow
isResizingEnabled(): TextView
isReturnKey(): KeyEvent
isRightArrowKey(): KeyEvent
isRunning(): Application, EventLoop, Script, Timer
isScrollable(): TextField
isSelectable(): TextField, TextView
isSelected(): ListItem, MenuItem
isSeparator(): MenuItem
isShiftKeyDown(): DragSession, KeyEvent, Mouse-Event
isTabKey(): KeyEvent
isTransparent(): Bitmap, Button, ContainerView, DragWell, Image, InternalWindow, Label, List-Item, ListView, Menu, MenuView, Popup, Root-View, ScrollBar, ScrollGroup, ScrollView, Text-Field, TextView, View, ViewProxy, WindowContent-View
isUpArrowKey(): KeyEvent
isUsingLiveConnect(): Script
isValid(): Bitmap
isValidArchive(): Plan
isVisible(): ExternalWindow, InternalWindow, Menu-View, RootView, Window
ITALIC: Font
itemAt(): ListView, Menu, Popup
itemCount(): Menu
itemForPoint(): ListView, MenuView
itemHeight(): MenuView

J

justification(): Label, TextField, TextParagraph-Format

K

key: KeyEvent
KEY_DOWN: KeyEvent
KEY_UP: KeyEvent
keyboardArrowHotSpot(): Application
keyboardArrowImage(): Application
keyboardArrowLocation(): Application
keyboardArrowPosition(): Application
keyboardRect(): View
keyDown(): Application, FoundationPanel, TextField, TextView, View
KeyEvent: netscape.application
keys(): Hashtable
keysArray(): Hashtable
keysVector(): Hashtable
keyUp(): Application, FoundationPanel, View
knobHeight(): Slider
knobImage(): ScrollBar, Slider
knobLength(): ScrollBar
knobRect(): ScrollBar, Slider
knobWidth(): Slider

L

Label: netscape.application
lastElement(): Vector
lastIndex(): Range
lastIndexOf(): Vector
layer(): InternalWindow
layout(): FoundationApplet, FoundationPanel
LayoutManager: netscape.application
layoutManager(): View
layoutParts(): InternalWindow
layoutPopupWindow(): Popup
layoutView(): ContainerView, GridLayout, Layout-Manager, PackLayout, ScrollGroup, View
leading(): FontMetrics
LEFT_ARROW_KEY: KeyEvent
LEFT_JUSTIFIED: Graphics
LEFT_MARGIN_CAN_CHANGE: View
leftIndent(): TextField, TextParagraphFormat
leftMargin(): BezelBorder, Border, EmptyBorder, InternalWindowBorder, LineBorder, TextParagraphFormat
length: Range
length(): Range, TextView

lengthOfContentViewForAxis(): Scrollable, ScrollView
lengthOfScrollViewForAxis(): Scrollable, ScrollView
lighterColor(): Color
lightGray: Color
LineBorder: netscape.application
lineCount(): TextView
lineIncrement(): ScrollBar
lineNumber(): DeserializationException, HTMLParsingException
lineSpacing(): TextParagraphFormat
LINK_COLOR_KEY: TextView
LINK_DESTINATION_KEY: TextView
LINK_KEY: TextView
linkWasSelected(): TextViewOwner
ListItem: netscape.application
ListView: netscape.application
listView(): ListItem
LOAD_TYPE: FileChooser
loadData(): Bitmap
loadInExternalWindow(): PlanLoader
loadPlan(): PlanLoader
loadsIncrementally(): Bitmap
localBounds(): View
LOG_OPTION: DebugGraphics
logStream(): DebugGraphics
LONG_ARRAY_TYPE: Codable
LONG_TYPE: Codable
longArrayAt(): ClassTable
longAt(): ClassTable
LOST_FOCUS: TextFieldOwner
lostFocus(): FoundationPanel
LOWERED: BezelBorder
LOWERED_BUTTON: BezelBorder
loweredBezel(): BezelBorder
loweredBorder(): Button
loweredButtonBezel(): BezelBorder
loweredColor(): Button

M

magenta: Color
mainRootView(): Application
mainWindow(): RootView
makeCurrentDocumentWindow(): Application
mapIdentifier(): Archive
marker(): TextViewHTMLContainer, TextViewHTMLMarker
maxAdvance(): FontMetrics
maxAscent(): FontMetrics
maxDescent(): FontMetrics
maxSize(): ImageSequence

maxValue(): Slider
maxX(): Rect
maxY(): Rect
Menu: netscape.application
menu(): ExternalWindow, MenuView
MenuItem: netscape.application
MenuView: netscape.application
menuView(): ExternalWindow, InternalWindow, Window
META_MASK: DragSession, KeyEvent
midX(): Rect
midY(): Rect
minHeight(): ListItem, MenuItem
minItemHeight(): ListView, MenuView
minItemWidth(): ListView, MenuView
minKnobLength(): ScrollBar
minSize(): Button, ContainerView, ExternalWindow, InternalWindow, Label, ListView, MenuView, Popup, ScrollBar, ScrollGroup, Slider, TextField, View, Window
minValue(): Slider
minWidth(): ListItem, MenuItem
MODAL_LAYER: InternalWindow
modalView(): Application
modifiers: KeyEvent
modifiers(): MouseEvent
MOUSE_DOWN: MouseEvent
MOUSE_DRAGGED: MouseEvent
MOUSE_ENTERED: MouseEvent
MOUSE_EXITED: MouseEvent
MOUSE_MOVED: MouseEvent
MOUSE_UP: MouseEvent
mouseDown(): Button, ColorWell, DragWell, FoundationPanel, InternalWindow, ListView, MenuView, Popup, RootView, ScrollBar, ScrollView, Slider, TextAttachment, TextField, TextView, View
mouseDownSound(): Button
mouseDrag(): FoundationPanel
mouseDragged(): Button, ColorWell, DragSession, InternalWindow, ListView, MenuView, ScrollBar, Slider, TextAttachment, TextField, TextView, View
mouseEnter(): FoundationPanel
mouseEntered(): MenuView, View
MouseEvent: netscape.application
mouseExit(): FoundationPanel
mouseExited(): MenuView, View
mouseMove(): FoundationPanel
mouseMoved(): MenuView, View
mousePoint(): RootView
mouseStillDown(): RootView
mouseUp(): Button, ColorWell, DragSession, FoundationPanel, InternalWindow, ListView,

MenuView, ScrollBar, TextAttachment, TextField, TextView, View
mouseUpSound(): Button
mouseView(): RootView
MOVE_CURSOR: View
moveBy(): ExternalWindow, Plan, Point, Polygon, Rect, View, Window
moveTo(): ExternalWindow, Point, Rect, View, Window
moveToBack(): ExternalWindow, InternalWindow, Window
moveToFront(): ExternalWindow, InternalWindow, Window
multipleItemsSelected(): ListView

N

N_RESIZE_CURSOR: View
name(): Bitmap, DrawingSequence, Font, Image, Sound, TargetProxy
NAME_TO_COMPONENT_KEY: Plan
namedObjects(): Script
nameToComponent(): Plan
NE_RESIZE_CURSOR: View
NEVER_DISPLAY: ScrollGroup
NEW_FONT_SELECTION: ExtendedTarget
newIdentifier(): ClassTable
NEXT_FRAME: DrawingSequence
nextElement(): Enumeration
nextFrame(): DrawingSequence
nextSelectableView(): TextField, View
NO_MODIFIERS_MASK: KeyEvent
NONE_OPTION: DebugGraphics
NoSuchElementException: netscape.util
notificationImage(): Alert
nullRange(): Range
numPoints: Polygon
NW_RESIZE_CURSOR: View

O

OBJECT_ARRAY_TYPE: Codable
OBJECT_TO_BOUNDS_KEY: Plan
OBJECT_TYPE: Codable
objectToBounds(): Plan
onscreenAtStartup(): InternalWindow
orange: Color
owner: MenuView
owner(): DrawingSequence, ExternalWindow, InternalWindow, MenuView, TextAttachment, TextField, TextView, Window

P

PackConstraints: netscape.application
PackLayout: netscape.application
padX(): PackConstraints
padY(): PackConstraints
PAGE_DOWN_KEY: KeyEvent
PAGE_UP_KEY: KeyEvent
pageSizeAsPercent(): ScrollBar
paint(): FoundationApplet, FoundationPanel
PALETTE_LAYER: InternalWindow
panel(): ExternalWindow, FoundationApplet, Root-View
PARAGRAPH_FORMAT_KEY: TextView
paragraphForIndex(): TextView
paragraphForPoint(): TextView
paragraphsForRange(): TextView
parameterNamed(): Application
PASTE: ExtendedTarget
paste(): TextField, TextView
pauseFocus(): TextField, TextView, View
peekNextEvent(): EventLoop
peersForSubview(): View
performanceDebug: Archive
performCommand(): Button, ColorChooser, Color-Well, DrawingSequence, ExternalWindow, Font-Chooser, InternalWindow, Label, ListView, Menu, Plan, PlanLoader, Popup, RootView, Script, ScrollBar, Slider, Target, TargetChain, Target-Proxy, TextField, TextView, ViewProxy
performCommandAndWait(): Application
performCommandLater(): Application
pink: Color
PLAIN: Font
Plan: netscape.constructor
plan(): PlanLoader
PlanLoader: netscape.constructor
planURL(): PlanLoader
play(): Sound
playbackMode(): DrawingSequence
Point: netscape.application
Polygon: netscape.application
popIFCContext(): FoundationApplet
popState(): DebugGraphics, Graphics
POPUP: Popup
Popup: netscape.application
popup(): PopupItem
POPUP_LAYER: InternalWindow
popupImage(): Popup
PopupItem: netscape.application
popupList(): Popup
popupWindow(): Popup
positionForTab(): TextParagraphFormat

positionOfContentViewForAxis(): Scrollable, Scroll-View
preferredLayoutSize(): PackLayout
prefix(): TextViewHTMLContainer, TextViewHTML-Marker
PRESSED_LINK_COLOR_KEY: TextView
previousSelectableView(): TextField, View
printAll(): FoundationPanel
processEvent(): Application, CommandEvent, Event-Loop, EventProcessor, MenuItem, RootView, Timer
processor(): Event
prototypeItem(): ListView, Menu, Popup
PUSH_TYPE: Button
pushIFCContext(): FoundationApplet
pushState(): DebugGraphics, Graphics
put(): Hashtable
putPlanInExternalWindow(): PlanLoader
putPlanInInternalWindow(): PlanLoader

Q

questionImage(): Alert

R

RADIO_TYPE: Button
RAISED: BezelBorder
RAISED_BUTTON: BezelBorder
raisedBezel(): BezelBorder
raisedBorder(): Button
raisedButtonBezel(): BezelBorder
raisedColor(): Button
Range: netscape.application
rangeFromIndices(): Range
rangeFromIntersection(): Range
rangeFromUnion(): Range
read(): Archive
readASCII(): Archive
readData(): ClassTable
readInfo(): ClassTable
readObject(): Deserializer, Unarchiver
Rect: netscape.application
rectForItem(): ListView
rectForItemAt(): ListView, MenuView
rectFromIntersection(): Rect
rectFromUnion(): Rect
rectsForRange(): TextView
red: Color
red(): Color
redraw(): RootView

redrawAll(): RootView
redrawTransparentWindows(): RootView
reenableDrawing(): View
releaseName(): Application
releaseObjects(): Plan
rememberWindows(): PlanLoader
remove(): Hashtable
removeAll(): Vector
removeAllCommandsForKeys(): View
removeAllElements(): Vector
removeAllImages(): ImageSequence
removeAllItems(): ListView, Popup
removeAttributeForRange(): TextView
removeCommandForKey(): View
removeElement(): Vector
removeElementAt(): Vector
removeElementIdentical(): Vector
removeEvent(): EventLoop
removeFirstElement(): Vector
removeFromSuperview(): View
removeImage(): ImageSequence
removeItem(): ListView, Menu, Popup
removeItemAt(): ListView, Menu, Popup
removeLastElement(): Vector
removeNames(): Script
removeObserver(): Application
removeOverrideCursor(): RootView
removeParts(): ScrollBar
removeRootIdentifier(): Archive
removeScrollBar(): ScrollView
removeSubview(): GridLayout, LayoutManager, Pack-
  Layout, View
removeTarget(): TargetChain
repeatDelay(): Button
repeats(): Timer
replaceElementAt(): Vector
replaceItem(): Menu
replaceItemAt(): Menu
replaceObject(): Decoder, Unarchiver
replaceRangeWithString(): TextField, TextView
replaceRangeWithTextAttachment(): TextView
REPRESENTATION_KEY: HTMLParsingRules
requestDraw(): MenuItem
reset(): DrawingSequence
resetDirtyViews(): RootView
reshape(): FoundationPanel
RESIGNED_FOCUS: TextFieldOwner
resize(): FoundationPanel
resizePartWidth(): InternalWindowBorder
resumeFocus(): TextField, TextView, View
RETURN_KEY: KeyEvent, TextFieldOwner
rgb(): Color
rgbForHSB(): Color

RIGHT_ARROW_KEY: KeyEvent
RIGHT_JUSTIFIED: Graphics
RIGHT_MARGIN_CAN_CHANGE: View
rightIndent(): TextField
rightMargin(): BezelBorder, Border, EmptyBorder,
  InternalWindowBorder, LineBorder, Text-
  ParagraphFormat
ROOT_COMPONENTS_KEY: Plan
rootComponents(): Plan
rootIdentifiers(): Archive
RootView: netscape.application
rootView(): ExternalWindow, FoundationPanel, Key-
  Event, MouseEvent, RootView, View
rootViews(): Application
rowCount(): ClassTable, GridLayout
rowForIdentifier(): Archive, ClassTable
rowHeight(): ListView
rulesForMarker(): HTMLParsingRules
run(): Application, EventLoop, FoundationApplet,
  Script
RUN_COMMAND: Script
runAlertExternally(): Alert
runAlertInternally(): Alert
runForIndex(): TextView
runForPoint(): TextView
runsForRange(): TextView
runWithLinkDestinationNamed(): TextView

S

S_RESIZE_CURSOR: View
save(): Plan
SAVE_TYPE: FileChooser
saveToStream(): Plan
SCALED: Image
Script: netscape.constructor
scriptText(): Script
SCROLL_LINE_BACKWARD: ScrollBar
SCROLL_LINE_FORWARD: ScrollBar
SCROLL_PAGE_BACKWARD: ScrollBar
SCROLL_PAGE_FORWARD: ScrollBar
Scrollable: netscape.application
scrollableObject(): ScrollBar
ScrollBar: netscape.application
scrollBarDidBecomeActive(): ScrollBarOwner,
  ScrollGroup
scrollBarDidBecomeInactive(): ScrollBarOwner,
  ScrollGroup
ScrollBarOwner: netscape.application
scrollBarOwner(): ScrollBar
scrollBarUpdatesEnabled(): ScrollView

scrollBarWasDisabled(): ScrollBarOwner, Scroll-Group

scrollBarWasEnabled(): ScrollBarOwner, ScrollGroup

scrollBy(): Scrollable, ScrollView

ScrollGroup: netscape.application

scrollItemAtToVisible(): ListView

scrollItemToVisible(): ListView

scrollLineBackward(): ScrollBar

scrollLineForward(): ScrollBar

scrollPageBackward(): ScrollBar

scrollPageForward(): ScrollBar

scrollPercent(): ScrollBar

scrollRangeToVisible(): TextView

scrollRectToVisible(): InternalWindow, ScrollView, View

scrollIsToVisible(): InternalWindow

scrollTo(): Scrollable, ScrollView

scrollToCurrentPosition(): ScrollBar

scrollTrayLength(): ScrollBar

scrollTrayRect(): ScrollBar

scrollValue(): ScrollBar

ScrollView: netscape.application

scrollView(): ScrollGroup

SE_RESIZE_CURSOR: View

SECOND_OPTION: Alert

SELECT_NEXT_ITEM: ListView, Popup

SELECT_NEXT_RADIO_BUTTON: Button

SELECT_PREVIOUS_ITEM: ListView, Popup

SELECT_PREVIOUS_RADIO_BUTTON: Button

SELECT_TEXT: TextField

selectedColor(): ListItem, MenuItem

selectedImage(): ListItem, MenuItem

selectedIndex(): ListView, MenuView, Popup

selectedItem(): ListView, MenuView, Popup

selectedItems(): ListView

selectedRange(): TextField, TextView

selectedStringValue(): TextField

selectedTextColor(): MenuItem

selectionColor(): TextField, TextView

selectionDidChange(): TextViewOwner

selectItem(): ListView, MenuView, Popup

selectItemAt(): ListView, Popup

selectOnly(): ListView

selectRange(): TextField, TextView

selectText(): TextField

selectView(): RootView

selectViewAfter(): RootView

selectViewBefore(): RootView

SEND_COMMAND: Button

sendCommand(): Button, ColorWell, ListView, Menu-Item, Popup, Slider

sendDoubleCommand(): ListView

serializeObject(): FormattingSerializer, Serializer

Serializer: netscape.util

SET_FONT: ExtendedTarget

setActive(): ScrollBar

setAllowsEmptySelection(): ListView

setAllowsMultipleSelection(): ListView

setAltImage(): Button

setAltTitle(): Button

setAnchor(): PackConstraints

setApplication(): FoundationApplet

setArchiveData(): Plan

setArchiveFormat(): Plan

setAttributes(): TextViewHTMLContainer, TextView-HTMLElement, TextViewHTMLMarker, TextView-HTMLString

setAttributesForRange(): TextView

setAttributesToReplacingTarget(): TargetProxy

setAttributesToReplacingView(): ViewProxy

setAutoResizeSubviews(): View

setAWTComponent(): AWTComponentView

setBackgroundColor(): ContainerView, ListView, Menu, Plan, ScrollGroup, ScrollView, Slider, Text-Field, TextView, WindowContentView

setBacktabField(): TextField

setBooleanArrayAt(): ClassTable

setBooleanAt(): ClassTable

setBorder(): ContainerView, DragWell, Internal-Window, Menu, Popup, ScrollGroup, Slider, Text-Field

setBordered(): Button

setBounds(): ExternalWindow, InternalWindow, Rect, View, Window

setBuffered(): View

setByteArrayAt(): ClassTable

setByteAt(): ClassTable

setCanBecomeDocument(): InternalWindow

setCanBecomeMain(): InternalWindow

setCaretColor(): TextField, TextView

setCharArrayAt(): ClassTable

setCharAt(): ClassTable

setCheckedImage(): MenuItem

setChildren(): TextViewHTMLContainer, TextView-HTMLElement, TextViewHTMLMarker, TextView-HTMLString

setClassNameForComment(): HTMLParsingRules

setClassNameForMarker(): HTMLParsingRules

setClickCount(): MouseEvent

setClipboardText(): Application

setClipRect(): DebugGraphics, Graphics

setCloseable(): InternalWindow

setCoalesce(): Timer

setColor(): ColorChooser, ColorWell, DebugGraphics, Graphics, Label, LineBorder, RootView, Window-ContentView

setColumnCount(): GridLayout

setCommand(): Button, ColorWell, CommandEvent, Label, ListItem, ListView, MenuItem, Popup, Script, Slider, TextField, Timer

setCommandForKey(): View

setCommandKey(): Label, MenuItem

setCommands(): TargetProxy, ViewProxy

setComponents(): Plan

setConstraints(): PackLayout

setContainsDocument(): ExternalWindow, Internal-Window, Window

setContentsChangedCommandAndTarget(): Text-Field

setContentView(): ScrollGroup, ScrollView

setCoordinates(): Rect

setCornerColor(): ScrollGroup

setCurrentFrameNumber(): DrawingSequence

setCurrentImageNumber(): ImageSequence

setCursor(): FoundationPanel

setData(): ColorWell, CommandEvent, DragSession, DragWell, ListItem, MenuItem, Timer

setDataType(): ColorWell, DragSession, DragWell

setDebugOptions(): DebugGraphics, Graphics

setDecreaseButton(): ScrollBar

setDefaultAttributes(): TextView

setDefaultConstraints(): PackLayout

setDefaultContainerClassName(): HTMLParsing-Rules

setDefaultMarkerClassName(): HTMLParsingRules

setDefaultSelectedView(): InternalWindow, Root-View

setDelay(): Timer

setDirectory(): FileChooser

setDirty(): View

setDisabledColor(): MenuItem

setDisabledTitleColor(): Button

setDoubleArrayAt(): ClassTable

setDoubleAt(): ClassTable

setDoubleCommand(): ListView

setDrawableCharacter(): TextField

setDrawsDropShadow(): TextField

setEditable(): TextField, TextView

setElementAt(): Vector

setEnabled(): Button, DragWell, ListItem, ListView, MenuItem, Popup, ScrollBar, Slider

setExpand(): PackConstraints

setFile(): FileChooser

setFilenameFilter(): FileChooser

setFillX(): PackConstraints

setFillY(): PackConstraints

setFilter(): TextField, TextView

setFlashColor(): DebugGraphics

setFlashCount(): DebugGraphics

setFlashTime(): DebugGraphics

setFloatArrayAt(): ClassTable

setFloatAt(): ClassTable

setFlowDirection(): GridLayout

setFocusedView(): InternalWindow, RootView, Text-Field, View

setFont(): Button, DebugGraphics, FontChooser, Graphics, Label, ListItem, MenuItem, TextField, TextView

setFrameCount(): DrawingSequence

setFrameHeight(): ImageSequence

setFrameRate(): DrawingSequence

setFrameWidth(): ImageSequence

setGraphicsDebugOptions(): View

setGrooveHeight(): Slider

setHasHorizScrollBar(): ScrollGroup

setHasVertScrollBar(): ScrollGroup

setHeight(): TextAttachment

setHidesWhenPaused(): ExternalWindow

setHighlighted(): Button

setHorizGap(): GridLayout

setHorizResizeInstruction(): View

setHorizScrollBarDisplay(): ScrollGroup

setHTMLParsingRules(): TextView

setIdentifierArrayAt(): ClassTable

setIdentifierAt(): ClassTable

setImage(): Button, ColorWell, ContainerView, Drag-Well, ImageAttachment, ListItem, MenuItem, RootView, Slider

setImageDisplayStyle(): ContainerView, RootView, Slider

setImagePosition(): Button

setImageStrip(): ImageSequence

setIncreaseButton(): ScrollBar

setIncrementResolution(): Slider

setIndentationLength(): FormattingSerializer

setInitialDelay(): Timer

setInsertionPoint(): TextField

setIntArrayAt(): ClassTable

setIntAt(): ClassTable

setInternalPadX(): PackConstraints

setInternalPadY(): PackConstraints

setIntValue(): TextField

setItemHeight(): MenuView

setJustification(): Label, TextField, TextParagraph-Format

setKeyboardUIEnabled(): Application

setKnobHeight(): Slider

setKnobImage(): ScrollBar, Slider

setKnobLength(): ScrollBar

setLayer(): InternalWindow

setLayoutManager(): View

setLeftIndent(): TextParagraphFormat

setLeftMargin(): TextParagraphFormat
setLimits(): Slider
setLineIncrement(): ScrollBar
setLineSpacing(): TextParagraphFormat
setLoadInExternalWindow(): PlanLoader
setLoadsIncrementally(): Bitmap
setLogStream(): DebugGraphics
setLongArrayAt(): ClassTable
setLongAt(): ClassTable
setLoops(): Sound
setLoweredBorder(): Button
setLoweredColor(): Button
setMainRootView(): Application
setMarker(): TextViewHTMLContainer, TextView-HTMLElement, TextViewHTMLMarker, TextView-HTMLString
setMenu(): ExternalWindow, MenuView
setMenuView(): ExternalWindow, InternalWindow, Window
setMinSize(): ExternalWindow, View, Window
setModifiers(): MouseEvent
setMouseDownSound(): Button
setMouseUpSound(): Button
setMouseView(): RootView
setName(): DrawingSequence, TargetProxy
setNamedObjects(): Script
setNames(): Script
setNameToComponent(): Plan
setObjectToBounds(): Plan
setOnscreenAtStartup(): InternalWindow
setOverrideCursor(): RootView
setOwner(): DrawingSequence, ExternalWindow, InternalWindow, MenuView, TextAttachment, TextField, TextView, Window
setPadX(): PackConstraints
setPadY(): PackConstraints
setPageSizeAsPercent(): ScrollBar
setPaintMode(): DebugGraphics, Graphics
setPlan(): PlanLoader
setPlanURL(): PlanLoader
setPlaybackMode(): DrawingSequence
setPopup(): PopupItem
setPopupImage(): Popup
setPopupList(): Popup
setPopupWindow(): Popup
setProcessor(): Event
setPrototypeItem(): ListView, Menu, Popup
setRaisedBorder(): Button
setRaisedColor(): Button
setRedrawAll(): RootView
setRelativeURL(): PlanLoader
setRememberWindows(): PlanLoader
setRepeatDelay(): Button

setRepeats(): Timer
setResetOnStart(): DrawingSequence
setResetOnStop(): DrawingSequence
setResizable(): ExternalWindow, InternalWindow, Window
setRightMargin(): TextParagraphFormat
setRootComponents(): Plan
setRootView(): FoundationPanel, InternalWindow, KeyEvent, MouseEvent
setRowCount(): GridLayout
setRowHeight(): ListView
setRuleForMarker(): HTMLParsingRules
setRulesForMarker(): HTMLParsingRules
setScriptText(): Script
setScrollable(): TextField
setScrollableObject(): ScrollBar
setScrollBarOwner(): ScrollBar
setScrollBarUpdatesEnabled(): ScrollView
setScrollPercent(): ScrollBar
setScrollIsToVisible(): InternalWindow
setSelectable(): TextField, TextView
setSelected(): ListItem, MenuItem
setSelectedColor(): ListItem, MenuItem
setSelectedImage(): ListItem, MenuItem
setSelectedTextColor(): MenuItem
setSelectionColor(): TextField, TextView
setSeparator(): MenuItem
setShortArrayAt(): ClassTable
setShortAt(): ClassTable
setSide(): PackConstraints
setSize(): Plan
setState(): Button, MenuItem
setString(): TextView, TextViewHTMLContainer, Text-ViewHTMLElement, TextViewHTMLMarker, Text-ViewHTMLString
setStringArrayAt(): ClassTable
setStringAt(): ClassTable
setStringClassName(): HTMLParsingRules
setStringValue(): TextField
setSubmenu(): MenuItem
setSupermenu(): MenuItem
setTabField(): TextField
setTabPositions(): TextParagraphFormat
setTarget(): Button, ColorWell, CommandEvent, Label, ListView, MenuItem, Popup, Script, Slider, TextField, Timer
setTargetProxyManager(): Plan, TargetProxy
setTextColor(): ListItem, MenuItem, TextField, Text-View
setTimeStamp(): Event
setTitle(): Button, ContainerView, ExternalWindow, FileChooser, InternalWindow, Label, ListItem, MenuItem, Window

setTitleColor(): Button, ContainerView
setTitleFont(): ContainerView
setTracksMouseOutsideBounds(): ListView
setTransparent(): Bitmap, Button, ContainerView, InternalWindow, ListView, Menu, MenuView, ScrollView, TextField, TextView, WindowContent-View
setType(): Button, Event, InternalWindow, MenuView, TargetProxy
setTypingAttributes(): TextView
setUncheckedImage(): MenuItem
setupContext(): TextViewHTMLContainer
setUpdateCommand(): Bitmap
setUpdateTarget(): Bitmap
setURL(): Plan
setUseSingleFont(): TextView
setUsingLiveConnect(): Script
setValidArchive(): Plan
setValidObjects(): Plan
setValue(): Slider
setVersionNumber(): Plan
setVertGap(): GridLayout
setVertResizeInstruction(): View
setVertScrollBarDisplay(): ScrollGroup
setViewClassName(): ViewProxy
setWidth(): TextAttachment
setWindow(): ColorChooser, FontChooser, Internal-WindowBorder
setWindowClipView(): RootView
setWrapsContents(): TextField
setWrapsUnderFirstCharacter(): TextParagraph-Format
setXORMode(): DebugGraphics, Graphics
SHIFT_MASK: DragSession, KeyEvent
SHORT_ARRAY_TYPE: Codable
SHORT_TYPE: Codable
shortArrayAt(): ClassTable
shortAt(): ClassTable
SHOULD_IGNORE_END_KEY: HTMLParsingRules
SHOULD_RETAIN_FORMATTING_KEY: HTMLParsing-Rules
SHOW: Window
show(): ColorChooser, ExternalWindow, FontChooser, InternalWindow, MenuView, Window
SHOW_COLOR_CHOOSER: ColorWell, Extended-Target
SHOW_FONT_CHOOSER: ExtendedTarget
showBehind(): InternalWindow
showColorChooser(): RootView
showFontChooser(): RootView
showInFrontOf(): InternalWindow
showingPopupForKeyboard(): Popup

showModally(): ExternalWindow, FileChooser, InternalWindow, Window
showPopupWindow(): Popup
showWindows(): PlanLoader
side(): PackConstraints
SIDE_BOTTOM: PackConstraints
SIDE_LEFT: PackConstraints
SIDE_RIGHT: PackConstraints
SIDE_TOP: PackConstraints
Size: netscape.application
size(): Font, Hashtable, Plan, Vector
sizeBy(): ExternalWindow, Rect, Size, TextView, View, Window
sizeTo(): ExternalWindow, Rect, Size, View, Window
sizeToFit(): Plan
sizeToMinSize(): TextView, View
Slider: netscape.application
Sort: netscape.util
sort(): Sort, Vector
sortStrings(): Sort, Vector
Sound: netscape.application
soundForAWTAudioClip(): AWTCompatibility
soundFromURL(): Sound
soundNamed(): Sound
source(): DragSession
sourceView(): DragSource, DragWell
START: DrawingSequence
start(): DrawingSequence, FoundationApplet, Timer
startFocus(): TextField, TextView, View
state(): Button, MenuItem
STOP: DrawingSequence
stop(): DrawingSequence, FoundationApplet, Sound, Timer
stopFocus(): TextField, TextView, View
stopRunning(): Application, EventLoop
streamFromURL(): Plan
string(): TextView, TextViewHTMLContainer, TextView-HTMLElement, TextViewHTMLMarker, TextView-HTMLString
STRING_ARRAY_TYPE: Codable
STRING_MARKER_KEY: HTMLParsingRules
STRING_TYPE: Codable
stringArrayAt(): ClassTable
stringAt(): ClassTable
stringForRange(): TextField, TextView
stringHeight(): FontMetrics
stringSize(): FontMetrics
stringValue(): TextField
stringWidth(): FontMetrics
stringWithoutCarriageReturns(): TextView
style(): Font
submenu(): MenuItem
subviewDidMove(): RootView, View

subviewDidResize(): InternalWindow, RootView, ScrollView, View
subviews(): View
suffix(): TextViewHTMLContainer, TextViewHTML-Marker
supermenu(): MenuItem
superview(): View
SW_RESIZE_CURSOR: View
sync(): Graphics

T

TAB_KEY: KeyEvent, TextFieldOwner
tabField(): TextField
tabPositions(): TextParagraphFormat
Target: netscape.application
target(): Button, ColorWell, CommandEvent, Label, ListView, MenuItem, Popup, Script, Slider, Text-Field, Timer
TARGET_CHAIN_TYPE: TargetProxy
TargetChain: netscape.application
targetForCommand(): TargetChain
TargetProxy: netscape.constructor
targetProxyManager(): Plan, TargetProxy
TEXT_ATTACHMENT_BASELINE_OFFSET_KEY: TextView
TEXT_ATTACHMENT_KEY: TextView
TEXT_ATTACHMENT_STRING: TextView
TEXT_COLOR_KEY: TextView
TEXT_CURSOR: View
TextAttachment: netscape.application
TextAttachment(): TextAttachment
textColor(): ListItem, MenuItem, TextField, TextView
textDidChange(): TextViewOwner
textEditingDidBegin(): ColorChooser, TextField-Owner, TextViewOwner
textEditingDidEnd(): ColorChooser, TextFieldOwner, TextViewOwner
textEditingWillEnd(): ColorChooser, TextFieldOwner
TextField: netscape.application
TextFieldOwner: netscape.application
TextFilter: netscape.application
TextParagraphFormat: netscape.application
TextView: netscape.application
TextViewHTMLContainer: netscape.application
TextViewHTMLElement: netscape.application
TextViewHTMLMarker: netscape.application
TextViewHTMLString: netscape.application
TextViewOwner: netscape.application
textWasModified(): ColorChooser, TextFieldOwner
textWillChange(): TextViewOwner
THIRD_OPTION: Alert

TILED: Image
Timer: netscape.application
timeStamp(): Event, Timer
title(): Button, ContainerView, ExternalWindow, File-Chooser, InternalWindow, Label, ListItem, Menu-Item, Window
TITLE_TYPE: Window
titleColor(): Button, ContainerView
titleFont(): ContainerView
TOGGLE_TYPE: Button
TOP_LEFT_POSITION: Application
TOP_MARGIN_CAN_CHANGE: View
TOP_RIGHT_POSITION: Application
topMargin(): BezelBorder, Border, EmptyBorder, InternalWindowBorder, LineBorder
toString(): Bitmap, Color, EventLoop, Font, Font-Metrics, Graphics, Hashtable, InternalWindow, KeyEvent, MouseEvent, Point, Range, Rect, Size, Sound, TextParagraphFormat, TextView, TextView-HTMLContainer, TextViewHTMLMarker, TextViewH-TMLString, Timer, Vector, View
tracksMouseOutsideBounds(): ListView
translate(): DebugGraphics, Graphics
translation(): Graphics
trimToSize(): Vector
type(): BezelBorder, Button, Event, FileChooser, InternalWindow, MenuView, TargetProxy
typingAttributes(): TextView

U

unarchiveFrom(): Plan
unarchiveIdentifier(): Unarchiver
unarchiveObjects(): Plan
Unarchiver: netscape.util
uncheckedImage(): MenuItem
underlineRect(): Label
union(): Size
unionRect(): Rect
unionWith(): Range, Rect
UNKNOWN_TYPE: Plan
UP_ARROW_KEY: KeyEvent
UPDATE: ScrollBar
update(): FoundationPanel
updateCommand(): Bitmap
updateCursor(): RootView
updateCursorLater(): RootView
updateRect(): Bitmap
updateScrollBars(): ScrollView
updateTarget(): Bitmap
url(): Plan
usesSingleFont(): TextView

V

value(): Slider
Vector: netscape.util
VERSION_NUMBER_KEY: Plan
versionForClassName(): ClassTable, Decoder, Unarchiver
versionNumber(): Plan
vertGap(): GridLayout
VERTICAL: MenuView, Scrollable
vertResizeInstruction(): View
vertScrollBar(): ScrollGroup
vertScrollBarDisplay(): ScrollGroup
vertScrollBarIsVisible(): ScrollGroup
View: netscape.application
viewClassName(): ViewProxy
viewExcludedFromModalSession(): RootView
viewForMouse(): ExternalWindow, InternalWindow, RootView, View, Window
ViewProxy: netscape.constructor
VIEWPROXY_CLASS_NAME: ViewProxy
viewWithContents(): Plan

W

W_RESIZE_CURSOR: View
WAIT_CURSOR: View
wantsAutoscrollEvents(): ListView, MenuView, TextField, TextView, View
wantsMouseEventCoalescing(): View
warningImage(): Alert
WHEN_IN_MAIN_WINDOW: View
WHEN_SELECTED: View
white: Color
width: Rect, Size
width(): Bitmap, DrawingSequence, Image, ImageAttachment, ImageSequence, TextAttachment, View
WIDTH_CAN_CHANGE: View
widthMargin(): Border
widthsArray(): FontMetrics
widthsArrayBase(): FontMetrics
willBecomeInvisible(): TextAttachment
willBecomeSelected(): TextField, TextView, View
willBecomeUnselected(): View
willBecomeVisibleWithBounds(): TextAttachment
willMoveTo(): InternalWindow
willProcessEvent(): Application
Window: netscape.application
window(): ColorChooser, FontChooser, InternalWindow, InternalWindowBorder, View
windowClipView(): RootView

WindowContentView: netscape.application
windowDidBecomeMain(): WindowOwner
windowDidHide(): WindowOwner
windowDidResignMain(): WindowOwner
windowDidShow(): WindowOwner
WindowOwner: netscape.application
windowSizeForContentSize(): ExternalWindow, InternalWindow, Window
windowVector(): PlanLoader
windowWillHide(): WindowOwner
windowWillShow(): WindowOwner
windowWillSizeBy(): WindowOwner
wrapsContents(): TextField
wrapsUnderFirstCharacter(): TextParagraphFormat
write(): Archive
writeASCII(): Archive
writeComment(): FormattingSerializer
writeData(): ClassTable
writeInfo(): ClassTable
writeObject(): Archiver, FormattingSerializer, Serializer

X

x: MouseEvent, Point, Rect
x(): View
xPoints: Polygon
xPositionOfCharacter(): TextField
xTranslation(): Graphics

Y

y: MouseEvent, Point, Rect
y(): View
yellow: Color
yPoints: Polygon
yTranslation(): Graphics

Index

I

IFC (Internet Foundation Classes)
API of, 7
Constructor (see Constructor)
features of, 3–7
images
Alert class, 139
alerts and, 212
background, 42–43, 269
Bitmap class, 43, 154–158, 217–218
buffered drawing, 39–40, 154–158
for buttons, 80
clipping, 40
for cursors, 43–44
DebugGraphics class, 40–41,
225–227
drag/drop (see drag-and-drop)
flickering, 37, 39, 154–155
Graphics class, 35, 40–41, 241–243
graphics context, 35
Image class, 10, 153–154, 245–246
ImageAttachment class, 180, 246
ImageSequence class, 10, 163–163,
247
netscape.application class and, 208
in popup menus, 264
importHTMLFromURLString( ), 178,
285
importHTMLInRange( ), 178, 285
importing HTML, 177–179
InconsistencyException, 318
inConstructionMode( ), 300
init( ), 12–13, 213
interfaces, packages and (list),
323–341
interiorRect( ), 110
internal padding, 126
InternalInfoDialog class (example),
141
InternalOptionDialog class, 145
InternalWindow class, 9, 61, 66–70,
247–249
pulldown menus in (example),
118–119
InternalWindowBorder class, 250
internalWindowWithContents( ), 198,
300
intValue( ), 91
isAltKeyDown( ), 48, 53
isApplet( ), 14, 214
isArrowKey( ), 53
isControlKeyDown( ), 48
isCurrentDocument( ), 64

isFunctionKey( ), 53
isInViewHierarchy( ), 30, 291
isMetaKeyDown( ), 48
isShiftKeyDown( ), 48, 53
isTransparent( ), 42, 292
itemAt( ), 258

J

Java
IFC and, 3
Java Beans, 7–8
JFC (Java Foundation Classes), 6, 8

K

keyboard events, 51–55, 250–251
KeyEvent class, 51, 250–251
modifiers for, 53–55
text fields and, 94–95
keyboard shortcuts, 119–120
label command keys, 252
keyboard user interface, 52–53
Target interface and, 76
keyDown( ), 51, 214, 292
KeyEvent class, 233
keys( ), 317
Keys application (example), 53–55
keys for text attributes, 183
keyUp( ), 51, 214, 292

L

Label class, 252
labels, multi-line, 178
layered windows, 68–69
layout management/managers, 7,
32–33, 121, 123–131
example layout, 128–131
GridLayout class, 123–125, 243–244
LayoutManager interface, 124,
252–253
PackConstraints class, 262–263
PackLayout class, 125–128, 263
resizing rules, 122–123
view constraints, 123, 128
layoutView( ), 124, 252, 291
left mouse button (see mouse events)
leftMargin( ), 110
lengthOfContentViewForAxis( ),
103–104, 274
lengthOfScrollViewForAxis( ), 103–104
lighterColor( ), 111
LineBorder class, 111, 253
lineNumber( ), 314

ownership (cont'd)
TextViewOwner interface, 180, 290
WindowOwner interface, 70–71, 298
(see also setOwner( ))

P

packages, classes/interfaces of (list), 323–341
PackConstraints class, 128, 262–263
PackLayout class, 123, 125–128, 263
example, 128–131
padding, 126
parameterName( ), 214
parent views (see views)
paste( )
TextField class, 93
TextView class, 180
pasting (see copying/cutting/pasting)
pauseFocus( ), 52, 292
peekNextEvent( ), 233
performance
drawing and, 39–40
efficiency of IFC, 7
keyboard user interface, 52–53
performCommand( )
Button class, 219
ColorWell class, 223
FontChooser class, 238
Target interface, 56, 73–75, 278
performCommandLater( ), 56–57
placement
layout management, 7, 32
views, 32
windows, 63, 235
Plan class, 197, 300–303
.plan files, 10, 197–200, 300–303
PlanLoader class, 303–304
platform independence, 4
play( ), 277
Point class, 263–264
Polygon class, 264
popState( ), 241
popup menus
Popup class, 6, 114–116, 264–266
PopupItem class, 266
TextPop class (example), 115–116
position
images on buttons, 80
scrollbar knob, 104
views, 291

positionOfContentViewForAxis( ), 103, 275
preferredLayoutSize( ), 127
previousSelectableView( ), 293
processEvent( )
EventLoop class, 233
EventProcessor interface, 234
processNextEvent( ), 233
processors, event, 56
programs (see applications)
properties (see attributes of objects)
proxies, target, 199
push buttons, 81
pushState( ), 241
put( ), 317

Q

questionImage( ), 139, 212
queue, event, 56, 150

R

radio buttons, 82–83
ContainerView class and, 83–84
Range class, 178, 266–267
read( ), 307
readASCII( ), 189, 307, 315
reading from archives, 189–190
readObject( ), 309, 320
Rect class, 27, 36, 267–268
rectangles, 27, 36
reenableDrawing( ), 292
relative coordinates, 27
releaseName( ), 214
releaseObjects( ), 199, 301
remove( ), 317
removeFromSuperview( ), 30, 291
removeItem( )
ListView class, 90
Menu class, 118
removeOverrideCursor( ), 44
removeSubview( ), 30
LayoutManager class, 252
View class, 291
replaceObject( ), 314
replaceRangeWithString( ), 280
replaceRangeWithTextAttachment( ), 180
resizing (see size)
resumeFocus( ), 52, 292
Return key, 91
RGBView class (example), 107–108

setImage( )
  Button class, 80, 219
  DragWell class, 229
  RootView class, 42, 269
setImageDisplayStyle( ), 225
setImagePosition( ), 80, 219
setImageStrip( ), 247
setIncrementResolution( ), 276
setInitialDelay( ), 291
setIntValue( ), 91
setKeyboardUIEnabled( ), 53, 214
setLayoutManager( ), 252
setLimits( ), 106, 276
setLoadInExternalWindow( ), 303
setLoadsIncrementally( ), 217
setLogStream( ), 40
setLoops( ), 277
setMainRootView( ), 27, 213
setMinSize( ), 292
setMouseView( ), 46
setNamedObjects( ), 304
setOverrideCursor( ), 44
setOwner( )
  Menu class, 118
  TextField class, 280
  TextView class, 285
  WindowOwner interface, 71
setPlanURL( ), 303
setPopupImage( ), 264
setPopupList( ), 115
setProcessor( ), 232
setPrototypeItem( ), 257
setRepeatDelay( ), 81
setRepeats( ), 291
setResizeable( ), 63
setScrollableObject( ), 101, 270
setScrollbarOwner( ), 272
setSelectable( ), 179
setStringValue( ), 280
setTabField( ), 280
setTarget( )
  Button class, 74
  ListView class, 89
  TextField class, 280
setTextColor( ), 179
setTitle( )
  Label class, 252
  ListItem class, 253
  Window interface, 296
setTransparent( ), 179
setTypingAttributes( ), 184
setValue( ), 107
setVertResizeInstruction( ), 292

setVertScrollBarDisplay( ), 98, 272
setViewClassName( ), 305
setWindow( )
  ColorChooser class, 223
  FontChooser class, 238
Shift key
  as event modifier, 48, 53
  Shift-Tab combination, 52
shortcuts, menu, 119–120
show( )
  ExternalWindow class, 65, 235
  InternalWindow class, 67, 247
  Window interface, 62, 296
showColorChooser( ), 132, 223
showFontChooser( ), 133, 238
showModally( )
  ExternalWindow class, 235
  FileChooser class, 134, 236
  Show( ) versus, 137
  Window interface, 62, 296
showStatus( ), 15
size
  borders, 110
  font metrics, 239
  ListView objects, 90
  MenuView objects, 117
  rectangles, 36
  resizing rules, 122–123
  ScrollGroup objects, 100
  Size class, 275–276
  sliders, 106
  text attachments, 279
  views, 32, 291
  windows, 63, 235, 296
sizeBy( ), 32, 63
sizeTo( ), 32, 63, 235
sizeToMinSize( )
  ListView class, 90, 255
  MenuView class, 117
Slider class, 106–108, 276–277
sort( )
  Sort class, 319
  Vector class, 321
sorting
  Comparable class for, 313
  Sort class, 319
sortStrings( ), 319
sound
  button events and, 87
  Sound class, 277–278
soundFromURL( ), 277
soundNamed( ), 277
source view, 166

About the Authors

Dean Petrich grew up in Minneapolis, MN, but now lives in sunny Pasadena, CA. He received degrees in physics from MIT (B.S. '89) and Princeton (Ph.D. '94) and, after post-doctoral work at CalTech, is now putting his physics skills to good use in the equity research group of First Quadrant, a money management firm. In his spare time, he likes to read, hike, and travel.

David Flanagan is a consulting computer programmer, user interface designer, and trainer. His previous books with O'Reilly & Associates include the best-selling *Java in a Nutshell, JavaScript: The Definitive Guide, X Toolkit Intrinsics Reference Manual,* and *X Volume 6C, Motif Tools: Streamlined GUI Design and Programming with the Xmt Library.* David has a degree in computer science and engineering from the Massachusetts Institute of Technology.

Colophon

Our look is the result of reader comments, our own experimentation, and feedback from distribution channels. Distinctive covers complement our distinctive approach to technical topics, breathing personality and life into potentially dry subjects.

The fish on the cover of *Netscape IFC in a Nutshell* is an opah fish, the only member of the family Lamprididae. This beautiful fish is strikingly colored, shading from steel blue at the top of its body down to green, with a rose-colored belly. Silvery spots cover its body; the fins and jaws are red. The opah fish can grow to a length of 6 feet and a weight of 500 pounds. Although the opah fish lives in warm waters worldwide, it is rarely caught.

Edie Freedman designed the cover of this book, using a 19th-century engraving from the Dover Pictorial Archive. The cover layout was produced with Quark XPress 3.3 using the ITC Garamond font.

The inside layout was designed by Edie Freedman and Nancy Priest and implemented in both FrameMaker 5.0, by Mike Sierra, and gtroff, by Lenny Muellner. The text and heading fonts are ITC Garamond Light and Garamond Book; the code appears in Letter Gothic. The illustrations that appear in the book were created in Macromedia Freehand 5.0 and Adobe Photoshop by Robert Romano. This colophon was written by Clairemarie Fisher O'Leary.

More Titles from O'Reilly

Developing Web Content

Building Your Own WebSite

By Susan B. Peck & Stephen Arrants
1st Edition July 1996
514 pages, ISBN 1-56592-232-8

This is a hands-on reference for Windows® 95 and Windows NT™ desktop users who want to host their own site on the Web or on a corporate intranet. You'll also learn how to connect your web to information in other Windows applications, such as word processing documents and databases. Packed with examples and tutorials on every aspect of Web management. Includes the highly acclaimed WebSite™ 1.1 on CD-ROM.

Web Client Programming with Perl

By Clinton Wong
1st Edition March 1997 (est.)
250 pages (est.), ISBN 1-56592-214-X

Web Client Programming with Perl teaches you how to extend scripting skills to the Web. This book teaches you the basics of how browsers communicate with servers and how to write your own customized Web clients to automate common tasks. It is intended for those who are motivated to develop software that offers a more flexible and dynamic response than a standard Web browser.

JavaScript: The Definitive Guide, Second Edition

By David Flanagan
2nd Edition January 1997
672 pages, ISBN 1-56592-234-4

In this second edition, the author of the best-selling, Java in a Nutshell describes the server-side JavaScript application, LiveWire, developed by Netscape and Sun Microsystems.

Using LiveWire, developers can easily convert JavaScript applications and any HTML pages containing JavaScript code, into platform-independent byte codes ready to run on any Netscape 2.0 Server. The book describes the version of JavaScript shipped with Navigator 2.0, 2.0.1, and 2.0.2, and also the much-changed version of JavaScript shipped with Navigator 3.0. LiveConnect, used for communication between JavaScript and Java applets, and addresses commonly encountered bugs on JavaScript objects.

HTML: The Definitive Guide, Second Edition

By Chuck Musciano & Bill Kennedy
2nd Edition April 1997 (est.)
520 pages (est.), ISBN 1-56592-235-2

The second edition covers the most up-to-date version of the HTML standard (the proposed HTML version 3.2), Netscape 4.0 and Internet Explorer 3.0, plus all the common extensions, especially Netscape extensions. The authors address all the current version's elements, explaining how they work and interact with each other. Includes a style guide that helps you to use HTML to accomplish a variety of tasks, from simple online documentation to complex marketing and sales presentations. Readers of the first edition can find the updates for the second edition on the Web at www.oreilly.com.

Designing for the Web: Getting Started in a New Medium

By Jennifer Niederst with Edie Freedman
1st Edition April 1996
180 pages, ISBN 1-56592-165-8

Designing for the Web gives you the basics you need to hit the ground running. Although geared toward designers, it covers information and techniques useful to anyone who wants to put graphics online. It explains how to work with HTML documents from a designer's point of view, outlines special problems with presenting information online, and walks through incorporating images into Web pages, with emphasis on resolution and improving efficiency.

WebMaster in a Nutshell

By Stephen Spainhour & Valerie Quercia
1st Edition October 1996
378 pages, ISBN 1-56592-229-8

Web content providers and administrators have many sources of information, both in print and online. WebMaster in a Nutshell pulls it all together into one slim volume—for easy desktop access. This quick-reference covers HTML, CGI, Perl, HTTP, server configuration, and tools for Web administration.

Java Programming

Exploring Java, Second Edition

By Patrick Niemeyer & Joshua Peck
2nd Edition June 1997 (est.)
500 pages (est.),
ISBN 1-56592-271-9

The second edition of *Exploring Java*, fully revised to cover Version 1.1 of the JDK, introduces the basics of Java, the object-oriented programming language for networked applications. The ability to create animated World Wide Web pages sparked the rush to Java. But what also makes this language so important is that it's truly portable. The code runs on any machine that provides a Java interpreter, whether Windows 95, Windows NT, the Macintosh, or any flavor of UNIX.

Java in a Nutshell, Second Edition

By David Flanagan
2nd Edition May 1997
650 pages, ISBN 1-56592-262-X

Java programmers migrating to 1.1 find this second edition of Java in a Nutshell contains everything they need to get up to speed.

Newcomers find it still has all of the features that have made it the Java book most often recommended on the Internet. This complete quick reference contains descriptions of all of the classes in the core Java 1.1 API, making it the only quick reference that a Java programmer needs.

Java Virtual Machine

By Troy Downing & Jon Meyer
1st Edition March 1997
440 pages, ISBN 1-56592-194-1

This book is a comprehensive programming guide for the Java Virtual Machine (JVM). It gives readers a strong overview and reference of the JVM so that they may create their own implementations of the JVM or write their own compilers that create Java object code. A Java assembler is provided with the book, so the examples can all be compiled and executed.

Java Language Reference, Second Edition

By Mark Grand
2nd Edition July 1997 (est.)
448 pages, ISBN 1-56592-326-X

The second edition of the *Java Language Reference* is an invaluable tool for Java programmers, especially those who have migrated to Java 1.1. Part of O'Reilly's Java documentation series, this complete reference describes all aspects of the Java language plus new features in Version 1.1, such as inner classes, final local variables and method parameters, anonymous arrays, class literals, and instance initializers.

Java AWT Reference

By John Zukowski
1st Edition March 1997
1100 pages, ISBN 1-56592-240-9

With AWT, you can create windows, draw, work with images, and use components like buttons, scrollbars, and pulldown menus. *Java AWT Reference* covers the classes that comprise the java.awt, java.awt.image, and java.applet packages. It offers a comprehensive explanation of how AWT components fit together with easy-to-use reference material on every AWT class.

Java Threads

By Scott Oaks and Henry Wong
1st Edition January 1997
252 pages, ISBN 1-56592-216-6

Java Threads is a comprehensive guide to the intricacies of threaded programming in Java, covering everything from the most basic synchronization techniques to advanced topics like writing your own thread scheduler.

Java Threads uncovers the one tricky but essential aspect of Java programming and provides techniques for avoiding deadlock, lock starvation, and other topics.

Java Programming *continued*

Java Network Programming

By Elliotte Rusty Harold
1st Edition February 1997
448 pages, ISBN 1-56592-227-1

Java Network Programming is a complete introduction to developing network programs, both applets and applications, using Java; covering everything from networking fundamentals to remote method invocation (RMI).

It also covers what you can do without explicitly writing network code, how you can accomplish your goals using URLs and the basic capabilities of applets.

Developing Java Beans

By Rob Englander
1st Edition June 1997 (est.)
300 pages (est.),
ISBN 1-56592-289-1

With *Developing Java Beans*, you'll learn how to create components that can be manipulated by tools like Borland's Latte or Symantec's Visual Cafe, enabling others to build entire applications by using and reusing these building blocks. Beyond the basics, *Developing Java Beans* teaches you how to create Beans that can be saved and restored properly; how to take advantage of introspection to provide more information about a Bean's capabilities; how to provide property editors and customizers that manipulate a Bean in sophisticated ways; and how to integrate Java Beans into ActiveX projects.

Java in a Nutshell, DELUXE EDITION

By various authors
1st Edition June1997 (est.)
ISBN 1-56592-304-9
includes CD-ROM and books

Java in a Nutshell, Deluxe Edition, is a Java programmer's dream come true in one small package. The heart of this Deluxe Edition is the Java reference library on CD-ROM, which brings together five indispensable volumes for Java developers and programmers, linking related info across books. It includes: *Exploring Java, 2nd Edition*; *Java Language Reference, 2nd Edition*; *Java Fundamental Classes Reference*; *Java AWT Reference*; and *Java in a Nutshell, 2nd Edition*, included both on the CD-ROM and in a companion desktop edition. This deluxe library gives you everything you need to do serious programming with Java 1.1.

Database Programming with JDBC and Java

By George Reese
1st Edition July 1997 (est.)
300 pages (est.),
ISBN 1-56592-270-0

Java and databases make a powerful combination. Getting the two sides to work together, however, takes some effort—largely because Java deals in objects while most databases do not.

This book describes the standard Java interfaces that make portable, object-oriented access to relational databases possible, and offers a robust model for writing applications that are easy to maintain. It introduces the JDBC and RMI packages and uses them to develop three-tier applications (applications divided into a user interface, an object-oriented logic component, and an information store). Covers Java 1.1.

How to stay in touch with O'Reilly

1. Visit Our Award-Winning Site

http://www.oreilly.com/

★"Top 100 Sites on the Web" —*PC Magazine*
★"Top 5% Web sites" —*Point Communications*
★"3-Star site" —*The McKinley Group*

Our web site contains a library of comprehensive product information (including book excerpts and tables of contents), downloadable software, background articles, interviews with technology leaders, links to relevant sites, book cover art, and more. File us in your Bookmarks or Hotlist!

2. Join Our Email Mailing Lists

New Product Releases
To receive automatic email with brief descriptions of all new O'Reilly products as they are released, send email to:
listproc@online.oreilly.com
Put the following information in the first line of your message (*not* in the Subject field):
subscribe oreilly-news "Your Name" of "Your Organization" (for example: subscribe oreilly-news Kris Webber of Fine Enterprises)

O'Reilly Events
If you'd also like us to send information about trade show events, special promotions, and other O'Reilly events, send email to:
listproc@online.oreilly.com
Put the following information in the first line of your message (*not* in the Subject field):
subscribe oreilly-events "Your Name" of "Your Organization"

3. Get Examples from Our Books via FTP

There are two ways to access an archive of example files from our books:

Regular FTP
- ftp to:
  ftp.oreilly.com
  (login: anonymous
  password: your email address)
- Point your web browser to:
  ftp://ftp.oreilly.com/

FTPMAIL
- Send an email message to:
  ftpmail@online.oreilly.com
  (Write "help" in the message body)

4. Visit Our Gopher Site

- Connect your gopher to:
  gopher.oreilly.com

- Point your web browser to:
  gopher://gopher.oreilly.com/

- Telnet to:
  gopher.oreilly.com
  login: gopher

5. Contact Us via Email

order@oreilly.com
To place a book or software order online. Good for North American and international customers.

subscriptions@oreilly.com
To place an order for any of our newsletters or periodicals.

books@oreilly.com
General questions about any of our books.

software@oreilly.com
For general questions and product information about our software. Check out O'Reilly Software Online at **http://software.oreilly.com/** for software and technical support information. Registered O'Reilly software users send your questions to:
website-support@oreilly.com

cs@oreilly.com
For answers to problems regarding your order or our products.

booktech@oreilly.com
For book content technical questions or corrections.

proposals@oreilly.com
To submit new book or software proposals to our editors and product managers.

international@oreilly.com
For information about our international distributors or translation queries. For a list of our distributors outside of North America check out:
http://www.oreilly.com/www/order/country.html

O'Reilly & Associates, Inc.
101 Morris Street, Sebastopol, CA 95472 USA
TEL   707-829-0515 or 800-998-9938
         (6am to 5pm PST)
FAX   707-829-0104

Titles from O'Reilly

Please note that upcoming titles are displayed in italic.

WebProgramming

Apache: The Definitive Guide
Building Your Own Web Conferences
Building Your Own Website
Building Your Own Win-CGI Programs
CGI Programming for the World Wide Web
Designing for the Web
HTML: The Definitive Guide
JavaScript: The Definitive Guide, 2nd Ed.
Learning Perl
Programming Perl, 2nd Ed.
Mastering Regular Expressions
WebMaster in a Nutshell
Web Security & Commerce
Web Client Programming with Perl
World Wide Web Journal

Using the Internet

Smileys
The Future Does Not Compute
The Whole Internet User's Guide & Catalog
The Whole Internet for Win 95
Using Email Effectively
Bandits on the Information Superhighway

Java Series

Exploring Java
Java AWT Reference
Java Fundamental Classes Reference
Java in a Nutshell
Java Language Reference
Java Network Programming
Java Threads
Java Virtual Machine

Software

WebSite™ 1.1
WebSite Professional™
Building Your Own Web Conferences
WebBoard™
PolyForm™
Statisphere™

Songline Guides

NetActivism   NetResearch
Net Law   NetSuccess
NetLearning   NetTravel
Net Lessons

System Administration

Building Internet Firewalls
Computer Crime: A Crimefighter's Handbook
Computer Security Basics
DNS and BIND, 2nd Ed.
Essential System Administration, 2nd Ed.
Getting Connected: The Internet at 56K and Up
Internet Server Administration with Windows NT
Linux Network Administrator's Guide
Managing Internet Information Services
Managing NFS and NIS
Networking Personal Computers with TCP/IP
Practical UNIX & Internet Security. 2nd Ed.
PGP: Pretty Good Privacy
sendmail, 2nd Ed.
sendmail Desktop Reference
System Performance Tuning
TCP/IP Network Administration
termcap & terminfo
Using & Managing UUCP
Volume 8: X Window System Administrator's Guide
Web Security & Commerce

Unix

Exploring Expect
Learning VBScript
Learning GNU Emacs, 2nd Ed.
Learning the bash Shell
Learning the Korn Shell
Learning the UNIX Operating System
Learning the vi Editor
Linux in a Nutshell
Making TeX Work
Linux Multimedia Guide
Running Linux, 2nd Ed.
SCO UNIX in a Nutshell
sed & awk, 2nd Edition
Tcl/Tk Tools
UNIX in a Nutshell: System V Edition
UNIX Power Tools
Using csh & tsch
When You Can't Find Your UNIX System Administrator
Writing GNU Emacs Extensions

Web Review Studio Series

Gif Animation Studio
Shockwave Studio

Windows

Dictionary of PC Hardware and Data Communications Terms
Inside the Windows 95 Registry
Inside the Windows 95 File System
Windows Annoyances
Windows NT File System Internals
Windows NT in a Nutshell

Programming

Advanced Oracle PL/SQL Programming
Applying RCS and SCCS
C++: The Core Language
Checking C Programs with lint
DCE Security Programming
Distributing Applications Across DCE & Windows NT
Encyclopedia of Graphics File Formats, 2nd Ed.
Guide to Writing DCE Applications
lex & yacc
Managing Projects with make
Mastering Oracle Power Objects
Oracle Design: The Definitive Guide
Oracle Performance Tuning, 2nd Ed.
Oracle PL/SQL Programming
Porting UNIX Software
POSIX Programmer's Guide
POSIX.4: Programming for the Real World
Power Programming with RPC
Practical C Programming
Practical C++ Programming
Programming Python
Programming with curses
Programming with GNU Software
Pthreads Programming
Software Portability with imake, 2nd Ed.
Understanding DCE
Understanding Japanese Information Processing
UNIX Systems Programming for SVR4

Berkeley 4.4 Software Distribution

4.4BSD System Manager's Manual
4.4BSD User's Reference Manual
4.4BSD User's Supplementary Documents
4.4BSD Programmer's Reference Manual
4.4BSD Programmer's Supplementary Documents
X Programming
Vol. 0: X Protocol Reference Manual
Vol. 1: Xlib Programming Manual
Vol. 2: Xlib Reference Manual
Vol. 3M: X Window System User's Guide, Motif Edition
Vol. 4M: X Toolkit Intrinsics Programming Manual, Motif Edition
Vol. 5: X Toolkit Intrinsics Reference Manual
Vol. 6A: Motif Programming Manual
Vol. 6B: Motif Reference Manual
Vol. 6C: Motif Tools
Vol. 8 : X Window System Administrator's Guide
Programmer's Supplement for Release 6
X User Tools
The X Window System in a Nutshell

Career & Business

Building a Successful Software Business
The Computer User's Survival Guide
Love Your Job!
Electronic Publishing on CD-ROM

Travel

Travelers' Tales: Brazil
Travelers' Tales: Food
Travelers' Tales: France
Travelers' Tales: Gutsy Women
Travelers' Tales: India
Travelers' Tales: Mexico
Travelers' Tales: Paris
Travelers' Tales: San Francisco
Travelers' Tales: Spain
Travelers' Tales: Thailand
Travelers' Tales: A Woman's World

International Distributors

UK, Europe, Middle East and Northern Africa (except France, Germany, Switzerland, & Austria)

INQUIRIES
International Thomson Publishing
  Europe
Berkshire House
168-173 High Holborn
London WC1V 7AA, UK
Tel: 44-171-497-1422
Fax: 44-171-497-1426
Email: itpint@itps.co.uk

ORDERS
International Thomson Publishing
  Services, Ltd.
Cheriton House, North Way
Andover, Hampshire SP10 5BE
United Kingdom
Tel: 44-264-342-832 (UK)
Tel: 44-264-342-806
  (outside UK)
Fax: 44-264-364418 (UK)
Fax: 44-264-342761 (outside UK)
UK & Eire orders:
  tpuk@itps.co.uk
International orders:
  itpint@itps.co.uk

France

Editions Eyrolles
61 bd Saint-Germain
75240 Paris Cedex 05
France
Fax: 33-01-44-41-11-44

FRENCH LANGUAGE BOOKS
All countries except Canada
Tel: 33-01-44-41-46-16
Email: geodif@eyrolles.com

ENGLISH LANGUAGE BOOKS
Tel: 33-01-44-41-11-87
Email: distribution@eyrolles.com

Australia

WoodsLane Pty. Ltd.
7/5 Vuko Place, Warriewood NSW
  2102
P.O. Box 935,
Mona Vale NSW 2103
Australia
Tel: 61-2-9970-5111
Fax: 61-2-9970-5002
Email: info@woodslane.com.au

Germany, Switzerland, and Austria

INQUIRIES
O'Reilly Verlag
Balthasarstr. 81
D-50670 Köln
Germany
Tel: 49-221-97-31-60-0
Fax: 49-221-97-31-60-8
Email: anfragen@oreilly.de

ORDERS
International Thomson Publishing
Königswinterer Straße 418
53227 Bonn, Germany
Tel: 49-228-97024 0
Fax: 49-228-441342
Email: order@oreilly.de

Asia (except Japan & India)

INQUIRIES
International Thomson Publishing
  Asia
60 Albert Street #15-01
Albert Complex
Singapore 189969
Tel: 65-336-6411
Fax: 65-336-7411

ORDERS
Telephone: 65-336-6411
Fax: 65-334-1617
Email: thomson@signet.com.sg

New Zealand

WoodsLane New Zealand Ltd.
21 Cooks Street (P.O. Box 575)
Wanganui, New Zealand
Tel: 64-6-347-6543
Fax: 64-6-345-4840
Email: info@woodslane.com.au

Japan

O'Reilly Japan, Inc.
Kiyoshige Building 2F
12-Banchi, Sanei-cho
Shinjuku-ku
Tokyo 160 Japan
Tel: 81-3-3356-5227
Fax: 81-3-3356-5261
Email: kenji@oreilly.com

India

Computer Bookshop (India) PVT.
  LTD.
190 Dr. D.N. Road, Fort
Bombay 400 001 India
Tel: 91-22-207-0989
Fax: 91-22-262-3551
Email:
  cbsbom@giasbm01.vsnl.net.in

The Americas

O'Reilly & Associates, Inc.
101 Morris Street
Sebastopol, CA 95472 U.S.A.
Tel: 707-829-0515
Tel: 800-998-9938
  (U.S. & Canada)
Fax: 707-829-0104
Email: order@oreilly.com

Southern Africa

International Thomson Publishing
  Southern Africa
Building 18, Constantia Park
138 Sixteenth Road
P.O. Box 2459
Halfway House, 1685 South Africa
Tel: 27-11-805-4819
Fax: 27-11-805-3648

O'REILLY™

O'Reilly & Associates, Inc.
101 Morris Street
Sebastopol, CA 95472-9902
1-800-998-9938

Visit us online at:
http://www.ora.com/
orders@ora.com

O'REILLY WOULD LIKE TO HEAR FROM YOU

Which book did this card come from?

_____

Where did you buy this book?
- ❏ Bookstore
- ❏ Direct from O'Reilly
- ❏ Bundled with hardware/software
- ❏ Computer Store
- ❏ Class/seminar
- ❏ Other _____

What operating system do you use?
- ❏ UNIX
- ❏ Windows NT
- ❏ Other _____
- ❏ Macintosh
- ❏ PC(Windows/DOS)

What is your job description?
- ❏ System Administrator
- ❏ Network Administrator
- ❏ Web Developer
- ❏ Other _____
- ❏ Programmer
- ❏ Educator/Teacher

❏ Please send me O'Reilly's catalog, containing a complete listing of O'Reilly books and software.

Name _____ Company/Organization _____

Address _____

City _____ State _____ Zip/Postal Code _____ Country _____

Telephone _____ Internet or other email address (specify network) _____

Nineteenth century wood engraving
of a bear from the O'Reilly &
Associates Nutshell Handbook®
Using & Managing UUCP.

BUSINESS REPLY MAIL
FIRST CLASS MAIL   PERMIT NO. 80   SEBASTOPOL, CA

Postage will be paid by addressee

O'Reilly & Associates, Inc.
101 Morris Street
Sebastopol, CA 95472-9902